THE ANATOMY OF A MOMENT

THE ANATOMY OF A MOMENT

Thirty-five Minutes
in History and Imagination

Javier Cercas

Translated from the Spanish by Anne McLean

B L O O M S B U R Y

NEW YORK · BERLIN · LONDON · SYDNEY

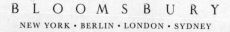

This work has been published with the help of a grant from the office of the Director
General of Books, Archives and Libraries of the Ministry of Culture of Spain.

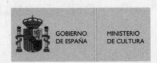

Published by Bloomsbury USA, New York

All papers used by Bloomsbury USA are natural, recyclable products made from
wood grown in well-managed forests. The manufacturing processes conform
to the environmental regulations of the country of origin.

Photograph on page viii, Spanish Cortes, 23 February 1981, © RTVE, 1981.
Photograph of Adolfo Suárez on page 114–5 © El País/Marisa Florez.

LIBRARY OF CONGRESS CATALOGING-IN-PUBLICATION DATA

Cercas, Javier, 1962–
[Anatomía de un instante. English]
The anatomy of a moment : thirty-five minutes in history and imagination /
Javier Cercas; translated from the Spanish by Anne McLean.—1st U.S. ed.
p. cm.
ISBN-13: 978-1-60819-491-9 (pb)
ISBN-10: 1-60819-491-4 (pb)
1. Spain—History—Coup d'état, 1981. I. Title.
DP272.C42813 2011
946.083—dc22
2010044463

Originally published in Spain as *Anatomía de un instante* by
Random House Mondadori, Barcelona

First U.S. Edition 2011

1 3 5 7 9 10 8 6 4 2

Typeset by Hewer Text UK Ltd, Edinburgh
Printed in the U.S.A. by Quad/Graphics, Fairfield, Pennsylvania

In memory of José Cercas

For Raül Cercas and Mercè Mas

he who made . . . the great refusal

Dante, *Inferno*, III, 60

Contents

PROLOGUE

EPILOGUE TO A NOVEL

I

In the middle of March 2008, I read that according to a poll published in the United Kingdom almost a quarter of Britons thought Winston Churchill was a fictional character. At that time I had just finished a draft of a novel about the 23 February 1981 coup d'état in Spain, and was full of doubts about what I'd written and I remember wondering how many Spaniards must think Adolfo Suárez was a fictional character, that General Gutiérrez Mellado was a fictional character, that Santiago Carrillo or Lieutenant Colonel Tejero were fictional characters. It still strikes me as a relevant question. It's true that Winston Churchill died more than forty years ago, that General Gutiérrez Mellado died less than fifteen years ago and as I write Adolfo Suárez, Santiago Carrillo and Lieutenant Colonel Tejero are still alive, but it's also true that Churchill is a top-ranking historical figure and, if Suárez might share that position, at least in Spain, General Gutiérrez Mellado and Santiago Carrillo, not to mention Lieutenant Colonel Tejero, do not; furthermore, in Churchill's time television was not yet the main fabricator of reality as well as the main fabricator of unreality on the planet, while one of the characteristics that defines the 23 February coup is that it was recorded by television cameras and broadcast all over the world. In fact, who knows whether by now Lieutenant Colonel Tejero might not be a television character to many people; perhaps even Adolfo Suárez, General Gutiérrez Mellado and Santiago Carrillo might also be to a certain extent, but not to the extent that he is: apart from people dressing up as him on comedy programmes and advertisements, the lieutenant colonel's public life is confined to those few seconds repeated each year on television in which, wearing his tricorne and brandishing his new standard-issue pistol, he bursts into the Cortes and humiliates the deputies assembled there at gunpoint. Although we know he is a real character, he is an unreal character; although we know it is a real image, it is an unreal image: a scene from a cliché-ridden Spanish film fresh from the hackneyed brain of a mediocre imitator of Luis García Berlanga. No real person becomes fictitious by appearing on television, not even by being a television personality more than anything else, but television probably contaminates everything it touches with unreality, and the nature of an historic event alters in some way when it is broadcast on television, because television distorts (if not trivializes and demeans) the way we perceive things. The 23 February coup coexists with this anomaly: as far as I know, it's the only coup in history filmed for television, and the fact that it was filmed is at once its guarantee of reality and its guarantee of unreality; added to the repeated astonishment the images produce, to the historic magnitude of the event and to the still troubling areas of real or assumed shadows, these circumstances might explain the unprecedented mishmash of fictions in the form of baseless theories, fanciful ideas, embellished speculations and invented memories that surround them.

Here's a tiny example of the latter; tiny but not banal, because it is directly related to the coup's televisual life. No Spaniard who'd reached the age of reason by 23 February 1981 has forgotten his or her whereabouts that evening, and many people blessed with good memories remember in detail – what time it was, where they were, with whom – having watched Lieutenant Colonel Tejero and his Civil Guards enter the Cortes live on television, to the point that they'd be willing to swear by what they hold most sacred that it is a real memory. It is not: although the coup was broadcast live on radio, the television images were shown only after the liberation of the parliamentary hostages, shortly after 12.30 on the 24th, and were seen live only by a handful of Televisión Española journalists and technicians, whose cameras were filming the interrupted parliamentary session and who circulated those images through the in-house network in the hope they'd be edited and broadcast on the evening news summaries and the nightly newscast. That's what happened, but we all resist having our memories removed, for they're our handle on our identity, and some put what they remember before what happened, so they carry on remembering that they watched the coup d'état live. It is, I suppose, a neurotic reaction, though logical, especially considering the 23 February coup, in which it is often difficult to distinguish the real from the fictitious. After all there are reasons to interpret the 23 February coup as the fruit of a collective neurosis. Or of collective paranoia. Or, more precisely, of a collective novel. In the society of the spectacle it was, in any case, one more spectacle. But that doesn't mean it was a fiction: the 23 February coup existed, and twenty-seven years after that day, when its principal protagonists had perhaps begun to lose for many their status as historical characters and enter the realms of fiction, I had just finished a draft of a novel in which I tried to turn 23 February into fiction. And I was full of doubts.

2

How could I even dream of writing a fiction about the 23 February coup? How could I dream of writing a novel about a neurosis, about a paranoia, about a collective novel?

There is no novelist who hasn't felt at least once the presumptuous feeling that reality is demanding a novel of him, that he's not the one looking for a novel, but that a novel is looking for him. I had that feeling on 23 February 2006. Shortly before this date an Italian newspaper had asked me to write an article on my memories of the coup d'état. I agreed; I wrote an article in which I said three things: the first was that I had been a hero; the second was that I hadn't been a hero; the third was that no one had been a hero. I had been a hero because that evening, after hearing from my mother that a group of gun-toting Civil Guards had burst into the Cortes during the investiture vote for the new Prime Minister, I'd rushed off to the university with my eighteen-year-old imagination seething with revolutionary scenes of a city up in arms, riotous demonstrators opposing the coup and erecting barricades on every corner; I hadn't been a hero because the truth is I hadn't rushed to the university with the intrepid determination to join the defence of democracy against the rebellious military, but with the libidinous determination to find a classmate I had a huge crush on and perhaps take advantage of those romantic hours, or hours that seemed romantic to me, to win her over; no one had been a hero because, when I arrived at the university that evening, I didn't find anyone there except the girl I was looking for and two other students, as meek as they were disoriented: no one at the university where I studied – not at mine or any other university – made the slightest gesture of opposing the coup; no one in the city where I lived – not mine or any other city – took to the streets to confront the rebellious Army officers: except for a handful of people who showed themselves ready to risk their necks to defend democracy, the whole country stayed at home and waited for the coup to fail. Or to triumph.

That's a synopsis of what I said in my article and, undoubtedly because writing it reactivated forgotten memories, that 23 February I followed with more interest than usual the articles, reports and interviews with which the media commemorated the twenty-fifth anniversary of the coup. I was left perplexed: I had described the 23 February coup as a total failure of democracy, but the majority of those articles, reports and interviews described it as a total triumph of democracy. And not just them. That same day the Cortes approved a declaration, which reads as follows: 'The lack of the slightest hint of social endorsement, the exemplary attitude of the citizenry, the responsible behaviour of the political parties and the trade unions, as well as the media and in particular the democratic institutions [. . .], sufficed to frustrate the coup d'état.' It would be difficult to accumulate more falsehoods in fewer words, or so I thought when I read that paragraph: my impression was that the coup had not lacked social endorsement, that the citizenry's attitude was not exemplary, the political parties' and unions' behaviour was irresponsible, and, with very few exceptions, the media and democratic institutions had done nothing to frustrate the coup. But it wasn't the spectacular discrepancy between my personal memory of 23 February and the apparent collective memory that most struck me and produced the presumptuous hunch that reality was demanding I write a novel, but something much less shocking, or more elemental – although probably linked to that discrepancy. It was an obligatory image on every single television report about the coup: the image of Adolfo Suárez turned to stone in his seat while, seconds after Lieutenant Colonel Tejero entered the Cortes, Civil Guards' bullets whizzed through the air around him and all the rest of the parliamentarians present there – all except two: General Gutiérrez Mellado and Santiago Carrillo – hit the floor seeking shelter from the gunfire. Of course, I had seen that image dozens of times, but for some reason that day I saw it as if I were seeing it for the first time: the shouts, the shots, the terrorized silence of the chamber and that man leaning back against the blue leather of his prime ministerial bench, solitary, statuesque and spectral in a desert of empty benches. It suddenly struck me as a mesmerizing and radiant image, meticulously complex, rich with meaning; perhaps because the truly enigmatic is not what no one has seen, but what we've all seen many times and which nevertheless refuses to divulge its significance, it suddenly struck me as an enigmatic image. That's what set off the alarm. Borges says that 'every destiny, however long and complicated, essentially boils down to a single moment – the moment a man knows, once and for all, who he is'. Seeing Adolfo Suárez on that 23 February sitting still while the bullets whizzed around him in the deserted chamber, I wondered whether in that moment Suárez had known once and for all who he was and what significance that remote image held, supposing it did hold some meaning. This double question did not leave me over the days that followed, and to try to answer it – or rather: to try to express it precisely – I decided to write a novel.

I got straight down to work. I don't know whether I need to clarify that the aim of my novel was not to vindicate the figure of Suárez, or to denigrate him, or even to evaluate him, but only to explore the significance of a gesture. I would be lying, however, if I were to say that Suárez aroused much sympathy in me: I was a teenager when he was in power and I never considered him anything other than a Francoist on the make who had prospered through back-breaking bowing, an opportunistic, reactionary, pious, superficial and smooth politician who embodied what I most detested about my country and whom, I'm very much afraid, I identified with my father, an obstinate supporter of Suárez; over time my opinion of my father had improved, but not my opinion of Suárez, or not much: now, a quarter of a century later, I had him down as a short-sighted politician whose principal merit consisted in having been in the place where he had to be and at the moment when he had to be there, something that had granted him a fortuitous prominence during a change, the one from dictatorship to democracy, which the country was going to undertake with or without him, and this reticence is the reason I watched with more sarcasm than astonishment the celebration of his consecration in his own lifetime as the great statesman of democracy – celebrations in which I always thought I recognized the scent of an even greater hypocrisy than is customary in these cases, as if no one believed it at all or as if, more than celebrating Suárez, the celebrants were celebrating themselves. But, instead of impoverishing them, the negligible esteem in which I held him enriched with complexity the character and his gesture, especially as I investigated his life story and researched the coup. The first thing I did was to try to obtain from Televisión Española a copy of the complete footage of Lieutenant Colonel Tejero's invasion of the Cortes. The procedure turned out to be trickier than expected, but it was worth the effort; the footage – most of which was shot by two cameras that kept running after the storming of the Cortes until they were unplugged by accident – is dazzling: the images we see every anniversary of 23 February last five, ten, fifteen seconds at most; the complete images last a hundred times longer: thirty-four minutes and twenty-four seconds. When they were shown on television, at midday on 24 February, the philosopher Julián Marías ventured the opinion that they deserved a prize for the year's best film; almost three decades later I feel that was faint praise: they are extremely dense images, of extraordinary visual power, brimming with history and electrified by truth, that I watched many times without their spell being broken. Meanwhile, during that initial period I read several biographies of Suárez, several books about the years when he was in power and about the coup d'état, leafed through the odd newspaper of the day, interviewed a politician or two, the odd military officer, a journalist or two. One of the first people I spoke to was Javier Pradera, an ex-Communist editor transformed into the éminence grise of Spanish culture and also one of the few people who on 23 February, when he was writing editorials for *El País* and the newspaper brought out a special edition with a genuinely anti-coup text he'd written, had shown himself willing to risk his neck for democracy. I told Pradera of my project (I deceived him: I told him I was planning to write a novel about 23 February; or maybe I didn't deceive him: maybe from the start I wanted to imagine that Adolfo Suárez's gesture contained all that 23 February meant in code). Pradera was enthusiastic; since he's not a man prone to enthusiasms, I raised my guard: I asked him why he was so enthusiastic. 'Very simple,' he answered. 'Because the coup d'état is a novel. A detective novel. The plot goes like this: Cortina sets up the coup and Cortina knocks it down. Out of loyalty to the King.' Cortina is Major José Luis Cortina; on 23 February Major José Luis Cortina was head of the special operations unit of CESID (Centro Superior de Información de la Defensa), the Spanish intelligence service: he had been a cadet at the military academy the same year as the King, was assumed to be close to the monarch and after 23 February had been accused of participating in the coup, or rather of unleashing it, and he'd been jailed, interrogated and absolved by the court martial that judged the case, but the suspicions hanging over him never entirely dissipated. 'Cortina sets up the coup and Cortina knocks it down': Pradera laughed sardonically; I laughed too: rather than the plot of a detective novel it seemed to me like the plot of a sophisticated version of *The Three Musketeers*, with Major Cortina in a role that blended D'Artagnan with Monsieur de Tréville.

I liked the idea. As it happens, a little while after talking to Pradera I read a book that fitted the fiction the old *El País* editorialist had in mind like a glove, except that the book wasn't fiction: it was a work of investigative journalism. Its author is the journalist Jesús Palacios; its thesis is that, contrary to what appearances seem to suggest, the 23 February coup was not an improvised and botched job by an imperfect combination of hard-core Francoist military officers and monarchist military officers with political ambitions, but rather 'a designer coup', an operation planned down to the last detail by CESID – by Major Cortina but also by Lieutenant Colonel Calderón, his immediate superior and at the time the strong man of the intelligence services – whose purpose was not to destroy democracy but to trim it or change its direction, getting the premiership away from Adolfo Suárez and putting a military man in his place at the head of a government of salvation made up of representatives of all the political parties; according to Palacios, with this objective Calderón and Cortina had counted not only on the implicit consent or impetus of the King, anxious to overcome the crisis to which the country had been driven by the chronic crises of Suárez governments: Calderón and Cortina had selected the operation's leader – General Armada, the King's former secretary – had encouraged its operational branches – General Milans del Bosch and Lieutenant Colonel Tejero – and had woven an intricate conspiratorial web of military men, politicians, businessmen, journalists and diplomats that assembled scattered and contrasting ambitions in the common cause of the coup. It was an irresistible hypothesis: suddenly the chaos of 23 February tallied; suddenly everything was coherent, symmetrical, geometric, just like in a novel. Of course Palacios' book wasn't a novel, and a certain knowledge of the events – not to mention the opinion of the most diligent scholars – allowed one to glimpse that Palacios had taken certain liberties with reality to keep it from contradicting his hypothesis; but I wasn't a historian, or even a journalist, just a writer of fiction, so I was authorized by reality to take as many liberties with her as necessary, because the novel is a genre that doesn't answer to reality, but only to itself. Happily I thought Pradera and Palacios were offering me an improved version of *The Three Musketeers*: the story of a secret agent who, with the aim of saving the monarchy, hatches a gigantic conspiracy destined to topple by means of a coup d'état (a *golpe de estado*) the King's Prime Minister, precisely the only politician (or almost the only one) who, when the moment arrives, refuses to comply with the will of the *golpistas* and remains in his seat while the bullets whizz around him in the Cortes.

In the autumn of 2006, when I decided I knew enough about the coup to develop that plot, I began to write the novel; for reasons that are beside the point, in the winter I abandoned it, but towards the end of the spring of 2007 I took it up again, and less than a year later I had a finished draft: it was, or wanted to be, the draft of a strange experimental version of *The Three Musketeers*, with Major Cortina as narrator and protagonist, and the action of which, instead of revolving around the diamond pendants presented by the Queen Consort of France, Anne of Austria, to the Duke of Buckingham, revolved around the solitary image of Adolfo Suárez sitting in the Cortes on the evening of 23 February. The text covered four hundred pages; I wrote it with unusual, almost triumphant fluidity, shooing away doubts by reasoning that the book was in an embryonic state and that only as I familiarized myself with its mechanism would the uncertainty finally clear away. This didn't happen, and as soon as I'd finished the first draft the feeling of triumph evaporated, and the doubts, instead of clearing away, multiplied. For a start, after having spent months groping through the ins and outs of the coup in my imagination, I now believed I fully understood what before I had only guessed with fear or reluctance, and that Palacios' hypothesis – which constituted the historical cement of my novel – was fundamentally false; the problem was not that Palacios' book was entirely wrong or even bad: the problem was that the book was so good that anyone who wasn't familiar with what happened on 23 February could end up thinking that for once history had been coherent, symmetrical and geometric, and not disorderly, turbulent and unpredictable, which is how it is in reality; in other words: the hypothesis upon which my novel was built was a fiction that, like any good fiction, had been constructed on the basis of facts, dates, names, analysis and conjecture, selected and arranged with a novelist's cunning until everything connects with everything else and reality acquires a homogeneous meaning. All right then, if Palacios' book was not exactly a work of investigative journalism, but rather a novel superimposed on a work of investigative journalism, was it not redundant to write a novel based on another novel? If a novel should illuminate reality through fiction, imposing geometry and symmetry where there is only disorder and chance, should it not start from reality, and not from fiction? Was it not superfluous to add geometry to geometry and symmetry to symmetry? If a novel should defeat reality, reinventing it in order to substitute it with a fiction as persuasive as itself, was it not indispensable to first know that reality in order to defeat it? Was it not the obligation of a novel about 23 February to renounce certain of the genre's privileges and try to answer to reality as well as to itself?

They were rhetorical questions: in the spring of 2008 I decided that the only way to erect a fiction on the 23 February coup was to know as scrupulously as possible the reality of the 23 February coup. Only then did I dive into the depths of the mishmash of theoretical constructions, hypotheses, uncertainties, embellishments, falsehoods and invented memories surrounding that day. For several months, while travelling frequently to Madrid and returning over and over again to the footage of the storming of the Cortes – as if these images were hiding in their transparency the secret key to the coup – I worked full-time at reading all the books I could find about 23 February and the years that preceded it, I consulted newspapers and magazines of the time, I delved into the summary of the trial, I interviewed witnesses and protagonists. I spoke to politicians, military officers, Civil Guards, spies, journalists, people who had experienced first-hand the politics of those years of change from Francoism to democracy and had known Adolfo Suárez and General Gutiérrez Mellado and Santiago Carrillo, and people who had experienced 23 February in the places where the result of the coup was decided: in the Zarzuela Palace, together with the King, in the Cortes, at Army General Headquarters, at the Brunete Armoured Division, at the central headquarters of CESID and at the central headquarters of AOME, the secret CESID unit commanded by Major Cortina. They were obsessive, happy months, but as my investigations advanced and my vision of the coup d'état changed I began to understand very quickly not only that I was going deeper into a shimmering labyrinth of almost always irreconcilable memories, a place with hardly any certainties or documents, where historians prudently had hardly ventured, but especially that the reality of 23 February was of such magnitude that for the moment it was invincible, or at least it was for me, and it was therefore futile for me to propose the exploit of defeating it with a novel; it took me longer to understand something even more important: I understood that the events of 23 February on their own possessed all the dramatic force and symbolic power we demand of literature and I understood that, even though I was a writer of fiction, for once reality mattered more to me than fiction or mattered to me too much to want to reinvent it by substituting it with an alternative reality, because none of what I could imagine about 23 February concerned me and excited me as much or could be as complex and persuasive as the pure reality of 23 February.

3

That's how I decided to write this book. A book that is, more than anything else – I'd better admit from the start – the humble testimony of a failure: incapable of inventing what I know about 23 February, illuminating its reality with fiction, I have resigned myself to telling it. The pages that follow aim to endow this failure with a certain dignity. This means from the outset trying not to deprive the events of the dramatic force and symbolic power they possess on their own, or even their unexpected occasional coherence and symmetry and geometry; it also means trying to make them a little bit intelligible, narrating them without hiding their chaotic nature or erasing the tracks of a neurosis or paranoia or collective novel, but with maximum clarity, with all the innocence I'm capable of, as if no one had ever told them before or as if no one remembered them any more, in a certain sense as if it were true that for almost everyone Adolfo Suárez and General Gutiérrez Mellado and Santiago Carrillo and Lieutenant Colonel Tejero were now fictional characters or at least contaminated by unreality and the 23 February coup an invented memory; in the best of cases I'd tell them as a chronicler of antiquity would have or as a chronicler from far in the future; and this meant finally trying to tell the 23 February coup as if it were a tiny story and at the same time as if this tiny story were one of the decisive stories of the last seventy years of Spanish history.

But this book is just as much – I'd better admit from the start – an arrogant attempt to convert the failure of my novel about 23 February into a success, because it has the nerve not to renounce anything. Or

almost anything: it won't renounce getting right up close to the pure reality of 23 February, and from there, although it's not a history book and
no one should kid themselves and search it for hitherto unknown facts or
relevant contributions to the knowledge of our recent past, it will not
entirely renounce being read as a history book;* nor will it renounce
answering to itself as well as answering to reality, and from there, although
it's not a novel, it won't entirely renounce being read as a novel, not even
as an incredibly strange experimental version of *The Three Musketeers*;
and most of all – and this is perhaps its worst impudence – this book will
not entirely renounce understanding by means of reality that which it
renounced understanding by means of fiction, and from there seeing
itself deep down as not being about 23 February, but only about an image
of or a gesture from Adolfo Suárez on 23 February and, collaterally, about
an image of or a gesture from General Gutiérrez Mellado and about an
image of or a gesture from Santiago Carrillo on 23 February. To try to
understand that gesture or that image is to try to answer the question I
posed to myself one 23 February when I presumptuously felt that reality
was demanding I write a novel; to try to understand it without the powers
and liberty of fiction is the challenge this book sets itself.

---

* Just as if it did aspire to be read as a history book, it takes as its starting point the first
documentary evidence of 23 February: the recorded images of the storming of the Cortes; it
cannot use, however, the second and almost final piece of evidence: the recordings of the
telephone conversations that took place during the evening and night of 23 February between
the occupiers of the Cortes and people outside. The recording was made on the orders of
Francisco Laína, Director of State Security and head of an emergency government formed that
evening on the King's orders by politicians belonging to the second line of state administration
in order to stand in for the hijacked government in the Cortes. The recording or part of the
recording was heard on the afternoon of the 24th by the National Defence Council presided
over by the King and Adolfo Suárez, in the Zarzuela Palace (and was surely decisive in the
government's issuing an immediate arrest warrant for the leader of the coup, General Armada);
it's possible it was also heard by the examining magistrate of the 23 February trial, who did not
allow it to be admitted as evidence because it had been obtained without judicial permission;
then it disappeared, and since then nothing certain has been known about it. There are those
who say it is in the archives of the intelligence services, which is false. There are those who say
it was destroyed. There are those who say that, if it wasn't destroyed, it can only be in the
archives of the Interior Ministry. There are those who say that it was in the archives of the Interior
Ministry and only disappeared from there a few years after the coup. There are those who say
that Adolfo Suárez took a copy of part of the recording with him when he left government.
There are many other conjectures. I don't know anything more.

PART ONE

THE PLACENTA OF THE COUP

Twenty-three minutes after six on 23 February 1981. In the chamber of the Congress of Deputies, the lower house of the Cortes, they are holding the investiture vote for Leopoldo Calvo Sotelo, who is about to be confirmed as Prime Minister to replace Adolfo Suárez, who resigned twenty-five days ago and is still acting Prime Minister after an almost five-year term in office during which the country had come to the end of a dictatorship and built a democracy. Sitting in their seats while waiting their turn to vote, the deputies chat, doze or daydream in the early evening torpor; the only voice that resounds clearly in the hall is that of Víctor Carrascal, Secretary of the Congress, who reads the list of deputies from the speakers' rostrum so that, as they hear their name, they stand up and support or refuse with a 'yes' or a 'no' Calvo Sotelo's candidacy, or they abstain. This is now the second vote and there is no suspense: in the first, held three days ago, Calvo Sotelo did not obtain the support of an absolute majority of the deputies, but in this second round he needs only the support of a simple majority, so – given that this majority is assured – unless something unexpected happens, in a few minutes the candidate will be elected Prime Minister.

But something unexpected happens. Víctor Carrascal reads the name José Nasarre de Letosa Conde, who votes 'yes'; then he reads the name Carlos Navarrete Merino, who votes 'no'; then he reads the name Manuel Núñez Encabo, and at that moment an anomalous noise is heard, perhaps a shout from the right-hand door to the chamber, and Núñez Encabo does not vote or his vote is inaudible or gets lost amid the perplexed commotion of the deputies, some of whom look at each other, wondering whether or not to believe their ears, while others sit up straight in their seats to try to establish what's happening, maybe less anxious than curious. Clear and disconcerted, the Secretary's voice enquires: 'What's going on?', mumbles something, asks again: 'What's going on?', and at the same time a uniformed usher comes in from the right, strides urgently across the central semicircle of the chamber, where the stenographers sit, and starts up the stairs between the deputies' benches; halfway up he stops, exchanges a few words with one of the deputies and turns around; then he goes up another three steps and turns around again. It is then that a second shout is heard, indistinct, from the left-hand entrance to the chamber, and then, also unintelligible, a third, and many deputies – and all the stenographers, and the usher as well – turn to look towards the left-hand entrance.

The angle changes; a second camera focuses on the left wing of the chamber: pistol in hand, Lieutenant Colonel of the Civil Guard Antonio Tejero calmly walks up the steps of the dais, passes behind the Secretary and stands beside the Speaker Landelino Lavilla, who looks at him incredulously. The lieutenant colonel shouts: 'Nobody move!', and a couple of spellbound seconds follow during which nothing happens and no one moves and nothing seems to be going to happen or happen to anybody, except silence. The angle changes, but not the silence: the lieutenant colonel has vanished because the first camera focuses on the right wing of the chamber, where all the parliamentarians who had stood up have taken their seats again, and the only one still on his feet is General Manuel Gutiérrez Mellado, Deputy Prime Minister of the acting government; beside him, Adolfo Suárez remains seated on the Prime Minister's bench, leaning forward, a hand gripping the armrest of his seat, as if he is about to stand up too. Four nearby shouts, distinct and indisputable, then break the spell: someone shouts: 'Silence!'; someone shouts: 'Nobody move!'; someone shouts: 'Get down on the floor!'; someone shouts: 'Everyone down on the floor!' The chamber rushes to obey: the usher and stenographers kneel down beside their table; some deputies appear to cringe in their seats. General Gutiérrez Mellado, however, goes out to face the rebellious lieutenant colonel, while Prime Minister Suárez tries to hold him back unsuccessfully, clutching at his jacket. Now Lieutenant Colonel Tejero appears in the frame again, coming down the steps from the speakers' rostrum, but he stops halfway, confused or intimidated by the presence of General Gutiérrez Mellado, who walks towards him demanding with categorical gestures that he immediately leave the chamber, while three Civil Guards burst in through the right-hand entrance and pounce on the scrawny old general, push him, grab him by the jacket, shove him, nearly throwing him to the ground. Prime Minister Suárez stands up and goes to his Deputy Prime Minister; the lieutenant colonel is halfway down the steps, undecided whether to go all the way down, watching the scene. Then the first shot rings out; then the second shot and Prime Minister Suárez grabs the arm of General Gutiérrez Mellado, who stands undaunted in front of a Civil Guard who orders him with gestures and shouts to get down on the floor; then the third shot rings out and, still staring down the Civil Guard, General Gutiérrez Mellado pulls his arm violently out of the Prime Minister's grip; then the burst of gunfire erupts. While the bullets rip visible chunks of plaster out of the ceiling and one after another the stenographers and the usher hide under the table and the benches swallow up the deputies until not a single one of them remains in sight, the old general stands amid the automatic-rifle fire, with his arms hanging down at his sides, looking at the insubordinate Civil Guards, who do not stop firing. As for Prime Minister Suárez, he slowly returns to his seat, sits down, leans against the backrest and stays there, inclined slightly to the right, solitary, statuesque and spectral in a desert of empty benches.

That's the image; that's the gesture: a translucent gesture that contains many gestures.

At the end of 1989, when Adolfo Suárez's political career was drawing to a close, Hans Magnus Enzensberger celebrated in an essay the birth of a new type of hero: heroes of retreat. According to Enzensberger, instead of the classic hero, the hero of triumph and conquest, the twentieth century's dictatorships have brought to light a new kind of modern hero, who is a hero of renunciation, reduction and dismantling: the first is a steadfast and principled idealist; the second, a dubious professional of fixing and negotiation; the first reaches the height of his achievement by imposing his positions; the second, by abandoning them, undermining himself. That's why the hero of retreat is more than a political hero: he is also a moral hero. Enzensberger gives three examples of this innovative figure: Mikhail Gorbachev, who at the time was trying to dismantle the Soviet Union; Wojciech Jaruzelski, who in 1981 had prevented a Soviet invasion of Poland; Adolfo Suárez, who had dismantled the Franco regime. Adolfo Suárez a hero? And not just politically, but a moral hero? For the right as well as the left that was a difficult one to swallow: the left could not forget – had no reason to forget – that, although after a given moment he wanted to be a progressive politician, and up to a certain point he managed to be, Suárez was for many years a loyal collaborator with Francoism and a perfect prototype of the arriviste that the Franco regime's institutionalized corruption favoured; the right could not forget – should not have forgotten – that Suárez never accepted his attachment to the right, that many policies he applied or advocated were not right-wing and no other Spanish politician of the second half of the twentieth century has exasperated the right as much as he did. Was Suárez then a hero of the centre, that political pipe dream he himself coined in order to harvest votes from the right and the left? Impossible, because the fanciful notion vanished as soon as Suárez left politics, or even before, the way magic vanishes as soon as the magician leaves the stage. Now, twenty years after Enzensberger's report, when illness has destroyed Suárez and he is regarded as a praiseworthy figure by all, maybe because he can no longer bother anybody, there is among the Spanish ruling class an agreement to accord him a starring role in the foundation of the democracy; but it's one thing to have participated in the founding of Spanish democracy and quite another to be a hero of democracy. Was he? Is Enzensberger right? And, if we forget for a moment that no one is a hero to their contemporaries and accept as a hypothesis that Enzensberger is right, does Suárez's gesture on the evening of 23 February not acquire the value of a founding gesture of democracy? Does Suárez's gesture not then become emblematic of Suárez as a hero of retreat?

The first thing that needs to be said is that this gesture is not a gratuitous gesture; Suárez's gesture is a gesture with meaning, although we might not know exactly what it means, just as the gesture of all the rest of the parliamentarians – all except Gutiérrez Mellado and Santiago Carrillo – has meaning and is not gratuitous, those who instead of remaining seated during the gunfire obey the *golpistas* and seek shelter under their benches: that of the rest of the parliamentarians is not, let's be honest, a terribly graceful gesture, which none of those involved has wanted to dwell on or return to, and rightly so, although one of them – someone as cold and calm as Leopoldo Calvo Sotelo – doesn't hesitate to attribute the Parliament's discredit to that desert of empty benches. The most obvious gesture Suárez's gesture contains is a gesture of courage; a remarkable courage: those who lived through that moment in the Cortes all remember the apocalyptic din of the bursts of automatic-rifle fire in the enclosed space of the chamber, the horror of an immediate death, the certainty that this Armageddon – in the words of Alfonso Guerra, deputy leader of the

Socialist Party, who was sitting opposite Suárez – could not end without a massacre, which is the same certainty overwhelming the television directors and technicians who watched the scene live from the Prado del Rey studios. That day the chamber was filled with about three hundred and fifty parliamentarians, some of whom – Simón Sánchez Montero, for example, or Gregorio López Raimundo – had demonstrated their valour in clandestinity and in Franco's prisons; I don't know if there's much to reproach them for: whichever way you look at it, remaining in your seat during the skirmish was an act so rash it verged on a desire for martyrdom. In wartime, in the unthinking heat of combat, it is not unusually rash; in peacetime and in the solemn, habitual tedium of a parliamentary session it is. I'll add that, to judge from the images, Suárez's rashness is not one dictated by instinct but by reason: when the first shot sounds Suárez is on his feet; at the sound of the second he tries to bring General Gutiérrez Mellado back to the bench; at the sound of the third and the outbreak of the firing he sits down, settles on his bench and leans against the backrest waiting for the shooting to stop, or a bullet to kill him. It is a lingering, reflexive gesture; it appears to be a practised gesture, and maybe in a certain way it was: those who saw Suárez frequently at that time attested that he had spent a lot of time trying to prepare himself for a violent end, as if hounded by a dark premonition (for several months he'd been carrying a small pistol in his pocket; during the autumn and winter more than one visitor to Moncloa, the prime ministerial residence, heard him say: 'The only way they're going to get me out of here is by beating me in an election or carrying me out feet first'); it could be, but in any case it's not easy to prepare oneself for a death like that, and it is especially difficult not to weaken when the moment arrives.

Given that it's a courageous gesture, Suárez's gesture is a graceful gesture, because every courageous gesture is, according to Ernest Hemingway, a gesture of grace under pressure. In this sense it is an affirmative gesture; in another it is a negative gesture, because every courageous gesture is, according to Albert Camus, the rebellious gesture of a man who says no. In both cases it is a supreme gesture of liberty; it is not contradictory to say that it is also a histrionic gesture: the gesture of a man playing a role. If I'm not mistaken, only a couple of novels completely centred on the 23 February coup have been published; they're not great novels, but one of them has the added interest that its author is Josep Melià, a journalist who was an acerbic critic of Suárez before becoming one of his closest collaborators. Operating as a novelist, at a certain point in his story Melià asks himself what the first thing was that Suárez thought when he heard the first shot in the chamber; he answers: the front page of tomorrow's *New York Times*. The answer, which might seem innocuous or malicious, is intended to be cordial; it strikes me most of all as true. Like any pure politician, Suárez was a consummate actor: young, athletic, extremely handsome and always dressed with the polish of a provincial ladies' man who enchanted mothers of right-wing families and provoked the mockery of left-wing journalists – double-breasted jackets with gold buttons, dark-grey trousers, sky-blue shirts and navy-blue ties – Suárez knowingly took advantage of his Kennedy-like bearing, understood politics as spectacle and during his many years of work at Radiotelevisión Española learned that it was no longer reality that created images, rather images that created reality. A few days before 23 February, at the most dramatic moment of his political life, when he announced his resignation as Prime Minister in a speech to a small group of Party members, Suárez could not help but insert a comment of the incorrigible leading man that he was: 'Do you realize?' he said to them. 'My resignation will be front-page news in every newspaper in the world.' The evening of 23 February was not the most dramatic moment of his political life, but the most dramatic of his whole life and, in spite of that (or precisely because of it), it's possible that while the bullets whizzed around him in the chamber an intuition trained over years of political stardom dictated the instantaneous obviousness that, no matter what role fate had reserved for him at the end of that barbarous performance, he would never again act before an audience so absorbed and so large. If that's true, he was not mistaken: the next day his picture monopolized the front page of the *New York Times* and that of all the newspapers and television screens in the world. Suárez's gesture, in this way, is the gesture of a man who's posing. That's what Melià imagines. But thinking it through perhaps his imagination is too slight; thinking it through, on the evening of 23 February Suárez was perhaps not posing just for the newspapers and television screens: just as he would from that moment on in his political life – just as if in that moment he'd known who he truly was – perhaps Suárez was posing for history.

That's maybe another gesture his gesture contains: a posthumous gesture, so to speak. Because the fact is that at least for its main leaders the 23 February coup was not exactly a coup against democracy: it was a coup against Adolfo Suárez; or if you prefer: it was a coup against the kind of democracy Adolfo Suárez embodied for them. Suárez only understood this hours or days later, but in those first seconds he could not have been unaware that for almost five years of democracy no politician had attracted the hatred of the *golpistas* as much as he had and that, if blood was going to be spilled that evening in the Cortes, the first to be spilled would be his. Maybe that might be an explanation of his gesture: as soon as he heard the first shot, Suárez knew he could not protect himself from death, knew that he was already dead. I admit this is an embarrassing explanation, which tastelessly combines emphasis with melodrama; but that doesn't make it false, especially since deep down Suárez's gesture is still a gesture of emphatic melodrama characteristic of a man whose temperament tended as much towards comedy as tragedy and melodrama. Suárez, it's true, would have rejected the explanation. In fact, whenever anyone asked him to explain his gesture he opted for the same reply: 'Because I was still Prime Minister of His Majesty's government and the Prime Minister of the government could not dive for cover.' The reply, which I believe sincere, is predictable, and betrays a very important characteristic of Suárez: his sacramental devotion to power, the disproportionate dignity bestowed by the office he held; it is also not a boastful reply: it presupposes that, had he not still been Prime Minister, he would have acted upon the same prudent instinct as the rest of his colleagues, protecting himself from the gunshots under his bench; but it is, furthermore or most of all, an insufficient reply: it forgets that all the rest of the parliamentarians represented the sovereignty of the people with almost the same claim as he had – not to mention Leopoldo Calvo Sotelo, who was going to be sworn in as Prime Minister that very evening, or Felipe González, who would be within a year and a half, or Manuel Fraga, who aspired to be, or Landelino Lavilla, who was the Speaker of the Cortes, or Agustín Rodríguez Sahagún, who was Minister of Defence and responsible for the Army. Be that as it may, one thing is beyond doubt: Suárez's gesture is not the powerful gesture of a man confronting adversity at the height of his powers, but the gesture of a man politically finished and personally broken, who for the last six months has felt that the entire political class was plotting against him and maybe now also feels that the seditious Civil Guards bursting into the chamber of the Cortes is the result of this same widespread conspiracy.

2

The first feeling is quite accurate; the second not so much. It's true that during the autumn and winter of 1980 the Spanish ruling class has devoted itself to a series of strange political manoeuvres with the objective of bringing down Adolfo Suárez's government, but it's only partly true that the attack on the Cortes and the military coup are the result of this widespread conspiracy. Two different things are involved in the 23 February coup: one is a series of political operations against Adolfo Suárez, but not against democracy, or not in principle; the other is a military operation against Adolfo Suárez and also against democracy. The two things are not entirely independent; but neither are they entirely united: the political operations were the context that fostered the military operation; they were the placenta of the coup, not the coup itself: the nuance is key in understanding the coup. For this reason we don't need to pay too much attention to the politicians of the time who state that they knew in advance what was going to happen in the Cortes that evening, or that many people in the chamber knew, or even that the whole chamber knew; they are almost certainly fictitious, vain or self-interested memories: the truth is, since the political operation and the military operation barely communicated, nobody or almost nobody in the chamber knew, and very few people outside knew.

What everyone in the whole country did know was that a coup d'état was in the air that winter. On 20 February, three days before the coup, Ricardo Paseyro, Madrid correspondent for *Paris Match*, wrote: 'Spain's economic situation is verging on catastrophe, terrorism is on the rise, scepticism towards institutions and their representatives is profoundly damaging the soul of the nation, the state is collapsing beneath the assault of feudalism and the excesses on the part of the autonomous governments, and Spain's foreign policy is a fiasco.' He concluded: 'There is the scent of a coup d'état, a *golpe de estado*, in the air.' Everyone knew what could happen, but no one or almost no one knew when, how and where; as for who, prospective candidates to carry out a coup d'état were not exactly in short supply in the Army, although it's certain that as soon as Lieutenant Colonel Tejero burst into the chamber everyone or almost every one of the deputies must have recognized him immediately, because his face had been in the newspapers ever since mid-November 1978 when *Diario 16* broke the news that he had been arrested for planning a coup based on taking the government hostage when the Cabinet was meeting at Moncloa and using the resulting power vacuum as an excuse to take over control of the state; after his arrest, Tejero was put on trial, but the military tribunal ended up imposing a laughable sentence and a few months later he was already at liberty and available for duty, that is without a concrete professional assignment, that is without any occupation other than making preparations for his second attempt with maximum discretion and the minimum number of people, which ought to prevent the leak that made the first one fall through. So, in the most absolute secrecy, counting on a very reduced number of military conspirators and with a very high degree of improvisation, the coup was hatched, and this explains to a great extent how, of all the threatened coups looming over Spanish democracy since the previous summer, this was the one that finally materialized.

The threats against Spanish democracy, however, had not begun the previous summer. A long time after Suárez left power a journalist asked him at what moment did he begin to suspect that a coup d'état might be in the works. 'From the moment I gained the use of prime ministerial reason,' Suárez answered. He wasn't lying. Less than an accident of history, in Spain the *golpe de estado* is a vernacular rite: all democratic experiments in Spain have been finished by coups d'état, and in the last two centuries there have been more than fifty; the last had been in 1936, five years after the installation of the Republic; 1981 was also five years since the starting point of the democratic process; combined with the difficult time the country was going through, that chance turned into a numerical superstition and that numerical superstition gnawed away at the coup d'état psychosis among the ruling class. But it was not just a psychosis, nor just a superstition. In reality, Suárez had even more reasons than any other democratic Spanish Prime Minister to fear a coup d'état from the very moment when he showed by his actions that his intention was not, as might have seemed at the beginning of his mandate, to change something so everything would stay the same, prolonging the content of Francoism by airbrushing its form, but to restore a political regime essentially similar to the one against which forty years before Franco and the Army had risen up in arms: it was not just that when Suárez came to power the Armed Forces were almost uniformly Francoist; they were, by Franco's explicit mandate, the guardians of Francoism. The most famous phrase of the transition from dictatorship to democracy ('Everything is tied up and well tied') was not spoken by any of the protagonists of the transition; it was spoken by Franco, which perhaps suggests that Franco was the true protagonist of the transition, or at least one of the protagonists. Everyone remembers that phrase spoken on 30 December 1969 in his year-end speech, and everyone interprets it for what it is: a guarantee issued by the dictator to his faithful that after his death everything would carry on exactly as it was before his death or that, as the Falangist intellectual Jesús Fueyo put it, 'after Franco, the institutions'; not everyone remembers, on the other hand, that seven years before Franco pronounced an almost identical phrase ('Everything is tied up and guaranteed') during a speech to an assembly of Civil War veterans gathered at Garabitas Hill, and on that occasion he added: 'Under the faithful and insurmountable guardianship of our Armed Forces.' It was an order: after his death, the Army's mission was to preserve Francoism. But shortly before he died Franco gave the military a different order in his will, and it was that they should obey the King with the same loyalty with which they'd obeyed him. Of course, neither Franco nor the military imagined that the two orders could come to be contradictory and, when the political reforms brought the country into democracy demonstrating that indeed they were, because the King was deserting Francoism, the majority of military officers wavered: they had to choose between obeying Franco's first order, preventing democracy by force, and obeying the second, accepting that it contradicted and annulled the first, and consequently accepting democracy. That wavering is one of the keys to 23 February; it also explains that almost from the very moment he reached the premiership in July 1976 Suárez would live surrounded by rumours of a coup d'état. At the beginning of 1981 the rumours were no more tenacious than they had been in January or April of 1977, but never had the political situation been as favourable for a coup as it was then.

From the summer of 1980 the country is in an ever deepening crisis. Many share the *Paris Match* correspondent's diagnosis: the economy is in bad shape, the decentralization of the state is dismasting the state and exasperating the Army, Suárez is proving incapable of governing while his party is disintegrating and the opposition is hard at work trying to bury him once and for all, the inaugural charm of democracy seems to have vanished in a few years and on the streets one senses a mixture of insecurity, pessimism and fear;* furthermore, there is terrorism, especially ETA terrorism, which is reaching unprecedented levels while venting its anger on the Civil Guard and the rest of the Armed Forces. The outlook is alarming, and talk begins to circulate of finding emergency solutions: not only from the eternal advocators of a military coup – unrepentant Francoists stripped of their privileges who fan the flames with daily patriotic harangues in the barracks – but also people of long-standing democratic affiliation, like Josep Tarradellas, an old Republican politician and former premier of the autonomous Catalan government who since the summer of 1979 had been asking for 'a touch on the rudder' to get the misdirected democracy back on course and who in July 1980 demanded 'a surgical coup to straighten the country out'. Touch on the rudder, surgical coup, change of course: this is the fearful terminology that impregnated conversations from the summer

---

* The word of the moment is disenchantment; if it made its fortune as a description of the time it's because it reflected a reality: in the second half of 1976, shortly after Suárez came to power, 78 per cent of Spaniards preferred political decisions to be made by representatives elected by the people, and in 1978, the year the Constitution was approved, 77 per cent defined themselves as unconditional democrats; but, according to the Metroscopia Institute, in 1980 barely half of Spaniards preferred democracy over any other form of government: the rest had doubts or didn't care, or supported a return to dictatorship.

of 1980 in the hallways of the Cortes, dinners, lunches and political discussions and newspaper and magazine articles in the political village of Madrid. Such expressions are simple euphemisms, or rather empty concepts, which everyone fills in according to their own interests, and which, aside from the resonances of coups they evoke, have only one point in common: for the Francoists as much as for the democrats, for Blas Piñar's or Girón de Velasco's ultraright-wingers as much as for Felipe González's Socialists and many of Santiago Carrillo's Communists and many of Suárez's own centrists, the only one to blame for that crisis is Adolfo Suárez, and the first condition for ending the crisis is to get him out of government. It is a legitimate and sensible wish, because for a long time before the summer Suárez has been an ineffective politician; but politics is also a matter of form – especially the politics of a democracy with many enemies inside and outside the Army, a recently unveiled democracy, the rules of which are still being rolled out and no one has yet mastered, and whose seams are still extremely fragile – and here the problem is not one of content, but of form: the problem was not getting rid of Suárez, but how to get rid of Suárez. The answer the Spanish ruling class should have given to this question is the only answer possible in a democracy as frail as that of 1981: through elections; this was not the answer the Spanish ruling class gave to the question and the answer was practically unvarying: at any price. It was a savage answer, to a great extent the result of arrogance, avarice for power and the immaturity of a ruling class that would rather run the risk of creating conditions favourable to the conduct of the saboteurs of democracy than continue tolerating the presence of the intolerable Adolfo Suárez in the government. There is no other way to explain that from the summer of 1980 onward politicians, businessmen, labour and Church leaders and journalists were deliriously exaggerating the gravity of the situation to be able to play daily with constitutionally questionable solutions that made the already stumbling government of the country stumble, inventing unparliamentary short cuts, threatening to jam the new institutional gears and creating a chaos that constituted the ideal fuel for a possible coup. In the great sewer of Madrid, which is how Suárez referred to the political village of Madrid during that time, those solutions – those surgical coups or touches on the rudder, those changes of course – were no secret to anyone, and rare was the day when the press made no mention of one of them, almost always to encourage it: one day they spoke of a caretaker government led by Alfonso Osorio – right-wing deputy and Deputy Prime Minister of Suárez's first government – and the next day they talked about an interim government led by José María de Areilza – also a right-winger and Minister of Foreign Affairs in the King's first government – one day they were talking about *Operación Quirinal*, bound to make Landelino Lavilla – Speaker of the Cortes and leader of the Christian Democrat sector of Suárez's party – Prime Minister of a coalition government and the next day they were talking about Operation de Gaulle, to make a prestigious military officer leader of a government of national unity, Álvaro Lacalle Leloup or Jesús González del Yerro or Alfonso Armada, the King's former secretary and eventual leader of the 23 February coup attempt; barely a week went by without voices that disagreed over just about everything coming together to agree on their demand for a strong government, which was interpreted by many as a demand for a government led by a military man or involving military officers, a government that would protect the Crown from the turbu-lence, that would correct the chaos of improvisation with which they had made the change from dictatorship to democracy and would put a stop to what some called its excesses, check the spread of terrorism, resuscitate the economy, rationalize the regional autonomy process and make the country calm again. It was a daily jumble of proposals, gossip and secret meetings, and on 2 December 1980 Joaquín Aguirre Bellver, parliamentary reporter for the far-right paper *El Alcázar*, described the political atmosphere in the Cortes: 'A Turkish-style coup, interim government, coalition government . . . A horse race *à la* General Pavía [. . .] At this stage anybody who doesn't have his own formula for the coup is a nobody. Meanwhile, Suárez walks the corridors alone, and no one pays him any attention.' Working things to the advantage of a coup, Aguirre Bellver conscientiously blends military coups in his list – the one led by General Evren a short time ago in Turkey or the one led by General Pavía in Spain a little more than a century before – with theoretically constitutional political operations. It was a deceitful, lethal blend; out of this blend arose 23 February: the political operations were the placenta that nourished the coup, supplying arguments and alibis; to openly discuss the possibility of offering the government to a military man or of asking the military for help in order to escape from the mess, the ruling class half opened the door of politics to an army clamouring to intervene in politics to destroy democracy, and on 23 February the Army burst through that door en masse. As for Suárez, the description Aguirre Bellver gives of him in the winter of the coup is very exact, and inevitably makes one think that the image of his solitary figure in the corridors of the Cortes prefigures his solitary image in the chamber during the evening of 23 February: it is the image of a lost man and a written-off politician who in the months before the coup feels that the entire political class, the entire ruling class of the country, is plotting against him. He is not the only one to feel this way: 'WE'RE ALL PLOTTING' is the headline of an article published at the beginning of December in the newspaper *ABC* by Pilar Urbano in which she refers to the machinations against Suárez by a group of journalists, businessmen, diplomats and politicians of various parties dining together in the capital. He is not the only one to feel this: in the great sewer of Madrid, in the political village, many feel that the whole of reality is plotting against Adolfo Suárez, and during the autumn and winter of 1980 there is barely a single member of the ruling class who consciously or unconsciously does not add his grain of sand to the great mountain of the conspiracy. Or what Suárez feels as a conspiracy.

3

Journalists are plotting against Suárez (or Suárez feels they are plotting against him). Of course, the far-right journalists are plotting, attacking Suárez daily because they consider that destroying him equals destroying democracy. It's true there are not many of them, but they're important because their newspapers and magazines – *El Alcázar, El Imparcial, Heraldo Español, Fuerza Nueva, Reconquista* – are almost the only ones that get inside the barracks, persuading the military that the situation is even worse than it actually is and that, unless out of irresponsibility, egotism or cowardice they allow themselves to be complicit with an unworthy political class that is driving Spain to the brink, sooner or later they'll have to intervene to save the endangered nation. The exhortations for a coup have been constant since the beginning of democracy, but since the summer of 1980 they are no longer sibylline: the 7 August issue of the weekly *Heraldo Español* had an enormous white horse rearing up on the cover and a full-page headline demanding: 'WHO WILL MOUNT THIS HORSE? WANTED: A GENERAL'; inside, a pseudonymously signed article by the journalist Fernando Latorre proposed avoiding a hard military coup by staging a soft military coup that would place a general in the premiership of a government of unity, bandied about a few names – among them that of General Alfonso Armada – and imperiously suggested the King should choose between two types of coup: 'Pavía or Prim: let he who can choose.' In the autumn and winter of 1980, but especially in the weeks before 23 February, these harangues were an everyday occurrence, especially in the newspaper *El Alcázar*, perhaps the most combative publication of the far right, and undoubtedly the most influential: three articles were published there between the end of December and the beginning of February signed by Almendros – a pseudonym that probably disguised the reserve general Manuel Cabeza Calahorra, who in his turn collected the opinions of a group of retired generals – calling for the interruption of democracy by the Army and the King, just as the reserve general Fernando de Santiago – who five years earlier had been one of the Deputy Prime Ministers in Suárez's first government – called for fifteen days before the coup in an article entitled 'Extreme Situation'; there, on 24 January, the editor-in-chief of the newspaper, Antonio Izquierdo, wrote: 'Mysterious unofficial emissaries, who claim to be well informed about everything, are going around these days communicating to well-known personalities in news and finance that "the coup is about to happen, within two months everything will be settled" '; and there, in spite of the stealth with which the coup was hatched, the night before 23 February some clued-up readers knew that the following day would be the great day: the front page of the 22 February issue of *El Alcázar* showed a photo three columns wide of the empty chamber of the Cortes, beneath which, as the paper had done on other occasions, a red sphere warned that the front page contained agreed information; the information could be found by joining with a straight line the point of a thick arrow pointing to the chamber (inside which could be read: 'All ready for Monday's session') to the text of the article by the editor that appeared to the right of the photo; the phrase of the article the straight line pointed to gave almost the exact time Lieutenant Colonel Tejero would enter the Cortes on the following day: 'Before the clock marks 18.30 next Monday.' So, although it is most likely that none of the deputies present in the Cortes on the evening of 23 February knew in advance what was going to happen, at least the editor of *El Alcázar* and some of his contributors did know. There are four questions: who provided them with that information? Who else knew? Who knew how to interpret that front page? Who was the newspaper trying to warn?*

---

* I don't have answers for these questions, but I do have some speculations. The newspaper probably obtained the information from General Milans del Bosch, who the next day would rebel against the government in Valencia, or from one of Milans del Bosch's direct collaborators,

EL ALCAZAR

Director: Antonio IZQUIERDO

Madrid, domingo, 22 de febrero de 1981 / 30 pesetas

Todo dispuesto para la sesión del lunes

UCD INTENSIFICA SU ACTIVIDAD EN BUSCA DE VOTOS

En cualquier caso, la victoria del señor Calvo Sotelo será inestable

(Pág. 10)

Un seguro perdedor

Con todo lo que se ha dicho en torno a la primera fase de la investidura presidencial, no se ha dicho algo importante: las 17 abstenciones (seis de Coalición Democrática, nueve de Minoría Catalana y dos de votos particulares) pueden decidir la suerte del candidato a la presidencia. Pero también y sustancialmente pueden decidir la suerte del PSOE y de todo el ala izquierda del Congreso de los Diputados. Las seis ausencias (dos del PSOE, una del Grupo Andalucista y tres de Herri Batasuna) podrían, a su vez, inclinar la balanza a favor de esa misma izquierda. La penosa realidad de UCD es que su candidato depende de que se mantengan las diecisiete abstenciones y las seis ausencias. Las abstenciones son negociables, claro está. Y no resulta ocioso suponer que a estas alturas —antes de que suenen las 16,30 horas del próximo lunes— los muñidores centristas habrán entrado en funcionamiento para sacar a esos grupos de su pasividad decisoria y para que emitan sus sufragios en favor de don Leopoldo Calvo Sotelo.

Pero, ¿a cambio de qué? Si Coalición Democrática, tras su libre sesión (tres votos afirmativos, seis abstenciones) se mantiene en su posición, el señor Calvo Sotelo no tiene otro camino que negociar, a tumba abierta, con la Minoría Catalana. ¿Qué puede negociar el candidato centrista con la Minoría Catalana? Sólo cuestiones que se escapan, política y moralmente hablando, a la capacidad de maniobra de todo Gobierno: cuestiones de Estado, de soberanía, de integridad... ¡Cara puede resultar la mínima victoria del centrismo! Cara e intolerable. Se dirá que de alguna forma hay que resolver la sesión del lunes, pero lo importante no es que se resuelva o no se resuelva la sesión del lunes. Es más importante que se prevea, a tiempo, lo que puede suceder tras esa sesión.

¿Disolución de las Cámaras y convocatoria de elecciones generales...? ¿Por qué? Existen otros indicios que pudieran presagiar el resultado positivo de otras operaciones, llevadas hasta ahora con la máxima cautela: formación de un Gobierno de «ancha base», como solicitaban anoche las movilizaciones de esas bases —en automóvil, porque los tiempos siguen cambiando que es una barbaridad— para anunciar una concentración prevista para hoy y posteriormente desautorizada. Es notorio que para la Corona existe una prueba hasta cierto punto atractiva por lo que pudiera tener de riesgo: un Gobierno socialista que estabilice o desestabilizara, con carácter irreversible, la permanencia de la propia institución. Eso dicen, al menos, los mejor informados. ¿No constituiría un primer paso ese Gobierno de «ancha base»? ¿Le pondrían reparos los socialdemócratas de Fernández Ordóñez, la figura más mimada por la oposición marxista? ¿Le haría reparos Manuel Fraga Iribarne, tras su demoledora actitud ante Calvo Sotelo y sus oportunas y recientes declaraciones dando por hecho que admitiría la colaboración del PSOE en un posible Gabinete? ¿Le harían ascos los liberales asidos al centrismo unico fórmula de supervivencia? ¿Se negarían a ello los grupos separatistas, forman o no en el ala izquierda de su «ente»? ¡Hay que ver qué lenguaje se gastan! si mantienen la certeza de que ese Gobierno facilitaría aún más sus pretensiones autonomistas?

Difícil jornada la del próximo lunes en el Palacio de la Carrera de San Jerónimo: en el mejor de los casos, la situación sería mala, porque la anunciada victoria por mayoría simple de Calvo Sotelo será una victoria pírrica, carvada de hipotecas y asaltante; y el menos posible conformaría el paso inmediato a un Gabinete de concentración, con discreta mayoría socialista —a nivel gubernamental— y un independiente frío, al estilo de López de Letona, de Cabeza del Ejecutivo... O un general con pedigree liberal y demócrata de toda la vida o de parte de ella. En pocas palabras: el panorama no es halagüeño para nadie. En cualquier caso, el señor Calvo Sotelo será un seguro perdedor. Porque será inequívoco: el Estado Español; o, si queréis, España. Pero el Estado vive preso del federalismo y de España con nadie se acuerda ya, salvo Juan Pablo II, que tuvo la inoportuna humorada —¡Dios se lo pague!— de evocar la epopeya civilizadora de nuestro pueblo en Asia: en Filipinas, donde no se rindieron los últimos soldados que defendían los flecos del Imperio: en Baler. ¡Quién recuerda ya aquellas fantásticas historias!

Antonio IZQUIERDO

SIN NOTICIAS DE LOS CONSULES SECUESTRADOS

(Pág. 7)

But not only far-right journalists are plotting against Suárez – and against democracy – democratic journalists are also plotting against him – or Suárez feels they are plotting against him. It is the feeling of a cornered man, but maybe it's not an inexact feeling. The final stages of Francoism and the beginnings of the transition had brought about a singular symbiosis between journalism and politics, a cronyism between politicians and journalists that allowed the latter to feel themselves protagonists of the first order in the change from dictatorship to democracy; by 1980, however, that complicity has broken, or at least the complicity has broken down between Suárez and the press, which considers itself disdained by power and attributes to this disdain the responsibility or part of the responsibility for the terrible time the country's going through. The wounded pride the press is feeling then is a translation of Suárez's wounded pride (and also a translation of the wounded pride the country is feeling) and, given that some significant journalists claim the mission of dictating the government's policies and consider Suárez little short of an impostor and in any case a deplorable politician, in much of the media the criticism of Suárez is brutally harsh and contributes to spurring on the coup d'état mentality, feeding the phantom of an emergency situation and giving space on their pages to constant rumours of political operations and hard or soft coups

---

or, more likely, from Juan García Carrés, former head of the vertical trade unions of the Franco era who in the months leading up to the coup acted as liaison between Milans del Bosch and Tejero: Milans del Bosch and García Carrés both maintained close links with *El Alcázar*. José Antonio Girón de Velasco, leader of a sector of the far right, president of the Confederation of Combatants and close friend of García Carrés, would probably likewise have known; also, generals in the reserves linked to Cabeza Calahorra and Fernando de Santiago and former Francoist ministers linked to Girón de Velasco, but not the far-right parliamentarian who had a seat in the Cortes: the leader of Fuerza Nueva, Blas Piñar. Undoubtedly more people knew, but not many more. In any case, this is especially fertile ground for fantasy or, indeed, for hallucination: on 5 February Manuel Fraga, leader of the right-wing party Alianza Popular, writes in his diary: 'Rumours everywhere [. . .]. A clairvoyant mentions a coup for the 24th'; on the 13th the police receive a report from an informer who is about to be fired for his lack of credibility that announces a coup for the 23rd; *Spic*, a monthly commercial aviation journal devoted to leisure and tourism, goes on sale on the 18th; one of the articles, signed by its editor, says: 'It is not true that I intend to launch a coup on Monday 23 February . . . besides, I don't know (*además no sé*)' (further hallucination: the word *además* contains 6 letters; the word *no* 2; the word *sé* another 2; result: 6.22, almost exactly the time Lieutenant Colonel Tejero bursts into the Cortes). It is important to say that on the 5th, on the 13th and even on the 18th the date and time of the coup had still not been fixed.

under way that, rather than prevent them, serves to prepare the ground for them. Furthermore, four and a half years in power – and especially four years as intense as those experienced by Suárez – have been more than enough to make many enemies: there are spiteful journalists who change their adulation in a very short time into scorn; there are critical journalists who turn into kamikaze journalists; there are editorial conglomerations – like the 16 Group, owners of *Diario 16* and *Cambio 16*, the most important political weekly of the time – that in the summer of 1980 initiate a ferocious campaign against Suárez instigated by the leaders of his own party; there are cases like that of Emilio Romero, undoubtedly the most influential journalist of the late stages of the Franco regime, who after being ousted by Suárez from his privileged position in the press of the Movimiento, the only party allowed to exist under Franco, developed a lasting hatred for the Prime Minister, and who, in his column in *ABC* a few days before the coup, proposed General Armada as a candidate to lead the government after the surgical coup or touch on the rudder that should displace Suárez. The case of Luis María Anson, a very prominent journalist in democratic times, is different and more complicated.

Anson was a veteran defender of the monarchist cause whom Suárez had helped in the early 1970s, when he thought he was going to be charged for insulting Franco as a result of an article published in *ABC*; later, in the mid-1970s, it was Anson who helped Suárez: encouraged by the future King, the journalist urged on Suárez's political career while in charge of the magazine *Blanco y Negro*, boosted his candidacy for Prime Minister of the government and celebrated his appointment in *Gaceta Ilustrada* with an enthusiasm unusual in the reformist press; finally it was Suárez who helped Anson again: just two months after reaching the premiership he appointed the journalist to the post of director of the state news agency EFE. Although Anson remained at the head of the agency until 1982, this mutual exchange of favours was cut short a few months later, when the journalist began to feel that Suárez was a weak politician and had a complex about his Falangist past and that he was handing power in the new democracy to the left, and turned into an implacable detractor of the Prime Minister's policies; implacable and public: Anson met periodically in the EFE agency canteen with politicians, journalists, financiers, Church officials and military officers, and in those meetings stirred up discontent against his erstwhile patron from very early on; also, according to Francisco Medina, as early as the autumn of 1977 he discussed a plan to rectify democracy – in reality a concealed coup d'état – inspired by the events of June 1958 that allowed General de Gaulle to return to power and found the French Fifth Republic: the idea was that the Army would put discreet pressure on the King to persuade Suárez to resign and oblige him to establish a theoretically apolitical government led by a technocrat, a government of unity or salvation that would place constitutional legitimacy in brackets for a time with the aim of re-establishing order, stopping the bloodbath of terrorism and overcoming the economic crisis; with the addition of a military officer leading the government, large doses of improvisation and recklessness, and a head-on crash with constitutional order, that was the plan the *golpistas* tried to execute on 23 February. Anson's relationship with General Armada – described in his memoir as 'a good friend' with whom he'd kept in touch over 'many years' – the rigid monarchical convictions that united them, the fact that certain witnesses claimed Anson figured as a minister in the government Armada planned to form as a result of the coup, EFE's resistance after 23 February to accepting the general's role as leader of the rebellion, Anson's belligerence towards Suárez's politics and his prestige as perpetual conspirator extended suspicions about the journalist over time. However, the truth is that Anson and Armada's relationship was not as close as the general made it out to be, that the journalist figured in the supposed list of Armada's government along with numerous democratic politicians ignorant of the role the general desired to assign them as guarantors of the coup, and that EFE's unwillingness to admit that the King's former secretary would have led the attempted military coup was a reflection of a quite generalized incredulity in the days immediately following 23 February; as for the idea of the coup, it was most probably that of the general himself – who had arrived in Paris as a student at the École de Guerre shortly after de Gaulle's ascent to power in France and had experienced its consequences up close – who conceived it and spread it so successfully that from the summer of 1980 it was circulating profusely throughout the political village of Madrid and there was hardly a political party that did not consider the hypothesis of placing a soldier at the head of a coalition or caretaker or unity government as one of the possible ways of expelling Suárez from power. In short, no serious indication exists that Anson was a direct promoter of Armada's candidacy for the leadership of a coalition government – and much less that he was linked to the military coup – although there is no reason to disregard that at some point in the autumn and winter of 1980 he might have considered that emergency solution to be reasonable, because it is certain that the journalist encouraged any effort designed to replace as soon as possible a head of government who, in his opinion as in that of almost all of the ruling class, was leading the Crown and the country to disaster.

4

Bankers and businessmen are also plotting against Suárez (or Suárez feels they're plotting against him) as well as the right-wing party that the bankers and businessmen back: Alianza Popular. It has not always been like this: businessmen and bankers have not always backed the party of the right, or they haven't always done so with as much enthusiasm. Although it is likely that deep down they despised Suárez since he came to power (and not only because they considered him ignorant of economic matters), the fact is that at the beginning of his mandate bankers and businessmen supported the new Prime Minister unreservedly because they understood that supporting him was supporting the monarchy and because the monarchy convinced them that this likeable nonentity, who had started out as an errand boy in the Movimiento edifice and knew it like the back of his hand after having swept every last corner of the place, was the ideal foreman to direct the demolition job of an obsolete architecture that for forty years had been of great use to them but now was hindering their business and embarrassing them before their European colleagues. Suárez came through: he carried out the task successfully; once completed, however, he should go: this was the opinion of the majority of bankers and businessmen. But Suárez didn't go; on the contrary: what happened was that the errand boy promoted to foreman fancied himself an architect and began to erect the brand-new edifice of democracy on the razed site of the edifice of the dictatorship. That's where the problem started: after years of seeking their approval, emboldened by the repeated endorsement of votes Suárez began to give them the brush-off, to refuse their advice and pats on the back, avoid them or ignore them or snub them or make gestures that they interpreted as snubs, and ended up not receiving them at Moncloa or taking their calls and not even acknowledging the warning and lessons with which they tried to return him to the fold. That's how they discovered to their cost something they'd suspected from the start, which was that the formerly obliging errand boy was concealing one of those cocky provincial upstarts who nurse like a grudge the dream of facing up to the strongest men in the capital. That was also how they discovered, as they noticed anxiously that business was getting worse and worse, the belated or improvised social democratic vocation afflicting Suárez and to which they indistinctly attributed his incapacity to rid himself of his upbringing as a young Falangist with the revolution pending, his eagerness to emulate Felipe González, the brilliant young Socialist leader, and his obsession with acquiring the credentials of democratic purity the approval of the newspaper *El País* could bestow. And that was how, over the course of 1980, they decided Suárez's policies were definitely doing nothing but making the economic crisis worse and tearing the state to pieces; they likewise decided that this plebeian was practising the premiership fraudulently, because his power came from the right, who had voted for him and who had supported him for four years, but he was governing for the left. The conclusion came swiftly: the erroneous premiership of this illicit, insolent upstart must be ended by whatever means necessary. From there in the autumn and winter before the coup bankers and businessmen boosted the nightmare of a country rushing towards catastrophe, they backed any and every political operation against Suárez's government that the right came up with and injected daily doses of disquiet into the disquiet of the most conservative sectors of the party that propped up government, with the aim of dismembering it, uniting the deserters with the minority Alianza Popular and forming with them a new government led by a politician or an independent technocrat or a high-ranking military officer, a coalition or interim or unity government, in any case a strong government underpinned by a new parliamentary majority. Because they must re-establish the natural order of things shattered by Suárez, and they called this majority the natural majority; since the natural leader of this natural majority could only be the leader of the Alianza Popular, the businessmen and bankers turned Manuel Fraga into their leader.

In the autumn and winter of 1980 that Fraga should be plotting against Suárez (or that Suárez should feel that Fraga was plotting against him) was an almost unavoidable fact, obeying not just political logic: after all, almost no one had more powerful reasons than Fraga to consider Suárez a usurper. Fraga had been the dictatorship's wunder-kind, for years he had sat in Franco's Cabinet meetings and at the beginning of the 1970s, with a superficial liberal plating, he seemed to be the man chosen by history to lead post-Francoism, understanding such a thing to be a reformed Francoism that stretched the limits of Francoism without breaking it, which was what Fraga understood. No one had ever denied he had the intellectual capacity to carry out this labour. The anecdote is very famous: trying to flatter the leader of Alianza Popular and humiliate Suárez, during the debate of the no-confidence motion tabled against him in May 1980, Felipe González declared from the speakers' rostrum in the Cortes that Fraga could fit the state inside his head; if the metaphor is valid, then it's also incom-plete: if it's true that Fraga could fit the state inside his head, then it's also true that there was absolutely no room for anything else in there. In this sense, as in almost all of them, Fraga was the antithesis of Suárez: honours student, exam ace, prolific writer, during the years of the regime change Fraga was a politician who gave the impression of know-ing everything and not understanding anything, or at least not understanding what needed to be understood, and that is that the limits of Francoism could not be stretched without breaking because Francoism was unreformable, or was only reformable if the reform consisted precisely in breaking it; this dramatic intellectual weakness – added to his genetic authoritarianism, his lack of cunning, the distrust he'd inspired for no reason in powerful sectors of the Franco regime since the late 1960s, and his lack of personal harmony with the monarch – explains why the Prime Minister chosen by the King to direct the regime change was not the predicted Fraga but the unexpected Suárez, and in later years Fraga's intimidating manner and political roughness as well as the strategic intelligence of Suárez (who at that time gave the impression of understanding everything or at least understanding what needed to be understood, even if he didn't know anything) diminished his space until the theoretical liberal of the early 1970s ended up confined in the corner of the reactionaries and condemned to give vent to his frustrated ambitions by dragging a string of Francoist diplodocuses across a desolate stony wasteland. In the months before the coup, however, the tables have turned: while Suárez sinks down understanding nothing, Fraga seems to be on top of the world, as if he knows and understands everything; although his power in the Cortes continues to be scant, because the laboriously moderate coalition with which he'd stood in the last elections has barely a handful of seats, his public image is no longer that of someone incurably nostalgic for Francoism: they miss him in the Royal Household, where for years he had a loyal ally in General Alfonso Armada; his relations with the Army and the Church couldn't be better; the same businessmen and bankers who used to exclude him flatter him and prominent figures from Suárez's party pursue him, as they've now chosen him as their true leader and plan with him the best way to bring down the government and put in its place a coalition or interim or caretaker or national unity government, anything except letting Suárez remain in power and completely ruin the country. Anything includes a coalition or interim or caretaker or unity government led by a soldier; if that soldier is his friend Alfonso Armada, so much the better. Like so many people in those days, perhaps more than anybody in those days, Fraga, who is aware that he is a political reference point for many in the military with *golpista* instincts, weighs up the possibility: his diaries of the time abound in notes about dinners with politicians and officers where it's considered; many outstanding members of Alianza Popular, such as Juan de Arespacochaga, former Mayor of Madrid, approve unreservedly; according to Arespacochaga, many members of the Party executive do as well. While he's meeting every second day with leading figures of Suárez's party, including his parliamentary spokesman, Fraga doubts, but he does not doubt that they have to somehow get rid of the subordinate who four years earlier, owing to the King's error or whim, got in the way of his prime ministerial destiny: before the summer he'd worried the country with the warning that 'if steps are not taken, the coup will be inevitable'; on 19 February, four days before the coup, he warned in the Cortes: 'If a touch on the rudder is wanted, the change of direction we all know necessary, we'll be found ready to collaborate. And if not, not [. . .] The boat must be brought into dry dock and the hull and engine thoroughly revised.' Suárez has not done the political transition well, and the moment has come to trim it or rectify it: that was exactly the objective of 23 February. Touch on the rudder, surgical coup, change of direction: that was exactly the terminology of the placenta of the coup. Otherwise, during the evening and night of 23 February the businessmen and bankers kept silent, not condemning or approving the coup, like almost everyone else, and only towards two in the morning, when the failure of the military uprising seemed sure after the King spoke against it on television, the director of the CEOE (the Confederation of Spanish Business Organizations), pressured by the head of the provisional government, finally resolved to publicly condemn the seizure of the Cortes and proclaim his respect for the Constitution. The political parties, and among them Alianza Popular, did not do so until seven in the morning.

5

Is the Church also plotting against Suárez? Does Suárez feel the Church is also plotting against him? Just as in recent times he has made enemies of the journalists and bankers and businessmen and of almost the entire political class of the country, shortly before the coup Suárez makes an enemy of the Catholic Church; the Church, for its part, abandons him to his fate, if not actually doing everything in its power to bring him down. For Suárez, a religious man, a weekly-Mass Christian, educated in seminaries and Acción Católica associations, very aware of the enormous power the Church still possesses in Spain and that its support is one of the few he has left in the disordered scattering of these final months, the setback is a terrible blow. The Church – or at least the upper echelons of the Church or an important part of the upper echelons of the Church – had favoured the change from dictatorship to democracy on the eve of Franco's death and, since Suárez had come to power, Cardinal Tarancón, president of the Spanish Episcopal Conference from 1971, established a complicity with him over the years that managed to weather the Church's determination to maintain its eternal privileged status in spite of political transformations. In the autumn of 1980, however, Suárez and Tarancón's relationship snaps; the provocation for the rupture is the divorce law, an unacceptable revolution for a large part of the Church and the Spanish right. By that time the law has been in the works for almost two years, always under the control of Christian Democrat ministers and always guarded by a personal pact between Suárez and Tarancón severely restricting its reach; but in September of that year, as a consequence of one of the

cyclical crises that rock the government, the law passes into the hands
of the leader of the Social Democrat sector of the Prime Minister's
party, who accelerates proceedings and manages to get the Congressional
Justice Committee to approve in mid-December a much more permis-
sive projected divorce law than the one agreed between Suárez and
Tarancón. His response is immediate: furious, feeling betrayed, he
breaks all links with Suárez, and from that moment on, wrong-footed
by the Prime Minister's feint – or by his weakness, which prevents him
from keeping his promises – Tarancón is left at the mercy of the
conservative bishops, partisans of Manuel Fraga, who also see their
positions reinforced by the arrival in Madrid of an extraordinarily
conservative papal nuncio representing the extraordinarily conservative
Pope John Paul II: Monsignor Innocenti. So Suárez is also left undefended on the religious flank; more than undefended: it is a fact that
the nunciature as well as members of the Episcopal Conference encouraged operations against Suárez organized by the Christian Democrats
of his party, and it's very likely that the nuncio and some bishops were
informed in the days before the coup that a trimming or rectification
of democracy with the backing of the King was imminent. It's hard to
believe all this had nothing to do with the Church's behaviour on 23
February. That afternoon the plenary assembly of the Episcopal
Conference was meeting at the Pinar de Chamartín Retreat, in Madrid,
with the aim of electing Cardinal Tarancón's replacement; on learning
the news of the assault on the Cortes the assembly broke up without
pronouncing a single word in favour of democracy or making a single
gesture of condemnation or protest at that outrage against liberty. Not
a single word. Not a single gesture. Nothing. It's true: like almost everyone else.

6

Of course the main opposition, the PSOE, the Spanish Socialist Party, is plotting against Suárez (or Suárez feels they're plotting against him). But, unlike Fraga and his party, the businessmen and bankers and even the journalists, the leaders of the PSOE have absolutely no experience of power and are barely beginning to penetrate the corridors of the great sewer of Madrid, so they operate with a naive rookie clumsiness that makes them easy to manipulate by those planning the coup.

The Socialists have been the surprise of the new democracy: run since 1974 by an impetuous group of young men with a clean democratic pedigree (albeit little or no relevance in the struggle against Franco), the PSOE is from then on a party clustered around the leadership of Felipe González, and in 1977, after the first democratic elections, becomes the second largest party in the country and the largest on the left, displacing Santiago Carrillo's Communist Party, which throughout the Franco period has been in practice the only party of clandestine opposition. The electoral triumph plunges the Socialists into a perplexed euphoria, and for the next two years they develop, as do Fraga's right and Carrillo's Communists, a politics of accords with Suárez that culminates in the passing of the Constitution, but at the beginning of 1979, when the first constitutional elections are about to be held, they understand their time has come: like so many people on the right and the left, they think that, once the edifice of Francoism has been demolished and the edifice of democracy erected with the Constitution, Suárez has finished the task the King assigned him; they don't despise Suárez (or not yet, or not in public, or not entirely) for being an upstart errand boy designated in haste as foreman and eventually self-styled architect, although they are absolutely sure that only they can success-fully administer democracy, establish it in the country and integrate the country into Europe; they think the country thinks like them and they also think, as jittery as hungry children in front of a cake-shop window, that if they don't win these elections they'll never win; they think they're going to win. But they don't win, and that disappoint-ment is mainly responsible for four decisions they make in the following months: the first consists of attributing their unexpected defeat to Suárez's final television appearance of the campaign, in which the Prime Minister managed to frighten an electorate wary of the Marxist radical-ism of a PSOE that according to its statutes was still a Marxist party but according to its deeds and words was already a social democratic party; the second is to interpret Suárez's televised intervention as a dirty trick, and to assume that you can't play fair with someone who plays dirty; the third consists of accepting that they would only get into government if they managed to destroy Suárez politically and person-ally, demolishing the reputation of the leader who had beaten them in two consecutive elections; the fourth is the corollary of the previous three: it consists of going all out for Suárez's head.

From the autumn of 1979 – once the term Marxism was eliminated from the PSOE statutes and Felipe González's power in the leadership of the Party reinforced – the offensive, increasingly endorsed by Suárez's inability to curb the country's deterioration, is merciless: the Socialists paint a daily apocalyptic picture of the Prime Minister's administra-tion, they dig up and throw in his face his past as a Falangist errand boy and Movimiento social climber, accuse him of ruining the democratic project, of being ready to sell Spain in order to remain in Moncloa, call him illiterate, a card sharp, a potential *golpista*. Meanwhile, they opt for dramatic effect, and in the middle of May 1980 propose a vote of no confidence against Suárez in the Cortes. The manoeuvre, destined in theory to make Felipe González Prime Minister, is a mathematical fail-ure because the Socialist leader does not obtain enough votes to remove Suárez from his post, but most of all it is a propagandistic success: during the debate the television cameras show a young, persuasive and prime ministerial González facing an aged and defeated Suárez unable even to defend himself from his adversary's attacks. This triumph, however, marks a limit: with the no-confidence motion the Socialists have used up the parliamentary mechanisms for taking the premiership; and this is when, goaded by desperation and fear and immaturity and greed for power, they begin to explore the limits of the recently debuted democracy, forcing its rules to the utmost without yet having mastered them; and this is when they turn into useful tools for the *golpistas*.

Since before the summer those recent arrivals in the salons, *tertulias* and restaurants of the political village of Madrid have talked and heard talk of *golpes de estado*, coups d'état, of governments of national unity, caretaker governments, governments of salvation, of de Gaulle-style operations; their attitude to this is ambiguous: on the one hand the rumours worry them; on the other hand they don't want to be left to one side when it comes to replacing Suárez, because they are impatient to prove that, as well as knowing how to operate in opposition, they know how to operate in government, and they also begin to consider the idea of forming a coalition or caretaker or unity government chaired by a military officer, a proposal for which in the last week of August they seek support in discussions with Jordi Pujol, premier of the Catalan autonomous government. Undoubtedly with this idea in mind, in the autumn the Socialists make enquiries into the Army's mood and about the murmurs of a military coup, and in mid-October, after an internal meeting during which Felipe González wonders whether all the warning lights of the democracy were not already flashing and in which they discuss the eventuality of the Party entering a coalition government, several PSOE leaders meet with General Sabino Fernández Campo, secretary to the King, and with General Alfonso Armada, his predecessor in the post, whose name had been on everyone's lips for months as a possible leader of a government of unity. Felipe González is involved in the interview with Fernández Campo; not in the interview with Alfonso Armada: it is conducted by Enrique Múgica, the Party's number three and until recently leader of the Congressional Defence Committee. In light of 23 February the conversation between Múgica and Armada takes on important significance, and its protagonists have told of it in public more than once. The interview, which lasts for almost four hours, is held on 22 October during a lunch given at the home of the Mayor of Lérida, in the province of which the general has been military governor since the beginning of the year, and is attended, as well as by the host, by Joan Raventós, leader of the Catalan Socialists. Múgica and Armada seem to get along personally; politically as well, at least on the crucial point: both agree that the situation of the country is catastrophic, which according to Armada is of great worry to the King and is putting the Crown in danger; both agree that the only one responsible for the catastrophe is Suárez and that Suárez leaving power is the only possible solution to the mess, although according to Armada the solution would not be complete unless an interim or unity government was immediately formed with the participation of the principal political parties and led by an independent, if possible from the military. Múgica does not say no to this last suggestion; then Raventós interjects and asks Armada if he would be willing to be the military officer who heads the government; Armada does not say no to this suggestion either. The lunch ends without promises or commitments, but Múgica writes up a report on the interview for the Party's executive committee, in the weeks that follow various members of that organization sound out leaders of minority parties about the possibility of forming a coalition government led by a soldier and over the course of the autumn and winter several different rumours spread around Madrid – the PSOE plans a new no-confidence motion supported by a sector of Suárez's party, the PSOE plans to enter a caretaker or interim government with Fraga's party and a sector of Suárez's party – united by the common denominator of a general with whom the Socialists intend to remove Suárez from Moncloa.

That was all. Or that's all we know, because at that time the leaders of the PSOE often discussed the role the Army could play in situations of emergency such as the one they believed the country was going through, which was a way of signalling the landing strip for military intervention. In any case, the long lunchtime chat between Enrique Múgica and General Armada in Lérida and the movements and rumours to which it gave rise constituted backing for Armada's *golpista* inclinations and a good alibi enabling the King's former secretary to insinuate or declare here and there in the months before the coup that the Socialists would readily participate in a unitarian government led by him or were even encouraging him to form one, and on the night of 23 February, again waving the banner of the PSOE's acquiescence, to try to impose that government by force. All this does not of course mean that during the autumn and winter of 1980 the Socialists were plotting in favour of a military coup against democracy; it only means that a strong dose of irresponsible bewilderment induced by an itching for power led them to press to a frightening degree the siege of the legitimate Prime Minister of the country and that, believing they were manoeuvring against Adolfo Suárez, they ended up manoeuvring unknowingly in favour of the enemies of democracy.

7

But more than anyone else it is his own party that is plotting against Suárez (that Suárez feels is especially plotting against him): the Unión de Centro Democrático. The word party is imprecise; in reality, the Union of the Democratic Centre is not a party but a painstaking cocktail of groups with disparate ideologies – from Liberals and Christian Democrats to Social Democrats, by way of the so-called Blues, who like Suárez came from the very belly of the Francoist machine – an electoral brand improvised in the spring of 1977 to stand in the first free elections for forty years at the inducement of Adolfo Suárez, who according to all prognostications would win thanks to the success of his trajectory as Prime Minister, during which he's managed to dismantle in less than a year the institutional framework of Francoism and call the first democratic elections. Finally the predictions are fulfilled: Suárez achieves the victory and over the two years that follow the UCD remains united by the glue of power, by Suárez's undisputed leadership and by the historical urgency of constructing a system of liberties. The spring of 1979 sees Suárez's stellar moment, the peak of his command and also that of his party: in December the Constitution had been passed, in March he won his second general election, in April his first municipal ones, the edifice of the new state seems on the point of being completed with the processing of the statutes of autonomy of Catalonia and the Basque Country; just at this moment of fulfilment, however, Suárez begins to sink into a sort of lethargy from which he will not emerge until he leaves the premiership, and his party begins to splinter irremediably. The phenomenon is strange, but not inexplicable, it's just that it doesn't have one single explanation, but several. I'll suggest two: one is political and it is that Suárez, who had been able to do the most difficult things, is unable to do the easiest; the other is personal and is that Suárez, who until then has appeared to be a politician of steel, collapses psychologically. I'll add a third explanation, at once political and personal: the jealousies, rivalries and discrepancies that germinate at the heart of his party.

In effect: at the end of March 1980, when the inefficient running of the country can no longer be hidden and pessimism is overwhelming in the opinion polls the government commissions, three bitter defeats at the ballot box (in the Basque Country, in Catalonia and in Andalusia) reveal unsatisfied ambitions in the UCD and ideological disagreements until then covered by the glitter of victory, so that any relevant matter (economic policy, autonomy policy, education policy, the divorce law, whether to join NATO) and more than one irrelevant matter provoke controversies that are postponed to avoid an internal explosion and that time does nothing but exacerbate; for his part, Suárez is increasingly absent, perplexed and locked away in the domestic labyrinth of Moncloa, and has lost the energy of his early years in government and seems unable to restore order to the rebellious ruckus his party has become, perhaps because he suspects that for quite a while, encouraged by his own weakness, like animals who've got the scent of fear in their prey the leaders of the theoretically fused groups of the UCD again consider him what maybe deep down they have never stopped considering him: a little provincial Falangist consumed by ambition, an ignorant nonentity, a textbook arriviste who had thrived in the corrupt environment of Francoism thanks to flattery and fiddling and who continued to thrive afterwards thanks to the King putting him in charge of dismantling with a card sharp's tricks and huckster's verbosity the whole Movimiento set-up, a rogue who years earlier was perhaps a necessary evil, because he knew the cesspits of Francoism better than anybody, but who is now driving the country to the brink with his risible statesman pretensions. This is how Suárez begins to suspect the leaders of his party see him; his suspicions are not groundless: arrogant lawyers, prestigious professionals from good families, high-ranking career civil servants, cultured, cosmopolitan men or men who think

themselves cultured and cosmopolitan, the UCD leaders have gone in
a few years from crawling to Suárez, investing him with the supremacy
of a charismatic leader, to denouncing ever more openly his personal
and intellectual limitations, his incompetence at governing, his abys-
mal qualities as a parliamentarian, his ignorance of democratic customs
– which authorizes him to believe that he can keep governing as he did
in his time as appointed Prime Minister, when he answered only to the
King – his snubbing of the Cortes and the deputies of his party in
the Cortes, his chaotic way of working, his pseudo-leftist populism
and his fugitive's isolation in Moncloa, where he lives sequestered by a
drove of incompetent and disorganized acolytes. In April 1980 that is
the reality which for Suárez then is only a suspicion: that all the leaders
of all the ranks of his party despise him, as do many of his seconds, and
all of them feel they could replace him and do a better job.

This private feeling among the UCD leaders soon finds public
confirmation, and Suárez's suspicion becomes a certainty. Knocked out
by Felipe González's devastating rhetorical skill during the debate triggered by the no-confidence motion tabled by the Socialists in May,
Suárez embarrasses the deputies of his party by shying away from
dialectical combat and allowing his ministers to be the ones to defend
the government from the rostrum while the deputy leader of the
Socialists, Alfonso Guerra, hurls an open secret at the Prime Minister.
'Half the UCD deputies get excited when they hear Felipe González
speak,' Guerra proclaims in the Cortes. 'And the other half get excited
when they hear Manuel Fraga.' Suárez survives the no-confidence vote
by the skin of his teeth, but he does so knowing that Guerra's sentence
is not a mere rhetorical thrust of parliamentary squabble, that his political prestige borders on nil, that his party is threatening to disintegrate
and that if he wants to avoid an end to his government and recover
control of the UCD he must immediately take the initiative. So, as
soon as he can, he summons all the Party chiefs together at a country
estate belonging to the Ministry of Public Works, in Manzanares el
Real, not far from Madrid. The conclave lasts three days and amounts
to the worst humiliation he's suffered so far in his political life; in fact,
it's easy to imagine that, barely has the debate begun, when his colleagues'
eyes reveal the truth to Suárez, and in them Suárez reads words like

Falangist, nonentity, upstart, sycophant, ignoramus, card sharp, huckster, rogue, populist, inept. But he doesn't have to imagine anything, because the reality is that during those three days the Party bosses of the UCD tell Suárez to his face what they've been saying behind his back for months, and if they don't finish him off once and for all it's because they have no viable replacement yet – none of them can count on the support of the others, and the rank and file of the Party is still with the Prime Minister – and because Suárez turns this to his advantage: after resisting as well as he can the criticisms they inflict on him from every angle, Suárez promises to mend his sorry prime ministerial ways and most of all makes a pledge to share power with them, to such an extent that from that moment on he is no longer in practice the head of the Party and government but has become a *primus inter pares*. Once the meeting ends, Suárez tries to fulfil the promise immediately; also the pledge, and at the end of August he designs with a few of his faithful a strategy that means reshuffling the Cabinet for the second time in a few months, giving important ministries to the UCD Party bosses. The arrangement is not short of counterweights damaging to his future – worst of all: it perhaps hastens the departure from the government of the Deputy Prime Minister Abril Martorell, a longstanding friend who in recent times has served as his shield as well as right-hand man – but convinces Suárez that he can smother the uprising with it and prolong his dying premiership and be compensated for the affronts received by proving to his critics that they're mistaken. The one who's mistaken, however, is him, because he doesn't know or can't understand that once respect for someone is lost it cannot be recovered, and inside his party the rebellion is unstoppable.

On 17 September, his new government recently constituted, Suárez, who appears at times to be waking from his lethargy, comfortably wins a confidence vote in the Cortes; since this should allow him to govern without problems in the upcoming months, it confirms for a few hours the optimism of his predictions. The next day, however, a riot breaks out. Miguel Herrero de Miñón – one of the leaders of the Christian Democrat sector of the Party – publishes an article in *El País* that pretends to be a reasoned clarification of the confidence motion but is in reality a frontal attack on his Prime Minister's way of practising politics. A few days later the UCD deputies elect Herrero de Miñón to the post of Party spokesman in the Cortes; given that Herrero de Miñón had run on a platform of being an antidote to Suárez's outrages and negligences, and given that he had sponsored a candidate who was defeated, this election represents a severe setback for the Prime Minister, who only then intuits that his summer promises and concessions have not dissolved the mounting rejection of him, but rather increased it. The intuition is now accurate, but belated: by this stage the powerful Christian Democrat sector of the UCD is publicly plotting to expel him from the premiership; the Liberals and Social Democrats and Blues have also begun to do so, and as autumn passes and winter begins even those most loyal to the Prime Minister secretly give up their loyalty and take positions in view of a future without him: pressured, wooed and backed up by journalists, businessmen, bankers, soldiers and clergymen, some aspire to form a new majority with Fraga; pressured, wooed and backed up by the Socialists' youthful vigour, unbridled ambition and absolute faith in themselves, others aspire to form a new majority with González; all or almost all – Christian Democrats and Liberals and Social Democrats and Blues, long-standing anti-Suárists and bandwagon anti-Suárists – argue about how to replace Suárez without going to the polls and who to put in his place. In the early days of 1981, while the UCD prepares for its second conference, which will be held at the end of January in Palma de Mallorca, the Party's confusion is total, and in these days a document demanding a greater degree of internal democracy, drawn up by the Prime Minister's adversaries, has already been signed by more than five hundred centrist delegates, which amounts to a very serious threat to the control Suárez still has over the Party rank and file, his last stronghold. As in the Alianza Popular, as in the PSOE, as in the whole political village of Madrid, in the UCD there are also discussions of the idea that a military officer or a prestigious politician at the head of a coalition or interim or caretaker or unity government might be the best instrument to get Suárez out of government and overcome the crisis; certain heavyweight deputies indulge it – especially deputies from the Christian Democrat sector well connected to the military, and especially to Alfonso Armada, with whom some have personally discussed the idea

– and in the middle of January the rumours that have been circulating with variable intensity since the summer proliferate, rumours of hard coups or soft and rumours of another motion of no confidence against the Prime Minister in the works, a motion probably presented by the PSOE but supported by a sector of the UCD if not organized from within it, which should guarantee its success and maybe the formation of the emergency government everyone's talking about and for which everyone starting with Suárez himself knows that General Armada is putting himself forward. In reality the rumours about the no-confidence motion are much more than rumours – there is no doubt that the motion is seriously discussed within the Party – but in any case the UCD is, one month before 23 February, a seething mob of politicians tirelessly scheming against the Prime Minister of the government much more than the political party that sustains the government. The coup grows in the midst of this mob: this mob is not the whole placenta of the coup, but it is a substantial part of the placenta of the coup.

8

All these things happen in Spain, where everyone and everything seems to be plotting against Adolfo Suárez (or where Adolfo Suárez feels everyone and everything is plotting against him). Outside Spain the situation is no more favourable for the Prime Minister; it was, but it isn't any more, among other reasons because since he came to power Suárez has done the opposite of what the world has done: while he was trying desperately to shift to the left, the world calmly shifted to the right.

In July 1976, when the King hands Suárez the leadership of the government, Europe awaits the pacific change from dictatorship to democracy with sympathy tempered by scepticism; the United States, with sympathy tempered by apprehension: at the time its ideal for Spain – from the strategic point of view a key country in case of war with the Soviet Union – is a docile parliamentary monarchy and limited democracy that prevents the existence of a legal Communist Party and brings the country into NATO. At the outset the appointment of Suárez, described as a young lion of Francoism, pleases the United States much more than Europe, but soon the preferences are reversed: Suárez legalizes the Communist Party, propels the country towards a full democracy and, in spite of the constant pressures brought to bear on him – including the pressure of his fellow UCD members – indefinitely postpones the application to join the Atlantic Alliance; not only that: convinced that by remaining on one side of the division into blocs imposed by the cold war Spain can play a more efficient or more visible international role than by enrolling as a supernumerary in the bloc under the American thumb, during his last year in government Suárez receives the Palestinian leader Yasser Arafat at Moncloa and sends an official observer to the Non-aligned Movement Summit. Four years earlier, these gestures of independence – which in Spain irritate the right and almost all the leaders within the Prime Minister's party but not an overwhelmingly anti-American public opinion – would have caused a faint worry mixed with astonishment in Washington; combined with the country's instability, in the autumn of 1980 they cause manifest alarm. Because in those four years things have changed radically, and not just for the United States: in October 1978 Karol Wojtyla was elected Pope of the Catholic Church; in May 1979 Margaret Thatcher was elected Prime Minister of the United Kingdom; in November 1980 Ronald Reagan was elected President of the United States. A conservative revolution spreads across the West and, with the aim of finishing off the Soviet Union by way of a ring of concentric pressure, Reagan relaunches the arms race and heats up the cold war. Given those circumstances, if there's one thing Washington doesn't want it's upheavals in southern Europe: in September it successfully supported a military coup in Turkey, and now harbours fears that the fragility of a left-leaning Suárez hounded by political and economic crises and by an increasingly strong Socialist Party, will end up creating favourable conditions for a revolution similar to the one in Portugal in 1974. So when in the months before 23 February the US Embassy and CIA station in Madrid begin to receive news of the imminence of a surgical coup or a touch on the rudder of Spanish democracy, their reaction, more than favourable, is enthusiastic, in particular that of Ambassador Terence Todman, an extremely right-wing diplomat who in previous years fully supported Latin American dictatorships as Assistant Secretary of State for Inter-American Affairs, who now manages to ensure that the only two Spanish politicians welcomed by President Reagan in the White House before the coup should be two significant Francoist politicians biding their time – Gonzalo Fernández de la Mora and Federico Silva Muñoz – and on 13 February meets with General Armada on an estate near Logroño. We do not know what was said at this meeting, but there are facts that demonstrate beyond doubt that the US government was informed of the coup before it took place:

from 20 February the US military bases of Torrejón, Rota, Morón and Zaragoza were in a state of alert and ships from the VI Fleet were stationed in the vicinity of the Mediterranean coastline, and all through the evening and night of the 23rd an AWACS electronic intelligence plane belonging to the 86th Communications Squadron deployed from the German base of Ramstein overflew the peninsula with the object of monitoring Spanish airwaves. These details were not known until days or weeks or months later, but on the night of 23 February, when the US Secretary of State, General Alexander Haig, sent a question about what was going on in Spain without a single word of condemnation of the assault on the Cortes or a word in favour of democracy – the attempted coup d'état did not go beyond 'an internal matter' as far as he was concerned – no one failed to understand the only thing there was to understand: that the United States approved of the coup and that, if it ended up succeeding, the US government would be the first to celebrate.

9

So in the final days of 1980 and the first of 1981 reality itself seems to plot against Adolfo Suárez (or Adolfo Suárez feels that reality itself is plotting against him): journalists, businessmen, bankers, right-wing, left-wing and centrist politicians, Rome and Washington. Even some Communist leaders make public or private statements in favour of a government of national unity led by a military officer. Even the leaders of the main trade unions are doing so, talking about extreme situations, emergency situations, not of a crisis of government but of state. Even the King does so, trying in his way to be rid of Suárez and spurring on some of those against him.

All these materials went into the making of the coup: the political manoeuvring against Adolfo Suárez was the organic matter of the coup; all these materials went into the making of the placenta of the coup. That said, maybe the word conspiracy might seem inadequate to define the campaign of political harassment against Adolfo Suárez; in other words: in the months before the coup Suárez undoubtedly felt that all of reality was plotting against him, but was this not a simple feeling of a politically finished and personally broken man unsubstantiated by facts? Was not what was really happening in Spain during this time a simple confluence of political strategies, interests and legitimate ambitions directed at removing an inept prime minister from power? It was, but that is exactly what political plotting is: the alliance of a collection of people against whoever holds power. And that is exactly what occurred in Spain in the final days of 1980 and the first of 1981. I repeat that the content of this conspiracy was legitimate, but its form was not, and at least in Spanish politics of the time, after forty years of dictatorship and less than four of democracy, the form was the content: stretching the very fragile forms of democracy to their limit, raising a dense political dust cloud while turning to military officers permanently tempted to destroy the political system as a means of ending Suárez's premiership, meant handing over to the enemies of democracy the instrument with which to finish off Suárez and the democracy. Only a few refused to participate in that suicidal gibberish; among them were General Gutiérrez Mellado and Santiago Carrillo, two of the very few front-line politicians who did not join the siege of the Prime Minister and thus avoided the error common to a ruling class whose conspiratorial passion against Adolfo Suárez led it consciously or unconsciously to plot against democracy. As for Suárez himself, he was of course a pure politician, and as such, in spite of the fact that he was politically finished and personally broken, he continued in those months fighting to stay in power; he was fighting for himself, but in fighting for himself and fighting to stay in power he was also fighting to sustain the edifice he'd constructed over the years he had been in office: although from the beginning the coup-inclined military considered Suárez the embodiment of the democracy – and for that reason when they finally launched the coup for them it was a coup against Suárez more than a coup against democracy – maybe Suárez never really embodied democracy until the days before the coup, and maybe he never fully embodied it until the evening of 23 February, while the bullets whizzed around him as he sat on his Prime Minister's bench in the Cortes, because never as much as in that moment did fighting for himself and to stay in power correspond with such precision to fighting for democracy.

10

I have kept the principal plotter out of sight: the Army. The 23 February coup was a military coup against Adolfo Suárez and against democracy, but who was plotting in the Army during the autumn and winter of 1980? And with what aim were they plotting? Were the intelligence services, then part of the Army, also plotting? Was CESID, which was the organization that grouped together most of the intelligence services? And, if they were, were they plotting to get Adolfo Suárez out of power or were they plotting in favour of a coup? Did CESID participate in the 23 February coup? This last is one of the most controversial points about the coup and, for obvious reasons, undoubtedly the one that's aroused the greatest number of speculations: exploring it also allows for exploration of the *golpista* manoeuvres that were being hatched within the Army during the months before the coup.

The trial of those involved on 23 February charged only two members of CESID: Major José Luis Cortina, head of AOME, the centre's special operations unit, and Captain Vicente Gómez Iglesias, Cortina's subordinate. The major was acquitted; the captain was found guilty: the legal truth of the 23 February coup therefore states that CESID as an institution did not participate in the coup, only one of its members did so and on his own initiative. Is the legal truth the actual truth? Naturally, those then responsible for the intelligence services – its commander, Marine Corps Colonel Narciso Carreras, and its director and strong man, Lieutenant Colonel Javier Calderón – have always denied not only that CESID participated in the coup, but having had the slightest hint that it was brewing, which in any case is as good as a recognition of a resounding failure, because one of the fundamental missions the government had assigned to the intelligence services – if not the fundamental mission – was to warn of the eventuality of a coup. Are Carreras and Calderón telling the truth? Did CESID really fail on 23 February? Or, on the contrary, did it not fail and did it know about the preparations under way for the coup and nevertheless not warn the government, because it was implicated in the rebellion? Two facts seem unquestionable from the outset: one is that, even supposing it didn't know in advance the exact details of the coup – the who, the when, the how and the where – CESID had reliable news of a plot against Adolfo Suárez and of the military conspiracies that in one way or another would eventually culminate in the events of 23 February; the other is that it informed the government. This at least is what emerges from a report habitually attributed to CESID, dated November 1980 and titled 'Panorama of Operations Under Way', a report that according to a version accepted by those who years later have published it in various books was sent to the King, Adolfo Suárez, General Gutiérrez Mellado and the Minister of Defence, Agustín Rodríguez Sahagún.

It is perhaps the most useful document we have to understand the immediate background to the coup, because it contains a contemporary, detailed and largely true description of the political and military plots of the day and a quite exact announcement of what would happen on 23 February. The report is divided into a prologue and three parts; each of the parts examines a type of operation: the first examines the civilian operations; the second, the military operations; the third, a mixed civilian-military operation. The prologue just sets out an obvious fact and a caution: the obvious fact is that the common denominator of the operations set out in the report is the desire to overthrow Adolfo Suárez to end 'the climate of anarchy and the current socio-political chaos'; the caution pointed out that, given the current anarchy and chaos, 'there is no reason whatsoever to expect there are not more operations under way', and rather 'we fear that these could be almost infinite'. The first part of the report describes four civilian operations, that is four political operations, three of them formulated within the Prime Minister's party and the fourth within the Socialist Party:

the report minimizes the viability of the first ones, but stresses the interest of each one of their organizers – Christian Democrats, Liberals and UCD Blues – in the civilian-military operation; it grants much more importance to the Socialist operation. This would be put into practice in the months of January or February 1981 and would consist of the tabling of a motion of no confidence by the PSOE, after making a pact with a large dissident UCD group, as the result of which Suárez would be removed from power and a government of national unity would be formed under the leadership of a military officer of liberal disposition and in the Crown's good books, which would neutralize the Army's *golpista* temptations and, supposing that its proponents could count on a suitable and willing officer with the King's approval, provide the project with 'almost total credibility'. The profile of the suitable and willing officer was the profile of General Armada or the profile generally assumed by General Armada, who, as the author of the report undoubtedly knew, had just met with Socialist leaders in Lérida. In this section note is also taken of the PSOE's interest in the civilian-military operation set out at the end, and which is no more than a variation of the Socialist operation.

The second part of the report examines three military operations: that of the lieutenant generals, that of the colonels and that of a group it calls 'the impromptus'. Here the author's information is especially copious and reliable. According to him, the three operations are autonomous although not lacking points of connection and at any moment could unite; furthermore all three are highly viable and dangerous. The lieutenant generals' operation, whose civilian point of reference is Manuel Fraga, would consist of a collective pronouncement by the Captaincy Generals – the centres of the Army's power in each of the military regions the country had been divided into – which, similar to what had happened two months before in Turkey, would grant the coup an institutional tone or appearance; the report omits the names of the lieutenant generals involved in the operation (and among them the most conspicuous: Jaime Milans del Bosch, Captain General of Valencia), but considers 'more than likely' that the coup will occur if the political deterioration continues. Like the previous one, the colonels' operation is not yet entirely ripe; unlike the previous one, the colonels, who are 'cold, rational and methodical,' are planning theirs with care and therefore – and owing to 'the human and professional quality' of the organizers – once activated 'would be unstoppable'; also unlike the previous one, this operation scorns the Crown: the colonels possess an 'advanced' social mentality, verging on a very nationalist and 'un-Marxist socialism' and their political ideal is not monarchy but a presidential republic. Again the report links the name of Manuel Fraga to this operation; again omits those of its proponents, perhaps one of whom might be Colonel José Ignacio San Martín, head of the main intelligence service of late Francoism and at this time chief of staff of the Brunete Armoured Division. As for the third operation, that of the so-called impromptus, according to the report this was the most dangerous: not only because it was the most violent and most imminent, but also because it lacked the slightest monarchical inclination. The impromptus considered that the only way to galvanize the Army around a coup was to launch a devastating attack against a key point in the country ('not ruling out summary executions if they encountered resistance or refusals to step down'): the report does not mention the Cortes, but does mention Moncloa, critical ministries, communication centres; according to the impromptus' predictions, once the sudden attack was perpetrated 'the rest of the Armed Forces would join it or at least not use force to prevent it' and, once the political class was 'totally' eliminated, the heads of the operation 'would put themselves under the orders of the verified military commanders, who would give definitive form to the total military coup'. According to the report, the impromptus' plan had a precedent in 'the famous *Operación Galaxia*', which is how the press had baptized the coup that Tejero had planned two years earlier but not managed to execute, the author's way of pointing out the lieutenant colonel as the protagonist of this new attempt.

Those were the civilian and military operations under way; the report then went on to consider the mixed civilian-military operation. This turns out to be a soft coup aimed at averting the risk of the three hard coups just described; its proponents are a group of unaffiliated civilians with political experience and a group of serving generals, 'with brilliant records and potential appeal'; the mechanism of implementation is formally constitutional, 'although such formality went no further than covering the minimal legal appearances to avoid the classification as a coup': it would consist of forcing Suárez's resignation through a continuous series of pressures from different directions (political parties, financial, business, ecclesiastic, military and journalistic means) which would culminate with pressure from the King, who would immediately propose, with the support of the main parties, a general 'with the backing of the rest of the military structure' as Prime Minister, who would form a 'caretaker government' or a 'government of national salvation' at least fifty per cent of which would comprise independent civilians or nominations by the UCD, PSOE and Alianza Popular. As well as eliminating terrorism and reviving the economy, this government – whose mandate would end the legislature in principle – would reform the Constitution, do away with the autonomous governments, reduce the power of the parties and make the Communist and nationalist ones illegal. It did not aim in principle to destroy democracy: it aimed to trim or restrict or shrink it and turn it into a semi-democracy. According to the report, this mixed operation not only counted on the support of leaders in the UCD and the PSOE, who would have been convinced that it was the only alternative to a hard coup; it was also seeking the approval of the proponents of the military operations, assuring them that, if the mixed option failed, the field could be cleared for their attempt ('in which they would find the same collaboration they'd lent to this one'). The report concluded with the claim: 'The viability of this operation is very high'; a date was even ventured: 'It is estimated that its period of implementation could culminate before the spring of 1981 (barring imponderables).'

This is a synopsis of the contents of the 'Panorama of Operations Under Way'. In the end there were imponderables, but not too many: fundamentally the news the report offered was exact; its predictions as well: after all the 23 February coup turned out to be an improvised attempt to put into practice the civilian-military operation under the cover of the four civilian operations and with the support of the three military operations; or spelled out with all the names: a failed attempt to hand power to General Armada using the force of the military plotters – Milans del Bosch's lieutenant generals, San Martín's colonels and Tejero's impromptus – to oblige the civilian plotters – the UCD,

Alianza Popular and the PSOE – to accept this emergency solution. So, if it's true that CESID prepared this report, there is no doubt – although not knowing exactly the who, the when, the how and the where of the coup – the intelligence service possessed in November 1980 information so reliable on the coup d'état conspiracies that it was able to predict without much margin of error what would end up happening on 23 February. It so happens, however, despite usually being attributed to CESID, the report is not the work of CESID: its author is Manuel Fernández-Monzón Altolaguirre, then a lieutenant colonel in the Army and head of the Ministry of Defence press office. Fernández-Monzón was a former member of the intelligence service who maintained many connections among his former colleagues and who for years sold politico-military reports to a select clientele of Madrid politicians, bankers and businessmen, as well as being at the time adviser to Luis María Anson in the news agency EFE. His report – which was sent to the Minister of Defence and indeed reached the King, the Prime Minister and his Deputy Prime Minister, and undoubtedly circulated around the political village of Madrid in the autumn and winter of 1980 – constitutes an apt summary of the seething swarm of plots on the eve of 23 February, especially the military plots. Although some of it was in the public domain, most of the news the report contained came from CESID, which demonstrates that the intelligence service knew the general design of operations under way, but did not know exactly, in the days before the attempted military coup, the who, the when, the how and the where of it. Did they know? Did CESID fail in its mission to inform and warn the government? Or did it not fail but not warn the government because it was on the side of the rebels? The most controversial question about 23 February still stands for the moment: did CESID participate in the coup d'état?

11

23 February

It was a Monday. A sunny day dawned in Madrid; towards half past one in the afternoon the sun stopped shining and gusts of winter wind swept the streets of the city centre; by half past six it was already getting dark. Just at that time – at twenty-three minutes past six to be more precise – Lieutenant Colonel Tejero entered the Cortes in command of an improvised troop made up of sixteen officers and a hundred and seventy NCOs and soldiers recruited from the Civil Guard Motor Pool, on Calle Príncipe de Vergara. It was the beginning of the coup. A coup whose elemental design did not correspond to the design of a hard coup but rather a soft coup, that is to the design of a bloodless coup that should only brandish the threat of weapons enough so that the King, the political class and the citizenry will bend to the will of the *golpistas*: after the Parliament was taken, the Captain General of Valencia, General Milans del Bosch, would declare martial law in his region and occupy its capital, Colonel San Martín and some officers of the Brunete Armoured Division would persuade their unit into rebellion and occupy Madrid, and General Armada would go to the Zarzuela and convince the King that, with the aim of solving the problem created by the rebellious military officers, he should allow him to go in his name to the Cortes to liberate the parliamentarian hostages and in exchange to form with the main political parties a coalition or caretaker or unity government under his premiership. Those four tactical movements corresponded to a certain extent to the four military operations

announced in November by Fernández-Monzón's report: the taking of
the Cortes, which was the most complicated movement (and the trigger), corresponded to the operation of the impromptus; the taking of
Valencia, which was the most well-prepared movement, corresponded
to the lieutenant generals' operation; the taking of Madrid, which was
the most improvised movement, corresponded to the colonels' operation; and the taking of the Zarzuela, which was the simplest (and most
essential) movement, corresponded to the civilian-military operation.
There was nevertheless an extremely important difference between the
coup as Fernández-Monzón's report predicted it and the coup as it
happened in reality: while in the first case the civilian-military operation functioned as the political means with which to prevent the three
military operations, in the second case the three military operations
functioned as the means of force with which to impose the civilian-
military operation. Furthermore, although the design of the coup
might be simple, its execution was not or certain aspects of its execution were not, but on the morning of 23 February few *golpistas* harboured
doubts about its success: all or almost all thought that not only the
Army but the King, the political class and a large part of the public
were predisposed to accept the victory of the coup; all or almost all
thought the entire country would welcome the coup with more relief
than resignation, if not with fervour. I put forward one piece of information: agents of CESID took part in two of the four movements of
the coup; and another: at least in one of those movements its intervention was not trivial.

This is how it is: at five o'clock in the afternoon of that day at the
Civil Guard Motor Pool, Major Cortina's subordinate in CESID,
Captain Gómez Iglesias, cleared away the final doubts of the officers
who would accompany Lieutenant Colonel Tejero in the assault on the
Cortes. Gómez Iglesias had been friends with the lieutenant colonel
since they'd been stationed together years before in the San Sebastián
Civil Guard headquarters, had possibly spent months keeping an eye
on Tejero on Major Cortina's orders, knew his friend's plans to perfection and in the last days was helping to bring them to fruition. The
help he lent him at that moment and in that place – an hour and a half
before the assault on the Cortes and in the office of Colonel Miguel

Manchado, commanding officer of the Motor Pool – was vital. Minutes before Gómez Iglesias' arrival in Colonel Manchado's office, the lieutenant colonel began trying incoherently to convince the officers gathered there to go with him to the Cortes to carry out a public-order operation of great national significance – that was the formula he used over and over again – an operation conducted on the orders of the King under the command of General Armada, who must be at the Zarzuela Palace by then, and General Milans del Bosch, who was going to declare a state of emergency in Valencia. None of the officers listening to him was unaware of the lieutenant colonel's rebellious record and *golpista* proclivities; although most of them had been in on the secret of his project for days or hours and approved of it, those who weren't expressed their doubts, especially Captain Abad, a very competent officer in command of a very competent and well-trained group of Civil Guards, which would be indispensable, once the Cortes was taken, for deploying outside to seal and control it; the entrance into the office of Gómez Iglesias, who was taking a short course at the Motor Pool at the time, changed everything: Abad's reluctance and the scruples that some of the other officers might still have been harbouring disappeared as soon as the captain assured them with his incontestable authority as a CESID agent that what Tejero had told them was true, and everyone gathered there got down to work immediately, filling the six buses Colonel Manchado provided with troops and organizing the departure for the Cortes, where according to the lieutenant colonel's plan the group should rendezvous with another bus that, at that very moment, on the other side of Madrid, Captain Jesús Muñecas Aguilar was filling with Civil Guards belonging to the Valdemoro Squadron of the First Mobile Command. That's how the initial movement of the coup got started, and those were the men who conducted it. Many who have investigated 23 February, however, hold that, as well as Captain Gómez Iglesias, several CESID agents collaborated at this point with the *golpista* lieutenant colonel; according to them, Tejero's column and Muñecas' column were coordinated or linked by vehicles driven by Major Cortina's men – Sergeant Miguel Sales, Corporals Rafael Monge and José Moya – provided with false number plates, low-frequency transmitters and walkie-talkies. To my mind, this can only be partly true: it's almost impossible that the two columns were linked by CESID agents, among other reasons because the transmitters their agents used at the time had a range of barely a kilometre and the walkie-talkies five hundred metres (besides, if they'd been linked they would have arrived at the Cortes at the same time, as undoubtedly was their aim, instead of one column a long time after the other, as actually occurred); it's possible on the other hand that some of the CESID vehicles were escorting the columns, not with the aim of leading them to the Cortes (which would be absurd: no resident of Madrid needs anyone to guide him there), but with that of clearing their route to prevent any obstacles from getting in their way.* Be that true or not – and we'll have to return to it – there is one sure thing: at least one CESID agent subordinate to Major Cortina lent decisive help to Lieutenant Colonel Tejero so the assault on the Cortes would be a success.

The second movement of the coup was also a success: the occupation of Valencia. At half past five that afternoon, after an unusually hectic morning in the Captaincy General building, Milans del Bosch had called together in his office the generals under his command in the city and was informing them what was going to happen an hour later: he spoke of the assault on the Cortes, the occupation of Madrid by the Brunete Armoured Division, of the publication of an edict declaring martial law in the region of Valencia and that this was all with the King's consent, who would be accompanied in the Zarzuela by General Armada, the ultimate authority of the operation and future leader of a government with his own promotion to President of the Joint Chiefs of Staff, the top position in the Armed Forces. Seconded by his deputy chief of staff, Colonel Ibáñez Inglés, and by his aide-de-camp, Lieutenant Colonel Mas Oliver, General Milans – one of the most prestigious military officers in the Spanish Army, one

---

* There are likewise indications that, along with the CESID agents, agents of the Civil Guard Information Service (SIGC) under the command of Colonel Andrés Cassinello participated in the seizure of the Cortes. According to a report by one member of that service published in the newspapers in 1991, at five o'clock on 23 February several officers and twenty Civil Guards of the Operations Group of the SIGC under the command of a lieutenant began to deploy in the Cortes and vicinity, and at five thirty had already combed the area to be sure that, when the moment came, the police in charge of the building's security would not oppose the entry of Lieutenant Colonel Tejero and his Civil Guards. This information has never been refuted.

of the most fervently Francoist, one of the most openly monarchical – had been the soul or one of the souls of the conspiracy: the coup had been incubated in Valencia, there Tejero's *golpista* compulsion had been given wings, there Milans had harmonized his plans with Armada's, from there they had acquired for the coup the support or benevolent neutrality of five of the eleven Captaincy Generals into which the Spanish military geography was divided (the II, with headquarters in Seville; the V, with headquarters in Zaragoza; the VII, with headquarters in Valladolid; the VIII, with headquarters in La Coruña; the X, with headquarters in the Balearic Islands), from there on the previous day they'd set in motion the mutiny of the Brunete Armoured Division in Madrid, from there he'd set himself up as the military leader of the rebels. On the eve of the coup Milans endeavoured to look after the details: several days before he'd had sent to headquarters, from the Valencian delegation of CESID, two confidential notes – one, on a possible terrorist attack by ETA; the other, on possible violent acts by left-wing trade unionists – which, although described with a minimal indication of reliability and based on false information, must have served him as additional cover for confining units to barracks and the application of martial law planned by the edict Colonel Ibáñez Inglés drew up at his insistence on the morning of 23 February; he also endeavoured to look after details on the day of the coup: the two notes from CESID had been prepared by some member of the intelligence services, but Milans considered that organization not to be an ally but a potential enemy of the coup, and one of the first measures he adopted after declaring the state of emergency was to arrest the head of CESID in Valencia and prevent any action by the organization by sending a detachment composed of a major and several soldiers to its offices in the city. At least in his territory Milans had or believed he had all the elements necessary to keep the coup under control: that morning he'd sent the commanding officers of the region sealed orders that should be opened only once they'd received a password ('Miguelete') by teletype and, when at six in the evening he closed the meeting of generals he'd called at headquarters and sent them back to their command posts to begin operations, nothing in Valencia seemed to predict the failure of the coup.

Nothing predicted it in El Pardo either, a few kilometres from Madrid, where the headquarters of the Brunete Armoured Division were located, the most powerful, modern and battle-hardened unit of the Army, and also the closest to the capital. Nothing predicted it in any case until about five in the afternoon, at the moment when, almost at the same time that Lieutenant Colonel Tejero overcame with the help of Captain Gómez Iglesias the suspicions of the officers recruited to accompany him to the Cortes and that General Milans informed his subordinates of the imminence of the coup, an anomalous meeting was taking place in the office of the commander of the division, General José Juste. The meeting was anomalous for several reasons, the first of which is that it had been called in a great rush by a mere major, Ricardo Pardo Zancada, whom the previous day General Milans had put in charge of inciting the Brunete Division to join the rebellion and occupy the streets of Madrid. Pardo Zancada was then a prestigious commissioned officer who had participated in agitation against the government and was close to the colonels' plot or kept close relations with some of them, especially with Colonel San Martín, his immediate superior and chief of staff of the division; his ideological and personal connection with Milans has also been close ever since the general commanded the Brunete Division in the second half of the 1970s. This explains how on Sunday morning Milans had summoned him urgently and that, without asking for clarifications or hesitating for an instant, after giving Colonel San Martín an account of that untimely phone call, Pardo Zancada jumps in his car and leaves for Valencia. Upon the major's arrival in the city after an almost four-hour drive, Milans tells him the plan for the following day just as the following day he'll tell his generals, and he entrusts him with the mission of inciting his unit to rebellion with the help of San Martín and Luis Torres Rojas, a general who had taken part in preparatory meetings for the coup and had held the command of Brunete before being removed from his post for a threat of rebellion and assigned to the military government of La Coruña; although he was confident that to incite the division to rebellion he'd need only the halo of an undefeated warrior that surrounded him and the insurrectional air they breathed there, as in almost all Army units, Milans also made Pardo Zancada listen to a telephone conversation with General Armada from which the major deduced that the King was informed of the coup. Pardo Zancada paid attention with all five senses and, in spite of the uncertainty he was plunged into by Milans' words and the dialogue between Milans and Armada – the plan struck him as poor, disjointed and unripe – he enthusiastically accepted the assignment; his questions had not cleared when at midnight, back in Madrid, he informed San Martín, but his enthusiasm had not waned either: both had been waiting for this moment for years, and both agreed that the clumsiness and improvisation with which the coup seemed to have been prepared did not authorize them to back out and prevent the triumph they undoubtedly considered certain.

The following morning was the most frenetic of Major Pardo Zancada's life: almost single-handedly, without the help of Torres Rojas – whom he tried to phone over and over again at his military government office in La Coruña – without the help of San Martín – who had left first thing for a training camp near Zaragoza to supervise tactical exercises in the company of General Juste – Pardo Zancada prepared the Brunete Armoured Division for a mission that he still didn't know and sketched out a programme of operations that each of its units should carry out: seizing the radio and television stations, taking up advance positions in strategic locations in Madrid – in the Campo del Moro, the Retiro, the Casa de Campo and the Parque del Oeste – their subsequent deployment in the city. Mid-morning he finally managed to speak with Torres Rojas, who rushed to catch a regular flight to Madrid dressed in his combat uniform and tank-driver beret, ready to stir his former unit to rebellion with his reputation as a tough leader loyal to his officers built up during his recent years in command. Pardo Zancada picked up Torres Rojas at Barajas airport just after two in the afternoon, and shortly afterwards had lunch with him in the headquarters canteen in the company of other commanders and officers surprised by the unexpected visit by their former general, at the same time that, in the Santa María de la Huerta parador, where he was lunching with General Juste on their way to Zaragoza, Colonel San Martín received a prearranged warning from Pardo Zancada according to which everything in the division was ready for the coup. At this moment San Martín must have hesitated: to return with Juste to headquarters meant risking that the commander of the Brunete might abort the plot; not to return meant perhaps excluding himself from the glory and yields of the triumph: the ambition to enjoy those, allied to the arrogance of the once all-powerful head of the Francoist intelligence services and his knowledge of the difficulties inherent in moving a division if the one doing it is not its natural commander, he convinced himself he could handle Juste and that he should return to his command post at El Pardo, which would eventually turn out to be one of the causes of the failure of the coup. This is how at half past four in the afternoon Juste and San Martín make a surprise reappearance at headquarters and this is how a few minutes before five, after troops have been confined to barracks, Major Pardo Zancada finally takes the floor to address the commanders and officers of all ranks he himself has summoned to that anomalous meeting and who now pack Juste's office. Pardo Zancada's speech is brief: the major announces that in a matter of minutes an event of great significance will occur in Madrid; he explains that this event will be followed by the occupation of Valencia by General Milans; he also explains that Milans is counting on the Brunete Division to occupy the capital; also, that the operation is directed from the Zarzuela Palace by General Armada with the consent of the King. The reaction of the majority of the meeting to Pardo Zancada's words wavers between repressed joy and expectant but not dissatisfied seriousness; the commanders and officers await the verdict of Juste, whom Torres Rojas and San Martín try to win over to the cause of the coup with calming words and appeals to the King, Armada and Milans, and whom San Martín convinces not to call his immediate superior, General Quintana Lacaci, Captain General of Madrid, who is not aware of anything. After a few minutes of anguished hesitation, during which the uprising of 1936 goes through Juste's head and the possibility that, if he opposes the coup, his officers might wrest away his command of the division and execute him then and there, at ten past five in the afternoon the commander of the Brunete Armoured Division makes an anodyne gesture – some of those present interpret it as a frustrated attempt to adjust his tortoiseshell glasses or to smooth his meagre grey moustache, others as a gesture of consent or resignation – pulls his chair up to his desk and pronounces three words that seem to be the penultimate sign that the coup will triumph: 'Well, carry on.'

At the very same time, barely five hundred metres from the Cortes, at Army General Headquarters in the Buenavista Palace, everything is ready for the final signal to occur. There, in his new office as Deputy Chief of the Army General Staff, General Alfonso Armada has just arrived from Alcalá de Henares, where that morning he had participated in a celebration commemorating the foundation of the Parachute Brigade, has changed out of his ceremonial uniform and into his everyday one and waits but not impatiently, without even turning on the radio to listen to the debate of investiture of the new Prime Minister, for some subordinate to burst in and tell him of the assault on the Cortes. But what Armada – perhaps the most monarchist military man in the Spanish Army, until four years ago the King's secretary, for the last several months many people's candidate in the political village of Madrid to lead a coalition or interim or unity government – is especially waiting for is the subsequent call from the King asking him to come to the Zarzuela and explain what's going on in the Cortes. Armada has good reasons to expect it: not only because he's sure that, after almost a decade and a half of being his most dependable confidant, the King trusts him more than anyone else or almost anyone, but also because after his painful exit from the Zarzuela the two had reconciled and in recent weeks he has warned the monarch on a great many occasions about the risk of a coup and insinuated that he knows its ins and outs and if it finally occurs he could control it. Then, once in the Zarzuela, Armada will take charge of the problem, just like he used to do in the old days: backed by the King, backed by the King's Army, he will go to the Cortes and, without having to make too much of an effort to convince the political parties to accept a solution that in any case the majority of them already considered reasonable long before the military took to the streets, he'll liberate the deputies, form a coalition or interim or unity government under his leadership and bring tranquillity back to the Army and the nation. That's what Armada expects will happen and that's what, according to the *golpistas'* predictions, will inevitably end up happening.

So at six in the evening on 23 February the essential elements of the coup were all ready and in the places assigned by the *golpistas*: six buses full of Civil Guards under the command of Lieutenant Colonel Tejero were about to leave the Motor Pool to head for the Cortes (and another under the command of Captain Muñecas was about to do so from Valdemoro); the military commanders of the region of Valencia had opened their sealed orders with Milans' instructions and, once the units were stocked up with fuel and ammunition, the barracks prepared to open their gates; the brigade and regiment commanders of the Brunete were just leaving headquarters for their respective command posts with operational orders drawn up by Pardo Zancada and approved by Juste containing concrete instructions on their priority objectives, deployment zones and occupation and surveillance missions; though not in his office but in that of General Gabeiras – his immediate superior and Chief of the Army General Staff, who just summoned him to discuss a routine matter – General Armada waits at Army General Headquarters for the phone call from the Zarzuela. Half an hour later Lieutenant Colonel Tejero bursts into the Cortes and the coup is unleashed. The taking of the Cortes was perhaps an easier than expected success: neither the police who guarded the building nor the deputies' bodyguards offered the least resistance to the attackers, and a few minutes after entering the chamber, when the interior as well as the exterior of the Cortes was under his control and the mood of his men was euphoric, Lieutenant Colonel Tejero telephoned Valencia euphorically to give the news to General Milans; it was an easy success, but not a complete success. Given that it was meant to be the gateway to a soft coup, Tejero's orders were that the occupation of the Cortes should be bloodless and discreet: he was only to suspend the session of investiture of the new Prime Minister, to detain the parliamentarians and maintain order pending the Army now in revolt coming to relieve him and his Civil Guards and General Armada, giving the hostages a political exit; miraculously, Tejero managed to keep the occupation bloodless, but not discreet, and that was the first problem for the *golpistas*, because a hail of bullets in the Cortes broadcast live on radio to the whole country gave the scenery of a hard coup to what was meant to be a soft coup or meant to keep up the appearance of a soft coup and made it difficult for the King, the political class and the general public to willingly give in to it. It could have been much worse, of course; if, as at the beginning seemed inevitable to those who heard the shooting on the radio (not to mention those who suffered it in the chamber), as well as indiscreet the operation had been bloody, then everything would have been different: because there's no turning back from deaths, the soft coup would have become a hard coup, and the bloodbath may have been inevitable. However, as things happened, in spite of the violence of the operation's *mise-en-scène* nothing essential stood in the *golpistas'* way ten minutes into the coup: after all a *mise-en-scène* is only a *mise-en-scène* and, although the shooting in the chamber would undoubtedly force certain adjustments to the plan, the reality is that the Cortes was hijacked, that General Milans had proclaimed martial law in his region and had sent forty tanks and one thousand eight hundred soldiers of the 3rd Maestrazgo Mechanized Division out onto the streets of Valencia, that the Brunete Armoured Division was in revolt and their AMX-30 tanks ready to leave the barracks and that in the Zarzuela the King was on the point of calling Army General Headquarters to speak to General Armada. If it's true that the fate of a coup is decided in its first minutes, then it's also true that, ten minutes after its start, the 23 February coup had triumphed.

PART TWO

A *GOLPISTA* CONFRONTS THE COUP

The frozen image shows the deserted chamber of the Congress of Deputies. Or almost deserted: in the centre of the image, leaning slightly to the right, solitary, statuesque and spectral in a desolation of empty benches, Adolfo Suárez remains seated on his blue prime minister's bench. On his left, General Gutiérrez Mellado stands in the central semicircle, his arms hanging down at his sides, his back to the camera, looking at the six Civil Guards who shoot off their guns in silence, as if he wanted to prevent them from entering the chamber or as if he were trying to protect the body of his Prime Minister with his own body. Behind the old general, closer to the viewer, another two Civil Guards spray the chamber with submachine-gun fire while, pistol in hand, from the steps of the speakers' rostrum, Lieutenant Colonel Tejero demands with gestures of alarm and inaudible shouted orders that his men stop the shooting that is pulverizing the instructions he has received. Above Prime Minister Suárez a few hands of hidden deputies appear between the uninterrupted red of the benches; in front of the Prime Minister, under and around a table covered with open books and a lit oil lamp, three stenographers and an usher curl up on the elaborate carpet of the central semicircle; closer, in the lower part of the image, almost blending in with the blue of the government benches, the crouching backs of a few ministers can be distinguished: a thread of crustacean shells. The whole scene is wrapped in a scant, watery, unreal light, as if it were going on inside an aquarium or as if the chamber's only illumination came from the baroque cluster of spherical glass lampshades that hang from one wall, in the top right of the image; perhaps for this reason the whole scene also has a suggestion of a dance or a funereal family portrait and a hunger for meaning not satisfied by the elements that compose it or by the fiction of eternity that lends it its illusory stillness.

But if we unfreeze the image the stillness vanishes and reality regains its course. Slowly, while the shots grow more intermittent, General Gutiérrez Mellado turns, puts his hands on his hips, turning his back on the Civil Guards and Lieutenant Colonel Tejero, observes the abandoned chamber, like a punctilious officer taking visual stock of the destruction when the battle has not yet entirely concluded; meanwhile, Prime Minister Suárez leans back in his seat, straightening up a little, and the lieutenant colonel finally manages to get the Guards to obey his orders and the chamber is overtaken by a silence exaggerated by the recent din, as dense as the silence that follows an earthquake or a plane crash. At this moment the angle changes; the image we now see shows the lieutenant colonel from the front, with his pistol held high, standing on the stairs to the speakers' rostrum; on his left, the Secretary of the Congress, Víctor Carrascal – still with the papers on his lap with the list of deputies that only a few seconds ago he was reciting monotonously during the investiture vote – watches in panic, lying on the ground, as two Civil Guards point their weapons at General Gutiérrez Mellado, who watches them in turn with his hands on his hips. Then, noticing out of the blue that the old general is still there, standing defiantly, the lieutenant colonel rushes down the stairs, pounces on him from behind, grabs him by the neck and tries to force him to the ground before the eyes of two Civil Guards and Víctor Carrascal, who at this moment hides his face in his arms as if he lacks the courage to see what is going to happen or as if he feels an incalculable shame at not being able to prevent it.

The angle changes again. It is also a frontal view of the chamber, but wider: the deputies lie tucked under their benches and the heads of a few of them cautiously peek over to see what's going on in the central semicircle, in front of the speakers' rostrum, where the lieutenant colonel has not managed to fell General Gutiérrez Mellado, who has stayed on his feet holding on with all his might to the armrest in front of the ministers' bench. Now he is surrounded by the lieutenant colonel and three Civil Guards, pointing their guns at him, and Prime Minister Suárez, barely a metre from the general, stands up from his seat and approaches him, also holding on to the armrest: for a moment the Civil Guards seem to be about to fire; for a moment, on the armrest in front of their bench, the hand of the young Prime Minister and the hand of the old general seem to seek each other, as if the two men wanted to face up to their destiny together. But the destiny does not arrive, the shots do not arrive, or not yet, although the Civil Guards close in round the general – no longer four but eight of them now – and, while one of them insults him and shouts the demand that he obey and lie down on the carpet of the central semicircle, the lieutenant-colonel approaches him from behind and trips him and this time almost manages to throw him down, but the general resists again, clinging to the armrest as to a life raft. Only then does the lieutenant colonel give up and he and his Guards walk away from the general while Prime Minister Suárez seeks his hand again, takes it for an instant before the general pulls away angrily, without taking his eyes off his aggressors; the Prime Minister, however, insists, tries to calm his rage with words, begs him to return to his seat and makes him see reason: taking him by the hand as if he were a child, pulls him towards him, stands up and lets him pass, and the old general – after unbuttoning his jacket with a gesture that reveals his white shirt, his grey waistcoat and his dark tie – finally sits down in his seat.

I

There is a second translucent gesture here that perhaps like the first contains many gestures. Like Adolfo Suárez's gesture of remaining seated on his bench while the bullets whizz around him in the chamber, General Gutiérrez Mellado's gesture of furiously confronting the military *golpistas* is a courageous gesture, a graceful gesture, a rebellious gesture, a supreme gesture of liberty. Perhaps it might also be, in a manner of speaking, a posthumous gesture, the gesture of a man who knows he is going to die or that he's already dead, because, with the exception of Adolfo Suárez, since the advent of democracy no one has stockpiled as much military hatred as General Gutiérrez Mellado, who as soon as the shooting started perhaps felt, like almost all of those present, that it could only end in a massacre and, supposing he were to survive it, the *golpistas* would not take long to get rid of him. I don't believe it is, however, a histrionic gesture: although he'd been practising politics for the last five years, General Gutiérrez Mellado was never essentially a politician; he was always a soldier, and therefore, because he was always a soldier, his gesture that evening was above all a military gesture and therefore also in some way a logical, obligatory, almost fatal gesture: Gutiérrez Mellado was the only soldier present in the chamber and, like any soldier, he carried in his genes the imperative of discipline and could not tolerate soldiers' insubordination. I'm not noting this fact to detract from the general in any way; I do so only to try to pin down the significance of his gesture. A significance that on the other hand we might not be able to pin down entirely if we don't imagine that, while he is facing up to the *golpistas*, refusing to obey them or while shouting his demand that they leave the Cortes, the general could see himself in the Civil Guards defying his authority by shooting over the chamber, because forty-five years earlier he had disobeyed the genetic imperative of discipline and had rebelled against the civilian power embodied in a democratic government; or in other words: perhaps General Gutiérrez Mellado's fury is not made only of a visible fury against some rebellious Civil Guards, but also of a secret fury against himself, and perhaps it wouldn't be entirely illegitimate to understand his gesture of confronting the *golpistas* as an extreme gesture of contrition by a former *golpista*.

The general would not have accepted this interpretation, or he would not have accepted it publicly: he wouldn't have accepted that forty-five years earlier he had been a rebellious officer who had supported a military coup against a political system fundamentally identical to the one he now represented in government. But no one escapes his biography, and the general's biography would correct him: on 18 July 1936, when he was a barely twenty-four-year-old lieutenant just out of the Artillery Academy, a member of the Falange and assigned to a regiment stationed a few kilometres from Madrid, Gutiérrez Mellado helped to incite his unit to join the rebellion against the legitimate government of the Republic, and on the 19th, until the military insurrection was crushed in Madrid, spent the morning on the roof of his barracks shooting with a conventional machine gun at the Breguet XIX planes from the Getafe airfield that had been bombing the rebel positions since dawn. The general never denied these facts, but he would have denied the comparison between the democracy of 1936 and that of 1981 and between the *golpistas* of 18 July and those of 23 February: he never repented publicly of having mutinied in 1936, he would never have admitted that the political regime against which he'd rebelled in his youth was fundamentally identical to the one he'd contributed to creating in his old age and now represented, and he always asserted that General Franco's coup d'état had been necessary because the democracy of 1936, which had allowed three hundred violent deaths in political incidents over a few months, was scandalously imperfect and unsustainable and had given up power to the streets, where the Army had simply picked it up. This or something very similar was the general's argument (an argument shared by the substantial segment of the Spanish right that still has not broken its historical devotion to Francoism); its incoherence is glaring: did the *golpistas* of 1981 not invoke reasons resembling those of 1936? Did they not assert that the democracy of 1981 was scandalously imperfect? Did they not assert that power was in the street, ready for someone to come along and pick it up? And did they not have as many or almost as many reasons to say so as the *golpistas* of 1936 did? How many deaths need to be on the table before a democratic regime is no longer one or is unsustainable and ends up making military intervention necessary? Two hundred? Two hundred and fifty? Three hundred? Four hundred? Wouldn't fewer be enough? In the week of 23 to 30 January 1977, when General Gutiérrez Mellado had been Deputy Prime Minister of Adolfo Suárez's first government for four months, ten people were murdered for political motives in Spain, fifteen were seriously injured and there were two kidnappings of high-ranking figures of the regime (Antonio María de Oriol y Urquijo, president of the Council of State, and General Emilio Villaescusa, president of the Supreme Council of Military Justice); in 1980 alone there were more than four hundred and fifty terrorist attacks, more than four hundred wounded, more than a hundred and thirty deaths, the equivalent of more than one attack a day, more than one person wounded a day, almost one death every three days. Was that a sustainable situation? Was the democracy that allowed it a real democracy? Was military intervention necessary in 1977 or in 1981? One answer to these questions is obvious: if, as General Gutiérrez Mellado said towards the end of his life, the Republic in 1936 was an unsustainable regime, then the constitutional monarchy in February 1981 was as well and it wasn't the general who was in the right but the Civil Guards who attacked the Cortes that evening.

But there is also another answer: a less logical but truer answer, and also more complex. The answer is that theory is one thing and practice quite another: in theory the general never renounced the 18 July uprising, and, like any other military man of his generation, perhaps he never even renounced Francisco Franco; in practice, however, and at least from the moment Adolfo Suárez brought him into politics and put him in charge of military affairs for his government, the general did nothing but renounce Francisco Franco and the uprising of 18 July.

Let me explain. A historiographical cliché has it that the change from dictatorship to democracy in Spain was possible thanks to a pact of forgetting. It's a lie; or, what amounts to the same thing, it's a fragmentary truth, which only begins to be completed by a contrary cliché: the change from dictatorship to democracy in Spain was possible thanks to a pact of remembering. Speaking in general, the transition – the historical period we know by that misleading name, which suggests the falsehood that democracy was an inevitable consequence of Francoism and not the result of a willed and improvised series of chances enabled by the decrepitude of the dictatorship – was a pact by which the vanquished of the Civil War agreed not to settle scores for what had happened during forty-three years of war and dictatorship, while, in compensation, after forty-three years of settling scores with the defeated, the victors accepted the creation of a political system that admitted both sides and was essentially identical to the system brought down by the war. That pact did not include forgetting the past: it included shelving it, avoiding it, setting it aside; it included agreeing not to use it politically, but it didn't include forgetting it. From the point of view of justice, the pact contained an error, because it meant shelving, avoiding or setting aside the fact that those ultimately responsible for the war were those who won it, who provoked it with a coup d'état against a democratic regime, and because it also meant relinquishing any compensation for the victims and the prosecution of those responsible for an ignominious settling of scores that included a plan to exterminate the defeated; but, from the political point of view – even from the point of view of political ethics – the pact was a wise move, because its result was a political victory for the defeated, who restored a system essentially identical to that which they'd defended in the war (though one was called a republic and the other a monarchy, both were parliamentary democracies), and because maybe the moral error would have been to try to settle scores with those who had committed the error of settling scores, adding ignominy to ignominy: that is at least what the politicians who made the transition thought, as if they'd all read Max Weber and thought like him that there was nothing ethically more abject than to practise spurious ethics that seek only to be right, ethics that, 'instead of being concerned with what the politician is interested in, the future and the responsibility towards that future, are concerned with politically sterile questions of past guilt', and which, falling into this guilty indignity, 'overlook the unavoidable falsification of the whole problem', a falsification that is the result of the predatory interest of victors and vanquished in obtaining moral and material advantages and for others to confess their guilt. In any case, if the politicians of the transition were able to fulfil the pact that this involved, not making use of the past in political combat, it was not because they'd forgotten it, but because they remembered it very well: because they remembered and they decided that it was undignified and abject to settle scores with the past in order to be right at the risk of mutilating the future, perhaps of submerging the country in another civil war. During the transition few people in Spain forgot, and the memory of the war was more present than ever in the memory of the political class and the population in general; that is precisely one of the reasons why no one or hardly anyone opposed the 23 February coup: during those years everyone wanted to avoid at any price the risk of repeating the savage orgy of bloodletting that had happened forty years earlier, and everyone transmitted that desire to a political class that was only its reflection. It was not a heroic desire, anxious for justice (or apocalypse); it was just a brave and reasonable bourgeois desire, and the political class fulfilled it, bravely and reasonably: although in the autumn and winter of 1980 the political class behaved with an irresponsibility that verged on sending the country back to barbarism, between 1976 and 1980 it was much less incompetent than its last two centuries of history might have predicted. All this is valid, especially, for the generation that had fought the war and conspired for such a thing never to happen again. All this is valid, without doubt, for General Gutiérrez Mellado, who, no matter what he said in public, at least since his arrival in government always acted like someone who rejected in advance being right or having been in the right, that is he acted as if he knew the truth: that the democracy he was helping to construct was essentially identical to the one he'd helped to destroy forty years earlier, and that he was in his way responsible for the catastrophe of the war. From that point, as if the general were also a hero of the retreat – a professional of renunciation and demolition who abandons his positions undermining himself – all his political accomplishments were directed, not at arguing over or recognizing his guilt, but at atoning for it, assuming responsibility for preventing another 18 July and disman-tling, to prevent it, the army that had provoked it: his own army, the Army of the Victory, Francisco Franco's Army. And from there as well – besides a gesture of courage and grace and rebellion, besides a supreme gesture of liberty, a posthumous gesture and a military gesture – his gesture of confronting the rebel Civil Guards in the chamber of the Cortes can be understood not only as a way of gaining a definitive pardon for the sins of his youth, but also as a summary or emblem of his two main aims over the five years since Adolfo Suárez named him Deputy Prime Minister and put him in charge of his government's defence policies: to subjugate military power to civilian power and to protect the Prime Minister from the fury of his comrades-in-arms.

2

At the beginning of September 1976, when he was Chief of the Army General Staff and just a few days before Adolfo Suárez brought him into politics by naming him Deputy Prime Minister of his first government, General Gutiérrez Mellado was one of the military officers most respected by his comrades-in-arms; only a few months later he was one of the most hated. There was no lack of people who attributed this sudden change to the errors of Gutiérrez Mellado's military policies; it's quite probable that there were errors, but it's beyond doubt that, had there not been, the result would have been the same: for the Army – for the majority in the Army, stonily entrenched in the mentality of Francoism – Gutiérrez Mellado's error was his unconditional support for Adolfo Suárez's democratic reforms and his role as the Prime Minister's military lightning rod and guarantor. He paid dearly for both: Gutiérrez Mellado spent the last years of his life a shadow of the proud soldier he'd once been, despised by his comrades-in-arms, trying in vain to make sense of their collective defection, admired by people whose admiration flattered him but didn't matter much to him and rejected by people whose affection he'd done nothing but seek. He loved the Army with a passion, and the hatred he sensed from its members destroyed him; it was also the cause of the drastic metamorphosis he underwent during his brief political career: at the beginning of the 1970s, when he found himself assigned to the High Command General Staff at the orders of General Manuel Díez Alegría – a liberal officer with enlightened touches of whom he considered himself a disciple from then on – Gutiérrez Mellado was a serious, cordial, calm and open-minded man; less than a decade later, when he left government after 23 February, he'd turned into a surly, nervous, distrustful and irritable man, reluctant to take an objection or criticism patiently. Politics crushed him: although in the 1970s he'd developed a strong vocation for politics – in part as a result of his contacts with military commanders from democratic countries, who had persuaded him of the Spanish Army's inefficiency, of the third-world anachronism of the role of guardian it played in the country and of his own capacity to carry out a reform that could not be postponed – he was not prepared for politics; although the military reform he drove through meant the modernization of an antiquated, needy, archaic, outsized and inoperative army, the political reform, the intransigence of his comrades and his own errors ended up hiding it; although his main aim was to divorce the Army from politics ('One is either in politics and leaves the military, or one is in the military and leaves politics,' he said), he did not manage to get his comrades-in-arms to accept a separation he applied first of all to himself, requesting his transfer to the reserves and becoming a retired general, nor did he manage to keep them from accusing him of still being in the military while being in politics; although he had spent his life among soldiers, he didn't seem to know the military mentality of his times, or maybe he resisted knowing it or admitting that he knew it: he never acknowledged the evidence that the majority of the Army did not accept democracy or only accepted it reluctantly; he never acknowledged the evidence that the majority of the Army resisted submitting to the civilian power embodied in the government and aspired to enjoy a broad degree of autonomy that would allow it, under the direct command of the King, to run itself in accordance with its own criteria and direct or guard the country's course; perhaps because he'd barely exercised direct command of troops, he didn't understand or had forgotten that in his relationship with his superiors a soldier does not want reasons, suggestions or exchanges of opinions, but orders, and that in the Army anything that is not an order runs the risk of being interpreted as a sign of weakness. These and other contradictions, that he could not avoid or reconcile – maybe because in the years he had to govern it was impossible to do so – left too many flanks open to the criticisms of those who from the start of the transition opposed the loss of the Army's power as the guarantor of the continuity of Francoism, and in the end overwhelmed him, so before he noticed the idea had spread among his comrades that he had betrayed the Army and the nation for dirty political ambition and a desire for public prominence, and he lacked sufficient prestige and power to contradict it.

It was a Calvary that began on the afternoon of 21 September 1976, when General Gutiérrez Mellado took on the deputy premiership of Adolfo Suárez's first government as a replacement for General Fernando de Santiago. That very morning de Santiago had threatened the Prime Minister that he'd resign if, as the Minister of Industrial Relations had announced, the left-wing trade unions were legalized; Suárez, who had inherited de Santiago from the government of his predecessor and knew that his unwavering Francoism would be an obstacle to his plans for reform, seized the opportunity and accepted his resignation (or imposed it), and as soon as de Santiago had left his office he phoned Gutiérrez Mellado and summoned him to offer him the post. He had spoken with him only on a couple of occasions, but he had no doubt that this was his man: everyone knew of his technical skill, his tolerant disposition and his modern military ideas and vocabulary, and more than a few people with influence over him – from the King to Díez Alegría himself – had recommended him as the general Suárez needed to renovate the Army. Besides, it was not the first time Suárez had offered him a ministry: when he formed his first government in July of that year the Prime Minister had proposed that he take the Internal Affairs portfolio, but Gutiérrez Mellado turned down the offer, claiming that he did not possess adequate knowledge to carry out the brief (which in itself gives the lie to the unbridled passion for power his enemies always reproached him for); now, however, he did not hesitate to accept: the Deputy Prime Minister's office had vast powers in defence matters, and in this sphere the general did consider that he knew what had to be done and was prepared to do it. As for the political project he would carry out for the government of which he was going to be Deputy Prime Minister, it is no secret that Gutiérrez Mellado was a man of few political ideas and fundamental conservatism, so he most likely thought at that moment, as almost everyone thought, as perhaps

Suárez himself thought, that the task of government would go no further than adapting the old structures of Francoism to the country's new reality; for the same reason it's likely that only as reality imposed its discipline and Suárez yielded to the discipline of reality that Gutiérrez Mellado finally came to understand – maybe with some confusion but when it was already too late, because he was too committed to Suárez and to what Suárez represented to go back – that the political system he was helping to construct was not essentially different from the one he'd helped to destroy half a century before, and that constructing it meant constructing a democratic army on top of Franco's Army.

Appointing Gutiérrez Mellado Deputy Prime Minister was a brilliant move on Suárez's part: the general's then still intact prestige calmed the military and the far right, guaranteeing with his prominent presence in the government that the Army was controlling the reforms; it also calmed those who sought to liberalize the regime and the still illegal democratic opposition, guaranteeing with his reputation as someone who was open to change that the reforms were serious; and it calmed an immense majority of people in the country in whom the memory of the war instilled a dread of sudden shocks, guaranteeing that the reforms were going to happen in an orderly way and without violence. On the other hand, for Gutiérrez Mellado accepting Suárez's appointment meant half-opening a breach in his military prestige, and he had barely taken up his post when the general realized that those who until then had admired or appreciated him would henceforth seize any opportunity to attack him. A gaffe by the government itself gave them the first, and the breach was open. A few days after Gutiérrez Mellado's appointment, General de Santiago sent a communiqué to his comrades-in-arms in which he justified his resignation as Deputy Prime Minister by stating that he considered validating the legalization of the left-wing unions banned by Franco with his presence in the government to be incompatible with his soldierly honour; this declaration was applauded and supplemented by General Carlos Iniesta Cano in an article published in *El Alcázar* in which he deemed it dishonourable for any soldier to accept the post de Santiago had left, and accused the new Deputy Prime Minister of perjury. Determined to crush the slightest hint of military defiance, Suárez decided to punish both officers with their immediate relegation to the reserve list; the measure was fair and brave, but it was also illegal and, when the government noticed its mistake, it had no choice but to retract it, which did nothing to avert the first press campaign against the general in the far-right media, poisoning the barracks, denouncing Gutiérrez Mellado's complicity with a government ready to bypass the law in order to humiliate the Army.

That was the first time they called him a traitor. The second happened seven months later, when his government legalized the Communist Party, but then it was no longer just a minority in the Army who resorted to the insult. For historians the episode is central in the change from dictatorship to democracy; for researchers interested in 23 February it is one of the remote origins of the coup; for General Gutiérrez Mellado it was something else: the crossing of a line with no turning back in his personal and political life. For forty years the Communist Party had been the *bête-noire* of Francoism; and also of the military, who felt that forty years before they'd defeated the Communists on the battlefield and were in no way prepared to permit their return to political life. It's likely that, when he came to power in July 1976, Suárez had no intention of legalizing the Communists, but not that he was unaware that their legalization might constitute the touchstone of his reform, because the Communists had been the main and almost sole opposition to Francoism and because a democracy without Communists would be an abbreviated democracy, perhaps internationally acceptable, but nationally insufficient. That in any case is what Suárez gradually came to understand during his first months in government and, after overcoming many doubts, what convinced him that he should make the decision to legalize the Communist Party even in the face of military opposition. It was 9 April 1977 and it was a historic jolt. In the following days, while the country began to emerge from its incredulity, the Army was on the brink of a coup d'état: except for Gutiérrez Mellado, the military ministers of the government said they learned the news from the press, the Minister for the Navy, Admiral Pita Da Veiga, resigned from his post, and the Minister for the Army, General Álvarez Arenas, called a meeting of the Senior Army Council in which insults to the government were voiced and threats made to bring the troops out onto the street, and out of which came a tough communiqué condemning the governmental decision; all the rage of the military officers converged on the Prime Minister (and, by default, on his Deputy Prime Minister): the accusations of perjury and treason were repeated and amplified; they added the accusation that he had deceived them. None of the accusations were baseless: there is no doubt that, by legalizing the Communist Party, Suárez was violating the principles of the Movimiento he had sworn to defend; further- more, it's true that in a certain sense he had deceived the Armed Forces.

Eight months before, on 8 September 1976, Suárez had called a meeting of the top military commanders in the Prime Minister's office to explain to them personally the nature and reach of the political changes he was planning. Present at the meeting were members of the High Command of the three branches of the Armed Forces – more than thirty generals and admirals in total, Gutiérrez Mellado among them – and, over three hours of uninterrupted talk, Suárez displayed all his dialectical skill and all his arts of seduction to convince those present that they had nothing to fear from reforms that, as he'd said months before in front of the Francoist Cortes, were going to be limited to 'elevating to the political category of normal what at street level is simply normal', and which, as those who listened to him understood (and Suárez did nothing to keep them from understanding), all in all were equivalent to a sophisticated reformulation of Francoism, or to its disguised prolongation. That was the crux of Suárez's speech; but the crucial moment of the encounter (or the one that time ended up turn- ing into the crucial moment of the encounter) didn't happen while Suárez was speaking, but while lavishing jokes, embraces and smiles on the little groups that gathered once he'd finished doing so. In one of them someone asked him what would happen with the Communist Party; the Prime Minister's answer was careful but categorical: as long as it had its current statutes, it would not be legalized. The meeting broke up a short time later amid the enthusiasm and cheers of the generals ('Prime Minister, long live the mother who bore you!' shouted General Mateo Prada Canillas), who left the Prime Minister's office convinced that the Communist Party would not go back to being legal in Spain and that Adolfo Suárez was a blessing for the country. Eight months later reality showed them their error. It cannot be said, however, that Suárez lied to the military that morning: on the one hand, the proviso contained within his answer to the key question ('as long as it had its current statutes') was a way of protecting himself against the future, and it's true that before legalizing the Party Suárez had the guile and prudence to accommodate it by getting the PCE to modify certain aspects of their statutes; on the other hand, Suárez didn't yet know in September of 1976 if he would legalize the Communist Party: he didn't know it in September, or in October, or in November, or in December, or even in January, because the transition was not a process designed in advance, but a continual improvisation that took Suárez into territories in which a few months earlier he could not even have imagined he'd set foot. But it can be said that Suárez tricked the military by letting them believe until the last moment that he wouldn't legalize the Communist Party, although only by adding immediately that he tricked almost everybody, including the Communists themselves, probably including himself. Some military men and democratic politicians have frequently reproached Suárez for this way of proceeding: for them, if the Prime Minister had warned the military in time they would have complied with his decision without rows or threats of rebellion (and in consequence wouldn't have begun the permanent plotting that culminated in the 23 February coup attempt); the argument seems flimsy to me, if not false: the proof is that convincing a solidly anti-Communist army of the legitimacy of the Communist Party ended up being a task that took years, incompatible in any case with the speed with which Suárez introduced his reforms that was definitely one of the fundamental reasons for their success. Be that as it may, whether or not it was necessary to trick the Army and with it almost everybody else, the fact is that as soon as they found out that Suárez had legalized their eternal enemy, ignoring or forgetting what they'd been promised or what they thought they'd been promised, the generals exchanged the enthusiasm and cheers with which they'd applauded him months earlier for the virtuous indignation of those who feel themselves to be victims of the misdeeds of a renegade.

They never trusted Suárez again. Neither Suárez nor General Gutiérrez Mellado, who not only complied with his Prime Minister's decision but also, once the Communists were legalized and the first democratic elections held in June 1977, remained as the only military officer in Suárez's government, and from that moment on became the favoured target of attacks that deep down were not aimed at him, but at Suárez. It was a ferocious and inflexible campaign that went on for years, that meant daily attacks in the press, personal insults, retrospective slander and periodic riots, and did not exclude from its unusual virulence those who worked either closely or distantly with him. Gutiérrez Mellado survived it as well as he could, but not all his collaborators had the same luck or the same fortitude: unable to hear himself called fucking traitor or destroyer of the Army any longer, shortly after the coup d'état General Marcelo Aramendi ended his life with a pistol shot in his office at Army General Headquarters. The aggression Gutiérrez Mellado coped with was no less cruel than that which broke General Aramendi, but it was incomparably more assiduous and more publicized. They accused him of cowardice and duplicity because he hadn't made war on them face to face and because he'd spent a great deal of his career in the intelligence services, a double accusation perhaps predictable in an army like Franco's, in which valour, more than a virtue, was barroom rhetoric, and in which the terrible reputation of the intelligence services had been established by a phrase attributed to Franco, a phrase by which, as Gutiérrez Mellado knew first-hand, Francoism endeavoured to abide: Spies get paid, not decorated; apart from predictable and stupid, the accusation was false: although it was true that almost from the beginning his military career had been linked to espionage, Gutiérrez Mellado had not only fought with a machine gun in his hand during the 18 July uprising, but also, converted later into one of the chiefs of the fifth column in Madrid, for three years he'd risked his life in the obscurity of the Republican rearguard much more often than the majority of the braggarts who were recriminating him for having gone through the war without firing a shot. They accused him of leading the UMD – the Unión Militar Democrática or Democratic Military Union, a tiny clandestine military association that in the fading years of Francoism tried to promote the creation of a democratic regime – when the reality is that, in spite of being personally and ideologically close to some officers incorporated in it, he fought unhesitatingly against it because in his judgement it was splitting the discipline of the Armed Forces and putting their unity at risk, and that, once its members were tried and expelled from the Army, he opposed allowing them to be readmitted to their posts, which did not prevent him from often interceding to stop the persecution his comrades unleashed against them (though not against the members of other also clandestine associations, such as the Unión Militar Patriótica or Patriotic Military Union, that advocated the prolongation of Francoism and at that time were perfectly at ease in the Army). They accused him of wanting to demilitarize the Civil Guard – something that started a campaign of newspaper articles, collections of signatures and public festivities in which Lieutenant Colonel Tejero took a spirited part – when the reality is that he was only trying to improve the corps' efficiency, without stripping it of military allegiance, by putting its public order and security functions under the auspices of the Ministry of the Interior. They accused him of wanting to pervert, revoke or crush Army ethics with his reform of Carlos III's Royal Ordinances – the code that had ruled military morality since passed by the Earl of Aranda in 1787 – when the reality is that he was just trying to adapt the institution's ultraconservative ethics to the ethics of the twentieth century, permeating them with the lay and liberal values of democratic society. They accused him of every despicable thing possible, and explored his biography with a microscope in search of fuel with which to rubbish his reputation: they dug up an incident that had happened forty years earlier, during the witch-hunt against Freemasonry unleashed by Francoist authorities at the end of the war, to maintain that he'd been involved in or committed or instigated a murder, that of Major Isaac Gabaldón, gunned down one night in July 1939 while, according to certain witnesses, carrying a file of documents accusing some of his colleagues in SIMP, Franco's intelligence service, of belonging to the Freemasons; Gutiérrez Mellado was one of the members of SIMP and, although the judge hearing the case declared that the major had been murdered by Republican partisans and found Gutiérrez Mellado and the other members of SIMP not guilty of all the charges against them, the incident cast a shadow over the beginning of his military career and was used at the end to sow new doubts about his loyalty to the Army and his personal honesty.

Gutiérrez Mellado's personal honesty and loyalty to the Army were, as far as we know, unquestionable; as far as we know, the general was a decent man, congenitally incapable of guile and deceit, and perhaps therefore not suited for the practice of politics, or at least for the practice of politics in convulsive times. This does not of course mean that all the accusations poured out against him can be qualified as false or unjust. Not everything about the general's military policies was right; but, given the exceptional circumstances he had to fight against, many of the mistakes he committed would have been hard to avoid, if not actually unavoidable. His promotions policy, for example, was the best instrument the government had at its disposal to purge the Armed Forces of its leaden Francoist hindrance. Since a hierarchical promotion ladder was sacrosanct in the Army, in this matter as in almost everything Gutiérrez Mellado was almost always caught in the crossfire: he either respected seniority, allowing the radical old guard to monopolize the top command positions and threaten the course of democracy, or he bypassed protocol and promoted reliable officers and in return infuriated the passed-over officers and gave ammunition to those in favour of an uprising. Gutiérrez Mellado confronted this insoluble dilemma on more than a few occasions; the best known, the most illustrative as well, took place in May 1979, when the new Chief of the Army General Staff was named after the retirement of General De Liniers. The candidates to replace him were General Milans del Bosch, then Captain General of Valencia, and General González del Yerro, then Captain General of the Canary Islands; Gutiérrez Mellado did not consider either of them, but instead had named General Gabeiras – a soldier who lacked standing among his colleagues but enjoyed the Deputy Prime Minister's full confidence – thereby finding it necessary not only to promote him in an artificial and hasty manner, but also to promote the generals above him in the pecking order to avoid accusations of cronyism and of completely ignoring military norms. The ruse was in vain, and the scandal in the barracks monumental, not to mention the indignation of Milans and González del Yerro. Could he have avoided both things by arranging the change of power at the top of the Army in a different way? Perhaps, but it's not easy to imagine how; what is easy to imagine is what would have happened if on 23 February Milans had been in Madrid in command of the Army General Staff instead of being in Valencia in command of a secondary military region (the same or almost the same applies to González del Yerro, who during the 23 February coup adopted a dangerously equivocal attitude): almost certainly it would have been much more difficult for the coup to fail. On the other hand, on 23 February Gabeiras proved to be, if not the forceful chief a democratic army would have needed to confront the coup, at least a loyal soldier, and in any case the episode of his appointment was only one of many that embittered the relationship between the government and the Armed Forces and allowed the far right to keep the barracks on a continuous war footing against the government, propagating the rumour that Gutiérrez Mellado's military policy was just one despotic arbitrariness after another with which democracy aimed to castigate the Army, demoralizing it and eliminating any trace of its former prestige.

But the military discontent that crucified Gutiérrez Mellado and led to the events of 23 February was not only fed by professional gripes, imaginary humiliations and political intransigence; the military *golpistas* were not within reason, but they had reasons, and some of them were very powerful. I'm not referring to the concern around 1980 with which they watched the deterioration of the political, social and economic situation, or to the undisguised disgust they felt – they, who had not only been charged by the Constitution of 1978 with the defence of the unity of Spain but felt bound to that command by an imperative buried in their DNA – at the proliferation of flags and nationalist claims and the decentralization propelled by the *Estado de las Autonomías* (State of Autonomies), a combination of words that for the immense majority of military men was simply a euphemism hiding or anticipating the controlled explosion of the fatherland; I'm referring to a much more wounding matter, definitely one of the direct causes of the coup d'état: terrorism, and in particular the terrorism of ETA, which at that time was viciously attacking the Army and the Civil Guard in the face of the indulgence of a left that had not yet divested the ETA militants of their aura of anti-Franco fighters. If it's easy to understand this attitude of the left: simply recall the disastrous role the Army, the Civil Guard and the police played for forty years in supporting the dictatorship, not to mention the voluminous list of their atrocities, it's impossible to justify: if the Armed Forces had to protect democratic society with all their resources against its enemies, then democratic society had to protect the Armed Forces with all its resources from the slaughter to which they were being subjected, or at least support its members. It did not, and the consequence of that error was that the Armed Forces felt abandoned by a considerable part of democratic society and that putting a stop to that slaughter became, in the eyes of a considerable part of the Armed Forces, an irresistible argument for putting a stop to democratic society.

Few people were as aware of this state of affairs as General Gutiérrez Mellado, few people made greater efforts to remedy it and few people suffered from it personally as much as he did, because it was he who the indignant military, spurred on by the far right, held responsible from the beginning for allowing the murders of their comrades-in-arms and the disdain with which part of the country viewed them. That indignation provoked repeated acts of insubordination against the general and public revolts, which in their way were announcements or foreshadowings of 23 February; terrorism was not always the cause or the excuse – they didn't always happen during the heat of funerals for murdered soldiers, Civil Guards or policemen: they also happened at briefings of the High Command, on routine visits to barracks, even at formal ceremonies or drinks receptions – but it was always the cause or excuse of the most tumultuous and violent ones. Perhaps the most serious took place on the afternoon of 4 January 1979, at Army General Headquarters, during the funeral rites for the military governor of Madrid, Constantino Ortín, killed the night before in an ETA attack, and it must be said, like the majority of military disturbances of those years, not the spontaneous result of the emotion of the moment, but an act prepared by a previous alliance of officers pushing for a coup and far-right groups. The scene, which has been described on numerous occasions by numerous witnesses, could have happened like this:

Gutiérrez Mellado, personal friend of General Ortín and sole member of the government who attends the ceremony, presides over the funeral. The parade ground of the General Headquarters is heaving with a huge military crowd. Beneath an overcast winter sky, the ceremony goes on in an atmosphere of sorrow but also of induced tension, until at a certain moment, just after the band plays a prayer and the infantry hymn and as the undertaker's employees pick up the coffin while the commanders, officers and NCOs lined up in front of the podium fall out, shouts against the government begin to break out here and there as well as insults against the Deputy Prime Minister, who is immediately accosted by several officers who jostle him violently, corner him against the south door of the parade ground, vilify and punch him. A few metres from where this is happening, another group of officers wrestle the coffin away from the undertaker's employees and, after threatening the sentry guarding the premises that they'll shoot the doors open, manage to leave with the coffin on their shoulders out on to Calle Alcalá, where a crowd shouting 'Power to the Army!' ecstatically greets the several hundred insurgent commanders and officers, merges with them and accompanies them for three kilometres through the centre of Madrid to La Almudena cemetery, while in an office in the Headquarters, far from the military uprising inundating the streets of the capital, a crestfallen Gutiérrez Mellado who's lost his glasses tries to recover from the humiliation among the handful of comrades-in-arms who've just prevented his lynching.

That is the scene: in order to protect his battered self-esteem, and that of his army, Gutiérrez Mellado always denied having been the victim of that outrage, but two years later he could not repeat the denial, because on the evening of 23 February the television cameras filmed the kind of affront, with more or less attenuating variants, that he'd become very familiar with in the privacy of the barracks. In this sense, as well, his gesture of confronting the *golpistas* in the Cortes chamber was a summary or an emblem of his political career; for this reason, it was the final battle of a merciless war against his own comrades that left him exhausted, ready for the scrap heap: like Adolfo Suárez, on 23 February Gutiérrez Mellado was a man who was politically finished and personally broken, his morale at a low ebb and his nerves undone by five years of daily skirmishes. It's possible, however, that on 23 February the general was at the same time a happy man: that evening

Adolfo Suárez was giving up power, and with his fall he had promised to give up a political career that without Adolfo Suárez he might never have embarked on.

He kept his promise: he was not prevented from doing so by Leopoldo Calvo Sotelo, who upon taking Suárez's place as Prime Minister proposed he should stay on in the government, nor by Suárez himself, who tried to recruit him for the party with which he returned to politics after 23 February, and Gutiérrez Mellado prepared to spend the rest of his days in retirement, with nothing else to do but preside over charitable foundations, play long games of cards with his wife and spend long summers in Cadaqués with his Catalan friends. During his five years of political work many of his comrades-in-arms had loathed him for trying in vain to put an end to Franco's Army and for successfully planning the bases of the Army of democracy; his retirement did not attenuate that feeling: the first request of the senior commanders of the Army to the Minister of Defence after he left government was that the general not come near their units, and not long after Gutiérrez Mellado had left his position as Deputy Prime Minister he had to give up organizing an act of redress conceived to counteract a renewed press campaign against him for fear that the proposal would divide the Armed Forces. He never set foot in an Army barracks again, except for the day when the Academy where he had done his officer training paid him a last-minute homage and the general was able to experience – at least while listening without shedding a single tear to the five-minute standing ovation that day from the cadets who filled the auditorium – the fictitious and sentimental certainty that all the unpleasantries of his years in government were justified. He died a short time after that misleading day, on 15 December 1995, when the Opel Omega he was driving to Barcelona to deliver a speech skidded on the ice around a curve and went off the road. With him disappeared the most loyal politician Adolfo Suárez ever had at his side, the last Spanish soldier to occupy a seat in the Cortes, the last brass hat in the history of Spain. Those who used to see him in his final years remember a humble, diminished, quiet and slightly absent man, who never gave statements to the press, who never spoke of politics, who never mentioned 23 February. He didn't like to recall that evening, undoubtedly because he didn't consider his gesture of confronting the mutinous Civil Guards as a gesture of courage or grace or rebellion, or even as a sovereign gesture of liberty or as an extreme gesture of contrition or as an emblem of his career, but simply as the greatest failure of his life; but whenever anyone managed to get him to talk about it he dismissed it with the same words: 'I did what they taught me at the Academy.' I don't know if he ever added that the man in charge of the Academy where they taught him that was General Francisco Franco.

3

Returning to an image in the film: standing, with his arms hanging at his sides and defying the six Civil Guards riddling the Cortes chamber with bullets, General Gutiérrez Mellado – as much as if he wants to prevent the rebels from entering the premises as to subjugate military power to civilian power – seems to want to protect with his own body the body of Adolfo Suárez, sitting behind him in the solitude of his prime ministerial bench. That image is another summary or emblem: the emblem or summary of the relationship between those two men.

Gutiérrez Mellado's loyalty to Adolfo Suárez was an unconditional loyalty from the beginning to the end of his political career. This can in part be attributed to the sense of gratitude and discipline of Gutiérrez Mellado, whom Suárez had turned into the highest-ranking military officer in the country after the King and the second most powerful man in the government; it's likely that it was due to the total confidence that he placed in Suárez's political wisdom and in his courage, his youth and his instinct. Suárez and Gutiérrez Mellado were nevertheless, aside from the political task uniting them, two opposite men in almost every respect: both, it's true, shared a rock-solid Catholic faith, both cultivated a certain dandyism, both were thin, frugal and hyperactive, both loved football and the cinema, both were good card players; but their affinities practically finished there: the first was an expert in the ruses of the Spanish card game *mus* and the second in the more aristocratic bridge, the first came from a provincial Republican family and the second was from pure Madrileño stock and a good monarchist family, the first was a disastrous student and the second got straight As, the first was always a professional of power and the second was always a military professional, the first possessed, in short, political intelligence, personal charm, a gift for handling people, the cheek of a neighbourhood posse leader that he used to practise the art of seduction with indiscriminate skill, while the technical intelligence and sobriety of character of the second tended to confine his social life to the circle of his family and a few friends. They were also separated by a more obvious and more important difference: Suárez was exactly twenty years younger than Gutiérrez Mellado; they could have been father and son, and it's almost impossible to resist interpreting the relation that united them as a strange and unbalanced paternal-filial relationship in which the father acted as a father because he protected the son but he also acted as the son because he didn't question the other's orders or doubt the validity of his opinions.

Gutiérrez Mellado's political devotion to Adolfo Suárez must have begun the first time they spoke, or at least that's how the general liked to remember it. It's likely their paths had crossed at some point towards the end of the 1960s, when Suárez was running Radiotelevisión Española and flattering the military with programmes about the Army broadcast during prime time and with bouquets of roses he sent to their wives with notes apologizing for taking up their husbands' time in off-duty hours, but it wasn't until the winter of 1975 that they were alone together for the first time. During that period, with Franco recently deceased, Suárez had just been named Minister Secretary-General of the Movimiento in the King's first government; for his part, Gutiérrez Mellado had already been a major general for several months and the government's delegate in Ceuta, and on one of his trips to the capital he requested a meeting with the new minister to talk to him about a sports centre to be built in the city. Suárez received him, and a meeting that should have been a mere formality went on for several hours, at the end of which the general left the office at 44 Calle Alcalá dazzled by the young minister's irresistible charm, original language and clarity of ideas, so at the beginning of July, when Suárez was put in charge of forming a government to the distressed surprise of most of the country, Gutiérrez Mellado might have been surprised, but not distressed, because by then he was already convinced of the exceptional worth of the new Prime Minister. Just three months later, Suárez summoned him to his side to turn him into his bodyguard and right-hand man in one, and nothing would ever come between them again. Gutiérrez Mellado was the first Deputy Prime Minister and the only unchanging minister of the six governments Suárez formed, but the friendship Suárez and Gutiérrez Mellado struck up was not just political. Not long after he joined the government, Gutiérrez Mellado moved with his family into one of the buildings that made up the Moncloa complex, where Suárez's family home was already established; from then on, barely a day passed when they didn't see each other: they worked next door to each other, and as time went on they began to share not only their workdays but also their leisure time, united by a respectful privacy that did not preclude confidences or long familiar silences, and only grew stronger during the months leading up to the coup while Suárez was every day losing, amid the ruins of his power and prestige, political allies, close collaborators and friendships that had lasted years. In those final moments of Suárez's premiership and of Gutiérrez Mellado's own political career he was, as well as politically finished and personally broken, a perplexed man: he didn't understand the country's ingratitude to the Prime Minister who had brought the dictatorship to an end and constructed the democracy; he understood the irresponsible frivolity of the political class even less – especially that of the members of the Prime Minister's government – embroiled in the foolish struggle for power while democracy was crumbling around them. That's why he was trying to pacify the internal rebellions of the UCD though no one paid him any attention, and that's why at least on one occasion and with the very same result he took advantage of Suárez's absence from a Cabinet meeting to shout angrily at its members and demand their loyalty to the man who had put them in their posts. Two anecdotes that speak for themselves date from that time. The first happened at five in the afternoon on 29 January 1981 in Moncloa, when, after Suárez announced his resignation to his ministers in a specially called Cabinet meeting, Gutiérrez Mellado stood up from his chair and improvised a very short speech that concluded with this request: 'May God reward you, Prime Minister, sir, for the service you have done for Spain'; the sentence was sincere, if not eloquent: what is eloquent is that the meeting should have broken up immediately without any other minister pronouncing a single public word of consolation or support for the resigning Prime Minister. The second anecdote is without a precise date or location, but it almost certainly took place in Moncloa, perhaps in the two weeks previous to the first one; if that is the case, it must have taken place in a half-renovated office that Suárez began to use then in the back part of the residence, an enormous tumbledown hall with huge temporary windows through which the winter wind blew in and with loose wires hanging out of the walls that looked like the work of a decorator given the task of turning that space into a metaphor of the dilapidation of Adolfo Suárez's final months in government. It could have been there and then, as I say, but it also might not have been: after all reality lacks the slightest decorative inclination. In any case it deserved to be there and then where, as Suárez himself recalled in public after the general's death, he said to him at the end of a conversation or inventory of setbacks and desertions: 'Tell me the truth, Prime Minister: apart from the King, you and me, is there anyone else on our side?'

4

No. The answer is no: there is no one else on their side. Or that is at least the self-pitying answer that Adolfo Suárez undoubtedly gave to himself at that moment and the self-vindicating answer he was still giving years later, when he told the anecdote about his friend, now dead (and perhaps for that reason he was telling it). But, even if it was self-pitying and self-vindicating, the answer was not false.

The image of Adolfo Suárez sitting alone in the Cortes chamber during the evening of 23 February is also an emblem of something else: an emblem of his virtually absolute solitude in the months leading up to the coup. Curiously, a year and a half before that date a photographer caught a similar image in the same place: sitting on his Prime Minister's bench, Suárez is dressed the same way he was on 23 February – dark jacket, dark tie, white shirt – and, although his posture is a little different from that which he adopted while the guns were firing on 23 February, to his right stretches the same desolation of empty seats. As in the image of 23 February, Suárez is posing; as in the image of 23 February, Suárez doesn't appear to be posing (Suárez was always posing in public: that was his strength; he often posed in private: that was his weakness). The image was taken on 25 September 1979, but, if we ignore certain differences of colour and framing, it could be confused with that of 23 February 1981, as if, instead of photographing Suárez, the photographer had been photographing the future.

Although the secret was not made public until a year later, in September 1979, when he was at the height of his power and his prestige, Suárez was already privately finished as a politician. Earlier I

pointed out one reason for his sudden collapse: Suárez, who had known how to do the most difficult thing – dismantle Francoism and construct a democracy – was unable to do the easiest: administer the democracy he'd constructed. I'll qualify that now: for Suárez the most difficult was the easiest and the easiest was the most difficult. It's not just a play on words: although he hadn't created Francoism, Suárez had grown up with it, he knew its rules inside out and managed them masterfully (that's why he was able to finish Francoism off, pretending he was only changing its rules); whereas, although he had created this democracy and established its rules, Suárez had difficulty managing within it, because his habits, his talent and his temperament were not made for what he'd constructed, but for what he'd destroyed. That was at once his tragedy and his greatness: that of a man who consciously or unconsciously works not to strengthen his positions, but rather, to resort to Enzensberger's term again, to undermine them. Since he didn't know how to use the rules of democracy and only knew how to exercise power the way it's exercised in a dictatorship, he ignored Parliament, ignored his ministers, ignored his party. In the new game he'd created his virtues rapidly turned into defects – his savoir-faire turned into ignorance, his daring to rashness, his assurance to coldness – and the result was that in a very short time Suárez was no longer the brilliant and resolute politician he had been during his first years in government – when everything in his head seemed to connect with everything else, as if he had a magnet inside him that attracted and ordered the most

insignificant fragments of reality and allowed him to operate without fear, because at each moment he had the certainty of knowing the most distant result of every action and the innermost cause of every effect – but became a clumsy, dull and hesitant politician, lost in a reality he didn't understand and unfit to manage a crisis his bad governance did nothing but deepen. Together with the jealousy, bickering and greed for power of the ruling class, these deficiencies triggered the generalized plotting against him from the summer of 1980 onwards that ended up spurring on the coup; together with the exhaustion produced by four incredibly tough years as Prime Minister and a character more complex and more fragile than those who knew him only superficially suspected, they also triggered his personal collapse.

From the summer of 1980 onwards Suárez spent his time practically cloistered at Moncloa, protected by his family and by a meagre handful of collaborators. He seemed to be affected by a strange paralysis, or by a hazy kind of fear, or maybe it was vertigo, as if at some moment of masochistic lucidity he'd understood that he was no more than a fraud and intended to avoid any social contact at all costs for fear of being unmasked, and at the same time as if he feared that an obscure longing for sacrifice was driving him to put an end to the farce himself. He spent hours and hours shut up in his office reading reports relating to terrorism, the Army, economic or international politics, but then he was unable to make decisions about these matters or even to meet with the ministers who needed to make them. He didn't attend Parliament, didn't give interviews, was barely seen in public and more than once did not want or could not manage to preside from start to finish over Cabinet meetings; he could not even find the energy to attend the funerals of three Basque members of his party murdered by ETA, nor those of the forty-eight children and three adults who died at the end of October as the result of an accidental propane gas explosion in a school in the Basque Country. His physical health was not bad, but his mental health was. There is no doubt that around him he saw only an obscurity of ingratitude, betrayal and contempt, and that he interpreted any attack on his work as an attack on his person, something that might also be attributed to his difficulties in adapting to democracy. He never fully understood that in the politics of a democracy nothing's personal, given that in a democracy politics is theatre and no one can act in a theatre without pretending to feel what they don't feel; of course, he was a pure politician and, as such, a consummate actor, but his problem was that he pretended with such conviction that he ended up feeling what he was pretending, which led him to confuse reality with its representation and political criticisms with personal ones. It's true that in the hunting party unleashed against him over the course of 1980 many of the criticisms he received were personal rather than political, but it's no less true that when he arrived in government he had also been the object of personal criticisms, only then the Prime Minister was still protected by the privileges of an authoritarian system and his neophyte enthusiasm turned them into spurs to his will and his mental strength neutralized them, attributing them to failings of their authors – errors of judgement, frustrated ambitions, unsatisfied vanity, bitterness – now, instead, exposed by liberty, submitted to pressing demands and with his defences decimated by the high-interest loan of almost five years of a term of office in often extreme conditions, he felt those personal criticisms to be an instrument of daily martyrdom, undoubtedly because he repeated them to himself, and against oneself there is no possible protection. Like all pure politicians, Suárez also felt an urgent need to be admired and loved and, like everyone in the political village of Francoist Madrid, he'd forged his career to a great extent on the basis of adulation, spellbinding his interlocutors with his sympathy, his insatiable desire to please and his tree-like repertoire of anecdotes until they were convinced not only that he was an extraordinary being but also that they were even more extraordinary than he was, and therefore he was going to make them the object of all his trust, his attention and his affection. For a man like that, all outward appearance, whose self-esteem depended almost entirely on the approval of others, noticing that his conjuring tricks no longer worked must have been a devastating experience, that the country's ruling class had taken his measure and the shine of his seduction had dimmed, that no one laughed at his jokes or was entranced by his opinions, that no one fell under the spell of his stories or felt privileged to be in his company, that no one believed his promises any more or accepted his declarations of eternal friendship, that those who had admired and flattered him looked down on him, that those who owed him their political careers and had pledged their loyalty betrayed him, that the best feeling he could now evoke among his equals was a mixture of weariness and mistrust and that, as the polls made sure to demonstrate to him daily starting in the summer of 1980, the whole country was fed up with him.

Politically alone and exhausted, personally lost in a labyrinth of self-pity, exasperation and disillusion, towards November 1980 Suárez began to think of resigning. If he didn't do so it was because he was held back by inertia or the instinct for power and because he was a pure politician and a pure politician never gives up power: he gets thrown out; also, maybe, because in the moments of euphoria interspersed in his dejection a scrap of courage and pride persuaded him that, although nothing that he might do from then on could outdo what he'd already done, only he could fix what he himself had done wrong. In those days he sought relief and stimulation in trips abroad, where his standing as the maker of Spanish democracy still remained intact; in the course of one of them, after attending the inauguration of the Peruvian Prime Minister Belaúnde Terry in Lima, Suárez gave one of his last interviews as Prime Minister to the journalist Josefina Martínez, and the result of that interview was a text so dark, so bitter and so sincere – so full of laments about ingratitude, incomprehension and the personal offences and insults of which he felt himself the object – that his advisers prevented its publication. 'I tend to say that I'm engaged in a boxing match in which I'm not willing to throw a single punch,' Suárez said to the journalist that day. 'I want to win the fight in the fifteenth round by exhausting the opponent . . . So I must have great stamina!' It's false that he didn't throw a single punch (he threw some, but he no longer had the strength to keep at it), but it's true that he had great stamina, and it's especially true that he saw himself like that many times in the autumn and winter of 1980: in the centre of the ring, staggering and blinded by blood, sweat and black eyes, with his arms hanging dead at his sides, breathing heavily under the shouts of the spectators and the heat of the lights, secretly longing for the final blow.

5

The final blow was landed by the King. Maybe he was the only one who could have delivered it: the King had given power to Suárez so maybe only the King could take it away from him; he did: he took his power, or at least spared no effort in getting Suárez to hand it back. This means that, like the majority of the Spanish political class, in the autumn and winter of 1980 the King was also in his way plotting against the Prime Minister of his government; this means that Gutiérrez Mellado was mistaken: the King wasn't on their side either.

The King had met Suárez in January 1969, during a vacation trip to Segovia in the company of a cortege that included his personal secretary and future leader of 23 February: General Armada. At the time Suárez was the civilian governor of the province and the King a precarious prince still a few months away from being sworn in by the Francoist Cortes as Franco's successor, but whose future as King was not entirely clear even to Franco himself, because it hung from a delicately balanced web that might break after his death. The two men got along well from the start; from the start they sensed that each needed the other: Suárez was not a monarchist, but he immediately became a monarchist, undoubtedly because he knew that, in spite of the balancing acts and uncertainties, Spain's most credible future was the monarchy and he didn't want to miss the future for anything in the world; as for the King, harassed and ignored by very influential sectors of Francoism – starting with Franco's own family – he urgently needed allies, and that young man only six years older than him, discreet, promising, diligent, obliging and talkative, must have seemed like a good ally at first sight.

The first day Suárez just had lunch with the Royal Family in a restaurant in Segovia, but during the following months the King returned several times to an estate in the province, in the Guadarrama sierra, and there a weekend complicity was forged between the two men that possibly ended up convincing the future monarch that, if he knew how to use his eagerness to please, his ambition and his quick and practical intelligence, Suárez could come to be much more than amusing company for him. It's unlikely they talked much about politics at the beginning, although it's almost certain that the King understood very soon that Suárez's brain was not fossilized by Francoism, that he knew how to lead and lacked elaborate political ideas; it's also unlikely that he didn't suspect that his main political idea consisted in prospering politically, and that his monarchism therefore depended exclusively on the Crown's ability to satisfy his aspirations.

From that moment on the King did as much as he could to promote Suárez's political career. In November of the same year he interceded to persuade Admiral Carrero Blanco to appoint him director general of Radiotelevisión Española, and Suárez didn't waste any time at all in proving to the monarch he hadn't been mistaken in betting on him. During the four years he ran the country's only television station he orchestrated an image campaign that introduced the until then fleeting and vague figure of the Prince into every home: he did not fail to record a single one of his trips, or a single one of his official acts, or a single one of his public appearances; his recently acquired monarchist vocation (or his convert's zeal) led him into confrontation on several occasions with his boss the Cabinet minister, especially when he refused to broadcast live and on the main channel the wedding of Franco's granddaughter to Alfonso de Borbón, the Prince's cousin, who also aspired to the throne, and whose matrimony raised hopes in the general's innermost circle of seeing power perpetuated in Franco's family. By that time, in the early 1970s, Suárez had already begun to put himself forward for a ministry, but he did not receive one until the death of Franco when the first government of the monarchy was formed and the King, who lacked sufficient strength to impose a prime minister to his taste and was obliged to inherit Arias Navarro – a hesitant mummy unable to settle up his Francoist debts – had enough to impose Suárez, to whom Arias Navarro assigned the key post of Minister Secretary General of the Movimiento after being convinced by Torcuato Fernández Miranda, then the King's main political adviser and President of the Cortes and of the Council of the Kingdom, two of the dictatorship's prime bastions of power. Only six months later the King managed to get rid of Arias Navarro and, after a series of intrigues by Fernández Miranda in the Council of the Kingdom – the body in charge of presenting the monarch with a trio of candidates for Prime Minister – chose Adolfo Suárez to head the government.

He wasn't the only possible choice. There were much more obvious candidates, with better monarchist credentials, better intellectual training and more political experience; but the King (or the King advised by Fernández Miranda) calculated that at that time such virtues were actually defects: a government under, let's say, José María de Areilza – a cultured, cosmopolitan man, eternally devoted to the Crown, well connected to the clandestine opposition and a favourite of many of the regime's reformers – or Manuel Fraga – former minister under Franco and later leader of the right – would have been an Areilza government or a Fraga government, because Fraga and Areilza both had very strong personalities and their own political projects; a Suárez government, on the other hand, wouldn't be a Suárez government, but the King's government, because Suárez (or this at least was the King's and Fernández Miranda's belief) lacked any political project and was ready to carry out the one the King entrusted to him and in the way in which it was entrusted. The King's project was democracy; more precisely: the King's project was some form of democracy that would allow the monarchy to take root; still more precisely: the King's project was some form of democracy not because he found Francoism repugnant or because he was impatient to give up the powers he'd inherited from Franco or because he believed in democracy as a universal panacea, but because he believed in the monarchy and because he thought that at that moment a democracy was the only way to root the monarchy in Spain. However, changing a dictatorship into a democracy without breaking the law was a very complex, perhaps unheard-of operation, and the King needed to monitor it closely, so he needed someone to manage it whose passion for power made him absolutely faithful and absolutely docile, a man of his age who wouldn't feel the temptation to guide him or impose on him and with whom he could maintain a fluid relation. Suárez fulfilled these conditions from the outset; others as well. He knew the Francoist political class and the corridors of power off by heart, every last nook and cranny of the system that had to be demolished, he was young, clever, quick, fresh, realistic, flexible, efficient, charming and smooth enough to persuade the opposition that everything was going to change while persuading the Francoists that nothing was going to change although everything was changing. Finally, as well as the daring of ignorance and the fearlessness of those who have nothing to lose, he possessed an exorbitant self-confidence and an unshakeable desire to win that should enable him to carry out the job they were going to give him, withstanding the furious attacks from all sides without wavering and without getting completely burnt before his time was up.

But naturally he ended up getting burnt. By the time that happened, however, Suárez had already done his duty to the King: in order to get the monarchy to take root he'd installed democracy, maybe a more complete or more profound democracy than he and the King had imagined in the beginning. He'd done his work well. Only by 1980 he seemed intent on ruining it. Because in the King's view as in that of almost the entire Spanish ruling class the problem was that, after constructing democracy, Suárez had thought himself able to run it, and his remaining in government did nothing but deepen a crisis of which he himself was the cause. The other problem was that the King proposed to solve this problem, and in order to do so lent a hand to the manoeuvring destined to replace Suárez that formed the placenta of the 23 February coup. He probably felt it was his obligation to do so. Like the entire political class, like Suárez himself, the King was trying out the rules of democracy for the first time, and hadn't yet assumed his new role as an institutional or symbolic figure without effective political power (or hadn't wanted to); as if he still retained the authority to install and remove prime ministers that he'd inherited from Franco and which he'd renounced by sanctioning the Constitution of 1978, he wanted to intervene in the politics of the country again beyond the limits imposed by the recent rules of the parliamentary monarchy. His error was not just the result of inexperience; it was also a result of habit and fear. During the idyll of his first years in government, Suárez had accustomed the King to being consulted on every step he took, having his wishes turned into commands; now, instead, full of his successes and Prime Minister not by virtue of the monarch's will but by the citizens' votes, Suárez abandoned his submissive ways and servile behaviour and began to disagree with the King and to make decisions not just regardless of his opinion, but against it (pressed by the United States, the King considered joining NATO urgent and Suárez did not; pressed by the military, the King considered removing Gutiérrez Mellado from government urgent and Suárez did not; in the months before 23 February they had serious arguments about matters that would be determining factors in the events of 23 February, especially about the appointment of General Armada as Deputy Chief of the Army General Staff, which the King considered necessary and Suárez dangerous); the King took Suárez's insubordination or eagerness for independence badly, undoubtedly blaming him in part for the bad way the country was going, and this ended up poisoning the relationship between the two men: four years earlier, three years earlier, two years earlier, Suárez would show up unannounced at the Zarzuela Palace and the King would make surprise visits to Moncloa just to have a glass of whisky with his friend, they improvised meetings or communiqués, rustled up dinners together with their wives or films with their families; now that spirit of camaraderie had evaporated, replaced by an increasingly irritating bargaining that included, as well as differences of opinion, unreturned calls by the King to Moncloa or insolently delayed answers and annoyingly long waits for Suárez in the Zarzuela. It may be that jealousy between two men who were disputing the prestigious paternity of the new democracy within the borders of Spain and beyond was also a factor. Fear undoubtedly was. The King had been born in exile, and had only recovered the throne for himself and his family through the use of large doses of intelligence, luck, skill and sacrifice; now he was panicked about losing it and, as leading politicians kept repeating, as did Zarzuela courtiers – among them his father, at loggerheads with the Prime Minister for a long time by then – Suárez's disrepute was not just contaminating democracy, but also the monarchy, if the two things

could be separated at that moment: even though Suárez was no longer
the King's Prime Minister, as he had been when he'd been hand-picked
in 1976, but that of the voters, who had twice elected him at the polls,
the majority of citizens still identified the King with Suárez, so Suárez's
fall could bring down the monarchy with him. This alarming, specious
and repeated argument must have contributed, straining his constitutionally compulsory neutrality, to the King asserting his duty and
assuming the right to play a part in Suárez's downfall. 'Let's see if you
can get rid of that one for me,' he was heard to say in the autumn and
winter of 1980, referring to Suárez, by numerous visitors to the Zarzuela.
'Because with that one we're heading for disaster.' The King didn't just
encourage the hounding of Suárez with the weight of his authority; he
also discussed with quite a few people ways of replacing him, and it's
very likely that, given the country's dismal situation, he may also have
thought, as a large part of the ruling class did, that democracy had been
brought in hastily, that perhaps a surgical coup with the aim of extracting abscesses and stitching up gashes was needed, and by that point
perhaps a simple change of government might no longer be enough to
straighten things out, but it was especially very likely that at some
moment he looked kindly on or at least considered or allowed people
to think he seriously considered the proposal of a coalition or caretaker
or unity government chaired by a monarchist military officer – and
there was no more monarchist military man than his former secretary
Alfonso Armada, with whom he undoubtedly discussed the matter in
the weeks before the coup – providing the proposal counted on the blessing of the political parties and was directed towards getting the country
back on course with a touch on the rudder and keeping democracy,
which five years earlier had been the instrument of the Crown's survival,
from turning into that of its demise.

Suárez knew it. He knew the King was no longer on his side. To put
it a better way: he knew it but he didn't want to admit that he knew it,
or at least he didn't want to admit it until he was left with no choice but
to admit it. In the autumn of 1980 Suárez knew the King considered
him to be mainly responsible for the crisis and that he harboured serious doubts about his ability to resolve it, but he didn't know (or didn't
want to admit that he knew) that the King cursed him every time he

spoke to a politician, a military officer or a businessman; Suárez also
knew that his relationship with the King was bad, but he didn't know
(or didn't want to admit that he knew) that the King had lost confidence in him and was exhorting his adversaries to throw him out of
power. Finally on 24 December Suárez was left with no choice but to
admit that he knew what he knew and in reality had known for several
months. That night the King's Christmas speech was shown on television; it had almost always been an ornamental speech, but on that
occasion it was not (and, as if wanting to underline that it was not, the
monarch appeared before the cameras alone and not accompanied by
his family, as he'd done up till then). 'Politics,' said the King among
other things that night, should be considered 'a means to achieve an
end and not an end in itself'. 'Let us strive to protect and consolidate
what is essential,' he said, 'if we do not want to risk being left without
a base or occasion to exercise what is incidental.' 'Looking back today
over our conduct,' he said, 'we should ask ourselves if we have truly
done what we needed to do to make us feel proud.' 'It is urgent,' he
said, 'that we examine our behaviour in the sphere of responsibility
proper to each of us, without the evasion that always looks for someone
else to blame.' 'I wish to invite those who have the government of
the country in their hands to reflect,' he emphasized. 'They must put the
defence of democracy and the common good above their limited and
transitory personal interests, or those of their group or party.' Those
were some of the sentences the King pronounced in his speech, and it's
impossible that Suárez would not have felt they were directed at him;
also, that he wouldn't have interpreted them for what they probably
were: an accusation of clinging to power as an end in itself, of protecting the incidental, which was his position as Prime Minister, above the
essential, which was the monarchy; an accusation of behaving irrespon-
sibly by looking for people to blame for his own faults and putting his
transitory and limited interests above the common good; a public and
confidential way, in short, of asking him to resign.

I do not know what Suárez's immediate reaction to the King's speech
was. But I know that Suárez knew two things: one is that although the
King had no legal right to ask for his resignation he did retain a moral
right over him for having made him Prime Minister four years earlier;

the other is that – having lost the support of the man on the street, of Parliament, of his party, of Rome and Washington, blind and staggering and sobbing in the centre of the ring amid the howling of the spectators and the heat of the lights – losing the King's support entirely meant losing his last support and receiving the final blow. That same day Suárez must have understood that his only choice was to resign. This does not contradict the fact that, according to some sources, in a meeting held on 4 January in La Pleta, the royal residence in the mountains, in Lérida, the King hinted that he should resign, and Suárez refused to do so. It could well be: death throes are death throes, and some resist dying, although they know they're already dead. The fact is that only three weeks after the high-noon Christmas warning from the monarch, Suárez told his closest allies that he was giving up the leadership of the government. On the 27th he told the King in his office in the Zarzuela. The King did not put on an act: he didn't ask him to explain the reasons for his resignation, he didn't make the slightest ceremonial pretence of refusing it or ceremonially ask if he'd considered his decision carefully, he didn't have a word of thanks for the Prime Minister who had helped him preserve the Crown either; he just summoned his secretary, General Sabino Fernández Campo, and told him as soon as he entered the office, looking at him but pointing a pitiless finger at Suárez: He's going.

6

On 29 January 1981, twenty-five days before the coup, Adolfo Suárez announced his resignation as Prime Minister in a televised speech. The question is inevitable: how is it possible that the man who claimed the only way he'd leave Moncloa was if he lost an election or feet first was leaving Moncloa voluntarily? Was Suárez not a pure politician and is a pure politician not a politician who never gives up power unless thrown out? The answer is that Suárez did not give up power voluntarily, but was thrown out: the man on the street threw him out, Parliament threw him out, Rome and Washington threw him out, his own party threw him out, his own personal collapse threw him out and in the end the King threw him out. There is another answer, which is the same: since he was an absolutely pure politician, Suárez left before the sum of those adversaries threw him out and with the aim of justifying himself before the country, thus thwarting the alliance that had formed against him and preparing his return to power.

With the exception of the 23 February coup – of which it was actually a basic ingredient – no event in recent Spanish history had unleashed as much speculation as Adolfo Suárez's resignation; however, of all the enigmas of 23 February maybe the least enigmatic might be Adolfo Suárez's resignation. Although it's impossible to exhaust the reasons that triggered it, it's possible to rule out the most truculent and publicized of them. Suárez did not resign because the military forced him to and he did not resign to prevent a military coup: as Prime Minister he was prone to many faults, but cowardice was not one of them, and there is no doubt that, no matter how crushed he might have been, if the military had pointed a pistol at his chest Suárez would have immediately ordered them to stand to attention; there is no doubt either that had he known a coup was in the works he would have got ready to stop it. The most remembered phrase from his resignation speech seems to belie this last assertion: 'As often happens in history,' said Suárez, 'the continuity of a project demands a change of personnel, and I don't want the democratic system of coexistence to be, once again, a parenthesis in the history of Spain.' This sacrificial declaration, suggesting that its author was sacrificing himself to save democracy that retrospectively seemed to become saturated with significance on 23 February, did not figure in the draft of the speech that Suárez sent to the Royal Household on the eve of his television appearance, but was added at the last minute and, in spite of at least one of the people who normally wrote and corrected his texts crossing it out of the speech, Suárez put it back in. It was perhaps a characteristic dramatic emphasis and of a piece with his particular resignation strategy, but not pretence. Although he didn't know that the placenta of a coup against democracy was growing in the country, Suárez was not unaware that the intrigues against him were also dangerous to democracy, because they aimed to get him out of power without elections and straining to the maximum the mechanisms of a recently introduced game; he was not unaware (or at least he suspected) that a no-confidence motion was being prepared in order to unseat him; he was not unaware (or at least he suspected) that this motion might have the backing of a portion of his own party, and might therefore triumph; he was not unaware that many felt the motion should bring a general in to lead a coalition or caretaker or unity government; he was not unaware that the King approved or was seriously considering the manoeuvre, or at least was allowing some to believe he approved or was seriously considering it; he was not unaware that the most likely military man to carry it out was Alfonso Armada, and that in spite of his objections the King was doing everything possible to bring his former secretary to Madrid as Deputy Chief of the Army General Staff. All this undoubtedly struck him as dangerous to his future, but – because it meant putting the brand-new mechanisms of the democratic game to the test by involving the Army in an operation that opened the doors of politics to a military reluctant to accept the system of liberties, if not impatient to destroy it – it also struck him as dangerous to the future of democracy: Suárez knew its rules and, although he didn't work well within them, he'd invented the game or thought he'd invented the game and was not ready to allow it to fail, for the simple reason that he was its inventor. To avoid the risk of the game failing he resigned.

But, although he was politically finished and personally broken, he also resigned for the same reason any pure politician would have done: in order to be able to keep playing; that is: so as not to be expelled by force from the table and the game and find himself shown out of the casino through the false door and with no possibility of returning. In fact, it's possible that Suárez, by announcing his resignation, intended to imitate a triumphant bluff by Felipe González, who in May of 1979 had quit the leadership of the PSOE, in dispute with the Party still defining itself as Marxist, and just four months later, when the PSOE hadn't managed to replace him and had expunged the word Marxist from its statutes, returned to his post welcomed by a huge crowd.* It's possible that Suárez was trying to provoke a similar reaction in his party; if he was, he was on the verge of achieving it. On 29 January, the very day Suárez announced his resignation from the premiership on television, the second UCD Party conference was due to begin in Palma de Mallorca; Suárez's strategy perhaps consisted of a surprise announcement of his resignation during the first day and then waiting for the commotion this provoked to ignite a revolt among the rank and file of the organization against the leaders who would put him straight back into the leadership of the Party and the government or would do so within a few short months. Bad luck (perhaps combined with the cunning of some of his adversaries in the

---

* Suárez contributed in his way to the success of González's bluff, and his contribution demonstrates that at that moment as well democracy mattered more to him than power: once González had resigned, the Prime Minister had the opportunity to facilitate a leadership takeover of the PSOE by a group of Marxists – Enrique Tierno Galván, Luis Gómez Llorente, Francisco Bustelo – whom he probably would have easily defeated in elections; he didn't do it: he facilitated González's return because, although he knew he was a much more considerable electoral adversary, he thought a young social democrat like him was much more useful for the stability of democracy than his adversaries. This is another proof that above all Suárez wanted the game he'd invented to work.

government) thwarted his plans: a strike of air traffic controllers forced the conference to be postponed for a few days right at the moment when Suárez had already communicated his intention to resign to several ministers and some of the rank and file leaders of his party, and the result of this setback was that, convinced that the scoop couldn't be kept secret for so long, he had to make his resignation known before he'd planned, so when the conference was finally held in the first week of February the time gone by since the announcement of his withdrawal had dampened the impact of the news, which was not enough to recover his lost power but was enough to allow him to take control of the leadership of the UCD, to be the member with the most votes from his fellow Party members and for the conference to give him a long and warm standing ovation.

There might be still another reason why Suárez resigned, a reason perhaps more decisive than all the previous ones, because it constitutes their basis and gives them an additional and deeper meaning: Suárez resigned as Prime Minister of the government to give himself legitimacy as Prime Minister of the government. It's a paradox, but Suárez is a paradoxical character, and the almost five years in which he remained in power were not for him in a certain sense anything but this: a permanent, agonizing and eventually futile fight to legitimize himself as Prime Minister. In July 1976, when the King put him in charge of the political reform, Suárez knew he was a legal prime minister, but he was not unaware – as he himself had said to a journalist who accosted him shortly after his appointment – that he was not a legitimate prime minister, because he wasn't backed up by the votes of the citizens to carry out the reforms; in December 1976, when he won the referendum on the Law for Political Reform by a crushing majority – the legal instrument that allowed him to carry out the reforms – Suárez knew that victory legitimized him to effect the change from dictatorship to democracy or to some form of democracy, but he was not unaware that it did not give him legitimacy to act as Prime Minister, because he had been chosen by the King and a prime minister of the government was only legitimate after having been chosen by the citizens in free elections; in June 1977, when he won the first free elections, Suárez knew he was a democratic prime minister because he had the legitimacy of the citizens' votes, but he was not unaware that he lacked the legitimacy of the law, because the laws of Francoism were still in force, and not those of democracy; in March 1979, when he won the first elections held after the passing of the Constitution, Suárez knew he had the full legitimacy of votes and laws, but that was when he realized he did not have moral legitimacy, because that was when the entire ruling class pounced to remind him – and perhaps he repeated it to himself, and against oneself there is no possible protection – that he'd never been anything but the King's messenger boy, a mere little provincial Falangist, a Francoist upstart, a nonentity consumed by ambition and a rogue intellectually unfit to preside over the government who had never conceived of politics except as an instrument of personal prosperity, and whose foolish eagerness for power kept him tied to the premiership while the entire country fell to pieces around him. So, since the spring of 1979 Suárez knew he possessed all the political legitimacy he needed to govern, but only a year later discovered that he lacked the moral legitimacy (or he'd been divested of it): the only way he found to acquire it was to resign.

That in reality is the meaning of his resignation speech on television, a speech that contains an individual response to the King's Christmas reproaches and a collective reproach to the ruling class that has denied him the longed-for legitimacy, but most of all contains a vindication of his political integrity, which, in a politician like Suárez, with no aptitude for distinguishing the personal from the political, also means a vindication of his personal integrity. Proudly, after all truthfully (although only after all), Suárez begins to explain to the country that he's leaving of his own volition, 'without anyone having asked me', and that he's doing so in order to demonstrate with his actions ('because words seem not to be enough and we need to demonstrate with deeds what we are and what we want') that the image of him that has been imposed as 'a person clinging to his position' is false. Suárez remembers his role in the change from dictatorship to democracy and states that he is not giving up the job of Prime Minister because his adversaries have defeated him or because he has been left without the strength to keep fighting them, which might not be true or not entirely true, but because he's reached the conclusion that his giving up power might be more beneficial to the country than his remaining in it, which it indeed probably is: he wants his resignation to be 'a moral salutary lesson' able to banish 'viscerality', 'the permanent discrediting of people', 'irrationally systematic attacks' and 'the useless wholesale discrediting' for ever from the practice of democratic politics: all those aggressions of which he has been feeling victim for many months. 'Something very important has to change in our attitudes and behaviour,' he says. 'And I want to contribute with my resignation so this change can be really immediate.' Furthermore, Suárez does not say he's retiring from politics – although he is giving up the leadership of his party; on the contrary: after declaring his optimism for the country's future and for the UCD's capacity to guide it, he maintains that politics 'is going to carry on being my fundamental reason for living'. 'I thank you all for your sacrifice, for your collaboration and for the repeated demonstrations of trust you've placed in me,' he finishes. 'I wanted to repay them with absolute devotion to my work and with dedication, self-denial and generosity. I promise that wherever I might be I shall remain identified with your aspirations. That I shall always be at your side and shall try, as long as I have the strength, to remain in the front line and with the same hard-working spirit. Thanks to every one of you and for everything.'

Let me repeat: the speech, including its good intentions and emotive rhetoric, means to be a moral as well as a political declaration. We have no reason to doubt his sincerity: by giving up the premiership Suárez intends to dignify democracy (and, in a certain sense, to protect it); but the ethical and political reasons are joined by reasons of personal strategy: for Suárez, resigning is also a way of protecting himself and dignifying himself to himself, recovering his self-esteem and his best self with the aim of preparing his return to power. That's why I said before that resigning as Prime Minister was his final attempt to legitimize himself as Prime Minister. Let me correct myself now. It wasn't his final attempt: it was the penultimate. The final one was on the evening of 23 February, when, sitting on his bench while the bullets whizzed around him in the Cortes chamber and words were no longer enough and he had to demonstrate with actions what he was and what he wanted, he told the political class and the whole country that, though he might have the dirtiest democratic pedigree in the great sewer of Madrid and had been a little provincial Falangist and Francoist upstart and an uneducated nonentity, he was indeed ready to risk his neck for democracy.

7

I have left one question pending, and now return to it: were the intelligence services plotting against the democratic system in the autumn and winter of 1980? Did the Higher Defence Intelligence Centre, CESID, participate in the coup d'état? The hypothesis is not only literarily irresistible, but historically plausible, and this is in part why it continues to be one of the most controversial points of 23 February. The hypothesis is plausible because it is not infrequent that in periods of political regime change the intelligence services – liberated from their old bosses and not yet entirely under the control of the new ones, or discontented with their old bosses for provoking the disappearance of the old regime – tend to operate autonomously and form focal points of resistance to change, organizing or participating in manoeuvres designed to make it fail. That's what happened in 1991 for example in the Soviet Union of Mikhail Gorbachev. Did it also happen ten years earlier in the Spain of Adolfo Suárez? In 1981 was CESID a focal point of resistance to change? Did CESID organize the 23 February coup? Did they participate in it?

General Gutiérrez Mellado might have been more clearly aware than any other Spanish politician of the danger that disaffected intelligence services could pose for democracy, because he had spent most of his career in them and knew their ins and outs first-hand; and vice versa: few Spanish politicians must have been more clearly aware than Gutiérrez Mellado of the utility that an intelligence service loyal to its new rulers could have for democracy. So in June 1977, as soon as Adolfo Suárez formed the first democratic government after the first free elections, Gutiérrez Mellado rushed to try to provide the state with modern, efficient and trustworthy intelligence services. In order to do this for a start he wanted to fuse the numerous intelligence agencies of the dictatorship into a single one, CESID, but the clenched resistance his project met allowed him to unite only the two main ones: SECED and the third section of the High Command General Staff. They were very different services: both were military, but the third section of the High Command tended towards foreign espionage and was characteristically more technical than political, while SECED tended towards interior espionage and was much more political than technical, because it had been conceived in the mid-1960s by then Major San Martín – the *golpista* colonel of the Brunete Armoured Division on 23 February – like a sort of political police in charge of keeping watch over Francoist orthodoxy. The failure of Gutiérrez Mellado's attempt to unify all the intelligence agencies happened again when he tried to modernize them: in 1981 CESID was still an insufficient and primitive, almost DIY intelligence service; its staff was skeletal and its structure rudimentary: made up of barely seven hundred people, it possessed fifteen or so delegations spread all over the country and was organized into four divisions (Interior, Exterior, Counterintelligence, and Communications and Statistics); in command of them was a director and a secretary general; alongside them – and supervised only by the Secretary General – was an elite unit: AOME, the special operations unit directed by Major Cortina. An unusual fact gives an idea of the difficulties Gutiérrez Mellado's intelligence service faced: in spite of one of the principal missions with which the general entrusted it being the control of the various coup plots and in spite of the existence of a section dedicated to this within the Interior Division, the so-called involution section, CESID members were not officially authorized to enter the barracks and inform about what was going on or being planned inside them (this task was reserved for the information service of the Army's Intelligence Division, the so-called Second B, which in practice blocked the news and fomented *golpismo*), so all that CESID knew about the Army it knew through unofficial channels, which did not prevent the Centre from breaking up, thanks to a tip-off, Lieutenant Colonel Tejero's first attempt at a coup d'état in November 1978, the so-called

Operation Galaxia. A no less unusual fact than the previous one gives an idea of the disorder that reigned in the intelligence service: by the time of 23 February, after little more than three years of existence, CESID had already had three directors, none of whom was an expert in espionage; all had been little short of compelled to accept the post and all considered it little short of despicable to investigate their comrades-in-arms. This means that, as well as insufficient and primitive, in 1981 CESID was also a chaotic and slapdash intelligence service. Does this also mean that it was untrustworthy?

After the fusion into CESID of the two principal espionage services of the dictatorship, the inheritance that predominated was that of SECED – the regime's political police: the branch of intelligence most addicted to Francoism – but Gutiérrez Mellado endeavoured to always keep the command of the centre in the hands of men from the third section of the High Command who enjoyed his complete confidence. The person who was effectively directing CESID on 23 February was not Colonel Narciso Carreras, its director, but Lieutenant Colonel Javier Calderón, its Secretary General. Calderón's trajectory is exceptional because it's characteristic of a tiny minority of military officers who, like Gutiérrez Mellado, were trying to liberate themselves from the ideological dependency of Francoism and create a favourable atmosphere for political change: educated in the late 1940s in and around the Colegio Pinilla – a military prep school that encouraged a socially-concerned Falangism from which emerged some members of the future, tiny and illegal Democratic Military Union (Unión Militar Democrática, UMD) – at the beginning of the 1970s Calderón began to work in the counterintelligence service of the third section of the High Command; a little while later he acted as defence counsel for Captain Restituto Valero, one of the leaders of the UMD, and participated in GODSA, a think-tank or a nascent party that aspired to promote in late Francoism an opening up of the regime and bet on Manuel Fraga as the driver of reform until, displaced and overtaken by Suárez, the former transformed into the skimmed Francoism of the Alianza Popular; in 1977, with the creation of CESID, Calderón joined its Counterintelligence Division, and in 1979 Gutiérrez Mellado turned him into the Centre's strongman. On 23 February Calderón's conduct was impeccable: CESID was, under his command, one of the few military agencies that placed itself from the beginning and unequivocally on the side of legality, famously contributing to keeping the Brunete Armoured Division from coming out onto the streets of Madrid (something which turned out to be of prime importance in the *golpistas'* defeat); his conduct after 23 February offers more doubts: CESID had notched up a resounding failure by not detecting the coup in advance and, in order not to squander all the Centre's credit, in the days following the 23 February coup Calderón attempted to silence the rumours about the participation of some of his men in the attempted coup, but the fact is that he did order an investigation to be opened and in the end he expelled those who had been suspected of connivance with the *golpistas*, including Major Cortina. Calderón's debatable way of proceeding after the coup cannot, however, hide the obvious, and that is that by 1981 the strongman of CESID was one of the few democratic military men in the Spanish Army, whose work in the intelligence service made it the opposite of a focal point of resistance to political change: that's why the far-right military officers' criticisms had CESID in their sights; that's why Calderón's name figured in all the lists of undesirable comrades-in-arms that were periodically published; that's why he was an entirely safe man for Gutiérrez Mellado, with whom before 23 February he'd had a good friendship, which was consolidated after 23 February and which explains why in 1987, as a result of the drug-induced death of one of Calderón's sons, the general created the Foundation to Help Fight Drug Addiction with his friend on the board of directors. No: Gutiérrez Mellado did not manage to set up powerful, unified, modern and efficient intelligence services, and the failure of CESID to predict the who, when, how and where of 23 February can be attributed to that failure; but the general did manage to set up trustworthy intelligence services: CESID as an agency contributed to the failure of the coup d'état, and there is no proof to the contrary that links it to its preparation or execution.

None except for the participation in the coup of some of its members. Because by this stage we already know several CESID agents – without doubt Captain Gómez Iglesias, possibly Sergeant Miguel Sales and Corporals Rafael Monge and José Moya – collaborated with Lieutenant

Colonel Tejero on the day of the coup: the first, persuading certain indecisive officers stationed at the Civil Guard Motor Pool to back up the lieutenant colonel in his assault on the Cortes; the latter, escorting Tejero's buses to their objective through the streets of Madrid. Those four agents belonged to AOME, Major Cortina's elite unit. Were they acting autonomously? Were they acting under Cortina's orders? Since neither Calderón nor CESID supported or organized the 23 February coup, did AOME support or organize it? Did Cortina support or organize it? That is the question still pending.

8

23 February

I don't know if the success or failure of a coup d'état is settled in its first minutes; I do know that at twenty-five to seven that evening, ten minutes after it began, the coup d'état was a success: Lieutenant Colonel Tejero had taken the Cortes, General Milans del Bosch's tanks were patrolling the streets of Valencia, the tanks of the Brunete Armoured Division were preparing to leave their barracks, General Armada was waiting for the King's phone call in his office at Army General Headquarters; at twenty-five to seven that evening everything was going as the *golpistas* had anticipated, but at twenty to seven their plans had changed and the coup was beginning to fail. There were high stakes riding on those crucial five minutes in the Zarzuela Palace. It was the King's hand to play.

Ever since the very day of 23 February there have been unceasing accusations that the King organized the 23 February coup, that he was somehow implicated in the coup, that in some way he had wanted it to triumph. It is an absurd accusation: if the King had organized the coup, if he'd been implicated in it or had wanted it to triumph, the coup would have triumphed without the slightest doubt. The truth is obvious: the King did not organize the coup but rather stopped it, for the simple reason that he was the only person who could stop it. Stating the above is not the same as stating that the King's behaviour in relation to 23 February was irreproachable; it was not, just as that of the majority of the political class was not: as with the political class, many extenuating circumstances can be found for the King – his youth, immaturity, inexperience, fear – but the reality is that in the months before 23 February he did things he shouldn't have done. He should not have abandoned the strict neutrality of his constitutional role as arbiter between institutions. He should not have encouraged the replacement of Suárez. He should not have encouraged or considered alternative solutions to Suárez. He should not have spoken to anyone or allowed anyone to speak to him about the possibility of replacing Suárez's government with a coalition or caretaker or unity government headed by a soldier. He should not have submitted the government to the utmost pressure to have it accept General Armada as Deputy Chief of the Army General Staff, authorizing him to conceive and propagate the idea that he'd been brought to Madrid to be made Prime Minister of a coalition or caretaker or unity government. He should not have been ambiguous; he should have been emphatic: he should not have allowed any politician, any businessman, any journalist, any soldier – especially any soldier – to even imagine that he might support forcibly constitutional manoeuvres that were straining the recently installed hinges of democracy, pushing ajar its doors for an army eager to finish it off. Like almost the entire political class, in the months before 23 February the King behaved imprudently at the very least and – because for the military he was not only the head of state, but also the head of the Armed Forces and Franco's heir – much more than that of the political class his own imprudence gave wings to the advocates of a coup. But on 23 February it was the King who clipped them.

It's not easy to reconstruct what happened in the Zarzuela Palace during the first fifteen minutes of the coup; they were moments of enormous commotion: it's not just that testimonies from the protagonists are scarce and contradict each other; the thing is that sometimes the protagonists contradict themselves. I am deliberately using the plural: the King is not the only protagonist; there is also – in a secondary but appreciable role – his secretary, Sabino Fernández Campo, in theory the third authority in the Royal Household, but in practice the first. Fernández Campo was by then a general with political experience, legal knowledge and wide-ranging military relations, who did not belong to the monarchist aristocracy and who four years earlier had replaced General Armada, with whom at first he maintained an excellent relationship that in the months before the coup had deteriorated, maybe because after a few years of distance from the Palace Armada had managed to get close to the King again and his shadow had begun to hover over the Zarzuela once again. It was Fernández Campo who on the evening of 23 February, after hearing the gunshots in the Cortes on the radio, sent word to the King, who was playing a game of squash with a friend and who, like his secretary, immediately understood they were facing a coup d'état. What happens next in the Zarzuela – what happens over the course of the night in the Zarzuela – happens in a few square metres, in the King's office and in Fernández Campo's, which was the outer office of the King's outer office. When the King arrives, he finds out almost at the same time about the assault on the Cortes and that Milans del Bosch has just issued an edict proclaiming a state of emergency in Valencia and, given that Milans is a solidly monarchist soldier whose fidelity he has taken great pains to cultivate, calls him on the telephone; Milans calms him down or tries to calm the King down: there's nothing to worry about, he is at his command as ever, has just assumed all the powers in the region to safeguard order until the hijacking of the Cortes is resolved. While the King is speaking to Milans, Fernández Campo manages to get in contact with Tejero thanks to a member of the Royal Guard who was attending the session of investiture of the new Prime Minister of the government in plain clothes and informs the royal secretary of what's happened from a phone booth and gives him a telephone number: Fernández Campo speaks to Tejero, forbids him to invoke the King's name, as he appears to have done when he burst into the Cortes, orders him to leave the Cortes immediately; before he finishes speaking, however, Tejero hangs up on him. That's when Fernández Campo calls General Juste, commander of the Brunete Armoured Division. He does so because he knows the Brunete – the most powerful, modern and hardened unit of the Army, and the nearest to the capital – is crucial for the triumph or failure of a coup; he also does so because he and Juste have been friends for many years. After the unplanned gunfire in the Cortes, which has endowed what had been intended as a soft coup with the scenery of a hard coup, the dialogue between Juste and Fernández Campo constitutes the second setback for the *golpistas* and the first stage of the dismantling of the coup. At the beginning of the conversation neither of the two generals speaks openly, in part because neither knows on which side of the coup his interlocutor will position himself, but especially because in Juste's office with him are General Torres Rojas and Colonel San Martín, who with Major Pardo Zancada are leading the uprising in the Brunete and who have convinced him to send his troops into Madrid with the argument that the operation has been ordered by Milans, enjoys the backing of the King and is being piloted from the Zarzuela Palace by Armada; Torres Rojas and San Martín listen carefully to the words Juste says to Fernández Campo, and they flow with difficulty down the telephone line, sinuous and plagued by guesswork, until the commander of Brunete mentions Armada's name and everything seems suddenly to fall into place for him: Juste asks Fernández Campo if Armada is at the Zarzuela and Fernández Campo answers no; then Juste asks if they're expecting Armada at the Zarzuela and Fernández Campo answers no again; then Juste says: Ah. That changes everything.

That's how the countercoup begins. The conversation between Juste and Fernández Campo goes on for a few more minutes, by the end of which the commander of the Brunete Division has understood that Torres Rojas, San Martín and Pardo Zancada have deceived him and the King does not endorse the operation; Juste hangs up the phone, picks it up again and calls his immediate superior and the highest military authority of the region of Madrid, General Guillermo Quintana Lacaci. By then Quintana Lacaci has spoken fleetingly with the King; like all the Captains General, Quintana Lacaci is an unwavering Francoist, but, unlike what almost all the other Captains General will do over the hours that follow, he has put himself unwaveringly under the orders of the King for whatever the King orders him to do: stop the coup or bring out the tanks; the King has thanked him for his loyalty and ordered him not to move his troops, so when Quintana Lacaci receives Juste's call announcing that the Brunete Division is ready to occupy Madrid on the orders of Milans, the Captain General flies into a rage: his subordinate has jumped the chain of command and has given an order with enormous implications without consulting him; he orders him to revoke it: he must confine the division to barracks and oblige those who have already taken to the streets or are preparing to do so to return to their units. Juste complies with the order and from that moment begins to put things into reverse, or tries to; he tries without much faith, without much energy, menaced by the mood of rebellion that has overtaken the Brunete headquarters and by the intimidating proximity of Torres Rojas and San Martín – who, on the other hand, paralysed by vertigo or fear, find neither sufficient energy nor faith to relieve him of his command of the unit and prevent him from putting the brakes on the coup – so it's mainly Quintana Lacaci who initiates a violent telephonic struggle, bristling with shouts, threats, insults and calls to order, with the Brunete regiment commanders, who minutes before were euphorically obeying the order to take Madrid and are now refusing to obey the countermand or postponing as long as they can, by way of excuses, evasions and military hair-splitting, the moment of doing so, hoping the military uprising will overflow the barracks and flood the capital and then the entire country. That, however, is not going to happen, although throughout the whole evening and night of 23 February it seems about to happen, and if it doesn't happen it's not just because fifteen minutes after the assault on the Cortes Quintana Lacaci (or Juste and Quintana Lacaci, or Juste and Quintana Lacaci on the King's orders) have set in motion the mechanism of the countercoup in Madrid, but also because at that very moment an even more important event is taking place, that entirely thwarts the *golpistas'* plans: the King (or Fernández Campo, or the King and Fernández Campo) have refused General Armada permission to come to the Zarzuela Palace.

The King and Armada spoke by telephone just after the King spoke to Milans and to Quintana Lacaci, but it wasn't Armada who phoned the King but rather the King who, just as the *golpistas* had anticipated (or just as Armada had anticipated), called Armada. That he should have done so, as he'd called Milans and Quintana Lacaci, is logical: Armada is at Army General Headquarters, in the Buenavista Palace, and the King calls there because he wants to keep the leadership of the military under control and find out any news they have there; although maybe that's not the only reason he calls him, maybe he's not just looking for power and information: since he's alarmed, since he knows it's a coup but doesn't know if it's with him or against him and perhaps cannot think of anything except preserving the Crown that had cost him years of effort to obtain, in those instants of panic and uncertainty the King is maybe also (or above all) seeking protection. Armada can provide all three of these things. Or at least it's logical that the King might think they can be supplied by Armada, his former tutor, his secretary for so long, the man who spent years getting him out of so many tight spots and was at his side during the difficult time of the restoration of the monarchy, the man whom, giving way to Adolfo Suárez's pressures, he'd expelled from his eternal post in the Royal Household less than five years ago and to whom, since he's wanted to be rid of Adolfo Suárez, he's begun to listen again, the man who so many times in recent months has warned him of the danger of a coup d'état whose threads he knows or perceives and can perhaps cut, and who so many times and with such vehemence has recommended a touch on the rudder to ward off that danger, the man he'd brought to Madrid against Adolfo Suárez's will as Deputy Chief of the Army General Staff, to have him nearby and available and perhaps – or this is at least what Armada desires or imagines, as so many desire or imagine – so he could direct the touch on the rudder by presiding over a unity government and in any case so he could inform and advise and control the Armed Forces and pacify their discontent, and eventually so he could help him in a situation like this. So, not even fifteen minutes after the beginning of the coup, the King calls Army General Headquarters and, after speaking to the Chief of the Army General Staff, General Gabeiras, asks him to pass the phone to General Armada, who is sitting beside him. The dialogue between the King and Armada is brief. Just as Milans has done minutes ago, Armada tries to calm the King down: the situation is serious, he tells him, but not desperate; and he can explain it: I'll just go up to my office, pick up a few papers and I'm on my way to the Zarzuela, Sire. The King is still listening to these words (or has just heard them and, wanting Armada to tell him what he knows, is about to say: Yes, come over here, Alfonso) when Fernández Campo walks into the office and questions the King in silence. It's Armada, the King answers, covering the receiver with his hand. He wants to come over. At this moment Fernández Campo, who has just spoken to Juste and run into the King's office to relay the conversation to him, must think two things at once: the first is that, if he lets him into the Zarzuela, Armada could take over the Palace, because in an emergency situation like that the King might prefer to trust his lifelong secretary, relegating him, who's barely been in the post for four years, to the background; the second is that, if as Juste has just told him the rebels are sure that Armada is at the Zarzuela directing the operation with the King's consent, that means that the former secretary is in on the coup or is somehow connected to the coup or has the intention of benefiting from the coup. Both thoughts convince Fernández Campo that he has to prevent Armada from coming to the Zarzuela, so he speaks to the King and then asks for the telephone. This is Sabino, Alfonso, he says to Armada. Fernández Campo does not ask Armada why Juste has mentioned his name, why the *golpistas* of the Brunete Division appeal to him, but Armada repeats what he's just told the King: the situation is serious, but not desperate; and he can explain it: I'm just going up to my office to pick up a few papers and I'm on my way to the Zarzuela, Sabino. And this is when Fernández Campo pronounces the final phrase: No, Alfonso. Stay there. If we need you we'll call you.

That was it: although Armada insisted that he must speak to the King in person, Fernández Campo's reiterated refusal obliged him to remain at Army General Headquarters, so that the former secretary could not approach the monarch and the fundamental piece of the coup could not fall into place. However, what would have occurred if the opposite had happened? What would have happened if that piece had also fallen into place? Let's imagine for a moment that it did. Let's imagine for a moment what would have occurred if everything had happened just as the *golpistas* had planned it, or as Armada had planned or as Armada and some of the *golpistas* might have imagined it would happen. Let's imagine for a moment that, for whatever reasons, Juste hadn't mentioned Armada's name in his conversation with Fernández Campo; or that, even though he'd mentioned it, Fernández Campo had not been suspicious of Armada or feared he'd oust him from his privileged position at the King's side or that he was involved in the coup or wanted to benefit from the coup; or that, even though Juste had mentioned Armada's name and Fernández Campo had been suspicious of him, the King had decided to trust his old lifelong secretary rather than his new secretary, or at least had decided he needed to know what it was his old secretary knew about the coup and how he proposed to confront it. Then the King would have said to Armada on the phone: Yes, Alfonso, come on over here, and Armada would have gone to the Zarzuela, where he undoubtedly would have explained to the King that what had happened was what he'd been predicting and fearing and warning him was going to happen for months, he would have explained that, in spite of the gunfire in the Cortes, he was certain that the rebels' plans were good and monarchist and he was sure that he could channel that military effusion – 'redirect' is the verb he might perhaps have used – to the advantage of the country and of the Crown. Then, maybe, he would have provoked in the Zarzuela a small and silent and almost invisible palace coup and Fernández Campo's authority and influence would have been substituted by Armada's authority and influence, and then the King (or the King advised by Armada) would next perhaps have ordered the Joint Chiefs of Staff, while waiting for the problem of the occupation of the Cortes to be solved and the parliamentarians freed, to assume all the powers of the government, and perhaps with the aim of keeping the peace in the streets and protecting democracy might also have ordered the Captains General to imitate Milans del Bosch and take control of their respective military regions, and the Joint Chiefs of Staff and the Captains General would have obeyed without a second's hesitation, not only because it was the head of the Armed Forces and head of state and Franco's heir who was ordering it, but also because Franco's heir and the head of the Armed Forces and of the state was ordering them to do what almost all of them had been wanting to do for a long time. Then, once the control of the institutions and order in the cities was secured, or at the same time as those two things were being secured, a unit of the Brunete Division might perhaps have relieved Lieutenant-Colonel Tejero's Civil Guards and might have quietly set up a cordon around the occupied Cortes, might have cleared the surrounding area and held the Cabinet and the deputies in the least ostentatious and least humiliating way possible while awaiting the appearance of the King's envoy. Then Armada would have appeared in the Cortes as the King's envoy and with the backing of the whole Army, he would have met with the main political leaders, he would have agreed with them that this situation, this use of force was totally unacceptable and would have persuaded them that the only way to fix it, and especially to save the threatened democracy, was to form a coalition or caretaker or unity government headed by himself, in short the option they'd all been driving forward over recent months to get the nation away from the edge of the precipice on which they all knew it was teetering. And then, once the government and deputies were persuaded that this was the best or only possible solution to the emergency (a solution on which the King would look kindly or that the King would not refuse if the Cortes approved it), everyone would have been set free and that very evening or that very night or the next day, with the soldiers back in their barracks or still in the streets, the session of investiture interrupted by Lieutenant Colonel Tejero would have been resumed, except that the Prime Minister elected in it would not have been Leopoldo Calvo Sotelo but Alfonso Armada, who would immediately have formed his government, a coalition or caretaker or unity government, a strong, stable, broad government that would have efficiently confronted Spain's great problems – terrorism, the disintegration of the state, the economic crisis, the loss of values – and that would not only have calmed down the military and the political class, the businessmen and bankers, Rome and Washington, but also the whole of the citizenry, who after a short time would have come out to demonstrate in all the regional capitals of Spain to celebrate the happy result of the coup and the continuation of democracy, and would have applauded the King's judicious attitude as the driving force behind the new political era and would have reinforced their trust in the monarchy as an indispensable institution to get the country out of the morass it was stuck in owing to the errors and frightful irresponsibility of certain politicians.

That is more or less what might have happened if Armada had got inside the Zarzuela and had won over the King and the final piece of the coup had fallen into place. I mean: that's more or less what Armada might have imagined would happen if his soft coup project triumphed;

the rest of the *golpistas*, many of the rest of the *golpistas*, were imagining a hard coup – with elections proscribed, political parties proscribed, autonomous governments proscribed, democracy proscribed – but what the political ringleader of the coup was imagining or might have imagined was more or less that. Maybe it was a ludicrous thing to imagine. Maybe it was a ludicrous plan. Now, when we know that it failed, it's easy to think it was; the truth is that it was an unpredictable plan – among other reasons because it is a universal rule that once you bring soldiers out of their barracks it's not easy to get them back in, and because most likely, had it succeeded, the soft coup would just have been a prelude for a hard coup – but I'm not so sure it was ludicrous: after all, it wouldn't have been the first time that a democratic parliament ceded to military blackmail, and Armada's plan also had the virtue of disguising as a negotiated way out of the hijacking of the Cortes and a rescue of democracy operation what in reality was simply a coup against democracy. It didn't work out, and it didn't because in the first minutes of the coup, when its success or failure was settled, two unpredictable things happened: the first is that the taking of the Cortes was not carried out with the agreed discretion and degenerated into gunfire, which tarnished what was meant to be a soft coup with the aesthetics of a hard coup and made it difficult for the King to endorse, preventing him from tolerating in principle a political manoeuvre whose letter of introduction was an outrage as strident as that; the second is that Armada's name came out of the *golpistas*' mouths before the general had the opportunity to explain the nature of the coup to the King and propose his solution, and that the distrust that the mention of Armada caused the King and Fernández Campo, with the addition of the rivalry between Fernández Campo and Armada, made the two of them decide to keep the former secretary away from the Zarzuela. And that is how, fifteen minutes after having started, the coup ran aground.

PART THREE

A REVOLUTIONARY
CONFRONTS THE COUP

The image, frozen, shows the deserted chamber of the Cortes. No, the image is frozen, but the chamber (or rather: its right wing, which is what the image is actually showing) is not deserted: Adolfo Suárez still remains sitting on his blue prime ministerial bench, still, statuesque and spectral. But he is no longer solitary: two minutes have passed since Lieutenant Colonel Tejero entered the Cortes and beside the Prime Minister, sitting on his right, is General Gutiérrez Mellado; further to his right are three ministers who have just retaken their seats, also blue, following both men's example; to his left, in the entrance hall, in the central semicircle, a group of Civil Guards intimidates the chamber with their weapons. A watery, sparse and unreal light envelops the scene, as if it were taking place inside a tank or inside a nightmare or as if it were only lit by the baroque cluster of spherical lamps hanging from one wall, in the top right-hand corner of the image.

Which suddenly unfreezes: I unfreeze it. Now, in the crackling and frightened silence of the chamber, the Civil Guards roam the entrance hall, the central semicircle, the four stairways among the benches, still looking for their place in the machinery of the operation; above Adolfo Suárez and the string of ministers beside him, from the desolation of empty benches, peek out one, two, three, four timid deputies struggling between curiosity and fear. Then the angle changes, and for the first time we have an image of the left wing of the chamber, where, as well as a few ministers, the Socialist Party and Communist Party deputies sit. What we see now is curiously similar and curiously different to what we've seen up till now, almost as if what's happening in the left wing of the chamber were an inverted reflection of what's happening in the right wing. Here, in the left wing, all the blue benches of the government are empty; the red benches of the deputies are too, or all except one: at the top edge of the image, in the first seat of the seventh row, just beside the press box, the floor of which is crowded with parliamentary reporters, one remains seated and smoking. The deputy is sixty-six years old, the gesture and the look behind his wire-framed glasses stony, the forehead so broad it blends into his baldness; he's wearing a dark suit, dark tie, white shirt. It's Santiago Carrillo, Secretary General of the Communist Party: like Suárez, like Gutiérrez Mellado, Carrillo has disobeyed the order to get down on the floor and has remained seated while the bullets riddle the chamber and his comrades seek shelter under the benches. He has disobeyed the order and now, two minutes after the gunfire, he's going to disobey it again: after a Civil Guard walks past him without saying anything, without even looking at him, the voice of someone invisible to us orders him to imitate his colleagues and get down on the floor; Carrillo makes as if to obey, but does not obey: he moves a little in his seat, looks like he's going to lie down or kneel down, but in the end leans to one side, the arm of the hand with the cigarette in it leaning on the armrest of the bench, in a posture as strange as it is forced, which allows him to pretend to the soldier that he's obeyed his order without actually having obeyed.

The angle changes again: the image again includes the right wing of the chamber, where we see Suárez, Gutiérrez Mellado, a few ministers of the government and the deputies of the party that keeps it in power. Nothing substantial has changed, except that there are more and more deputies' heads dotting the desert of empty benches: while the shot of the right wing alternates with a frontal shot of the Cortes' dais (on the steps of which Víctor Carrascal is still lying, sheltered there since the assault caught him reading out the list of deputies' names from the podium during the investiture vote), Suárez and the ministers lined up next to him remain in their seats, the Civil Guards continue roaming up and down the chamber, every once in a while you hear their commanding voices and unintelligible comments. Right behind one of them in the lower left of the image, at the bottom of one of the stairways between the benches, a woman appears with a Civil Guard holding her by the arm; the two of them cross the central semicircle, stepping over the prone bodies of the ushers and stenographers, and disappear off the lower right edge of the image, towards the exit. The woman is Anna Balletbó, Socialist deputy for Barcelona, who is visibly pregnant and whom the attackers set free. As soon as she's left, a crash of breaking glass is heard in the chamber; the noise alarms the Guards and their submachine guns point to the upper part of the room, the deputies also all turn in unison in that direction, but a moment later – because it turns out to be a banal incident: undoubtedly a belated consequence of the gunfire at the beginning – everything goes back to how it was, the silence goes back to how it was and the angle changes again and the image shows Santiago Carrillo again in the midst of a desolation of empty benches, old, disobedient and smoking away, sitting alone in the left wing of the chamber. Soon, on the orders of a Guard, in the first row of benches some ministers stand up and take their seats, their faces upset, their hands humiliatingly visible on the bench's armrests: we recognize Rodolfo Martín Villa, Minister for Territorial Administration; José Luis Álvarez, Transport Minister; Íñigo Cavero, Culture Minister; Alberto Oliart, Health Minister; Luis González Seara, Minister of Higher Education and Research. When the angle changes again and the camera again shows an image of the right wing of the chamber, something catches the eye that until then had gone unnoticed: just behind Adolfo Suárez, on the side stairway to the benches, a deputy has remained lying face down since the first shots were fired; it catches the eye because now the deputy is moving and, pale and dishevelled, he turns around on all fours while Adolfo Suárez also turns for a moment and notices – as we notice – that it is Miguel Herrero de Miñón, spokesman of his parliamentary group and one of his harshest critics within the UCD. Martial, brazen, pistol in hand, seconds later an officer from the traffic subsection of the Civil Guard makes his appearance in the entrance hall of the chamber: it is Lieutenant Manuel Boza. Instead of entering the chamber, the officer stays there, just a few metres from Suárez, observing the chamber and observing Suárez; he takes a step forward, then another and, when he's very close to the Prime Minister, he addresses him with a surly gesture of silent violence, he says something as if provoking him or as if spitting on him, he's probably insulting him; at first Suárez doesn't hear him or pretends not to hear him, but then he turns towards him and for a moment the two men hold each other's gaze in silence, motionless, and a moment later they stop looking at each other and the lieutenant climbs the side stairway and disappears into the top of the chamber. A short time later clear, commanding voices are heard (clear but also indecipherable), and then a muffled noise begins to rise while the images show alternately the right wing and the left wing of the chamber, as if wanting to offer a panoramic view of what's happening; and what's happening is that, obeying the order of one of the Civil Guards, the more than two hundred people who until that moment remained lying on the floor begin to stand up and retake their seats: in the left wing the first to do so are the journalists in the press box, then the members of the Communist group and finally the Socialists, so that in just a few seconds all the deputies are again visible on their benches. All, including Santiago Carrillo, who unlike the others has not had to get up because he never got down on the floor. And who carries on smoking while the image freezes.

I

This is the third man, the third gesture; a translucent gesture, like the two previous ones, but also a double, reiterated gesture: when the *golpistas* interrupt the investiture session Carrillo disobeys the general order to get down and remains in his seat while the Civil Guards shoot up the chamber, and two minutes later disobeys a specific order from one of the hijackers and remains in his seat while pretending to get down. Like that of Suárez, like that of Gutiérrez Mellado, Carrillo's is not a random or unreflexive gesture: with perfect deliberation Carrillo refuses to obey the *golpistas*; like that of Suárez and that of Gutiérrez Mellado, Carrillo's gesture is a gesture that contains many gestures. It is a courageous gesture, a graceful gesture, a rebellious gesture, a supreme gesture of liberty. It is also, like that of Suárez and that of Gutiérrez Mellado, a posthumous gesture, in a manner of speaking, the gesture of a man who knows he's going to die or who's already dead; like many deputies, as soon as he sees Lieutenant Colonel Tejero, Carrillo understands that his entry into the chamber is the beginning of a coup d'état, and as soon as the shooting starts he understands that if he survives the gunfire the *golpistas* will execute him: he is not unaware that, with the exception of Suárez and Gutiérrez Mellado, there is no one the far-right military officers hate as much as him, who symbolizes in their eyes the quintessence of the Communist enemy. Like that of Suárez, Carrillo's gesture is also a histrionic gesture: Carrillo is a pure politician, just like Suárez, and therefore a consummate actor, who chooses to die on his feet with an elegant, photogenic gesture, and who always said he didn't dive under his seat on the evening of 23 February for the same scenic, representative and insufficient reason Suárez always put forward: he was Secretary General of the Communist Party and the Secretary General of the Communist Party could not lie down. Like that of Gutiérrez Mellado, Carrillo's gesture is a military gesture, because Carrillo had joined the Communist Party half a century earlier the way someone joins a military order and his whole life story had been preparing him for a moment like this: he was raised in a family of professional revolutionaries, since he'd reached the age of reason he'd been a professional revolutionary, in his youth he was imprisoned several times, he'd confronted political gunmen, survived a death sentence, knew the clamour of combat, the brutality of three years of war and the uprooting of forty years of exile and clandestinity. Maybe there was more: maybe there's another similarity between Carrillo's gesture and that of Gutiérrez Mellado, a less apparent but more profound similarity.

Like Gutiérrez Mellado, Carrillo belongs to the generation that fought the war; like Gutiérrez Mellado, Carrillo did not believe in democracy until very late in life, even though he'd been defending a democratic republic during the war; like Gutiérrez Mellado, Carrillo participated as a young man in an armed insurrection against the government of the Republic: the uprising in Asturias, forming part of its revolutionary committee when he was barely nineteen years old; like Gutiérrez Mellado, Carrillo never publicly repented for having rebelled against democratic legality, but, also like Gutiérrez Mellado, at least since the mid-1970s he did nothing but repent with his actions for having participated in that rebellion. I don't mean to equate the desperate proletarian revolt Carrillo advanced in October 1934 with the military coup of the rich and powerful that Gutiérrez Mellado advanced in 1936; I am just saying, however understandable it may have been – and reasons to understand it abound – that the revolt was an error and that, especially from the moment when the transition began and the Communists started to play a decisive role in it, Carrillo acted as though it had been, deactivating the ideological and political mechanisms that might have led to the repetition of the error, a little bit the way since joining the government Gutiérrez Mellado set about deactivating the ideological and political mechanisms of the Army that forty years earlier had provoked the war. Not just that: Carrillo – and with him the old guard of the Communist Party – also gave up the chance to settle scores from an ignominious past of war, repression and exile, as if he considered trying to settle scores with those who had committed the error of settling scores for forty years a way of piling ignominy on ignominy, or as if he'd read Max Weber and felt like him that there was nothing more abject than practising an ethic that sought only to be right and that obliges people to spend time discussing the errors of an unjust and enslaved past with the aim of taking moral and material advantage of other people's confession of guilt, instead of devoting themselves to constructing a just and free future. As the head of the Communist old guard, during the transition and to make democracy possible, Carrillo signed a pact with the victors of the war and administrators of the dictatorship that included the renunciation of using the past politically, but he didn't do so because he'd forgotten the war and the dictatorship, but because he remembered them very well and was ready to do anything to keep them from happening again, as long as the victors of the war and administrators of the dictatorship accepted ending it and replacing it with a political system that welcomed victors and vanquished and was essentially identical to that which the vanquished had defended in the war. Carrillo was ready to do anything, or almost anything: to give up the myth of the revolution, the egalitarian ideal of Communism, the nostalgia of the defeated Republic, the very idea of historical justice . . . Because with Franco's death, justice dictated a return to the Republican legitimacy violated forty years earlier by a coup d'état and the resulting war, prosecution of those responsible for Francoism and complete reparation to its victims; Carrillo renounced all of that, and not only because he lacked the strength to achieve it, but also because he understood that often the most noble ideals of men are incompatible with each other and trying to impose at that moment in Spain the absolute triumph of justice was to risk provoking the absolute defeat of liberty, turning absolute justice into the worst injustice. Many left-wingers, in favour of letting justice be done though the world should perish (*Fiat justitia et pereat mundus*), bitterly reproached him for these concessions, which for them were a form of betrayal; they did not forgive him, in the same way many

right-wingers did not forgive Suárez and Gutiérrez Mellado for theirs:
like the Communist old guard, to build democracy Carrillo gave up his
lifelong ideals and chose harmony and liberty over justice and revolution, and in this way he also turned into a professional of demolition
and dismantling who fulfilled himself completely by undermining
himself, like a hero of the retreat. Like Suárez's and Gutiérrez Mellado's
detractors, Carrillo's detractors claim there was more calculated personal
interest and pure eagerness for political survival involved than authentic conviction; I don't know: what I do know is that this judgement of
intentions is politically irrelevant, because it forgets that, however
ignoble, personal motives do not cancel out the error or wisdom of a
decision. What's relevant, what's politically relevant, is that, given that
the decisions he adopted gave rise to the creation of a fairer, freer political system than any Spain had ever known in its history, and essentially
identical to the one that was defeated in the war (although one was a
republic and the other a monarchy, both were parliamentary democracies), at least on this point history has proven Carrillo right, whose
gesture of courage and grace and liberty and rebellion when faced with
the *golpistas* on the evening of 23 February thus acquires a different
significance: like that of Gutiérrez Mellado, it is the gesture of a man
who having combated democracy constructs it like someone expiating
a youthful error, who constructs it by destroying his own ideas, who
constructs it by denying his own people and denying his very self, who
stakes himself entirely on it, who finally decides to risk his neck for it.

The last gesture I recognize in Carrillo's gesture is not a real gesture;
it's an imagined gesture or at least a gesture that I imagine, maybe
whimsically. But if my imagination were truthful, then Carrillo's
gesture would contain a gesture of complicity, or of emulation, and its
story would go as follows. Carrillo is sitting in the first seat of the
seventh row in the left wing of the chamber; right opposite and below
him, in the first seat of the first row in the right wing, sits Adolfo
Suárez. When the firing begins, Carrillo's first impulse is that dictated
by common sense: the same way his comrades in the Communist old
guard sitting beside him, who like him joined the Party the way one
joins a militia of self-denial and danger and have known war, prison
and exile and maybe also feel that if they survive the gunfire they'll be

executed, Carrillo instinctively forgets for a moment about courage, grace, liberty, rebellion, even his actor's instinct, and prepares to obey the Guards' orders and shelter from the bullets under his bench, but just before he does he notices that opposite him, below him, Adolfo Suárez remains seated in his Prime Minister's bench, solitary, statuesque and spectral in a desert of empty benches. And then, deliberately, thoughtfully – as if in a single second he understood the complete significance of Suárez's gesture – decides not to duck.

2

It's a whim, maybe it's not truthfully imagined, but the reality is the two were much more than accomplices: the reality is that by February 1981 Santiago Carrillo and Adolfo Suárez had spent four years tied by an alliance that was political but was also more than political, and which only Suárez's illness and loss would finally break.

History fabricates strange figures, frequently resigns itself to sentimentalism and does not disdain the symmetries of fiction, as if it wanted to endow itself with meaning that on its own it did not possess. Who could have predicted that the change from dictatorship to democracy in Spain would not be plotted by the democratic parties, but by the Falangists and the Communists, irreconcilable enemies of democracy and each other's irreconcilable enemies during three years of war and forty post-war years? Who would have predicted that the Secretary General of the Communist Party in exile would set himself up as the most faithful political ally of the last Secretary General of the Movimiento, the single fascist party? Who could have imagined that Santiago Carrillo would end up turning into an unconditional protector of Adolfo Suárez and into one of his last friends and confidants? No one did, but maybe it wasn't impossible to do: on the one hand, because only irreconcilable enemies could reconcile the irreconcilable Spain of Franco; on the other, because unlike Gutiérrez Mellado and Adolfo Suárez, who were profoundly different in spite of their superficial similarities, Santiago Carrillo and Adolfo Suárez were profoundly similar in spite of their superficial differences. The two of them were both pure politicians, more than professionals of politics they were professionals of power, because neither of the two conceived of politics without power or because both acted as if politics were to power what gravity is to the earth; both were bureaucrats who had prospered in the inflexible hierarchy of political organizations ruled by totalitarian methods and inspired by totalitarian ideologies; both were democratic converts, belated and a bit forced; both were long accustomed to giving orders: Suárez had held his first political post in 1955, when he was twenty-three, and since then had risen step by step up all the rungs of the Movimiento ladder until reaching its top and becoming Prime Minister; Carrillo had spent more than three decades dominating the Communist Party with the authority of the high priest of a clandestine religion, but before his twentieth birthday he was already leader of the Socialist Youth, when barely twenty-one he became Councillor for Public Order of the Defence Junta of Madrid at one of the most urgent moments of the war, at twenty-two he'd become a member of the politburo of the PCE and from there on never stopped monopolizing positions of responsibility in the Party and the Communist International. The parallels don't stop there: both cultivated a personal vision of politics, at once epic and aesthetic, as if, rather than the slow, collective and laborious work of bending reality's resistance, politics were a solitary adventure dotted with dramatic episodes and intrepid decisions; both had been educated in the street, lacked any university training and distrusted intellectuals; both were so tough they almost always felt invulnerable to the inclemencies of their trade and both possessed uncomplicated ambition, unlimited confidence in themselves, a changeable lack of scruples and a recognized talent for political sleight of hand and for the conversion of their defeats into victories. In short: deep down they seem like twin politicians. In 1983, when after the coup d'état neither Carrillo nor Suárez were what they had been any more and were trying to mend their political careers in fits and starts, Fernando Claudín – one of Carrillo's closest friends and collaborators for over thirty years of Communist militancy – wrote the following about the eternal Secretary General: 'He lacked the least bit of knowledge of political and constitutional law, and made no efforts to acquire any. Economics, sociology and other subjects that might have allowed him to express fully formed opinions on most parliamentary debates were not his strong suits either [. . .] His only speciality was "politics in general", which tends to translate as talking a little bit about everything without going into anything in depth, and the Party machinery, in which, of course, no one could hold a candle to him. As had always happened to him, he couldn't find time to study, always absorbed by Party meetings, interviews, secret discussions, delegations and other such activities. The iron will he showed for other tasks, especially holding on to power within the Party and making his way towards it in the state, unfortunately failed him when it came to acquiring education that would have stood him in better stead in the exercise of these functions.' Twin politicians: if we admit that Claudín is right and that the previous quote defines some of Santiago Carrillo's weaknesses, then we just need to replace Party with the word Movimiento for it to define also some of Adolfo Suárez's weaknesses.

It's possible that these similarities were blindingly obvious to both as soon as they met at the end of February 1977, but it's certain that neither of the two would have sealed the pact they sealed with the other had they not both understood long before that they needed each other to prevail in politics, because at that moment Suárez had the power of Francoism but Carrillo had the legitimacy of anti-Francoism, and Suárez needed legitimacy as much as Carrillo needed power; something else is certain: since they were both pure politicians, they would not have sealed that pact if they hadn't believed that the country could do without their individual alliance, but not that of the collective alliance between the two irreconcilable Spains they represented, and which also needed each other. In spite of that, one might well assume that for Suárez, raised in the Manichaean claustrophobia of the dictatorship, it would be surprising to recognize his intimate kinship with the dictatorship's official bad guy; one might also assume that Carrillo's surprise would be even greater upon realizing that a young provincial Falangist was competing advantageously with the skill of an experienced old politician – whose heroic reputation in war and exile, international prestige and absolute power in the Party lent him the image of a demigod – forcing him to liquidate in a few months the strategy for post-Francoism he'd planned and maintained for years and to follow the path the younger man had marked out.

The story of that liquidation and its consequences is in part the story of the change from dictatorship to democracy and without it the unbreakable link between Santiago Carrillo and Adolfo Suárez that lasted for years cannot be understood; neither can 23 February; nor, perhaps, the twin gesture of these two twins on the evening of 23 February, while the bullets whizzed around the chamber of the Cortes. The story begins at some moment in 1976. Let's say it begins on 3 July 1976, the same day the King appoints Adolfo Suárez Prime Minister amid generalized stupor. By then, after thirty-six years of exile, Santiago Carrillo had been living clandestinely in Madrid for six months, in a house on the Viso housing estate, convinced that he needed to gauge the country's reality and cement his hold on the Party within the country so the Communists would be able to assert themselves as the most numerous, most active and best organized political force of opposition to the regime in the emerging post-Francoism. By then exactly a year had gone by since Carrillo initiated the dismantling or undermining or ideological demolition of the PCE with the aim of presenting it to Spanish society as a modern party free of the old Stalinist dogmatism: in July 1975 along with Enrico Berlinguer and Georges Marchais – leaders of the Italian and French Communists – he'd founded Euro-Communism, an ambiguous and heterodox version of Communism that proclaimed its independence from the Soviet Union, its rejection of the dictatorship of the proletariat and its respect for parliamentary democracy. By then it had been exactly three decades since the PCE had elaborated the so-called policy of national reconciliation, which in practice meant that the Party renounced the aim of overthrowing the regime by force and was confident that a non-violent national strike could paralyse the country so that power would be handed over to a provisional government composed of all the parties of the democratic opposition, whose first task would be to call free elections. By then, however, Carrillo had already become aware that, in spite of this still being official Party policy, the anti-Francoist organizations on their own lacked the strength to finish off the prolongation of Francoism embodied at that moment by the monarchy; he was no less aware, if the objective was bloodlessly to install a democracy in Spain, sooner or later the political parties of the opposition would have to end up negotiating with reform-inclined representatives of the regime – now that they could no longer break Francoism to impose democracy they had to negotiate the rupture of Francoism with Francoists lucid enough or resigned enough to accept that the only future for Francoism was democracy – a change of strategy that did not begin to be glimpsed in official PCE doctrine until the beginning of 1976 when the Secretary General introduced a terminological nuance into his speech and stopped talking about the 'democratic rupture' to talk about the 'negotiated rupture'.

So, Carrillo received the unexpected news of Suárez's appointment at a moment of total uncertainty and certain despondency, knowing that, although it seemed strong, his party was still weak, and that, although it seemed weak, Francoism was still strong. His response to the news was as unexpected as the news itself, or at least it was for the officials and members of his party, which like the democratic opposition and regime's reformers and the majority of public opinion considered the choice of the last Secretary General of the Movimiento meant the end of their liberalizing hopes and the triumph of the reactionaries of the regime. On 7 July, four days after the appointment of Suárez and barely a few hours after he announced on television that his government's aim was to achieve democratic normalization ('That the governments of the future may be the result of the free will of the Spanish people,' he'd said), Carrillo published in the weekly *Mundo Obrero*, clandestine organ of the PCE, an article full of benevolent scepticism towards the new Prime Minister: he didn't believe that Suárez was capable of fulfilling his promises, he wasn't even sure if they were sincere, but he recognized that his language and tone were not those of a usual Falangist leader and that his good proposals deserved to be given the benefit of the doubt. 'The Suárez government,' he concluded, 'could serve to bring about the negotiation that leads to the agreed rupture.'

Carrillo's prediction was spot on. Or almost: Suárez not only brought about the negotiation that led to the rupture; he also formulated it in terms no one was expecting: for Carrillo, for the democratic opposition, for the regime's reformers, the political dilemma of post-Francoism consisted in choosing between the reform of Francoism, changing its form but not its content, and the rupture with Francoism, changing its form to change its content; Suárez took only months to decide the dilemma was false: he understood that in politics the form is the content, and therefore it was possible to realize a reform of Francoism that was in practice a rupture with Francoism. He understood gradually, as he came to understand that it was imperative to break with Francoism, but as soon as he took up his post and made a programmatic declaration in which he announced free elections before 30 June of the coming year Suárez began a cautious series of interviews with the leaders of the illegal opposition to sound out their intentions and explain his project. Carrillo remained on the sidelines; at that moment Suárez was in a hurry for everything, except for talking to Carrillo: although he sensed that without the Communists his political reform lacked credibility, for the moment he was not suggesting the legalization of the Party, maybe especially because he was sure that would be an unacceptable measure for the Francoist mentality of the Army and of the social sectors he needed to shepherd towards democracy or towards some form of democracy. Carrillo, however, was in a hurry to talk to him: Suárez had promised in his first speech as Prime Minister to meet with all the political forces, but the promise hadn't been kept and, although he still didn't know if Suárez really meant to break with Francoism or simply reform it, Carrillo did not want to run the risk that the country might be heading for some form of democracy without the presence of the Communists, because he thought that would indefinitely prolong the Party's clandestinity and condemn it to ostracism and maybe extinction. So in the middle of August Carrillo takes the initiative and a little while later manages to get in contact with Suárez through José Mario Armero, head of the news agency Europe Press. The first interview between Carrillo and Armero is held in Cannes, at the end of August; the second is held in Paris at the beginning of September. Neither of the two encounters produces concrete results (Armero assures Carrillo that Suárez is heading for democracy and asks him for patience: conditions are not yet right for legalizing the PCE; Carrillo offers his help in constructing the new system, does not demand the immediate legalization of his party and claims that it won't reject the monarchy if it amounts to an authentic democracy); but neither of the two encounters is a failure. On the contrary: starting in September and all through the autumn and winter of 1976 Carrillo and Suárez remain in contact through Armero and Jaime Ballesteros, Carrillo's right-hand man in the PCE leadership. And that's when a strange complicity begins to tie them together through the intervening persons: like two blind men touching each other's features in search of a face, for months Carrillo and Suárez put their proposals, their loyalty, their intelligence and their cleverness to the test, they glimpse common interests, discover secret affinities, admit they should understand each other; both understand that they need democracy to survive and that they need each other, because neither of the two holds the key to democracy but each of them holds a part – Suárez has power, Carrillo legitimacy – which completes what the other holds: while he insists over and over again on speaking to him in person, Carrillo realizes with increasing clarity the difficulties Suárez is facing, the biggest of which stems from the resistance of a powerful section of the country to the legalization of the PCE; while the social pressure in favour of a democratic regime pushes him day by day to recognize that Francoism is only reformable with a reform that means its rupture and begins to dismantle the framework of the regime and holds dialogues with the leaders of the rest of the opposition political forces – on whom he absolutely does not press the legalization of the PCE: in general they don't believe in running any risk that might endanger the promised elections – Suárez understands with increasing clarity that there will be no credible democracy without the Communists and that Carrillo is keeping his party under control, has retired his revolutionary ideals and is ready to make as many concessions as might be necessary to get the PCE into the new political system. From a distance, the two men's initial caution and mutual distrust begin to dissolve; in fact, it's possible that towards the end of October or beginning of November Suárez and Carrillo were outlining a strategy to legalize the Party, an implicit strategy, elaborated not with words but with inferences, that would turn out to be a total success for Suárez and only a relative success for Carrillo, who accepts it because he has no alternative, because by this stage he has already assumed the form of political change that Suárez is proposing to be valid and because he entertains the hope that his success will also be total.

The strategy has two parts. On the one hand, Suárez will do his best to legalize the PCE before the elections in exchange for Carrillo persuading the Communists to forget their aim of a frontal rupture with Francoism and that they'll only achieve legitimacy and will only construct a democracy through the reform of the Francoist institutions that the government is brewing, because that reform is in practice a rupture; Carrillo immediately fulfils this part of the deal: in a clandestine meeting of the executive committee of the PCE held on 21 November, the Secretary General discards the Party's tactical programme during Francoism, convincing his people that neither a democratic rupture nor an agreed rupture is any longer any use but only the reforming rupture proposed by Suárez. The second part of the strategy is more complex and more dangerous, and maybe therefore satisfies Carrillo's and Suárez's intimate propensity for politics as an adventure. In order to legalize the PCE, Suárez needs Carrillo's party to oblige the government to increase the margin of tolerance for the Communists, to make them increasingly visible, to give them their naturalization papers with the aim of getting the majority of citizens of the country to understand that not only are they harmless for the future democracy, but that the future democracy cannot be constructed without them. This progressive *de facto* legalization, that should facilitate the *de jure* legalization, took the form of a duel between the government and the Communists in which the Communists didn't want to finish off the government and the government didn't want to finish off the Communists, and in which both knew in advance (or at least suspected or guessed) when and where they were going to hit their adversary: the blows of this false duel were blows for propaganda effect that included a general strike that did not manage to paralyse the country but did put the government in a tight spot, massive sales of *Mundo Obrero* on the streets of Madrid and massive distribution of Party membership cards, French and Swedish television reports showing Carrillo driving through the centre of the capital, a notorious clandestine press conference in which the Secretary General of the PCE – along with Dolores Ibárruri, the myth par excellence of the anti-Francoist resistance, demonized or idealized in equal measure by a great part of the population – announced between conciliating words that he'd been in Madrid for months and had no plans to leave, and finally the arrest of Carrillo himself, who once in prison the government could no longer expel from the country without breaking the law and could not keep hold of either in the midst of the national and international scandal occasioned by his capture, so that a few days later Carrillo was set free and converted into a Spanish citizen with full rights.

It was a step with no way back towards the legalization of the PCE: once forced to legalize the Secretary General, the legalization of the Party was just a matter of time. Carrillo knew it and so did Suárez; but Suárez had time and Carrillo did not: the legalization of the rest of the parties had begun to happen at the beginning of January, and he was still not sure that Suárez would fulfil his part of the deal, or that he wouldn't postpone his fulfilment until after the elections, or that he wouldn't postpone it indefinitely. By the middle of January Carrillo urgently needed to dispel Suárez's doubts, but it was reality that dispelled them for him, because that was when a lethal confusion of fear and violence took over Madrid, and when the false duel the two were engaged in was on the verge of ending because the whole country was on the verge of exploding. At a quarter to eleven on the night of 24 January, when Carrillo had been legally residing in Spain for less than a month, five partners of a Communist law firm are gunned down by a far-right hit squad in their office at 55 Calle Atocha. It was the macabre apotheosis of two days of carnage. On the morning of the previous day another far-right gunman had shot a student to death during a demonstration in favour of an amnesty law, and that same afternoon a student died as the result of the impact of a smoke canister launched by the forces of Public Order against a group of people protesting the previous day's death, while just a few hours earlier the GRAPO – an ultraleft terrorist group that since 11 December had been holding Antonio María de Oriol y Urquijo, one of the most powerful, affluent and influential representatives of orthodox Francoism – kidnapped General Emilio Villaescusa, president of the Military Supreme Court. Four days later GRAPO was still going to murder two more national policemen and a Civil Guard, but on the night of the 24th Madrid is already living in an almost pre-war atmosphere: explosions and gunshots are heard in different spots around the capital, and ultraright gangs sow terror in the streets. Added to the other episodes of those bloody days, the slaughter of its Atocha members marks for the PCE a brutal challenge destined to provoke a violent response in its ranks that, provoking in its turn a violent response from the Army, would abort the incipient democratic reforms; but the Communists do not respond: the executive committee orders its members to avoid any demonstration or confrontation in the streets and to display all the serenity possible, and the order is carried out to the letter. After arduous negotiations with the government – which fears that any spark will ignite the conflagration the far right is seeking – the Party obtains permission to install a funeral shrine for the lawyers in the Palace of Justice on the Plaza de las Salesas, and also for the coffins to be carried on the shoulders of their comrades to the Plaza de Colón. And so they do just after four o'clock on Wednesday afternoon; the television cameras film a spectacle that overwhelms the centre of Madrid; the images have been shown many times: in the midst of a sea of red roses and closed fists and a silence and order imposed by the Party leadership and respected by the rank and file with a discipline honed in clandestinity, tens of thousands of people overflow the Plaza de las Salesas and the adjacent streets to pay their last respects to the murdered men; some stills show Santiago Carrillo walking among the crowd, guarded by a wall of militants. The ceremony ends without a single incident, in the same great silence in which it began, converted into a proclamation of concord that dispels all the government's doubts about the PCE's repudiation of violence and spreads a wave of solidarity with Party members all over the country.

According to his then closest collaborators, it's very possible that Suárez secretly made the decision to legalize the Communist Party that very day; if so, it's very possible that on that very day Suárez decided that before doing so he'd need to meet their leader in person. The fact is that barely a month later, on 27 February, the two men met in a house near Madrid belonging to their mediator, José Mario Armero. The encounter was organized in the strictest confidence: although for Carrillo it entailed no danger, for Suárez it entailed plenty, and for that reason two of the three people he consulted – his Deputy Prime Minister, Alfonso Osorio, and Torcuato Fernández Miranda, President of the Cortes and of the Council of the Kingdom and his political mentor for the last few years – strongly advised him against it, reasoning that if his meeting with the clandestine Communist leader came to be known the political earthquake would be formidable; but the King's support of Suárez, his faith in Carrillo's discretion and his trust in his lucky star and in his talent to seduce persuaded him to run the risk. He was not mistaken. Years later Suárez and Carrillo both described the encounter as love at first sight: it may well have been, but the truth is that necessity had united them long before they met; it may well have been, but the truth is that for the seven consecutive hours their face-to-face meeting lasted, while they smoked cigarette after cigarette in the presence of Armero and in the silence of an uninhabited country house, Carrillo and Suárez behaved like two blind men who've suddenly recovered their sight to recognize a twin, or like two duellists who exchange a false duel for a real duel into which both are putting their all to break their rival's spell. The winner was Suárez, who as soon as the first handshake and jokes of introductions were concluded disarmed Carrillo by telling him of his Republican grandfather, his Republican father, the Republican dead of his family on the losing side of the war, and then finished him off with protests of modesty and praise of Carrillo's political experience and top-class statesmanship; defeated, Carrillo offered words of understanding, realism and caution designed to try once more to convince his interlocutor that he and his party not only were not a danger to his democracy project, but with time would turn into its principal guarantee of success. The rest of the interview was devoted to talking a little bit about everything and not committing to anything except to continue to back each other up and consult each other on important decisions, and when the two men went their separate ways in the early hours of the morning neither of them harboured the slightest doubt: both could rely on the other's loyalty; both were the only two real politicians in the country; both, once the PCE was legalized, the elections held and democracy installed, would end up together holding the reins of the future.

Events wasted no time in eroding this triple certainty, but it continued ruling Suárez's and Carrillo's behaviour for the four years that Suárez remained in government; nothing provided it with as much consistency as the way in which the Communist Party was finally legalized. It happened on Saturday 9 April, just over a month after the meeting between the two leaders, in the middle of the chaos of the Easter holiday and after which Suárez, knowing that public opinion had swiftly changed in favour of the measure he was getting ready to adopt, still sought to protect himself against the predictable outrage of the military and the far right with a legal report from the *Junta de Fiscales* (Attorney General's office) supporting the legalization; Carrillo also protected him, or did what he could to protect him. On Suárez's advice, the Secretary General had gone on vacation to Cannes, where he heard that very Saturday morning from José Mario Armero that the legalization was effective immediately and that Suárez asked two things of him: the first was that, in order not to irritate the Army and the far right still further, the Party should celebrate without raucousness; the second was that, in order to prevent the Army and the far right being able to accuse Suárez of complicity with the Communists, once the news was broadcast Carrillo should issue a public statement criticizing Suárez or at least distancing himself from him. Carrillo complied: the Communists celebrated the news discreetly and its Secretary General appeared that very day before the press to say a few words he'd agreed with the Prime Minister. 'I don't believe Prime Minister Suárez to be a friend of the Communists,' proclaimed Carrillo. 'I consider him rather to be anti-Communist, but an intelligent anti-Communist who has understood that ideas are not destroyed with repression and banning. And who is ready to confront ours with his own.' It was not enough. During the days following the legalization a coup d'état seemed imminent. Suárez appealed to Carrillo again; Carrillo again complied. At midday on 14 April, while the first legal meeting of the central committee of the PCE in Spain since the end of the Civil War is being held on Calle Capitán Haya Santiago, José Mario Armero summons Jaime Ballesteros, his contact with the Communists, to the café of a nearby hotel. Right now Suárez's head is not worth a cent, Armero tells Ballesteros. The military is on the verge of rising in revolt. Either you give us a hand or we're all going to hell. Ballesteros speaks to Carrillo, and the next day, during the second stage of the central committee meeting, the Secretary General interrupts the session to make a dramatic statement. 'We find ourselves today in the most difficult meeting we've had since the war,' says Carrillo in the midst of a glacial silence. 'In these hours, I'm not saying these days, these hours, it may be decided whether we move towards democracy or if we go into a very serious regression that will affect not only the Party and all the democratic forces of opposition, but also the reformist and institutional forces . . . I don't believe I'm being overly dramatic, I'm saying what's happening at this minute.' Immediately and without giving anyone time to react, as if he'd written it himself Carrillo reads a piece of paper perhaps drafted by the Prime Minister that Armero had handed to

Ballesteros and which contains the solemn and unconditional renunciation of some of the symbols that have represented the Party since it was
founded as well as the approval of some the Army considers threatened
by its legalization: the red-and-yellow flag, the unity of the fatherland
and the monarchy. Perplexed and fearful, used to obeying their leader
unquestioningly, the members of the central committee approve the
revolution imposed by Carrillo and the Party hastens to announce the
good news at a press conference during which its leadership council
appears in front of a surprising, enormous, improvised monarchist flag.

The coup d'état does not materialize, although the 23 February coup
began to be hatched then – because the military never forgave Suárez
for legalizing the Communist Party and from that moment on did not
stop plotting against the treacherous Prime Minister – but the PCE
could only digest such pragmatism and so many concessions snatched
from them by the threat of a coup d'état with much difficulty. According
to Carrillo's predictions, the result of his pact of prudence over the last
year and of half a century's monopoly of anti-Francoism would be an
electoral triumph of millions of votes that would turn his party into the
second biggest in the country after Suárez's party and would turn him
and Suárez into the two great protagonists of democracy; it didn't
happen like that: like a mummy that disintegrates on exhumation, in
the elections of 15 June 1977 the PCE received just over 9 per cent of the
vote, less than half of what they expected and less than a third of that
of the PSOE, which surprisingly took over the leadership of the left
because it was able to absorb the caution and disenchantment of many
Communist sympathizers and also because it offered an image of youth
and modernity in contrast to the old candidates of the PCE coming
back from exile, the Communist old guard starting with Carrillo
himself who evoked for voters the frightening past of the war and
blocked the renovation of the Party by the young Communists from
inside the country. Although Carrillo never felt defeated, Suárez had
won again: for the Prime Minister the legalization of the PCE was an
unqualified success, because it made democracy credible by integrating
the Communists, blocked the man he considered his most dangerous
rival at the polls and gained him a lasting ally; for the Communists'
Secretary General it was not a failure, but nor was it the success he'd

hoped for: although the legalization of the PCE assured that Suárez's reform truly was a rupture with Francoism and that the consequence of the rupture would be a real democracy, the things they were forced to concede by the way it was carried out, abandoning the symbols and diluting the traditional postulates of the organization, made the dream of making the Communist Party the hegemonic party of the left even more distant. The response of the PCE to this electoral fiasco was what was maybe to be expected from an organization marked by a history of assent to the dictates of its Secretary General and imbued with its unappeasable historic mission of an ideology in retreat: instead of admitting their errors in the light of reality with the aim of correcting them, they attributed their own errors to reality. The Party convinced itself (or more precisely the Secretary General convinced the Party) that it hadn't been them but the voters who'd been mistaken: two short months of legality had not been able to counteract forty years of anti-Communist propaganda, but the PSOE would waste no time in demonstrating their immaturity and inconsistency and the following elections would return to the PCE their rightful role of first party of the opposition that the Socialists had usurped, given that in Spain there were no serious parties other than the PCE and the UCD or any real political leaders other than Santiago Carrillo and Adolfo Suárez.

Unexpectedly, after the first elections Carrillo's predictions seemed to be starting to come true and he could for a time dazzle his comrades with the illusion that the defeat had in reality been a victory or the best preparation for victory. 'Of all the Spanish political leaders,' wrote *Le Monde* in October 1977, 'Santiago Carrillo is undoubtedly the one who has come to the fore most rapidly and with most authority in recent months.' That's how it was: in a very short time, all over the country, Carrillo won a vigorous reputation as a responsible politician who contributed to making the PCE appear to be a solid party capable of governing and that deserved much greater relevance than its poor electoral results seemed to indicate. His understanding with Suárez was perfect, and his whole political strategy of those years revolved around a proposal that meant to institutionalize it and to armour-plate the democracy they would construct between the two of them or that he thought they should construct between the two of them: the government of national unity. The formula resembled in name only what the majority of the ruling class was discussing or sponsoring in the months before 23 February (and which facilitated it): this was no government headed by a soldier but a government headed by Suárez and supported by the UCD and the PCE although with the cooperation of other political parties; according to Carrillo, only the fortitude of a government like that could bring stability to the country while they drew up the Constitution, strengthened democracy and warded off the danger of a coup d'état, and the Pacts of Moncloa – an important ensemble of social and economic measures designed to overcome the national economic crisis stemming from the first worldwide oil crisis, negotiated by Carrillo and Suárez and then signed by the main political parties and ratified by the Cortes in October 1977 – constituted for the Secretary General of the PCE the foretaste of this unitary government. Carrillo reiterated his proposal over and over again and, although at some moment he had hints that Suárez was thinking of accepting it, the government of national unity never came to be formed: it's very possible that Suárez would have happily governed along with Carrillo, but he probably never considered it seriously, maybe because he feared the reaction of the military and of a large part of society. In spite of that, Carrillo continued to sustain Suárez in the certainty that sustaining Suárez meant sustaining democracy, which made him an indispensable support of the system and meant that, although he didn't obtain the benefit of power, he obtained national and international respect: after the signing of the Pacts of Moncloa Carrillo received a standing ovation in the Cortes from the UCD deputies and a welcome into the country's most conservative forums for debate; around the same time he travelled to the United Kingdom and France and became the first Secretary General of a Communist Party allowed to enter the United States, where he was hailed by *Time* magazine as 'the apostle of Euro-Communism'. In the short term this was the result of his alliance with Suárez: during those years Carrillo personified a sort of oxymoron, democratic Communism; in the long term the result was his undoing.

Just as happened with Suárez, the beginning of the decline of Carrillo's political career coincided with the exact moment of its peak. In November 1977, during his triumphant trip to the United States, Carrillo announced without consulting his party that at their next conference the PCE would abandon Leninism. Deep down, it was the logical consequence of the dismantling or demolition or undermining of Communist principles that he'd begun years before – the logical consequence of the attempt to bring into being the oxymoron of democratic Communism he called Euro-Communism – but if months earlier accepting the monarchy and the red-and-yellow flag had been difficult for many, the abrupt abandonment of the Party's invariable ideological vector all through its history was even more so, because it meant such a radical change of direction that it placed the PCE in practice on the borders of socialism (or social democracy) and also demonstrated that the democratization of the Party on the outside did not assume a corresponding democratization behind closed doors: the Secretary General carried on without restrictions dictating PCE policy and governing it in accord with so-called democratic centralism, a Stalinist method that had nothing democratic about it and was entirely centralist, because it was based on the all-embracing power of the Secretary General, on the extremely hierarchical organizational structure and the uncritical obedience of the rank and file. That was when the Party's unanimity began to split for all to see, and when Carrillo noticed with astonishment that his authority was becoming a matter for discussion among his comrades: some – the so-called reformists – rejected his individualism and his authoritarian methods and demanded more internal democracy, while others – the so-called pro-Soviets – rejected his ideological revisionism and confrontation with the Soviet Union and demanded a return to Communist orthodoxy; each as much as the other criticized his unshakeable support for Adolfo Suárez's government and his unshakeable ambition to make common cause with him. But the submissive or disciplined habit of consenting to the dictates of the Secretary General still dominated the spirit of the Communists and, given that the promise of power operated over political parties like a binding agent, these divergences remained more or less buried in the PCE until the next elections, in March 1979: that's how Carrillo managed in April 1978 to get the 9th Party Conference to adopt Euro-Communism and abandon Leninism. However, a new electoral failure – in the March elections the PCE experienced a slight increase in votes but barely reached a third of the number their direct

Socialist competitors received – brought the discrepancies virulently out into the open; in a very short space of time, Carrillo was no longer able to convince his people that this defeat was in reality a victory and that they had to keep backing Suárez and confronting the Socialists who were taking over their political space and their electorate, and during the following years the Communists sank into a succession of increasingly profound internal crises, aggravated by their loss of influence in the politics of the country: with the new distribution of power resulting from the elections, with the end of the politics of accord between all the parties after the approval of the Constitution, after 1979 Suárez didn't need Carrillo to govern any more and sought the support of the Socialists and not the Communists, turning them into an isolated irrelevant party which barely mattered for the resolution of the big problems, and furthermore whose leader had squandered the statesman's halo he'd sported just a few months ago. As happened to Suárez at the same time, Carrillo's loss of prestige in the country's politics translated into a loss of prestige in his party's politics. While the protests against the national leadership of the PCE intensified, revolts were being prepared in Catalonia and in the Basque Country, and in Madrid some members of the executive committee stood up to the Secretary General: in July 1980, at the same time as the Party bosses of the UCD rebelled against Adolfo Suárez in a meeting held on a country estate in Manzanares el Real and the movements to remove him from power were getting under way, several high-ranking members of the PCE called Carrillo to the house of Ramón Tamames – the most visible leader of the so-called reformist sector – with the aim of exposing the Party's problems to him, reproaching him for his errors and calling his leadership into question; it was an unprecedented scene in the history of Spanish Communism, but it was repeated at the beginning of November in the heart of the central committee, when Tamames went so far as to propose that the secretary generalship should be turned into a collective position, almost like a few months earlier, at the Manzanares el Real meeting, the UCD Party bosses had demanded Suárez share his power over the Party and the government with them. Unlike Suárez, Carrillo did not give in, but by then his organization was already irremediably divided between reformers, pro-Soviets and Carrillistas, and in January 1981 that division was consummated in the breaking away of the PSUC, the Communist Party of Catalonia, which constituted just a hint of the ferocious internal fights that would tear apart the PCE for the next year and a half and would go on almost uninterruptedly until the virtual extinction of the Party.

So on the eve of 23 February Santiago Carrillo was not in such a different situation from that of Adolfo Suárez. Their time at the height of their powers had passed: both were now politically hounded, personally diminished, lacking credit with public opinion, furiously attacked within their own parties, embittered by the ingratitude and betrayals of their fellows or what they felt as ingratitude and betrayals of their fellows, two exhausted and disoriented men who'd lost their touch, increasingly hindered by defects that just a few years before had been invisible or hadn't seemed like defects: their personal notion of power, their talent for political exchange, their inveterate bureaucratic habits of totalitarian structures and incompatibility with the application of the democracy they'd built. Undermining even their demolition of the systems in which they'd grown up and which they'd manipulated as few others could – one Communism and the other Francoism – both had ended up fighting for survival amid the rubble of their former dominion. Neither of the two managed it, and on the eve of 23 February it was already obvious that neither of the two would manage it. At that time their personal relationship was meagre, because they'd turned into two fitters and a fitter is absorbed in the task of fitting. They probably looked at each other out of the corner of their eye every once in a while, remembering not so old times when together they sorted out the country's destiny with sparkling pyrotechnics of false duels, four-handed sparring, wordless pacts, secret meetings and great accords of state, and the iron alliance they'd forged in those years certainly remained immutable: in the autumn and winter of 1980 Carrillo was one of the few front-line politicians who did not participate in the political manoeuvring against Suárez that laid the ground for 23 February, and never mentioned surgical coups or a touch on the rudder unless denouncing that sinister terminology and that flirting with the Army that constituted ideal ammunition for *golpismo*; denouncing it outside of his party and within his party: there were also advocates of political shock therapy in the PCE of the time, but when Ramón Tamames twice proclaimed to the press his agreement with a unity government headed by a military officer, Carrillo was quick to use the occasion to defend Suárez, once again fulminating against his main adversary in the Party with a devastating diagnosis: 'Ramón's raving.' On the eve of 23 February Carrillo was still clinging to Suárez the way one shipwrecked man clings to another, he was still thinking that supporting Suárez meant supporting democracy, he was still keeping his eyes open against the risk of a coup d'état and still considering that his formula of a government of national unity with Suárez was the only way to prevent it and to thwart the collapse of what four years earlier they had begun to construct between the two of them. Of course, by that time the idea of governing with Suárez was unworkable; doubly unworkable: because neither he nor Suárez controlled his own party any more and because, although four years before their personal alliance represented a collective alliance between Franco's two irreconcilable Spains, by the time of 23 February it's more than likely that he and Suárez no longer represented anybody or hardly anybody, and represented only themselves. But it's possible that on the evening of the coup, while both remained in their seats in the midst of the gunshots and the rest of the deputies obeyed the *golpistas'* orders and lay down on the floor, Carrillo might have felt a sort of vengeful satisfaction, as if that instant corroborated what he'd always believed, and that he and Suárez were the only two real politicians in the country, or at least the only two politicians ready to risk their necks for democracy. I can't resist imagining that, if it's true that they both cultivated an epic and aesthetic conception of politics as an individual adventure flecked with dramatic episodes and intrepid decisions, that instant also condensed their twin conception of politics, because neither of the two experienced a more dramatic episode than that burst of gunfire in the Cortes nor ever took a more intrepid decision than the one they both took to remain in their seats while the bullets whizzed around them in the chamber.

3

Did they represent only themselves? Did they no longer represent anybody or hardly anybody?

I don't know what the first words were that Adolfo Suárez and General Gutiérrez Mellado said when they saw Lieutenant Colonel Tejero burst into the Cortes, and I don't think it's important to know; I do, however, know the first words Santiago Carrillo said – because not only he himself but some of his comrades in nearby seats recalled them on various occasions – and of course they're not important. What Carrillo said was: 'Pavía's arrived earlier than expected.' It was a cliché: for more than a century the name Pavía in Spain has been a metonym for the expression *golpe de estado*, because the coup d'état staged by General Manuel Pavía – a soldier who according to legend burst into the Cortes on horseback on 3 January 1874 – was until 23 February 1981 the most spectacular abuse the democratic institutions had suffered, and from the beginning of this democracy – and especially after the summer of 1980, and especially in the political village of Madrid obsessed since the summer of 1980 with the rumours of an impending coup d'état – rare was the comment on a coup d'état that didn't contain the name Pavía.* But Carrillo's phrase being a commonplace, and not having any importance, doesn't mean it's not interesting, because reality suffers from a curious propensity to deal in commonplaces, or allow

* One of the most resonant belongs to the deputy leader of the Socialist Party, Alfonso Guerra. 'If Pavía's horse comes into the Cortes,' said Guerra, 'Suárez will be riding it.' The prediction was not very accurate, although it sums up quite well the opinion that many held of the Prime Minister at that moment.

itself to be colonized by them; it also takes pleasure sometimes – as I
mentioned earlier – in fabricating strange figures, and one of those
figures is that General Pavía's coup seems to anticipate 23 February, and
what it was meant to be.

History repeats itself. Marx observed that great events and characters
appear in history twice, first as tragedy and then as farce, just as in
moments of profound transformation men, frightened by their responsibility, invoked the spirits of the past, adopted their names, their
mannerisms and slogans to represent with this prestigious disguise and
detachable language a new historical scene as if it were a seance. In the
case of 23 February Marx's intuition is valid though incomplete. The
legend is partially false: General Pavía did not burst into the Cortes on
horseback, he did so on foot and with a detachment of Civil Guards
under his orders and ejected the parliamentarians of the First Republic
at gunpoint and precipitated a coup d'état that the conservative press
had been advocating for months as a remedy against the disorder the
country had sunk into, a coup that led to the formation of a government of national unity led by General Serrano, who prolonged the
regime's agony for less than a year with a peculiar Republican dictatorship until General Martínez Campos finished it off with a military
uprising. A valid intuition though incomplete: Pavía's coup was a tragedy, but Tejero's coup was not a farce, or not entirely, or only because
its failure prevented the tragedy, or we only imagine that it was now
because tragedy plus time equals farce; Tejero's coup was, indeed, an
echo, a parody, a seance: Tejero aspired to be Pavía; Armada aspired to
be Serrano, and it could be imagined that, had the coup triumphed,
Armada's unity or coalition or caretaker government would not have
done anything but agonizingly prolong, with a peculiar authoritarian
democracy or a peculiar monarchist dictatorship, the life of a mortally
wounded regime.

There is still another parallel between the coup of 1874 and that of
1981, between Pavía's coup and Tejero's coup. Engravings of the time
show the deputies of the First Republic greeting the rebellious Civil
Guards' entrance into the chamber with gestures of protest, facing up
to the attackers; that's another legend, except this time it's not partially
but totally false. The 1874 deputies' attitude to the coup was almost

identical to that of the 1981 deputies: just as the 1981 deputies hid beneath their benches as soon as the first shots were fired, as soon as the first shots were heard in the corridors of the Cortes the 1874 deputies fled in terror from the chamber, which was empty when the Civil Guards arrived. Thirty years after Pavía's coup, Nicolás Estévanez, one of the deputies present in the Cortes, wrote: 'I don't deny my share of responsibility for the incredible shame of that day; we all behaved indecently.' Thirty years have not yet passed since Tejero's attempted coup and, as far as I know, none of the deputies present in the Cortes on 23 February has written anything similar. Whether or not one of them does so in the future, I'm not sure any of them behaved indecently; hiding from gunfire under a bench is not a very splendid gesture, but I don't think anyone can be blamed for doing so: much as it's possible that the majority of the parliamentarians present in the chamber were ashamed of not having remained in their seats, and much as it's certain that democracy would have been grateful if at least certain of them had done so, I don't think anyone is indecent for seeking shelter when bullets are flying. Besides, at least in 1981 – in 1874, too, I think – the deputies' attitude was a mirror image of that of the majority of society, because there was barely a gesture of public rejection of the coup in all of Spain until in the early hours of the morning the King appeared on television condemning the attack on the Cortes and the putsch was given up as a failure: apart from the head of the provisional government named by the King, Francisco Laína, or the premier of the autonomous Catalan government, Jordi Pujol, on the evening of 23 February all or almost all the responsible politicians who hadn't been taken hostage by Tejero – party leaders, senators, regional deputies and premiers, civil governors, mayors and councillors – restricted themselves to awaiting the outcome of events, and some hid or escaped or tried to escape abroad; apart from the newspaper *El País* – which brought out a special edition at ten at night – and *Diario 16* – which brought one out at midnight – there was barely a media organization that came out in defence of democracy; apart from the Police Trade Union and the PSUC, the Catalan Communist Party, there was barely a political or social organization that issued a statement of protest and, when some trade union discussed the possibility of mobilizing its membership, it was immediately dissuaded from doing so with the argument that any demonstration could provoke further military action. Furthermore, that evening the memory of the war closed people up in their houses, paralysed the country, silenced it: no one put up the slightest resistance to the coup and everyone took the hijacking of the Cortes and the occupation of Valencia by tanks with moods that varied from terror to euphoria by way of apathy, but with identical passivity. That was the popular response to the coup: none. I'm very much afraid that, as well as not being a splendid response, it was not a decent response: although in those moments the order disseminated by the Zarzuela Palace and the provisional government was to keep calm and act as if nothing had happened, the fact is that something had happened and that nobody or hardly anybody said to the *golpistas* from the opening moments that society did not approve of that outrage. Nobody or hardly anybody told them, which forces the question of whether Armada, Milans and Tejero had committed an error in imagining the country was ripe for the coup, and in supposing that, had it achieved its objective, the majority would have accepted it with less resignation than relief. It also forces the question of whether the deputies who on 23 February hid under their benches did not embody the popular will better than those who did not duck. In short: maybe it's an exaggeration to say that by the winter of 1981 Santiago Carrillo and Adolfo Suárez didn't represent anybody, but to judge by what happened on the evening of 23 February you wouldn't say they represented many people.

4

It's true: history fabricates strange figures and does not reject the symmetries of fiction, just as if with that formal design it were seeking to endow itself with a significance it did not possess on its own. The story of the 23 February coup abounds with them: they're fabricated by the events and the men, the living and the dead, the present and the past; perhaps the one formed by Santiago Carrillo and General Gutiérrez Mellado in one of the rooms of the Cortes that night is not the least strange.

At a quarter to eight in the evening, when more than an hour had already passed since the captain of the Civil Guard had announced from the speakers' podium the arrival at the Cortes of a competent military authority who would take charge of the coup, Carrillo saw from his bench that some Civil Guards were taking Adolfo Suárez out of the chamber. Like all the rest of the deputies, the Secretary General of the PCE deduced that the *golpistas* were taking the Prime Minister away to kill him. That they should do so didn't surprise him, but it did that half an hour later they took out General Gutiérrez Mellado and, not only him, but Felipe González. A little while later his surprise was dispelled: a Civil Guard, machine gun in hand, ordered him to stand up and forced him to leave the chamber; with him left Alfonso Guerra, deputy leader of the PSOE, and Agustín Rodríguez Sahagún, Minister of Defence. They took the three of them to a place known as the clock room, where Gutiérrez Mellado and Felipe González already were, but not Adolfo Suárez, who had been confined alone in the ushers' cloak-room, a few metres from the chamber. They pointed him towards a chair at one end of the room; Carrillo sat down, and for the next fifteen hours he barely moved from there, his gaze almost always fixed on a big chiming clock made by a nineteenth-century Swiss clockmaker called Alberto Billeter; on his left, very near, sat General Gutiérrez Mellado; opposite him, in the centre of the room with his back to him, was Rodríguez Sahagún, and further on, facing the wall (or at least that's how they remembered it when they remembered that night), González and Guerra. At each of the doors rebel soldiers armed with machine guns stood guard; there was no heating, or no one had turned it on, and a skylight in the ceiling open to the February dew kept the five men trembling with cold all night.

Like his companions, during the first hours of being shut up in the clock room Carrillo thought he was going to die. He thought he should prepare himself to die. He thought he was prepared to die and at the same time he wasn't prepared to die. He feared the pain. He feared his murderers would laugh at him. He feared weakening at the last moment. It won't be any big deal, he thought, looking for courage. It'll just be an instant: they'll put a pistol to your head, pull the trigger and it'll all be over. Maybe because it's not death but the uncertainty of death that we find intolerable, this last thought calmed him; two more things calmed him: one was the pride of not having obeyed the order of the rebel soldiers and remaining in his seat while the bullets whizzed around him in the chamber; the other was that death would liberate him from the torment his Party comrades were subjecting him to. How peaceful you're going to be, he said to himself. What a relief never to have to deal with so many irresponsible bastards ever again. What a relief not to have to smile at them ever again. As soon as he began to think that maybe he wasn't going to die the anxiety returned. He didn't remember exactly when it had happened (perhaps when the sound of aeroplanes flying over the Cortes came in through the skylight; perhaps when Alfonso Guerra returned from the toilet giving them stealthy encouraging glances; undoubtedly as time went by and news of the military authority announced by the *golpistas* failed to arrive); the only thing he remembered was that, once he'd accepted that he might not die, his mind turned into a whirlwind of conjecture. He didn't know what was happening in the chamber or what had happened outside the

Cortes, he didn't know if Tejero's operation was part of a wider operation or was an isolated operation, but he knew it was a coup d'état and he was sure that its triumph or failure depended on the King: if the King accepted the coup, the coup would triumph; if the King did not accept the coup, the coup would fail. He wasn't sure about the King; he didn't even know if he was still at liberty or if the *golpistas* had taken him prisoner. He wasn't sure what the Cortes' attitude would be when the military authority showed up, supposing that he showed up: it wouldn't be the first time that, coerced by weapons, a democratic Parliament handed power over to a military, he thought. He wasn't only thinking about Pavía; half his life had been spent in France and he remembered in 1940, coerced by the German Army after the debacle of the war, how the French National Assembly had handed power over to Marshal Pétain, and in 1958, coerced by its own army in Algeria, had handed it over to General de Gaulle. Now, he thought, the same thing could happen, or something similar, and he wasn't sure whether the deputies would refuse to bow down to blackmail: he was sure of Adolfo Suárez, he was sure of the old guard of his party (not the youngsters), he was sure of himself; but he wasn't sure of anyone else. As for the fact that the *golpistas* had isolated him with those precise companions, as the hours went past and he sensed increasing hope that the coup was paralysed, he began to think that maybe they had done so to keep a close rein on the most representative or most dangerous leaders, or those with the power to negotiate with them when the moment came. But he didn't know what there would be to negotiate, or with whom they'd have to negotiate it, or even in truth if there was any possibility of negotiating, and the whirlwind carried on spinning.

He spent the night sitting beside General Gutiérrez Mellado. They didn't say a single word to each other, but exchanged countless looks and cigarettes. In spite of being almost the same age and having shared the corridors of the Cortes for almost four years, they didn't know each other well, they'd barely spoken except on chance or formal occasions, they barely had anything in common except for friendship with Adolfo Suárez: almost everything else divided them; most of all, history divided them. They both knew it: the difference is that Gutiérrez Mellado, who thought he knew it more specifically, never mentioned it (at least not in public), while Carrillo did so on several occasions. In an interview on his ninetieth birthday, the former Secretary General of the PCE recalled that during those hours of captivity, while listening to Gutiérrez Mellado's bronchitic cough and seeing him sitting there elderly and exhausted, he thought more than once of the strange and ironic figure destiny was forcing them to compose. In 1936 this general was one of the leaders of the fifth column in Madrid, he thought. And I was the Public Order officer and my mission was to fight against the fifth column. At that moment we were mortal enemies and tonight here we are together, and we're going to die side by side. Carrillo glimpsed the figure, but not its precise form, because the data he had was not precise: had it been he would have discovered that the figure was still more ironic and strange than he imagined.

The first part of the figure consists of the crucial point of his biography: on 6 November 1936, when the Civil War had barely started, Carrillo began to turn into the villain of Francoism and the hero of anti-Francoism. He'd just turned twenty and, like Gutiérrez Mellado except from the opposite trench, was anything but the champion of concord he'd turn into in later years ('Concord? No!' he wrote at the beginning of 1934 in *El Socialista* newspaper. 'Class war! Mortal hatred of the criminal bourgeoisie!'). For several months he'd been head of the JSU, the unified Socialist and Communist youth wings, and that very day, as a result of his gradual ideological radicalization but also of his certainty that this was the best way to contribute to defending the Republic against Franco's coup, he'd joined the Communist Party. The Republic, however, seemed about to be defeated. For several days Madrid had been in a panic, with the troops of the Army of Africa at its gates and the streets invaded by thousands of refugees who were fleeing Francoist terror in a mass exodus. Convinced that the fall of the capital was inevitable, the government of the Republic had escaped to Valencia and left the impossible defence of Madrid in the hands of General Miaja, who at ten o'clock that night called a meeting at the War Ministry to constitute the Defence Junta, the new government of the city in which all the parties supporting the fugitive government should be represented; the meeting went on until very late, and it was decided to entrust the position of Security Chief to the leader of the JSU: Santiago Carrillo. But after that

general meeting an improvised restricted meeting was held, in the course
of which the Communists and the anarchists organized an expeditious
arrangement for the secondary problem posed during the first meeting;
a secondary problem in the midst of the life-and-death emergency of
the defence of Madrid, I mean: the prisons of the capital – Modelo, San
Antón, Porlier and Ventas – were overflowing with about ten thousand
prisoners; many of them were fascists or rebel officers who'd been offered
the opportunity to join the Army of the Republic and had turned the
offer down; Franco could take the city at any moment – in fact, there
was fighting two hundred metres from the Modelo prison – and in that
case the officers and fascists locked up there would go immediately to
swell the ranks of the mutinous Army. We don't know how long the
meeting lasted; we do know that its participants resolved to divide the
prisoners into three categories and apply the death penalty to the most
dangerous ones: the fascists and rebel officers. Before dawn on that very
morning the executions started at Paracuellos del Jarama, just over thirty
kilometres from the capital, and during the three weeks that followed
more than two thousand Francoist prisoners were executed without any
trial whatsoever.

It was the biggest massacre perpetrated by the Republicans during
the war. Did Carrillo participate in that improvised restricted meeting?
Did he make the decision to carry out the slaughter or take part in the
decision? Francoist propaganda, which made the Paracuellos executions into the epitome of Republican barbarism, always insisted he did:
Carrillo, it claimed, was the person responsible for the slaughter, among
other reasons because it would have been impossible to remove such a
huge number of inmates from the prisons without counting on the
Security Chief of the Office of Public Order; for his part, Carrillo
always defended his innocence: he simply evacuated inmates from the
prisons to avert the risk of them joining up with the Francoists, but his
jurisdiction ended with the capital and the crimes occurred outside it
and should be imputed to the groups of uncontrolled elements that
prospered in the heat of the disorder of war reigning in Madrid and the
surrounding area. Was the Francoist propaganda right? Is Carrillo
right? The historians have argued over the matter ad nauseam; in my
opinion, the investigations by Ian Gibson, Jorge M. Reverte and Ángel

Viñas are those that get closest to the truth of events. There's no doubt about the Communist and anarchist authorship of the murders and that they weren't the work of uncontrollables; it's certain that the inspiration came from the Communists, that Carrillo did not give the order to commit them, and that, as far as the documentary evidence shows, he was not directly implicated in them. According to Viñas, the order might have come from Alexander Orlov, Soviet NKVD agent in Spain, it might have been transmitted by Pedro Checa, strongman of the PCE, and executed by the Communist Segundo Serrano Poncela, Public Order delegate on the Public Order Council. The preceding does not exonerate Carrillo of all responsibility for the events: there is no record of his participation in the restricted meeting after the meeting of the Defence Junta in which the executions were planned – not decided: the decision was already made – but Serrano Poncela answered to him and, although it's likely that the executions on the first days happened without Carrillo knowing, it's very difficult to accept that those on the days that followed wouldn't have reached his ears. Carrillo can be accused of not having intervened to stop them, of having looked the other way; he cannot be accused of having ordered or organized them. Not intervening to stop such an atrocity is unjustifiable, but maybe understandable if one makes an effort to imagine a young man just past adolescence, newly joined member of a militarized party whose decisions he was not in a position to argue with or contradict, recently arrived in a post the reins of power of which he had not yet completely mastered (although as he did so he put a stop to much of the arbitrary violence infesting Madrid) and especially overwhelmed by the chaos and the vast demands of the defence of a desperate city, where militiamen were falling like flies on the outskirts and the bombs and shelling were killing people every day (and which astonishingly resisted Franco's siege for another two and a half years). Making the effort to imagine these things is not, I insist, trying to justify the deaths of more than two thousand people: it's just not to fail completely to understand the real horror of war. Carrillo understood it and that's why – and although probably in the Spain of the 1980s very few would dare to exonerate him of direct responsibility for the murders – he never denied his indirect responsibility for them. 'I cannot say, if Paracuellos happened while I was in charge of Security,' he declared in 1982, 'that I am totally blameless for what happened.'

That's the first part of the figure; below I describe the second. During the months that Carrillo ran the Office of Public Order of Madrid Gutiérrez Mellado was not, as many years later the Secretary General of the PCE believed, one of the leaders of the fifth column in the capital. Some time later he would be, but in the early hours of 6 November, just at the moment when the contrasting myth that would pursue Carrillo for the rest of his life was born – the myth of the hero of the defence of Madrid and the myth of the villain of the Paracuellos executions – Gutiérrez Mellado had been locked up for three months in the second corridor on the first floor of the San Antón prison, because the future general was one of the many officers who, after having tried to incite their garrisons to revolt against the legitimate government of the Republic in July and having been taken prisoner, had rejected the offer to join the Republican Army to defend the capital from the Francoist advance; that means that Gutiérrez Mellado was also one of the officers who, on 7 November, after the restricted meeting of Communist and anarchist leaders that followed the first meeting of the Defence Junta of Madrid the night before, should have been taken out of the prison along with dozens of his comrades and executed at dusk in Paracuellos. Miraculously, because of the disorder in which the operation was carried out, Gutiérrez Mellado was not taken out and shot that evening and somehow survived the *sacas* that followed in the San Antón prison until 30 November when the executions finished. Because both spent years fighting in the same trenches and became standard-bearers to the concord they combated in their youth, it's impossible that Carrillo was still the villain of Paracuellos for Gutiérrez Mellado in 1981, but not that at some moment of the night of 23 February, while exchanging cigarettes and glances with him in the icy and humiliating silence of the clock room, the general would have intuited with all precision the strange irony that had brought him to die beside the same man who, as he probably believed (and he probably believed it because he too understood the real horror of war), one night forty-five years earlier had ordered his death. If it's true that he believed it, perhaps it would have mattered to him to know he was mistaken.

5

After the coup d'état Santiago Carrillo's political star was rapidly eclipsed. He'd constructed democracy, risked his life for it on 23 February, but democracy had stopped needing him or didn't want anything more to do with him; neither did his own party. Throughout 1981 the PCE continued debating the labyrinth of internal conflicts that had been tearing them apart since four years earlier when their Secretary General announced the abandonment of the Party's Leninist essence; clinging to his post and to his old authoritarian conception of power, Carrillo tried to conserve the unity of the Communists under his command through purges, sanctions and disciplinary action. The result of this attempt at catharsis was lamentable: these actions, sanctions and purges provoked more purges, more sanctions and more actions, and by the summer of 1982 the PCE was a party on the point of collapse, with less than half the number of members it had just five years before and with an increasingly reduced and precarious social presence, broken in three pieces – the pro-Soviets, the reformers and the Carrillistas – unrecognizable to those who had belonged to it in the clandestine exuberance of late Francoism, when it was the biggest party of the opposition, or during the initial optimism of democracy, when it still seemed destined to be. Carrillo himself was unrecognizable: the hero of the defence of Madrid had been left behind, the myth of the anti-Francoist struggle, the internationally respected leader, the symbol of the new Euro-Communism, the Secretary General invested with the authority of demigod and the strategist able to turn any defeat into victory, the founder of democracy whom his own adversaries considered a solid, lucid, pragmatic, necessary statesman; now he was just a nervous petty tyrant on the defensive in a tangential party, embroiled in abstruse ideological debates and infighting where ambition was disguised as purity of principle and accumulated rage as longing for change, a waning politician with the manners of a Communist brontosaurus and the antiquated language of an apparatchik, lost in a cannibalistic labyrinth of conspiratorial paranoia. During those months of personal torment and political death throes Carrillo couldn't even avoid the exasperated gesture of using the memory of 23 February to defend himself from the PCE rebels (or to attack them): he did so in meetings where his comrades were jeering at him – 'If Lieutenant Colonel Tejero didn't manage to get me on the floor, it's hardly likely that you're going to keep me quiet here,' he said while they tried to shout him down at a function held on 12 March 1981 in Barcelona – and he did so at meetings of the Party organs, reproaching the leaders who were left in charge of the organization on the night of the coup for ineptitude or lack of courage to respond to the Army's uprising by organizing mass demonstrations; perhaps he also did so (or at least his detractors took it like this) by favouring a painting by the Communist José Ortega, who depicted him sitting up straight in the chamber of the Cortes during the evening of 23 February, while the rest of the deputies except Adolfo Suárez and Gutiérrez Mellado – on the canvas two modest figures compared with the panoramic figure of the Secretary General – shelter under their benches from the *golpistas'* gunshots.

It was all for naught. The October 1982 general election, the first one after the coup d'état, gave an absolute majority to the Socialist Party and allowed the formation of the first left-wing government since the war, but was a political death sentence for Santiago Carrillo: the PCE lost half its votes, and its Secretary General was left with no choice but to offer his resignation to the executive committee. He resigned from his post, but didn't renounce power; Carrillo was a pure politician and a pure politician doesn't give up power: he gets thrown out of it. Like that of Suárez before the coup, Carrillo's withdrawal after the coup was not a definitive withdrawal but a tactical one, meant to maintain control of the Party from a distance and await a favourable moment for his return: he managed to place at the head of the secretary generalship a loyal and malleable substitute (or one whom he initially thought to be loyal and malleable), he continued to be a member of the executive committee and the central committee and retained the post of Party spokesman in the Cortes. There, with his paltry four deputies, they didn't even manage to form their own parliamentary group and were forced to join the so-called mixed group, a group of all sorts of parties with minimal representation in the Cortes; and there he re-encountered Adolfo Suárez, who was trying to come back to political life after his resignation as Prime Minister and had just founded the CDS, a party with which he'd scraped in with half the paltry parliamentary representation obtained by Carrillo. And there they were again, indestructible twins, united in their last public adventure by the vice of politics, by the votes of citizens and by parliamentary norms, reduced by the political system they'd set up with their own four hands as if history wanted to make another figure out of them: five years after exchanging a dictatorship for a democracy, they were now two practically invisible deputies except as tiresome icons of an epoch the whole country seemed impatient to get over.

Neither of the two resigned himself to that secondary role. During the next three years Carrillo continued practising politics as far as he could in the Cortes and in the Party, where he fought to the end to keep control of the machinery and to guide his successor. Arguments between the two of them soon arose, and in April 1985 Carrillo was finally dismissed from all his posts and reduced to the condition of rank and file member; it was a covert expulsion, and his pride would not tolerate it: he immediately left the Party, in the company of a group of faithful, founded the Spanish Workers' Party (Partido de los Trabajadores de España, PTE), an organization that demonstrated its predictable irrelevance within a short time and in 1991 sought to join the PSOE, his fierce adversary during four decades of Francoism and one and a half of democracy. Making a virtue of necessity, Carrillo interpreted this gesture as a way of closing a personal circle, as a gesture of reconciliation with his own biography: as a young man, the same day the myth of the hero of Madrid and the villain of Paracuellos was born, he'd abandoned the Socialist Party of his family, his childhood and adolescence to join the Communist Party; as an old man he went back the opposite way: he abandoned the Communist Party to join the Socialist Party. Of course, nobody accepted that interpretation, although it's very possible that it really was a symbolic gesture: a symbolic recognition that, after a lifetime dedicated to reviling democratic socialism (or social democracy), it was democratic socialism (or social democracy) that was the inevitable result of the dismantling or undermining or ideological demolition of Communism that he'd begun years before. Perhaps it was also a gesture of rebelliousness, a final manoeuvring by a pure politician: although at seventy-six he no longer aspired to hold decisive positions, maybe he hadn't yet renounced the idea of influencing from his vantage point of experienced old leader the young and all-powerful Socialists in government. Whatever it might have been, finally his gesture came to nothing: the PSOE took in the rest of the PTE members, but convinced him whether with fine words or the private intention of humiliating him that, given his political trajectory, it would be best for everyone not to formalize his admission to the Party.

This was the embittered culmination of his political career. What happened later did nothing to contradict that. Pushed out of active politics, writing newspaper articles and airing his opinions in his cracked, monotone, phlegmatic voice on radio discussions and television programmes, with his constant cigarette, during his last years of life Carrillo seemed to climb up on to the venerable pedestal of the fathers of the nation. He only seemed to. Beneath the occasional homage and the respect the media and institutions paid him flowed an adverse current as stubborn as it was powerful: the right never stopped associating his name with the horrors of the war and inventing new iniquities from his past, and to the end of his days he could barely appear at a public event without gangs of radicals trying to harass him with insults and attempts at physical aggression; as for the left, the rejection Carrillo provoked was less noisy and more subtle, but secretly maybe no less bitter, especially among his former comrades or among the heirs of his former comrades or among the heirs of the heirs of his former comrades: his former comrades professed for him an enduring aversion of old parishioners subdued by his domination, that deep down was also (or at least was for many) an enduring aversion for

themselves for having belonged to a church where Carrillo was adored
like a high priest; making Felipe González's wickedness his, his former
comrades' heirs blamed him for managing in five years of democracy
what Franco hadn't managed in forty of dictatorship: destroying the
Communist Party; as for the heirs of his former comrades' heirs, they
denigrated him by repeating unknowingly, hardened by ignorance and
by the presumptuous impunity of youth, an old accusation: for them
– *Fiat justitia et pereat mundus* – it had been Carrillo's personal ambition and his complicity with Adolfo Suárez, added to his ideological
revisionism, his wavering politics and his strategic errors, that had
forced the left to make a disadvantageous pact with the right to
exchange the dictatorship for democracy and had prevented the restitution of the legally elected Republic overthrown by Franco's victory in
the war, complete restitution to the victims of Francoism and prosecution of those responsible for forty years of dictatorship. None of them
were right, but it's absurd to deny that they were all partially right and
that – although it would be good to know exactly what Carrillo's
comrades and the heirs of his comrades and the heirs of his comrades'
heirs were doing on the evening of 23 February, while he was risking his
neck for democracy – to a certain extent Carrillo was essentially a failure, because, except for that of reconciling the irreconcilable Spain of
Franco with democracy, all the great projects he undertook in his life
failed: he tried to make a revolution to take power by force and failed;
he tried to win a just war and failed; he tried to bring down an unjust
regime and failed; he tried to reform Communism to take power by
ballot and failed. He's living out his last years surrounded by the false
respect of almost everyone and the true respect of a very few. He has
been many things, but he's never been a fool or faint-hearted, and it's
possible that around him he sees only a scorched landscape of ideals in
ruins and defeated hopes.

During this final stage his friendship with Adolfo Suárez remained
intact. Both had given up political activity at the same time, in 1991,
and over the course of the ten years that followed their connection
grew more frequent and closer. They met often; they laughed a lot; they
tried in vain not to talk politics. By the winter of 2001 Carrillo began
to suspect that his friend was ill. In June of the following year, on the

occasion of the official celebration of twenty-five years of democracy, Suárez made one of his now rare public appearances and declared to the press that José María Aznar, who then had been in the Moncloa for six years, was the best Prime Minister since the restoration of democracy. The dithyramb provoked numerous comments; Carrillo's was taken by creatures of habit as an old dog's cynicism ready to be rude about a friend to get a laugh from society: 'Adolfo's not well: I think he's suffering from brain damage.' A little while later he visited Suárez at his house in La Florida, a housing development on the outskirts of Madrid. He found him the same as ever, or the same as he ever found him in those days, but at a certain moment Suárez told him of the long solitary walks he took through the neighbourhood and Carrillo interrupted him. You shouldn't go out alone, he said. They could give you a fright. Suárez smiled. Who? He said. ETA? He didn't let him answer: If they've got the balls, let them come and find me, he said. And then Carrillo watched him act out verbally the starring role of a scene from a Western: one day he went out on his own and, while he was walking through a nearby park, three armed terrorists jumped him, but before they could match him he spun around, pulled his pistol and disarmed them with three shots; then, after warning them that the next time he'd shoot to kill and that if they didn't comply with the rule of law and the democratic will of the people they were going to spend the rest of their lives in prison, he handed them over bound hand and foot to the authorities.

He didn't see Adolfo Suárez again. Or at least that's what Carrillo told me the only time I met him, one morning in the spring of 2007. The appointment was for noon at his home, a modest apartment in a building on Plaza de los Reyes Magos, in the Niño Jesús neighbourhood, very close to the Parque Retiro. By then Carrillo was in his nineties, but he looked the same as he did in his sixties; perhaps his body seemed a little smaller and his frame a little more fragile, his scalp a little balder, his mouth a little sunken, his nose a little softer, his eyes a little less sarcastic and friendlier behind his bifocals. While we were together he smoked a whole pack of cigarettes; he talked with neither bitterness nor pride, with an urge for precision assisted by an irreproachable memory. I asked him all about the years of political change, about the legalization of the PCE and about 23 February; he talked to me most of all about Adolfo Suárez ('Having worked in a university you'll have known lots of educated idiots, right?' he asked me twice. 'Well, Suárez was just the opposite'). The conversation lasted more than three hours during which we sat face to face in his study, a small room, every wall covered floor to ceiling in books; on his desk were more books, papers, a full ashtray; through a half-open window giving on to the street came the sound of children playing; behind my interlocutor, leaning on a shelf, a photo of 23 February dominated the room: the front-page photo from the *New York Times* in which Adolfo Suárez, young, brave and dishevelled, is leaving his bench to confront the Civil Guards who are jostling General Gutiérrez Mellado in the chamber of the Cortes.

6

The question about the intelligence services is still pending, although now it's another one. We know that CESID headed by Javier Calderón as such did not organize or participate in the coup, but rather opposed it, but we also know that several members of the elite CESID unit headed by Major José Luis Cortina, AOME, collaborated with Lieutenant Colonel Tejero in the attack on the Cortes (without doubt Captain Gómez Iglesias, who at the last moment persuaded certain indecisive officers to back up the lieutenant colonel; possibly Sergeant Miguel Sales and Corporals José Moya and Rafael Monge, who escorted Tejero's buses to their target); the question therefore is: did AOME organize or support 23 February? Did Major Cortina organize or support 23 February? In reality, it's impossible to answer these two questions without answering two prior questions: who was Major Cortina? What was AOME?

Outwardly, José Luis Cortina's biography offers many similarities to that of Javier Calderón, with whom he began in the 1970s a friendship that endures to this day; but the similarities are only outward, because Cortina is a much more complex and more ambiguous character than the former Secretary General of CESID, someone described with admirable consistency by those who know him best as an authentic man of action and at the same time as a virtuoso of camouflage: a twelve-faced character, as Manuel Vázquez Montalbán wrote after interviewing him. Like Calderón, Cortina was raised within the socially concerned Falangism of the Colegio Pinilla, except that Cortina's political vocation was always much more solid than Calderón's and led him in the 1960s to join little radical groups on the left wing of the Falange, like the Social

Revolutionary Front, which aimed, without leaving the fold of the regime, to renovate or purify it with pro-Marxist injections and sympathy for the Cuba of Fidel Castro. This ideological hodgepodge, not infrequent among the politicized youth of the day, afforded him the odd run-in with the Army intelligence service and with the police, but also relations with members of the opposition to Francoism, in particular with the Communists. Having graduated from the Military Academy at the top of his class – the 14th, the same as the King's – Cortina did not become part of the intelligence services until 1968, when, just turned thirty, he was co-opted by the High Command General Staff to organize the first special operations unit of the intelligence services, SOME (Sección Operativa de Medios Especiales), in which he worked until the mid-1970s. By then he'd tempered his pseudo-revolutionary impulses, like Calderón and like his brother Antonio, with whom he always shared ideas and political projects, he participated in GODSA, the think-tank or embryonic political party that linked up with Manuel Fraga in the search for a ruptureless reform of Francoism and then moved away from him (or many of its members did) as soon as it was clear that the monarchy was betting on Suárez's reform with a rupture; like Calderón, at that time Cortina acted as defence lawyer for one of the anti-Franco military officers of the Democratic Military Union: Captain García Márquez. Finally, in the autumn of 1977, shortly after the creation of CESID after the first democratic elections, its first director charged him with setting up the special operations unit of the centre, AOME, which he led until a few weeks after 23 February when the judge had him arrested for his presumed participation in the coup. From the political point of view, towards the beginning of the 1980s Cortina was a faithfully monarchist military officer who, although four years earlier he'd unhesitatingly accepted the democratic system, now thought like a good part of the political class (and unlike Calderón, tied by loyalty to Gutiérrez Mellado) that Adolfo Suárez had made a bad job of democracy or had spoiled it, that the system had entered into a profound crisis that threatened the Crown, and that the best way of getting out of this crisis was the formation of a coalition or caretaker or unity government under the auspices of a soldier with the characteristics of General Armada, whom Cortina knew well and to whom he was also linked through his brother Antonio, who had a good friendship with the general and had continued his political career in the ranks of Manuel Fraga's Alianza Popular; from the technical point of view, from the point of view of his espionage work, nothing defines Cortina better than the very nature of AOME.

Although it was part of CESID, AOME didn't share its organizational chaos or its precariousness of resources; on the contrary: perhaps it was one of the few units of the Spanish intelligence services comparable to units of the Western intelligence services. The merit was entirely due to its founder: Cortina commanded AOME for four years, enjoying almost complete autonomy; his only hierarchical link to CESID was Calderón, who didn't supervise the unit in practice but simply requested from it, on behalf of the various divisions of the centre, information the major would later obtain without answering to anybody about his manner of obtaining it. Like all those of similar characteristics in the Western intelligence services, AOME was a secret unit within the secret service itself, to a certain extent secret even to the secret service. Its structure was simple. It was made up of three operational groups subdivided into two subgroups which in turn were subdivided into three teams, each of which was made up of seven or eight people and allocated three or four vehicles and a personal transmitter with which to communicate with the rest of the members of the team and vehicles; each team was assigned a task and each agent had a speciality: photography, communications, locks, explosives, etc. As well as these three operational groups, AOME had its own academy from very early on, where every year it taught a course on intelligence techniques that allowed it to instruct students in sophisticated methods of information gathering and to choose those most suitable to carry out its missions, always the most exposed CESID jobs: tailings, phone tapping, clandestine entries into residences and offices, seizures. The nature of such activities explains why those who carried them out led semi-clandestine lives, including within CESID itself, the members of which did not know the identities of AOME agents or the location of the unit's secret headquarters, four houses on the outskirts of Madrid known respectively as Paris, Berlin, Rome and Jaca. This inscrutability could perhaps only be maintained, furthermore, thanks to a sort of sect mentality; according to those who were under his orders during those years, Cortina managed to inspire this mentality in his two hundred or so men and managed to form them into a compact elite who imagined themselves as something like a chivalrous order disciplined and loyal to their chief and to a slogan shared with other Army units: 'If it's possible, it's already done; if impossible, we'll get right on it.'

That, broadly speaking, was Major José Luis Cortina; that, broadly speaking, was AOME. Given the major's personal characteristics and given the organizational and operational characteristics of the unit he commanded, always on the border of legality or beyond, always operating covertly and without any external overseeing, there is no doubt that Cortina's AOME could have supported the 23 February coup while Calderón's CESID opposed it; given the internal cohesion with which Cortina endowed AOME, it's very improbable that its members could have acted without the major's authorization or knowledge. I'm not saying impossible (after all, the unit's internal cohesion demonstrated that it was not entirely without cracks, because it was AOME members who, after 23 February, denounced the participation of their comrades and Cortina himself in the coup d'état; after all, although maybe Captain Gómez Iglesias had been put in charge of watching Tejero months before by Cortina, at the last moment he could have joined the coup without consulting Cortina, guided by his old friendship and the communion of ideas that united him to the lieutenant colonel); I'm saying it's very improbable. Is that what happened? Did Major Cortina organize and support 23 February? And if he did, why did he? To back up Armada's government with force? Or did he support the coup just enough to be on the winning side if the coup triumphed and fight it just enough to be on the winning side if the coup failed? Or did he support it as a double agent, or as an agent provocateur, joining the coup to control it from within and make it fail? All these hypotheses have been proposed at one time or another, but it's impossible to try to answer these five questions without first trying to answer five prior questions: did Cortina know beforehand the who, the when, the how and the where of 23 February? Was Cortina in contact with Armada and the rest of the *golpistas* in the days before 23 February? What exactly did Cortina do the night before 23 February? What exactly did Cortina do on 23 February? What exactly happened in AOME on 23 February?

7

23 February

At twenty to seven in the evening, when fifteen minutes had passed since the assault on the Cortes and the King was preventing General Armada from coming to the Zarzuela, the coup d'état ran aground. That doesn't mean that at this moment, with the Cabinet and parliamentarians held hostage, the region of Valencia in revolt and the Brunete Armoured Division threatening Madrid, the coup no longer had any outcome other than failure; it only means that, as well as the coup, at this moment the countercoup was already under way, and from then on and until shortly after nine the *golpistas'* plans were put on hold, waiting for more military units to join the uprising.

The countercoup command post was located in the Zarzuela, in the King's office, where he remained for the rest of the night in the company of his secretary, Sabino Fernández Campo, the Queen, his son Prince Felipe – then a thirteen-year-old boy – and an aide-de-camp, while the adjoining salons of the Palace were filling up with relatives, friends and members of the Royal Household who answered or made phone calls or discussed the events. Although according to the Constitution he was no more than symbolic head of the Armed Forces, whose effective command resided in the Prime Minister and the Minister of Defence, in that exceptional situation the King acted as commander-in-chief of the Army and from the first moment began to issue orders to his comrades-in-arms to respect legality. At first, with the aim of having a stand-in for the sequestered government, the King approved a proposal according to which all executive powers would be placed in the hands of the Joint Chiefs of Staff, the highest organ in the hierarchy of the Armed Forces, but hastened to withdraw his approval as soon as someone – perhaps Fernández Campo, perhaps the Queen herself – made him see that this measure meant relegating civilian power in favour of military power and in practice sanctioning the coup; this false step aborted in time made clear in the Zarzuela the need to constitute a covering civilian government, which was done before eight o'clock that night, calling together a group of secretaries of state and undersecretaries from the ministries under the leadership of the Director of State Security, Francisco Laína. By that time, however, the King's main worry was not Lieutenant Colonel Tejero, who had the Cortes under his control, or General Milans, who had the region of Valencia in a state of rebellion, or the conspirators at the Brunete Armoured Division, who in spite of the countermands of their division commander and the Captain General of Madrid had not yet refused to join the coup, or even General Armada, around whom more and more suspicions converged as the *golpistas* put forward his name (Tejero referred to him, Milans referred to him, the conspirators at Brunete referred to him); the King was mainly worried about the Captains General.

These were almost a dozen generals who held a viceregal control over the eleven military regions into which the country was divided. All of them were Francoists: all had fought the war with Franco, almost all of them had fought on the Russian front with the Blue Division alongside Hitler's troops, all were ideologically attached to the far right or had good relations with it, all had accepted democracy reluctantly and out of a sense of duty and by 1981 many considered the Army's intervention in the country's politics to be indispensable or advisable. In the days before 23 February Milans, operating from the headquarters of the III military region, had obtained explicit or implicit support for his cause from five of the Captains General (Merry Gordon, chief of the II region; Elícegui, of the V; Campano, of the VII; Fernández Posse, of the VIII; Delgado, of the IX), but when the coup was barely under way and the King and Fernández Campo began to telephone them one by one and they had to state their positions, none of them clearly seconded Milans. They did not, however, unhesitatingly respect the King's authority either; they would have done if the King had ordered them to bring their troops out on to the streets, but, given that the order that came from the Zarzuela was exactly the opposite, all the Captains General except for two (Quintana Lacaci, in Madrid, and Luis Polanco, in Burgos) struggled with their doubts throughout the whole evening and night, urged from one side by Milans' telephonic harangues and his appeals to military honour and the salvation of Spain and the commitment to duty, and on the other subject to the respect for the King and at times by reticence or by the prudence of their second-in-commands, maybe fascinated by the vertigo of reliving in old age the insurrectional epic of their youth as officers under Franco and aware that any one of them backing the coup could swing it in favour of the *golpistas* – decisive for the intervention of the rest of their comrades and compelling all together the King to freeze or suppress a political regime they all detested – but also aware that this very backing could ruin their service records, annul their pleasant retirement plans and condemn them to spend the rest of their days in a military prison. Those generals probably had high opinions of themselves, but, to judge by what happened on 23 February, barring exceptions they only showed themselves to be a handful of cowardly, dishonourable, swaggering and spoiled-rotten soldiers: if they had been honourable soldiers they would not have wavered for a second before putting themselves at the King's orders to protect the legality they'd sworn to defend; if they hadn't been honourable soldiers but had been brave they would have done what their ideals and their guts were telling them to do and would have ordered their tanks on to the streets. With few exceptions, they did neither one thing nor the other; with few exceptions, their behaviour fluctuated between the embarrassing and the grotesque: for example, General Merry Gordon, commander of the II region, who had promised to be on Milans' side, spent the evening and the night in bed, laid out by an overdose of gin; or General Delgado, commander of the IX region, who set up an improvised headquarters in a restaurant on the outskirts of Granada where he remained shielded from the vicissitudes of the coup and without coming out in favour of it or against it until after midnight when he considered the situation was cleared up and returned to his office headquarters; or General Campano, commander of the VII region, who did not stop searching for strategies that would allow him to join the coup while protecting him from an eventual accusation of *golpismo*; or General González del Yerro, chief of the unified command of the Canary Islands (equivalent to the XI military region), who was willing to collaborate in the coup on the condition that it would not be Armada but he himself who would occupy the leadership of the resulting government. The anecdotes could be multiplied, but the category is always the same: except for Milans, no Captain General openly supported the coup, but, except for Quintana Lacaci and Polanco, no Captain General openly opposed it. In spite of that, and also in spite of the fact that throughout the whole evening and evening the pieces of news that arrived at the Zarzuela from the regional headquarters varied from one minute to the next and seemed to be or were frequently contradictory, it's very possible that before nine that evening the King had a reasonable certainty that barring something unforeseen turning the situation around drastically the Captains General were not going to dare to disobey his orders for the moment.

But something unforeseen could still happen, and a turnaround as well: the King had smothered part of the rebellion, but he hadn't extinguished it. The most flammable points between seven and nine that evening were the Cortes and the Brunete Armoured Division, the most crucial unit to the triumph of the coup. What happened during those two hours at the Brunete is inexplicable; inexplicable unless one admits that as much cowardice or indecision as overcame the Captains General also overcame the *golpistas* of the Brunete Division. Persuaded by them that the operation had the King's consent, in the minutes before the coup the commander of Brunete, General Juste, had issued the order to all his units to leave for Madrid, but before seven, after talking to the Zarzuela Palace and receiving unequivocal orders from General Quintana Lacaci – his immediate superior – Juste had issued the countermand; many regiment commanders, however, continued to show unwilling to obey it and some of the more fiery among them – Colonel Valencia Remón, Colonel Ortiz Call, Lieutenant Colonel De Meer – were looking for excuses or courage with which to send their troops out on to the streets, sure that it would take no more than one armoured vehicle in the centre of Madrid to dispel the scruples or vacillations of their comrades-in-arms and resolve the triumph of the coup. They didn't find either of the two things, but most of all they didn't find the *golpista* ringleaders within the division (General Torres Rojas, replacing Juste according to the conspirators' plans, Colonel San Martín, chief of staff, and Major Pardo Zancada, charged by Milans with putting the operation into action), or any of the other commanders and officers who were agitating in the midst of the generalized jumpiness: like so many other soldiers during the years before the coup, many had been lavish with their threats against the government with flag-waving boasts, but when the moment came to put them into practice they were unable to wrest command from the weak and doubtful Juste and, although it is true that during the first hours of the coup Torres Rojas and San Martín were still trying to convince Juste to rescind his countermand of the departure order, the truth is they did so with scant conviction, and the pressures they exerted against the commander of the Brunete Division vanished a little after eight when, docilely obeying his superiors' orders, Torres Rojas left headquarters and returned on a regular flight to his post in La Coruña.

Meanwhile, while those at the Brunete were chomping at the bit, in and around the Cortes the formidable stir raised by the parliamentarians being taken hostage seemed to be gradually calming down. The first two hours there following the start of the coup had been demented. As the evening went on, Madrid turned into a ghost town (a city without any open bars or restaurants, with no taxis and barely any traffic, with empty streets where gangs of extreme right-wingers strutted about chanting slogans, smashing windows and intimidating the few passersby as people shut themselves up in their houses and sat glued to the radio or television, which for a while had broadcast nothing but military music or classical music, because since before eight the public radio and television stations had been occupied by a detachment commanded by a captain from the Brunete Division), opposite the façade of the Cortes, on the other side of Carrera de San Jerónimo, the salons and stairways of the Hotel Palace began to seethe with military men of every force and rank, journalists, photographers, radio broadcasters, onlookers, drunks and crackpots, and almost immediately a little crisis cabinet was set up in the manager's office composed among others of General Aramburu Topete, Director General of the Civil Guard, and General Sáenz de Santamaría, Inspector General of the national police, two loyal members of the military who'd arrived at the Cortes building shortly after the assault and who, as soon as they understood that the hostage situation could go on for an unpredictable length of time, set up two security cordons – one of national police, the other of Civil Guards – with the aim of sealing off the building and keeping control of the maelstrom around it. It took them hours to achieve these two things, if they really did achieve them; in fact, vociferous groups of supporters of the *golpistas* besieged Carrera de San Jerónimo all night long and, from the first minutes of the seizure to the last, soldiers, police and Civil Guards in uniform or plainclothes entered the Cortes at will without anyone knowing with certainty if they were going in to join Tejero and his men or to find out their intentions, to declare support for their cause or to undermine their morale, to take them news from outside or to collect news from inside to inform the authorities, to parley with them or to snoop; even more: many people who approached the Cortes building in the first moments of the coup claim that, in the midst of that uproar, no one seemed to have been absolutely clear whether Aramburu's Civil Guards and Sáenz de Santamaría's police had surrounded the building to subdue the assailants or for their protection, to prevent more contingents of soldiers or civilians from reinforcing their numbers or to give them free entry, to repel the coup or to encourage it. It was an erroneous impression, or at least it became increasingly erroneous as the circumstances of the coup became clear, and, although they may never have gained absolute control over the cordon and didn't entirely seal off the Cortes, towards eight in the evening Aramburu and Sáenz de Santamaría had at least managed to get the blockade of the rebels organized and put a stop to the improvised attempts to bring the seizure to an end in an expeditious manner, removing their fear that an outburst of violence between supporters and opponents of the coup might precipitate with a massive Army intervention the turnaround the *golpistas* were longing for.* Two

* The fear of the consequences of an armed confrontation also served to dissuade Francisco Laína, head of the provisional government, from carrying out a project he was pushing until well into the night – taking the occupied Cortes by force with a special-operations company of the Civil Guard – and which after much doubt and discussion he finally rejected, convinced by Aramburu and Sáenz de Santamaría that Tejero and his men were prepared to repel the attack and that it could only end in a massacre.

of those attempts had happened very early: the first took place half an hour after the assault on the Cortes and featured Colonel Félix Alcalá-Galiano of the national police; the second took place just five minutes later and featured General Aramburu himself. Different versions circulate about what happened in both cases; the most plausible are the following:

Colonel Alcalá-Galiano is one of the first of the high-ranking military commanders to arrive at Carrera de San Jerónimo after the start of the coup. When he does so he has just spoken to General Gabeiras, Chief of the Army General Staff, who had ordered him to enter the Cortes and arrest or eliminate Lieutenant Colonel Tejero. Alcalá-Galiano obeys: he enters the building, locates Tejero and, while speaking to him, awaits his opportunity to capture or kill him; at a certain moment in the conversation, however, Tejero is called to the telephone to speak to Milans' deputy chief of staff in Valencia, Colonel Ibáñez Inglés, who when he hears that Alcalá-Galiano is in the Cortes orders Tejero to disarm and arrest him immediately, but the lieutenant colonel doesn't even have time to try, because Alcalá-Galiano has taken the astute precaution of listening in on another telephone to the conversation between the two rebels and then has the skill, amid strained jokes and friendly words between acquaintances and comrades-in-arms, to persuade Ibáñez Inglés to rescind the order and Tejero lets him return to the street. As for General Aramburu's attempt, it is much less subtle or devious, much more awkward as well. As soon as he arrives at Carrera de San Jerónimo, shortly after Alcalá-Galiano has come back out of the Cortes, Aramburu walks over to the entrance in the company of two of his adjutants and demands to speak to the leader of the mutineers; seconds later Lieutenant Colonel Tejero appears, pistol in hand, his expression and gestures defiant, and without any preambles the general gives him the categorical order to vacate the building and surrender. Aramburu is head of the Civil Guard and therefore the highest authority of the corps to which the lieutenant colonel belongs, but Tejero is not daunted and, brandishing his weapon while a group of rebel Civil Guards aim theirs at Aramburu, answers: 'General, sir, before surrendering I'd shoot you and then myself.' Aramburu's reply is instinctive and consists of reaching for his pistol, but one of his two adjutants holds his arm, prevents him from drawing his weapon and manages to bring the skirmish to a close with no further violence than insubordination and with Aramburu leaving the Cortes furious and stunned, convinced that Tejero's resolution augurs a protracted siege.

This episode took place towards seven in the evening. By then, once past the assailants' initial shouts and gunfire and the panic and stupor of the parliamentarians, journalists and guests who were in the chamber, the Cortes was filled with the rarefied air of a nightmare, or many of those who remained there remember it like that, almost as if the session of confirming the new Prime Minister of the government might be carrying on in a different dimension, or as if just tiny horrific or ridiculous details had been altered, making it subtly unreal. The parliamentarians were walking along the wide corridor that rings the chamber as usual, except with heads bowed, humiliated, fear etched on their faces, escorted by Civil Guards who accompanied them to the toilets and hearing the commanding voices and shouts of jubilation of the *golpistas* resounding through the offices and hallways; sometimes the toilets seemed full of people like in the recesses of the plenary sessions, except the politicians and journalists lined up at the urinals did not exchange the usual unimportant comments, but only sighs of uncertainty, anguish, self-pity or black humour; also as in the recesses of any plenary session, the usual-sized crowd had gathered in the bar, at that time situated by the main entrance of the old building, and the waiters were serving drinks, bringing bills and receiving tips, except that the clientele wasn't made up of politicians and journalists but Civil Guard officers, NCOs and constables armed with Cetme assault rifles and Star submachine guns who hurled encouragement, curses, sharp remarks and patriotic brazenness back and forth across the bar, and except that the *carajillos*, gin-and-tonics, cognacs, shots of whisky and glasses of beer greatly exceeded the usual amount. As for the chamber, after the irruption of the *golpistas*, an ominous silence reigned there interrupted by the coughs of parliamentarians and the occasional orders of the Civil Guards; the silence froze when, ten minutes after the start, a captain walked up the steps to the rostrum to announce the arrival of a military authority who would take charge of the coup, and was shattered when a short time later Adolfo Suárez stood up from his bench and demanded to speak to Lieutenant Colonel Tejero, provoking a commotion that was on the verge of unleashing another burst of gunfire, and ended when the Civil Guards got the Prime Minister to sit down again by way of shouts and threats. Minutes later, undoubtedly to boost the morale of his men and weaken that of his hostages, Tejero announced that Milans had decreed a general mobilization in Valencia. It was not the only announcement of this type the rebels would make from the rostrum over the course of the night: at a certain moment an officer read out to the parliamentarians the war-measures edict Milans had enacted in Valencia; at another, a Civil Guard read out news favourable to the *golpistas* transmitted by press agencies; at another, shortly before midnight, Tejero proclaimed that several military regions – the II, III, IV and the V – had accepted Milans as the new Prime Minister of the government. This news was all the deputies received about what was happening outside the Cortes during the first hours of the seizure; or almost all: circulating in a fragmentary and confused way as well was the news picked up secretly from a transistor radio by former Deputy Prime Minister Fernando Abril Martorell, who sent around airbrushed bulletins to keep his comrades' spirits up. Of course, he didn't keep anybody's spirits up, at least not in those initial hours, when not a single one of the events occurring in the chamber – not even the fact that the announced military authority had not arrived, not even the fact that the assailants had allowed those who were not parliamentarians to leave the Cortes – served to assuage the deputies' anxiety: for a long time the cataclysm seemed inevitable and the tension, anger and brutal behaviour of the Civil Guards did not abate, and around half past seven, after the repeated flickering of the lights in the room made the kidnappers fear a deliberate power cut that would be the prologue to an attempt to get them out of the Cortes by force, Lieutenant Colonel Tejero doubled the guard on the access routes to the chamber and shouted to his men that in the case of a power cut they were to open fire at the slightest sign or sound of anything out of the ordinary, and then he ordered some chairs to be chopped up to set up a bonfire in front of the podium to replace the possible lack of light, which made the deputies shudder, convinced that any fire would automatically spread in that thickly carpeted, wood-lined enclosure. That shudder was just a foretaste of the one that ran through the chamber at twenty to eight, at the moment when several Civil Guards took Adolfo Suárez away and then, successively, General Gutiérrez Mellado, Felipe González, Santiago Carrillo, Alfonso Guerra and Agustín Rodríguez Sahagún. The six of them left the room in the midst of a horrified silence, some white as chalk, all trying to maintain their fortitude, or feign it, and the majority of their colleagues watched them leave with the premonition they would be executed and that the *golpistas* had the same fate in store for many of them. The foreboding did not leave them for most of the night, because the deputies only began very slowly to set aside the fear of a bloodbath and to cherish the hope that the *golpistas* had simply isolated their leaders to negotiate a way out of the coup they never actually negotiated with a military authority they never actually saw.

That was the situation towards 8.30 or nine on the night of 23 February: with the Cortes held hostage, the region of Valencia in revolt, the Brunete Armoured Division and the Captains General still devoured by doubts and the entire country plunged into a frightened, resigned and expectant passivity, the rebels' coup seemed blocked by the Zarzuela's countercoup, and also seemed to be waiting for someone – the rebels or the Zarzuela – to unblock it, removing it from the parentheses in which the partial failure of the first and partial success of the second had enclosed it. That was when two opposed and determining movements started up, one launched from Army General Headquarters, in the Buenavista Palace, and the other from the Zarzuela, one in favour of the coup and the other in favour of the countercoup. Towards 7.30 or eight in the evening, while the King and Fernández Campo were still sounding out the Captains General and demanding they confine their troops to barracks, in the Zarzuela they had begun to discuss the possibility that the King might appear on television with a message to dispel any misunderstanding of his rejection of the assault on the Cortes and reiterate the order to defend legality he'd already issued by telephone and by telex to Milans and the rest of the Captains General; the idea immediately gained urgency, but before they could come up with a satisfactory way to do it the Royal Household had to confront an earlier problem: for the moment it was impossible to record and broadcast the monarch's address because the radio and television studios in Prado del Rey were occupied by a detachment of Brunete cavalry; so the Zarzuela Palace mobilized over the following minutes to remove the *golpistas* from there, until the Marquis of Mondéjar, head of the Royal Household and Cavalry general, after discovering that the occupying force belonged to the 14th Villaviciosa Cavalry Regiment, commanded by Colonel Valencia Remón, finally managed to get his comrade-in-arms to withdraw his men, and a little while later the Zarzuela requested the recently liberated television station to send round a mobile team to record the King's message.

That was the beginning of the first of the two opposing movements, the movement against the coup. The second, the movement in favour of the coup, possibly started to ferment in the minds of the rebel ringleaders not long after the King forbade Armada access to the Zarzuela, and must have strengthened as they understood that the King was not going to support the coup in principle and the Captains General were not in principle disposed to do so either; deep down, the movement was no more than an almost obligatory variation of the original coup plan: in the original plan Armada would arrive at the occupied Cortes from the Zarzuela and, with the explicit backing of the King and of the entire Army, form a coalition or caretaker or unity government under his premiership in exchange for the deputies' liberty and the Army's return to barracks; in this almost obligatory variation Armada would arrive at the Cortes with the same proposal, except not from the Zarzuela but from Army General Headquarters, where he had his command post as Deputy Chief of the Army General Staff, with all the explicit or implicit backing he was able to claim, starting with the backing of the King. For the *golpistas* the movement was more arduous and more unsure than the one originally planned, because no one knew how much support Armada could count on in those circumstances, but, given the unexpected negative reaction towards the coup on the part of the King, it was also, I repeat, almost obligatory, or it was for Milans and for Armada: Milans had acted openly ordering his troops on to the streets and refusing to withdraw them, so he now had no option but to carry on, pushing Armada to carry out the anticipated

plan, though it might be under worse conditions than those anticipated; as for Armada, who had remained stationary and almost
ambushed in Army General Headquarters, trying not to make any
gesture that would give away his involvement in the coup, the movement entailed additional risks, but could also afford some advantages:
if the movement triumphed, Armada would end up leading the government, just as the original plan anticipated, but if it failed it would
cleanse him of the suspicions that had been accumulating around him
since the beginning of the coup, allowing him to appear as the self-
sacrificing though frustrated negotiator of the liberation of the Cortes.
It is probable that towards nine that night Milans and Armada had
each on his own arrived at the conclusion that this movement was
necessary. In any case, half an hour later Milans called the Buenavista
Palace and asked to speak with Armada, at that moment the highest
authority at Army General Headquarters in the absence of General
Gabeiras, who was meeting with the Joint Chiefs of Staff at their headquarters on Calle Vitruvio. The conversation, long and complicated,
was the first the two *golpista* generals held that night, and from then
on, for many of those who soon heard of it, the stalemate of the coup
d'état seemed about to be unblocked; the reality is that it simply entered
a different phase.

PART FOUR

ALL THE COUPS OF THE COUP

The image, frozen, shows the left wing of the chamber of the Congress of Deputies: on the right are the benches, completely occupied by parliamentarians; in the centre, the press gallery is packed with journalists; on the left the Congress table, in profile, with the speakers' rostrum in the foreground. The image is the usual image of a plenary session of the Cortes in the first years of democracy; except for two details: first, the hands of the ministers and deputies are all visible on the armrests in front of their benches; the second one is the presence of a Civil Guard in the chamber: he's stationed in the left corner of the central semicircle, facing the deputies with his finger on the trigger of his automatic assault rifle. These two details destroy any illusion of normality. It is thirty-two minutes past six on the evening of Monday 23 February and exactly nine minutes earlier Lieutenant Colonel Tejero had burst into the Cortes and the coup d'état had begun.

Nothing essential varies in the scene if we unfreeze the image: the Guard armed with the automatic weapon keeps watch to the left and right, taking little steps hushed by the carpet of the central semicircle; the parliamentarians seem petrified in their benches; a silence broken only by a murmur of coughing dominates the chamber. Now the angle changes and the image includes the central semicircle and the right wing of the chamber: in the central semicircle the stenographer and an usher stand up after having spent the last minutes lying on the carpet, and the Secretary of the Congress, Víctor Carrascal – who at the beginning of the coup had been caught by surprise directing the roll-call voting to confirm Leopoldo Calvo Sotelo as the new Prime Minister to replace Adolfo Suárez – stands stiffly under the speakers' rostrum smoking; as for the right wing of the chamber, all

*the ministers and deputies remain there, sitting in their seats, the majority
with their hands visible on the armrests, the majority of them still. Adolfo
Suárez does not belong to this majority, and not only because his hands are
not in sight, but because he does not stop moving in his seat; in reality, he
has not stopped moving since the firing ceased and General Gutiérrez
Mellado returned to sit beside him after his confrontation with the Civil
Guards: restless, he's been turning around to his left, to his right, looking
behind him, he's lit one cigarette after another, he's crossed and recrossed his
legs unceasingly; now he has his back to the chamber, looking at the group
of Civil Guards controlling the entrance, as if he's looking for someone,
maybe Lieutenant Colonel Tejero. But if that's who he's looking for he
doesn't find him, and when he turns around again he sees, at a Civil
Guard's gesture, Víctor Carrascal is ceding his place under the podium to
an usher and, with a cigarette in one hand and the list of deputies' names
in the other, he walks up the steps to the congressional platform, stands at
the speakers' rostrum, drops his suddenly useless papers on the lectern, raises
his eyes and looks to his right and left with an expression halfway between
confusion and entreaty, as if it suddenly struck him as absurd or ridiculous
or dangerous to have climbed up there and he were begging for a place to
hide, or as if in the expectant expressions of his comrades he had just read
that they thought the golpistas had ordered him up there to say something
or to resume the voting where it had been interrupted, and he was trying to
correct the misunderstanding.*

*But the misunderstanding corrects itself. A minute after Víctor Carrascal
goes up to the speakers' rostrum, a captain of the Civil Guard takes his place
to address some words to the whole chamber. The captain is called Jesús
Muñecas and he is lieutenant colonel Tejero's most trusted officer that
evening, as well as having been one of his strongest supporters during the
days before the coup. The lieutenant colonel has asked him to calm
the deputies down and, after examining the chamber for a moment from the
hall – just as a cautious orator might inspect the conditions of the setting in
which he has to give a speech, to adapt it to them – with his automatic
weapon in one hand and his tricorne in the other he walks up to the speakers' rostrum. Nevertheless, as soon as the officer begins his speech someone
disconnects voluntarily or involuntarily the camera that is showing it to us
and, after offering a few nervous and fleeting shots of the captain, the image*

melts into blackness. Luckily there is another camera, situated in the left wing of the chamber, which is still functioning and which, before the captain finishes his address, shows him to us again, almost imperceptible, just a blurry uniformed profile on the extreme right of the image. What on the other hand is perceptible with absolute clarity are his words, which resound through the chamber in the midst of absolute silence. The captain's words are precisely these: 'Good evening. Nothing's going to happen, but we're going to wait a moment for a competent military authority to come to arrange . . . what has to be done and what he himself . . . will tell all of us. So stay calm. I don't know if it'll be a matter of a quarter of an hour, twenty minutes, half an hour . . . I imagine not longer. An authority who is competent, military of course, will be the one who determines what will take place. Of course nothing's going to happen. So you can all calm down.' Nothing more: the captain has spoken with a clear voice, accustomed to giving orders, though not without the odd vacillation or without two sequential stresses – his second mention of the word competent and the word military – betrayed the vigorously neutral tone of his speech's coercive emphasis. Nothing more: the captain walks down the steps of the speakers' rostrum and, while he blends into the group of Civil Guards who've been listening to him from the hall of the chamber, the image freezes again.

Who was the competent authority? Who was the military man whose arrival the hijacked parliamentarians were awaiting in vain throughout the evening and night of 23 February? Ever since the day of the coup this has been one of the official enigmas of the coup; it has also been one of the most exploited deposits of the insatiable embellishments that surround it. In fact, there is hardly a politician of the era who has not proposed his hypothesis on the identity of the soldier, and there is no book on 23 February that has not devised its own: some claim it was General Torres Rojas, who – after relieving General Juste of his command of the Brunete Armoured Division and occupying Madrid – would lead his troops to the Cortes to relieve Lieutenant Colonel Tejero; others argue that it was General Milans, who would arrive in Madrid from Valencia in the name of the King and the rebel Captains General; others conjecture that it was General Fernando de Santiago, Gutiérrez Mellado's predecessor in the post of Deputy Prime Minister and member of a group of generals in the reserves who had been plotting for some time in favour of a coup; others maintain it was the King himself, who would appear in the Cortes to address the deputies in his capacity as head of state and of the Armed Forces. Those four names do not exhaust the number of candidates; there are even those who increase the intrigue not by adding a candidate to the list but by omitting the name of theirs: in 1988 Adolfo Suárez claimed there were only two people who knew the identity of the military officer, and one of them was him. Naturally, there was no one more interested in feeding the mystery than the *golpistas* themselves. In this task Lieutenant Colonel

Tejero excelled, declaring during the 23 February trial that at one of the meetings before the coup Major Cortina had identified the military authority who would come to the Cortes by a code name: the White Elephant; it's very possible that Tejero's testimony was just a fantasy designed to add confusion to the confusion of the first hearing, but some journalist mentioned it in his report and in this way managed to fill in the missing proper name with the energy of a symbol and prolong to this day the vitality of the enigma. An enigma that is no enigma, because the truth is once again obvious: the announced military man could only be General Armada, who in accordance with the *golpistas'* plans would arrive at the Cortes from the Zarzuela and, with the King's authorization and the backing of the mutinous Army, would liberate the parliamentarians in exchange for their acceptance of the formation of a coalition or caretaker or unity government under his leadership. That was what was anticipated and, if it's true that the White Elephant was the code name of the announced soldier, Armada was the White Elephant.

2

Armada was the White Elephant and the military officer announced in the Cortes and the leader of the operation, but those who executed it were General Milans and Lieutenant Colonel Tejero. The three of them wove the plot of the coup. Was there a plot behind the plot? Also from the very day of the coup speculation began over the existence of a civilian plot hidden behind the military plot, a plot that seemed to involve a group of Franco's former ministers, radical tycoons and journalists who had operated in the shadow of the military and inspired and financed them. The fact that the court that prosecuted those involved in 23 February tried only one civilian eventually turned this hidden plot into another of the official enigmas of the coup.

The speculation is not unfounded, but fundamentally it was false. There is a rule rarely broken: when about to embark on a coup d'état, the Army closes in on itself, because at the hour of truth soldiers trust only soldiers; in this case the rule did not prove baseless, and the enigma of the so-called civilian plot is no enigma either: with the exception of the involvement of the odd specific civilian like Juan García Carrés – head of the Francoist Syndicate of Diverse Activities and a personal friend of Tejero's, who was the only civilian prosecuted in the trial for his role as liaison between the lieutenant colonel and General Milans in the months before the coup – behind the rebellious military there was no civilian plot at all: neither former ministers and leaders nor men from Francoist groups like José Antonio Girón de Velasco, nor Gonzalo Fernández de la Mora, nor bankers like the Oriol y Urquijo family, nor journalists like Antonio Izquierdo – editor of *El Alcázar* – nor any of the rest of the members of the far right who've often been mentioned directly ran or inspired the coup, because Armada, Milans and Tejero didn't need any civilian to inspire a military operation and because they wouldn't allow any civilian to interfere in their plans in any more than an anecdotal way (they wouldn't even allow García Carrés to participate in the main preparatory meeting for the coup: he attended, but Milans forced him to leave to avoid civilian interference); as for financing it, the 23 February coup was paid for with funds from the democratic state, which financed the Army.* It's nevertheless true that conspicuous members of the far right – including some of those mentioned above – had magnificent relations with the *golpistas* and maybe knew in advance who was going to stage the coup and where and how and when they were going to stage it; it's also true they'd spent years encouraging it and that, in spite of the often irreconcilable differences that separated them, had the harder version of the coup triumphed, they might have been called upon by the soldiers to administer it, and in any case they would have celebrated with enthusiasm. All this is true, but it's not enough to implicate that group of civilians in the preparations for the coup, a strictly military operation, which, had it achieved its objectives, expected applause from more than just the minority circle of the far right and which, judging by the popular and institutional response to the coup and by the pure logic of things, would most probably have received it. It is said that when the judge presiding at the court martial of José Sanjurjo for the attempted coup d'état of August 1932 asked the general who backed his putsch the soldier's reply was the following: 'Had it triumphed, everyone. Starting with yourself, your honour.' It's best not to deceive ourselves: it is most likely that, had it triumphed, the 23 February coup would have been applauded by an appreciable part of the citizenry, including politicians, organizations and social sectors that condemned it once it failed; years after 23 February Leopoldo Calvo Sotelo put it like this: 'What doubt can there be that

---

* There is one qualification to be made here: the two and a half million pesetas with which Tejero bought six second-hand buses and a few dozen raincoats and anoraks for his Civil Guards to use in the assault on the Cortes – and which in the haste of the last moment were left unused. The origin of this money is unclear; the most credible version claims it was supplied by Juan García Carrés and came from his personal patrimony or from other contributions from associates of the reserve general Carlos Iniesta Cano.

if Tejero had triumphed and Armada's coup had come to fruition, perhaps a million people wouldn't have come out to demonstrate their support, as they did in Madrid on 27 February in support of democracy, maybe there would only have been eight hundred thousand shouting: "*¡Viva Armada!*" ' This is what the *golpistas* expected, and it was not an unfounded expectation; trusting in the approval of the civil society does not mean, however, I insist, that it was directed by civilians: although the far right was clamouring for a coup d'état, on 23 February there was no civilian plot behind the military plot or, if it did exist, it was woven not only by the far right, but also by a whole immature, reckless and bewildered ruling class that, in the midst of the apathy of a society disillusioned with democracy or with the operation of democracy after the hopes at the end of the dictatorship, created favourable conditions for the coup. But this civilian plot was not behind the military plot: it was behind and in front of and around the military plot. The civilian plot was not the civilian plot of the coup: it was the placenta of the coup.

3

Armada, Milans and Tejero. They were the three protagonists of the coup; between the three of them they wove the plot: Armada was the political boss; Milans was the military boss; Tejero was the operational boss of the detonator for the coup, the assault on the Cortes. In spite of their similarities, they were three different men who embarked on the coup guided by disparate political and personal motivations; it may be that the latter are no less important than the former: although history is not governed by personal motivations, behind every historical event there are always personal motivations. The similarities between Armada, Milans and Tejero do not explain the coup; their differences don't explain it either. But without understanding their similarities it's impossible to understand why they organized the coup, and without understanding their differences it's impossible to understand why it failed.

Armada was the most complex of the three, maybe because much more than a military man he was a courtier; an old-school courtier, I should add, like a member of the retinue of a medieval monarch portrayed with the customary anachronisms by a Romantic dramatist: scheming, elusive, haughty, ambitious and sanctimonious, apparently liberal and profoundly traditionalist, an expert on protocol, pretence and the tricks of Palace life endowed with the unctuous manners of a prelate and the countenance of a sad clown. Unlike the immense majority of the high command of the military at the time, the monarchy ran in Armada's veins, because he belonged on all sides to a family of the monarchist aristocracy (his father, also a soldier, grew up with

Alfonso XIII and had been tutor to his son Don Juan de Borbón, the King's father); he was the godson of Queen María Cristina, Alfonso XIII's mother, and held the title of the Marquis of Santa Cruz de Rivadulla. Like all the military high command of the era, Armada was Francoist to the core: he'd fought the three years of the Civil War with Franco, gone to the Russian front with the Blue Division, he'd made his military career in Franco's Army and, thanks to an agreement between Franco and Don Juan de Borbón, in 1955 had become Prince Juan Carlos' private tutor. From that moment on his relationship with the future King grew ever closer and more intense: in 1964 he was named chief adjutant of the Prince's Household, in 1965 secretary of the Prince's Household and in 1976 secretary of the King's Household. Over the course of almost a decade and a half, during which Juan Carlos emerged from adolescence to become an adult and went from being Prince to King, Armada's influence over him was enormous: as the first effective authority of the monarch's milieu (the first theoretical authority was the Marquis of Mondéjar, head of the King's Household), the general controlled his agenda, designed strategies, wrote speeches, screened visitors, organized trips, planned and directed campaigns and attempted to guide Juan Carlos' political and personal life. He did manage to and the King developed a notable degree of dependence on and affection for him, and it's very likely that the privilege of proximity to the monarch and the authority he exercised for a long time over the Palace, allied to his innate patrician arrogance and with the success of the proclamation of the monarchy after four decades of uncertainty, inculcated in Armada the certainty that his destiny was united to that of the King and that the Crown had a future in Spain only if he continued to protect it.

The first half of this certainty vanished in the summer of 1977, shortly after the first democratic elections. It was then that the King informed Armada he'd have to leave his post. The dismissal didn't come into effect until the autumn, but according to an opinion shared by those who knew him the general took the news like a banishment order and privately attributed his fall from grace to Adolfo Suárez's growing influence over the monarch. The attribution was fair: the King had named Suárez Prime Minister against the advice of Armada – who favoured keeping Arias Navarro in the premiership or replacing him with Manuel Fraga, and in any case a Francoist monarchy or a restricted democracy with broad powers reserved for the Crown – and, from the very moment of the new Prime Minister's appointment, confrontations between the two of them were constant: they had acrimonious disagreements over the kidnappings of General Villaescusa and Antonio María de Oriol y Urquijo, which Suárez initially thought the work of the far right and Armada of the far left, over the legalization of the Communist Party, which Armada considered a betrayal of the Army and a surreptitious coup d'état, over letters sent by Armada on Palace letterhead canvassing for votes for Manuel Fraga's party during the electoral campaign of 1977, over a projected divorce law, over just about everything. Suárez would not tolerate interference from the King's secretary, whose legitimacy to argue with his decisions he did not recognize and whom he soon considered an obstacle to political reform; for this reason, when he felt his authority reinforced after his victory in the first democratic elections, the Prime Minister insistently requested the King replace his secretary, and taking advantage of the occasion to emancipate himself from the old tutor of his youth, the King eventually gave way. Armada never forgave Suárez. He had never had the slightest bit of respect for him and never imagined he'd turn into his rival and executioner: he'd had frequent contact with him since the days when Suárez ran Radiotelevisión Española, the national broadcasting corporation, and he'd resorted to his services to promote the Prince's then precarious and vague public image, and his opinion of the future Prime Minister mustn't have been very different from that of so many others who at the beginning of the 1970s considered him a servile and diligent nonentity and an unscrupulous commoner converted to the cause of the monarchy purely out of personal ambition; the fact that this upstart was the one to distance him from the King only helped to harden the hostility he felt for him from that moment on. Armada always denied it, but just leafing through his memoirs, published two years after the coup, one encounters venomous allusions to the Prime Minister at every turn; he writes of Arias Navarro, Suárez's predecessor: 'He cannot be blamed for the later problems, nor for the loss of the values that history and tradition tell us are the soul of Spain. It is *others* who have caused this situation' (the italics are his); of Manuel Fraga, who according to him should have occupied Suárez's place, he claims: 'Life is like that and often sacrifices the best to give passage and positions of responsibility to insolent people with neither ideas nor scruples.' One doesn't need great deductive gifts to guess who this insolent one with neither ideas nor scruples who provoked the loss of Spain's soul might be.

Armada didn't resign himself to his exile from the Zarzuela. On leaving the Palace he went back to his military career with assiduous proclamations of enthusiasm, first as professor of tactics at the Army's Higher Education College and later as director of general services at Headquarters, but he spent the following three years nursing his grudge against Adolfo Suárez as well as the *idée fixe* of recovering his place at the King's side. The post of secretary had been filled by Sabino Fernández Campo – a personal friend who he hoped would facilitate his return to court, perhaps as master of the Royal Household – and, through him and friends who still remained in the Palace, he did his utmost to maintain contact with the Zarzuela, sending reports or messages to the King, sending personal greetings to members of the Royal Family on their birthdays, saints' days and Christmas, and seeking a place at his audiences and public receptions, convinced that sooner or later the monarch would understand his error and summon him back to his side to re-establish a relationship on which the former secretary continued to think the future of the Crown in Spain depended. At the beginning of 1980 Armada was named military governor of Lérida and commander of the 4th Urgell Mountain Division; among his duties required by protocol was to pay respects to the Royal Family on their winter ski trips to the region, and that facilitated the renewal of relations between the general and the King: they saw each other once in the month of February, had dinner a couple of times in the spring. That reconciliation, that return to the confidence of former times came about at the moment when the King was losing confidence in Suárez and when his collapse and the country's crisis seemed to confirm Armada's predictions, and the former royal secretary's political ambition and courtier's mentality might have interpreted that coincidence as an omen that the time for revenge was nigh: Suárez had removed him from power and the fall of Suárez could mean his return to power. The year 1980 did nothing to correct this interpretation, and the months before the coup even less, when, as Suárez grew more and more distanced from the King, Armada drew closer – often meeting with him in private, discussing the political and military situation and the replacement of the Prime Minister, securing a prime posting for him in Madrid – almost as if he and Suárez were two royal favourites vying for the favour of the King who was seeking a way to replace one with the other. That's probably what Armada thought on the eve of 23 February and that's why the coup for him was not just a way to recover a restricted democracy or Francoist monarchy that had been his political ideal from the start, but also a way to finish off Adolfo Suárez and – entirely recovering the King's favour – to recover and multiply the power Suárez had taken away from him.

For Milans the 23 February coup was something quite different, not because he was not moved by personal concerns, but because deep down Milans was a quite different kind of man from Armada. Not superficially: like Armada, Milans was a soldier with aristocratic roots; like Armada, Milans professed a double fidelity to Francoism and to the monarchy. But, unlike Armada, Milans was more Francoist than monarchist, and he was especially much more of a soldier. Son, grand-son, great-grandson and great-great-grandson of eminent *golpista* soldiers – his father, his great-grandfather and his great-great-grandfather all reached the rank of lieutenant general, his grandfather was the Captain General of Catalonia and commander of Alfonso XIII's Military Chamber – and by 1981 Milans represented better than anyone, with his eventful profile of an old warrior and his considerable military curriculum, not just in Franco's Army, but in the Army of the Victory. In 1936, as a cadet at the Infantry Academy, he entered the saints' calendar of Francoist heroes by defending the Alcázar de Toledo for the two and a half months the Republican siege lasted: there he received his first war wound; in the six years that followed he received quite a few more, three of them fighting with the VII Battalion of the Spanish Legion in Madrid, on the Ebro and in Teruel, and the last with the Blue Division in Russia. He returned to Spain with the rank of captain and his chest covered in medals, among them the Army's most coveted:

a Laureate Cross of San Fernando, an individual military medal, two collective ones, five military crosses, three red crosses for military valour and a Nazi Iron Cross. No Spanish soldier of his generation could boast a similar campaign-service record, in spite of being the only one of them to obtain General Staff diplomas from all three branches of the Armed Forces, at the death of Franco nobody embodied better than Milans the prototype of the wind-and-weather military man idealized by Francoism, a man of succinct ideas, allergic to desk work and books, direct, efficient, visceral and without duplicity. In this sense Milans could not be further removed from the Palace deviousness of Armada; nor, of course, from the clumsiness or softness in the exercise of command, the technical mentality, intellectual curiosity and reflective and tolerant inclinations of Gutiérrez Mellado. I do not mention his name by chance: just as it is perhaps impossible to understand Armada's actions on 23 February without understanding his bitterness towards Adolfo Suárez, it is perhaps impossible to understand Milans' actions on that day without understanding his aversion to Gutiérrez Mellado.

Although Milans and Gutiérrez Mellado had known each other for a long time, Milans' animosity did not have a remote origin; it was born when Gutiérrez Mellado agreed to join Suárez's first government and grew as the general turned into the Prime Minister's most loyal ally and designed and put into practice a plan whose objective consisted of terminating the privileges of power conceded to the Army by the dictatorship and turning it into an instrument of democracy: Milans not only felt personally passed over and humiliated by the promotion policies of Gutiérrez Mellado, who did everything he could to keep him away from the top command positions and thus spare him *golpista* temptations; sheltered in his ultraconservative ideas and devotion to Franco, he also suffered as an insult Gutiérrez Mellado's aspiration to dismantle Franco's victorious Army, which he considered the only legitimate guarantee of the legitimate ultraconservative state founded by Franco and in consequence the only institution qualified to prevent another war (like the far right, like the far left, Milans was allergic to the word reconciliation, to his mind a simple euphemism for the word treason: several members of his family had been murdered during the conflict, and Milans felt that a worthy present could not forget the past, but must be founded on its permanent remembrance and on the prolongation of the triumph of Francoism over the Republic, which for him equalled the triumph of civilization over barbarism). Milans found in these two personal offences argument enough to condemn Gutiérrez Mellado to the condition of an upstart prepared to violate his oath of loyalty to Franco in order to satisfy his filthy political ambitions; this explains why he encouraged with all the means within reach, including chairmanship of the founding board of *El Alcázar*, a savage press campaign that left not a single nook of Gutiérrez Mellado's personal, political or military life unexplored in search of ignominy with which to persuade his comrades-in-arms that the man who was carrying out a treacherous purge of the Armed Forces lacked the slightest inkling of moral or professional integrity; and this explains also why, as soon as Gutiérrez Mellado entered the government, Milans came to embody the Army's resistance to Gutiérrez Mellado's military reforms and to the political reforms that allowed them: between the end of 1976 and beginning of 1981 the Army barely saw a protest against the government, a serious disciplinary incident or a whisper of conspiracy Milans was not mixed up in or in which Milans' name was not invoked. He boasted of never having deceived anybody and of never hiding his intentions, and during those years – first as commander of the Brunete Armoured Division and then as Captain General of Valencia – frequently used the threat of a coup: he liked to joke about it ('Your Majesty,' he said to the King over drinks at the end of one of the monarch's visits to Brunete. 'One more rum and I'll order the tanks out on to the streets!'); the first time he really did so was after a tumultuous meeting of the High Command of the Armed Forces held on 12 April 1977, three days after Adolfo Suárez legalized the PCE with the support of Gutiérrez Mellado and contrary to what he had himself promised the military or contrary to what the military believed he'd promised. 'The Prime Minister gave his word of honour that he would not legalize the Communist Party,' Milans said that day to his comrades-in-arms. 'Spain cannot have a Prime Minister without honour: we should order our tanks out on to the streets.' In the almost three years he was in command of the Captaincy General of Valencia similar expressions were frequently on his lips. 'Don't worry, Señora,' he was heard to say more than once to the ladies who flattered him at receptions, urging him to become the saviour of the nation in danger. 'I won't retire without ordering the tanks out on to the street.' He kept his word in the nick of time: on 23 February he was just four months away from being retired to the reserves; he also kept faith with his *golpista* and monarchist genes, given that, in spite of being a staunch Francoist, his coup did not aspire to be a coup against the monarchy, but rather with the monarchy. Like Armada, who was sure he'd be able to dominate the Zarzuela that day with his authority as the King's former secretary, on 23 February Milans was guilty of pride: he considered himself the most prestigious officer in the Army and believed his illusory aspect of invincible general would be enough to drag the rest of the Captains General along on an uncertain adventure and to bring the Brunete to mutiny without having prepared them to do so. He achieved neither one thing nor the other, and that was one of the reasons why the 23 February coup did not end up being what Milans had anticipated: a way of getting even for the humiliations Gutiérrez Mellado had inflicted on him and on his Army and also a way – recovering under the King's command the foundations of the state installed by Franco – of recovering for the Army of the Victory the power Gutiérrez Mellado had wrenched away.

The final protagonist of the coup was Lieutenant Colonel Tejero. He is the icon of the coup and it's obvious that he had an icon's vocation and that his appearance like that of a Civil Guard from a local vignette or from a Lorca poem or from a Berlanga film – robust body, bushy moustache, fervent look in his eye, nasal voice and Andalusian accent – contributed to his vocation as an icon; but it's also obvious that he was not the impetuous mediocrity the cliché of 23 February wanted him to be and the whole country insisted on constructing after 23 February, as if a collective guilty conscience for the complete lack of opposition to the coup needed to demonstrate to itself that only a lunatic could assault the Cortes at gunpoint and therefore the coup was just a nonsense that didn't need to be resisted because it was doomed to failure from the start. It's not true: Tejero was absolutely not a fairground madman; he was something much more dangerous: he was an idealist prepared to bend reality to his ideals, prepared to maintain loyalty to those he considered his own at any price, prepared to impose good and eliminate evil by force; on 23 February Tejero also proved to be many other things, but only because he was first and foremost an idealist. That Tejero's ideals strike us as perverse and anachronistic does not qualify the goodness or evil of his intentions, because evil is often concocted from good and perhaps good from evil; much less does it authorize us to attribute his misdemeanour to a picturesque derangement: if Tejero had been deranged he would not have prepared for months and carried out successfully a complex and dangerous operation like the assault on the Cortes, he would not have been able to keep the almost absolute control he kept over the hostage-taking for the seventeen and a half hours it lasted, he would not have known how to play his cards and would not have manoeuvred to achieve his objectives with the serene rationality with which he did so; if he had been deranged, if he'd taken his madness to its limit, perhaps the seizure of the Cortes would have ended in slaughter and not the negotiation with which it ended once he was certain the coup had failed. The reality is that Tejero was a technically competent officer who had been assigned to positions of maximum responsibility – like the command of the San Sebastián Civil Guard – and who, though his fiery and emotional idealism provoked the suspicion of his commanders and comrades, also inspired the devotion of his subordinates. It is unnecessary to add that he was a fanatic from having ingested tons of patriotic pabulum, a moralist blinded by the vanity of virtue and a megalomaniac with an indomitable yearning for prominence. By temperament and by mentality he was quite distant from Armada, but not from Milans. Like Milans, Tejero considered himself a man of action, and he was; the difference is that Milans had been one most of all during his youth in an open civil war while Tejero had been one most of all as an adult during an undercover war in the Basque Country. Like Milans, Tejero dreamt of a utopia of Spain as a barracks – a radiant place of order, brotherhood and harmony regulated by reveilles and taps under the radiant rule of God – the difference is that Milans accepted the gradual conquest of utopia while Tejero aspired to put the revolution into immediate effect. Like Milans, Tejero was a Francoist above all; the difference is that, precisely because he belonged to a later generation

than Milans and hadn't seen the war or known any Spain other than
Franco's Spain, Tejero was if possible even more Francoist than Milans:
he idolized Franco, he was ruled by the triad in capital letters of God,
Fatherland and the Military, his mortal enemy was Marxism, that is
Communism, that is the Anti-Spain, that is the enemies of the utopia
of Spain as barracks, who should be eradicated from the native soil
before they managed to poison it. This last of course formed part of the
far right's rhetorical bible in the 1970s, but for Tejero's literal sentimentalism it also constituted an exact description of reality and an ethical
command: in Tejero it grew into a finished fusion between patriotism
and religion and, as Sánchez Ferlosio says, 'It's when there is God that
all is permitted; as there is no one more ferociously dangerous than the
just, with right on their side.' From there, as for the whole of the far
right, for Tejero, Santiago Carrillo came to represent something like
what Adolfo Suárez represented for Armada and Gutiérrez Mellado for
Milans: the personification of all the misfortunes of the nation and, in
the midst of his hysterical egocentrism that allowed him to feel himself
to be the personification of the nation, the personification of all its
misfortunes; and from there as well, because the fusion between patriotism and religion dehumanizes the adversary and turns him into evil,
as soon as he glimpsed the return to Spain of the Anti-Spain his escha-
tological fanaticism imposed the duty to finish it off, and from then on
he exchanged his military record for a record of rebellion.

The percussion cap for this string of insubordination was what Tejero
considered the unmasked manifestation of the Anti-Spain: terrorism.
During the 23 February trial his defence lawyer described an episode
that happened after the murder at the hands of ETA of one of the Civil
Guards under his command at the Guipúzcoa station; more than an
event it was an image, a gruesome but not faked image: the image of
the lieutenant colonel bending over the corpse destroyed by an explosion and standing up with his lips and uniform stained with the blood
of his subordinate. It's very probable that Tejero never knew how to or
wanted to or could experience terrorism as anything but a savage intimate aggression, and there is no doubt that it was terrorism that turned
him into a chronic rebel and saturated him with justification as long as
the state showed itself incapable of putting a stop to it and part

of society seemed indifferent to the ravages it caused among his comrades-in-arms. In January 1977, not long after the murder of one of his men, the lieutenant colonel was relieved of his command in Guipúzcoa and placed under a month's arrest for sending a sarcastic telegram to the Minister of the Interior, who had just legalized the Basque flag while, as he repeated every time the incident was mentioned, the city of San Sebastián was filled with burning Spanish flags; in October of the same year he was relieved of his command in Málaga and again placed under arrest for another month after forbidding an authorized demonstration pistol in hand with the argument that ETA had just killed two Civil Guards and all of Spain should be in mourning; in August 1978, while the political parties discussed the projected Constitution, he was arrested for fourteen days for publishing in *El Imparcial* an open letter to the King in which he requested that he, as head of state and of the Armed Forces, prevent the approval of any text that did not include 'some of the values for which we believe our lives are worth risking', that he enact a law capable of ending the massacre of terrorism and finishing off 'the apologists of this bloody farce, whether or not they might be parliamentarians and sit among the fathers of the nation'; in November 1978 he was arrested and tried for planning a coup that anticipated the 23 February coup – the so-called Operation Galaxia: the idea was to take the Cabinet hostage in the Moncloa Palace and, with the help of the rest of the Army, then oblige the King to form a government of national salvation – but less than a year later was released from prison in the middle of 1980 after the court sentenced him to an insignificant term which he'd already served, and which convinced him that he could try again without running any greater risk than to spend a short and comfortable time in jail, converted into a semi-secret hero of the Army and a resounding hero of the far right. That was when he acquired a passion for notoriety; that was when the obsession with a coup became lodged in his brain; that's when he began to prepare 23 February. The idea was his: he gave birth to it and nursed it and raised it; Milans and Armada wanted to adopt it, subordinating it to their ends, but by that time the lieutenant colonel already felt himself to be its proprietor and when, on the night of 23 February, he came to realize that the two generals were pursuing the triumph of a different coup than the one he'd bred, Tejero preferred the failure of the coup over the triumph of a coup that wasn't his, because he thought the triumph of Milans and Armada's coup did not guarantee the immediate realization of his utopia of Spain as barracks and the liquidation of the Anti-Spain that no one personified better than Santiago Carrillo, or because for Tejero the coup d'état was more than anything a way to finish off Santiago Carrillo or what Santiago Carrillo personified and – recovering the radiant order of brotherhood and harmony regulated by reveilles under the radiant rule of God that had been abolished with the arrival of democracy – to recover what Santiago Carrillo, or what Santiago Carrillo personified to him, had wrenched away.

Tejero understood it quite well: it's not just that the three protagonists of the coup were profoundly different and were acting on different political and personal motivations; it's that each of them was pursuing a different coup and on the night of 23 February the two generals were trying to make use of the coup conceived by the lieutenant colonel in order to impose their own: Tejero was against democracy and against the monarchy and his coup was essentially meant to be a coup similar in content to the coup that in 1936 tried to overthrow the Republic and provoked the war and then Francoism; Milans was against democracy, but not against the monarchy, and his coup was essentially meant to be a coup similar in form and content to the coup that in 1923 overthrew the parliamentary monarchy and installed the monarchist dictatorship of Primo de Rivera, that is a military *pronunciamiento* to return to the King the powers he'd handed over by sanctioning the Constitution and, maybe after an intermediate phase, to lead to a military junta that would serve as a means of support to the Crown; finally, Armada was not against the monarchy nor (at least in a frontal or explicit way) against democracy, but only against the democracy of 1981 or against the democracy of Adolfo Suárez, and essentially his coup was meant to be a coup similar in form to the coup that led General de Gaulle to the presidency of the French Republic in 1958 and in content a sort of palace coup that should allow him to play with more authority than ever his role as the King's right-hand man, turning him into the Prime Minister of a coalition or caretaker or unity government with the mission of reducing democracy to the point of turning it into a semi-democracy or a substitute for democracy. The 23 February coup was an extraordinary coup because it was a single coup and three different coups in one: before 23 February Armada, Milans and Tejero believed their coup was the same one, and this belief allowed the coup to happen; during the course of 23 February Armada, Milans and Tejero discovered that their coup was in reality three different coups, and this discovery provoked the failure of the coup. That's what happened, at least from the political point of view; from the personal point of view what happened was even more extraordinary: Armada, Milans and Tejero staged in a single coup three different coups against three different men or against what three different men personified for them, and those three men – Suárez, Gutiérrez Mellado and Carrillo: the three men who'd carried the weight of the transition, the three men who had staked the most on democracy, the three men who had most to lose if democracy were destroyed – were precisely the only three politicians present in the Cortes who showed themselves willing to risk their necks by facing up to the *golpistas*. This triple symmetry also forms a strange figure, maybe the strangest figure of all the strange figures of 23 February, and the most perfect, as if its form were suggesting a signifi-cance that we were incapable of grasping, but without which it's impossible to grasp the significance of 23 February.

4

They were three traitors; I mean: for those to whom they owed loyalty through family ties, social class, beliefs, ideas, vocation, history, common interest or simple gratitude, Adolfo Suárez, Gutiérrez Mellado and Santiago Carrillo were three traitors. Not just to them; they were for many more people, and in a certain sense they are objectively: Santiago Carrillo betrayed the ideals of Communism by undermining its revolutionary ideology and placing it on the threshold of democratic socialism, and betrayed forty years of anti-Francoist struggle by declining to see justice done to those responsible for and complicit in Francoist injustice and forcing his party to make real, symbolic and sentimental concessions imposed by his pragmatism and by his lifelong pact with Adolfo Suárez; Gutiérrez Mellado betrayed Franco, betrayed Franco's Army, betrayed the Army of the Victory and its radiant utopia of order, brotherhood and harmony regulated by reveilles under the radiant rule of God; Suárez was the worst, the total traitor, because his treason made possible the treason of the others: he betrayed the single fascist party in which he'd been raised and to which he owed all that he was, he betrayed the political principles he'd sworn to defend, he betrayed the Francoist leaders and barons who trusted him to prolong Francoism and he betrayed the military with his veiled promises to keep the Anti-Spain in check. In their way, Armada, Milans and Tejero could imagine themselves as classical heroes, champions of an ideal of triumph and conquest, paladins of loyalty to clear, immovable principles who aspired to reach fulfilment by imposing their positions; Suárez, Gutiérrez Mellado and Carrillo gave up doing so from the

moment they began their task of retreat and demolition and dismantling and sought fulfilment by abandoning their positions, undermining
themselves unknowingly. The three of them committed political and
personal errors during the course of their lives, but that brave renunciation defines them. Deep down Milans was right (as were the
ultraright-wingers and ultraleft-wingers of the day): in the Spain of
the 1970s the word reconciliation was a euphemism for the word treason, because there was no reconciliation without treason or at least
without some betrayal. Suárez, Gutiérrez Mellado and Carrillo betrayed
more than anyone, and therefore were often called traitors. In a certain
sense they were: they betrayed their loyalty to an error in order to
construct their loyalty to a truth; they betrayed their own people in
order not to betray themselves; they betrayed the past in order not to
betray the present. Sometimes you can be loyal to the present only by
betraying the past. Sometimes treason is more difficult than loyalty.
Sometimes loyalty is a form of courage, but other times it is a form of
cowardice. Sometimes loyalty is a form of betrayal and betrayal is a
form of loyalty. Maybe we don't know exactly what loyalty is or what
betrayal is. We have an ethics of loyalty, but we don't have an ethics of
betrayal. We need an ethics of betrayal. The hero of retreat is a hero
of betrayal.

5

Let me recapitulate: the 23 February coup was an exclusively military coup, led by General Armada, plotted by General Armada himself, General Milans and by Lieutenant Colonel Tejero, encouraged by the Francoist far right and facilitated by a series of political manoeuvres through which a large part of the country's ruling class intended to put an end to Adolfo Suárez's premiership. All right then: when did it all begin? Where did it all begin? Who began it all? How did it all begin? There is no protagonist, witness or investigator of the coup who doesn't have answers to these questions, but there are barely two identical answers. In spite of being contradictory, many of them are valid; or might be: segmenting history is an arbitrary exercise; strictly speaking, it's impossible to pin down the exact origin of a historic event, just as it's impossible to pin down its exact end: every event has its origins in a previous event, which originates in another previous event, which originates in another, and so on, because history is like matter and within it nothing is created or destroyed: it only transforms. General Gutiérrez Mellado said more than once that the 23 February coup originated in November 1975, at the same moment when, after being proclaimed King before the Francoist Cortes, the monarch declared that he intended to be King of all Spaniards, which meant that his aim was to bring to an end the irreconcilable two Spains that Francoism perpetuated. It is an opinion accepted by many that the coup began on 9 April 1977, when the Army felt that Suárez had deceived it by legalizing the Communist Party and had betrayed Spain by giving naturalization papers to the Anti-Spain. There are those who choose to situate the beginning of the plot in the Zarzuela Palace itself, some months later, the day when Armada found out he'd have to give up the secretariat of the Royal Household, or, better yet, some years later, when the monarch began to contribute to the political manoeuvres against Adolfo Suárez with his words and his silences and when he considered or let it be believed that he was considering the possibility of replacing the government led by Suárez with a coalition or caretaker or unity government led by a military man. Maybe the simplest or least inexact would be to go back a little bit further, just to the day at the end of the summer of 1978 when the front page of every newspaper handed Lieutenant Colonel Tejero the formula for the coup he'd been brooding on for some time by then and which would grow over the following months like a tapeworm in his brain: on 22 August that year, the Sandinista commander Edén Pastora launched an assault on the National Palace in Managua and, after holding hostage for several days more than a thousand politicians with links to the dictator Anastasio Somoza, managed to liberate a large group of Sandinista National Liberation Front political prisoners; the Nicaraguan guerrilla leader's audacity dazzled the lieutenant colonel and, superimposed on the nineteenth-century memory of General Pavía's Civil Guards dissolving the Parliament of the First Republic by force, catalyzed his *golpista* obsession and inspired first the so-called Operation Galaxia, which just a few weeks later he unsuccessfully tried to execute, and finally the 23 February coup. Perhaps with the exception of the first of them – too vague, too imprecise – any of the conjectures mentioned might serve as the origin of the coup, or at least as the starting point for explaining it. I dare to choose another, no less arbitrary but maybe more apt for what I propose to do in the pages that follow: describe the plot of the coup, an almost seamless fabric of private conversations, confidences and understandings that I can often only try to reconstruct from indirect testimonies, stretching the limits of the possible until they touch the probable and with the pattern of the plausible trying to outline the shape of the truth. Naturally, I cannot guarantee that everything I am about to tell is true; but I can guarantee that it is concocted with truth and especially that it is the closest I can get to the truth, or to imagining it.

Madrid, July 1980. At the beginning of this month two events took place in the capital that we can suppose were simultaneous or almost simultaneous: the first was a lunch Lieutenant Colonel Tejero had with an emissary of General Milans; the second was the arrival at the Zarzuela Palace of a report sent by General Armada. We know the context in which they occurred: in the summer of that year ETA was killing left, right and centre, the second oil crisis was laying waste to the Spanish economy and, after being swept aside in several regional elections and suffering a humiliating motion of no-confidence from the Socialists, Adolfo Suárez seemed to be refusing to govern as he rapidly lost the Parliament's confidence, his party's confidence, the King's confidence and the confidence of a country, which in turn seemed also to be rapidly losing confidence in democracy or in the functioning of democracy. The coup plotters' lunch was held at a restaurant in the centre of the capital and was attended, as well as by Tejero, by Lieutenant Colonel Mas Oliver, General Milans' aide-de-camp, by Juan García Carrés, personal friend of Tejero's and the link between the two, and perhaps by retired General Carlos Iniesta Cano. Although it was through an intermediary, it was the first contact between Milans and Tejero, and there was talk of politics but most of all the talk was of the project of assaulting the Cortes conceived by Tejero, and days or weeks later, at another similar lunch, again through his aide-de-camp Milans charged the lieutenant colonel with studying the idea and keeping him informed of progress; in spite of awaiting ratification from a military tribunal of the sentence handed down by a court martial in the month of May for his involvement in Operation Galaxia, and in spite of suspecting that he was being followed, Tejero immediately began preparations for the coup and during the following months, while keeping in contact with Milans through Mas Oliver, he took photographs of the Cortes building, found out about the security measures that protected it and rented an industrial warehouse in the city of Fuenlabrada where he stored clothing and six buses he'd bought with the intention of camouflaging and transporting his troops on the day of the coup.

Thus began the plot captained by Milans, a military operation that remained secret until it burst out on 23 February. The arrival at the

Zarzuela Palace of the King's former secretary's report marked the beginning of a series of more or less public movements later baptized with the name *Operación Armada* (meaning 'Armed Operation' but also a play on the general's name) and destined to lead Armada to the head of the government, a political operation initially independent of the previous one but over the course of time converging with it, which would turn Armada into the leader of both: the military operation ended up being the battering ram of the political operation and the political operation ended up being the military operation's alibi. The text of the report received at the Zarzuela Palace had been handed by Armada to Sabino Fernández Campo, the King's secretary, and it was the work of a law professor whose identity we do not know; it was just a few pages long, and in them, after a description of the deterioration the country was going through, its author proposed as a remedy to the political chaos that Adolfo Suárez should leave power by way of a no-confidence vote backed by the PSOE, by Manuel Fraga's right wing and by dissident sectors of the UCD; the manoeuvre should conclude with the formation of a unity government led by an independent figure, perhaps from the military.

That was the content of the report. We don't know if the King read it, although we do know that Fernández Campo read it and that no one at the Zarzuela Palace made any comment on it to Armada at the time, but in the following weeks, while the rumour went round that the PSOE was preparing a new no-confidence motion against Adolfo Suárez, the text circulated through offices, newspaper editorial rooms and news agencies, and in a very short time the hypothesis of a unity government led by a military man as a life raft against the sinking of the country had reached every corner of the Madrid political village. 'I know the PSOE is weighing up the possibility of bringing a soldier in to be Prime Minister of the government,' Suárez declared to the press at some point in July; and he added: 'I think it's crazy.' But many didn't consider it crazy; more than that: during the months of July, August and September the idea seemed to permeate Spanish political life like a ubiquitous murmur, transformed into a plausible option. A general was being sought: there was a unanimous accord that it should be a prestigious, liberal military officer, with political experience, on good terms with the King and able to bring together the approval of the parties of the right, of the centre and of the left and assemble them in a government that would spread optimism, impose order, tackle the economic crisis and put a stop to ETA and to the danger of a coup d'état; bets were placed: given the identikit portrait of the redeeming general appeared to fit his political and personal features, the name of Alfonso Armada figured on every list. It's very possible that people close to him, like Antonio Cortina – brother of the head of AOME and distinguished member of Manuel Fraga's Alianza Popular – promoted his candidacy, but it's beyond doubt that no one did as much as Armada himself. Taking advantage of his frequent trips from Lérida to Madrid, where he still had his family home, and taking advantage especially of his summer holidays, Armada increased his presence at dinners and lunches with politicians, military officers, businessmen and bankers; in spite of the fact that since his departure from the Zarzuela his encounters with the monarch had been only sporadic, in those meetings Armada took on his former authority as royal secretary to present himself as interpreter not only of the King's thinking, but also of his desires, in such a way that, in a toing and froing of double meanings, insinuations and half-spoken words that decades of courtly ruses had taught him to wield with dexterity, anyone who talked to Armada ended up convinced that it was the King who was talking through him and all that Armada was saying the King was also saying. Of course, it was false, but, like all good lies, it contained a part of the truth, because what Armada was saying (and what everyone thought the King was saying through Armada) was a wisely balanced combination of what the King was thinking and what Armada would have liked the King to think: Armada assured everyone that the King was very anxious, that the situation of the country had him very worried, that the Army's permanent restlessness had him very worried, that his relations with Suárez were bad, that Suárez didn't listen to him any more and his clumsiness, negligence, irresponsibility and foolish attachment to power were putting the country and the Crown at risk, and that he would look very kindly on a change of Prime Minister (which entailed exactly what the King was thinking at that moment); but Armada also said (and everyone thought the King was saying it through Armada) that these were exceptional circumstances that demanded exceptional solutions and that a government of national unity composed of leaders of the main political parties and led by a military officer was a good solution, and he let it be understood that he himself, Armada, was the best candidate possible to head it up (all of which entailed exactly what Armada would have liked the King to be thinking and maybe partly through Armada's influence what he would come to think at some point, but not what he was thinking at that moment). Towards the middle or end of September, while the monarch's former secretary was returning to his post in Lérida and his presence was dwindling in Madrid and the political year was getting under way again after the holidays, Operation Armada seemed to lose the wind from its sails in the gossip shops of the capital, as if it had just been an excuse to while away the idle hours of summer heat without news; but what actually happened was something else, and the thing is that, although in the gossip shops of the capital it got buried by the breakdown of the government and Suárez's departure and by the avalanche of operations against the Prime Minister that were beginning to shape the placenta of the coup, Operation Armada remained very much alive in the mind of its protagonist and those around him who continued to consider it the ideal form for the touch on the rudder or surgical coup so many thought the country needed. Armada maintained good relations with politicians in the government, in the party that kept it in power and in the right-wing party – including its leader: Manuel Fraga – and during his summer encounters all had welcomed his promotional periphrases with sufficient interest to authorize him to trust that when the moment came all would accept him as a replacement for Suárez; Armada did not, however, know the Socialist leaders, whose agreement was necessary for his operation, and in the first weeks of the autumn the possibility arose of talking to them. He didn't get to speak with Felipe González (as might have been his aim), but he did speak to Enrique Múgica, the number three of the PSOE who was in charge of military affairs within the party; a few pages ago I described their meeting: it was held on 22 October in Lérida and was a success for Armada, who came out of it with the certainty that the Socialists not only sympathized with the idea of a unity government led by a military officer, but also with the idea that the officer should be him. Nevertheless, like the constitutionalist's report he'd sent to the Zarzuela in July and his summer propaganda campaign in the salons of the political village of Madrid, the meeting with the PSOE was for Armada a simple preparatory manoeuvre for the central manoeuvre: winning the King over to Operation Armada.

On 12 November the King and Armada met in La Pleta, a mountain cabin in the Arán Valley that the Royal Family used when they went skiing. The encounter formed part of the obligations or courtesies required by protocol of the military governor of Lérida, but the King and his former secretary had not seen each other for a long time – probably since the previous spring – and the conversation went on long past the bounds of protocol. The two men talked about politics: as by then he did with so many people, it's very possible that the King may have ranted and raved against Suárez and expressed his alarm over the state of the country; as the unity government led by a military officer was a hypothesis that was in the streets and had arrived at the Zarzuela by various routes, it's possible that the King and the general talked about it: in such a case, Armada would certainly have been in favour of the idea, although neither of the two would have mentioned his candidacy for the position; but what they undoubtedly talked most about was military discontent, which the King feared and Armada exaggerated, which might explain why the King would have asked the general to investigate it and inform him. This request was the reason or the excuse for Armada's next move. Barely five days later the former royal secretary travelled to Valencia to meet with Milans, aware that there was no more discontented officer than Milans in the whole Army and that any *golpista* intrigue would start from or lead to Milans, or be adjacent to him. The two generals had known each other since the 1940s, when they'd both fought in Russia with the Blue Division; their friendship had never been a close one, but their long-standing monarchist adhesion distinguished them from their comrades-in-arms and represented an added connection that afternoon and once on their own – after a lunch at headquarters accompanied by their wives and Lieutenant Colonel Mas Oliver, Milans' aide-de-camp, and Colonel Ibáñez Inglés, his deputy chief of staff – allowed them to expose their projects clearly to each other, or at least allowed Milans to do so. Both agreed on the diagnosis of the calamitous state of the country, a diagnosis shared by the media, political parties and social organizations entirely free of suspicion of far-right sympathies; they also agreed on the convenience of the Army intervening in the matter, although they disagreed on the way of doing so: with his customary frankness, Milans declared himself willing to head up a monarchist coup, he talked of distant meetings with generals in Játiva, or perhaps in Jávea, and of recent meetings in Madrid and Valencia, and it's even probable that already during that first meeting he mentioned the operation being planned by Tejero, from whom he continued to receive news thanks to his aide-de-camp. For his part, Armada talked of his conversation with the King or invented several conversations with the King and an intimacy with the monarch that no longer existed or that didn't exist as it once had – the King was anguished, he said; the King was fed up with Suárez, he said; the King thought it necessary to do something, he said – and he talked of his political soundings in the summer and autumn and of his project of forming a unity government under his leadership which would name him, Milans, President of the Joint Chiefs of Staff; he also told him that the King approved of this emergency measure, and reasoned that their two projects were complementary because his political project might need the help of a military push, and that in any case they were both pursuing common objectives and for the good of Spain and the Crown they should act in a coordinated way and maintain contact.

Convinced that Armada was speaking in the King's name, eager to convince himself of it, Milans accepted the deal, and in this way *Operación Armada* gained a military battering ram: through Milans the former royal secretary subdued the military officers in favour of a coup and could wield the threat or reality of force at the moment most convenient to his aims. It was like cresting a hill. Until that moment Operation Armada was a purely political operation meant to impose itself through purely political means; from that moment on it was more than a political operation, since it was keeping in reserve the resource of a military coup in case of not being able to impose itself through purely political means. The difference was obvious, although Armada probably did not want to perceive it, at least not yet: he probably told himself that his meeting with Milans had been just his way of carrying out the task of finding out information for the King and cooling the Captain General's *golpista* fervour in the meantime; furthermore, as if seeking to contribute to his voluntary blindness, the months of November and December filled with events that Armada perhaps read as omens of a non-violent triumph of the purely political operation: while the Army's malaise was revealed by new scandals – on 5 December several hundred generals, commanders and other officers boycotted a ceremony at the General Staff Academy in protest at a government decision – and while murmurs circulated in Madrid that a group of Captains General had asked the King for Adolfo Suárez's resignation and that another no-confidence motion against the Prime Minister was being drawn up, some leaders of political parties were flocking to the Zarzuela Palace to express their alarm at the deterioration of the situation and to champion the need for a strong government to put a stop to the unbearable weakness of Suárez's government. These favourable signs or what Armada could interpret as favourable signs seemed to receive the Crown's public endorsement when shortly before the end of the year, in his televised Christmas message, the King told anyone looking to understand it – and the first to understand it was Adolfo Suárez – that his support for the Prime Minister had come to an end.

Perhaps it was the gesture that Armada had been waiting for since his departure from the Zarzuela: his adversary fallen into disgrace, deprived of royal confidence and protection, for Armada's pride and courtesan mentality it was the moment to recover and augment his place as the King's favourite that Suárez had done all he could to steal, becoming head of his government in those times of difficulty for the Crown. This hunch encouraged him to tighten his siege of the monarch. During the Christmas holidays, Armada was with the King at least twice, once at the Zarzuela and again at La Pleta, where the Royal Family spent the first days of January. They spoke at length again, and in these conversations the former royal secretary was able to accumulate evidence that the King's favour for which he'd been longing for almost five years was returning; not fictitious evidence: worried for the future of the monarchy, reluctant to accept the role of institutional arbiter without authentic power assigned him by the Constitution, the

King sought resources with which to weather the crisis, and it's absurd
to imagine he'd refuse those offered or those he thought the man who'd
helped him overcome so many obstacles in his youth might be able to
offer. Although we have only Armada's testimony about what was
discussed in those conversations with the King, we can take a few
things as certain or as very likely: it is certain or very likely that, as well
as stressing both a gloomy opinion of Suárez and of the political
moment, Armada talked of the rumours of a no-confidence motion
against Suárez and of the rumours of a unity government, that he
revealed himself to be in favour of it and in a more or less elliptical way
proposed himself as a candidate to lead it, emphasizing that his monarchist and liberal profile corresponded to the profile of the leader
designed by the media, social organizations and political parties, many
of which (according to Armada again) had already given him their
blessing or insinuated that they would; it's certain or very likely that
the King would have let Armada talk and wouldn't have contradicted
him and that, if he hadn't done so before, would now have begun to
consider seriously the proposal of a government of unity led ·by a
soldier, whether or not it was Armada, as long as he could count on the
approval of the Cortes and on a constitutional framework that Armada
considered guaranteed; it's certain that, while both stressed their
gloomy opinion of the military moment, Armada was the more exasperated by it and would have talked of his visit to Milans, presenting
himself as a brake on the Captain General of Valencia's interventionist
ardour, craftily doling out information about his projects or threats and
without going into any details prejudicial to his own ends (it's unlikely
for example that he would have mentioned Tejero and his relationship
with Milans); it is also certain that the King asked Armada to continue
keeping him up to date on what was happening or being plotted in the
barracks; also, that he promised to find him a posting in the capital.
The reason for this promise must not be simple or singular: the King
undoubtedly was thinking that having Armada posted far from Madrid
was making his access to the most abundant and accurate news about
the Army difficult; he undoubtedly thought that placing him in a
central position within the military hierarchy could help to block the
coup; he undoubtedly wanted to have him nearby in order to be able

to turn to him in any contingency, including perhaps that of leading a coalition or caretaker or unity government. Maybe there were even more reasons. Whatever the case, the King hastened to fulfil this promise and, in spite of the drastic opposition of Suárez, who mistrusted more than ever the machinations of the former royal secretary, got the Minister of Defence to reserve for Armada the post of Deputy Chief of the Army General Staff. Supplied with this future appointment, with his many hours of proximity to the King and a concrete proposal, as soon as the Royal Family's holidays in Lérida were over Armada went back to Valencia with his wife to see Milans again.

It happened on 10 January and was the last time the two 23 February leaders spoke face to face before the coup. What Armada said that day to Milans was that the King shared their point of view regarding the political situation and his own imminent return to Madrid as Deputy Chief of the Army General Staff was the platform devised by the monarch from which to turn him into Prime Minister of a government of unity, the formation of which could only be a question of weeks, the time it would take for a victorious motion of no-confidence against Adolfo Suárez to crystallize; therefore, concluded Armada, this was the time to halt the military operations under way, subordinating them to the political operation: it was a question of bringing all the various coup plots together under a single command and a single project, to be able to deactivate them when the political operation triumphed or, if no other option remained because the political operation failed, to be able to reactivate them in order to triumph. This proposal defined by Armada and accepted by Milans was what dominated a meeting held eight days later in the Madrid home of the Captain General of Valencia's aide-de-camp, on Calle General Cabrera; attending it, summoned by Milans himself, were several reserve generals – among them Iniesta Cano – several active generals – among them Torres Rojas – and several lieutenant colonels – among them Tejero – whereas, faithful to a strategy of never talking about the coup in the presence of more than one person and looking for alibis for any hypothetically compromising move (therefore always talking alone with Milans and always visiting Valencia accompanied by his wife and on the pretext of settling private matters), Armada gave a last-minute excuse and did not attend the conclave. Given that it was the most well attended by those preparing the coup, and the most important from the point of view of the military operation, what was discussed at it is well known: during the 23 February trial several of those who were present gave similar versions, and years later some who were there and who eluded prosecution at the time would do so as well. It was Milans who was firmly in command of the meeting. The Captain General of Valencia assumed control of the coup projects in various stages of germination in which those present were involved and explained Armada's plan the way Armada had explained it to him, stressing it was all being done under the auspices of the King; likewise, after Tejero set out the technical details of his operation, Milans defined the basic mechanism they'd have to deploy at the chosen moment: Tejero would take the Cortes, he would take the region of Valencia, Torres Rojas would take Madrid with the Brunete Armoured Division and Armada would accompany the King at the Zarzuela Palace while the rest of the Captains General, whose complicity would have been previously secured, would join them by taking their respective regions and thus sealing the coup; it was, furthermore – as Milans repeated over and over again – a simple project, and its realization was not going to be necessary if, as he expected, Armada set in action his purely political project within a reasonable space of time; Milans even made clear what he understood as a reasonable space of time: thirty days.

Not even fifteen had gone by when the *golpistas'* plans seemed to be pulverized. On 29 January Adolfo Suárez announced his resignation on television. Despite the fact that for many months the ruling class had been shouting their demand for it, the news surprised everyone, and it can be imagined that in the first instant Armada would have rightly thought that Suárez had resigned to abort the political operations directed against him, Operation Armada among them; but it can equally be imagined in the second instant the general would try to convince himself that, far from complicating things, Suárez's resignation simplified them, since it saved the uncertain formality of the no-confidence motion and left his political future in the hands of the King, whom the Constitution granted the authority to propose a new Prime Minister after consulting with parliamentary leaders. It was at this moment that Armada decided to present his candidacy to the King without subterfuge and bring to bear all the pressure he could to make him accept it. He did so at a dinner alone with the monarch, a week after Suárez's resignation. By then Armada felt that everything was conspiring in his favour, and the proof is that, undoubtedly on his advice, days earlier Milans had gathered his people again or some of his people on Calle General Cabrera to assure them that the coup was on ice until further notice because the fall of the Prime Minister and Armada's immediate transfer to Madrid meant the coup was unnecessary and that Operation Armada was under way: on the morning after Suárez's resignation the newspapers were full of hypotheses of coalition or caretaker or unity governments, the political parties were offering to participate in them or looking for support for them and Armada's name was on everyone's lips in the political village of Madrid, put forward by people in his circle like the journalist Emilio Romero, who on 31 January proposed the general as new Prime Minister in his column in *ABC*; three days later the King telephoned Armada and told him he'd just signed the decree of his appointment as Deputy Chief of the Army General Staff and that he should pack his bags because he was coming back to Madrid. At this ideal juncture Armada had his dinner with the King, over the course of which the former secretary earnestly reiterated his reasoning: the need for a surgical coup or a touch on the rudder that would remove the danger of a coup d'état, the convenience of a government of unity led by a military officer and the constitutional nature of such a solution; he also offered to assume the leadership of the government and assured him or let him understand that he could count on the support of the main political parties. I don't know how the King reacted to Armada's words; there's no reason to rule out that he might have had doubts, and one reason not to rule it out is that, although the UCD had already proposed Leopoldo Calvo Sotelo as Suárez's successor, the King took another eleven days before presenting his candidacy to the Cortes: it's very unlikely that in the obligatory rounds of consultations with the leaders of the political parties, before the presentation of the candidate, he would have even mentioned Armada's name, but he would undoubtedly have talked about coalition or caretaker or unity governments; as well as this delay, another reason invites us not to rule out that the King might have had doubts: many people were advocating an exceptional way out and had been for a long time that, without violating the Constitution in theory, would not involve an automatic application of the Constitution, and he had absolute confidence in Armada and could think that a government led by the general and supported by all the political parties would calm the Army down, would help the country overcome the crisis and strengthen the Crown. We don't have to rule out that he had doubts, but the truth is that, for whatever reasons – perhaps because he understood in time that straining the Constitution meant putting the Constitution in danger and putting the Constitution in danger meant putting democracy in danger and that putting democracy in danger meant putting the Crown in danger – the King decided to apply the Constitution to the letter and present to the Cortes the candidacy of Leopoldo Calvo Sotelo on 10 February.

That was the end of Operation Armada, the end of the purely political operation; from that point on the possibility of the King's former secretary attaining the leadership of a coalition or caretaker or unity government by parliamentary means was ruled out. Armada now had only two alternatives open to him: one consisted of forgetting his ambitions and convincing Milans to forget the military operation and of Milans convincing Tejero and the other plotters in turn to forget the military operation; the other consisted of thawing out the military operation and using it as a battering ram to impose by force a political recipe he hadn't been able to impose by purely political means. Neither Armada nor any of the rest of the plotters even considered the first alternative; neither Armada nor any of the rest of the plotters abandoned the second at any moment, so it was the military alternative that ended up winning. It's quite true that the circumstances of that month didn't make victory a difficult one, because in the three weeks previous to 23 February the conspirators perhaps felt that reality was urgently demanding the coup, wielding a last arsenal of arguments to finally persuade them that only an uprising by the Army could prevent the extinction of the nation: on 4 February, the same day the Episcopal Conference published a very harsh document against the divorce law, a group of pro-ETA deputies interrupted the King's first speech to the Basque Parliament with a chorus of patriotic chanting and songs; on the 6th the body of an engineer kidnapped by ETA from the Lemóniz nuclear power plant turned up; on the 13th the ETA militant Joseba Arregui died at the Carabanchel prison hospital, and over the following days political tension was rife: during a wild parliamentary session the opposition accused the government of tolerating torture, there were public confrontations between the Ministry of the Interior and the Ministry of Justice, there were resignations of functionaries and then immediately a police strike that included the resignation of its whole board; on the 21st, finally, ETA kidnapped the Uruguayan consul in Pamplona and the Austrian and Salvadorean consuls in Bilbao. During those convulsive days Armada saw the King twice, once on the 11th and again on the 13th, both times at the Zarzuela Palace: at the first, during the funeral of Queen Frederica of Greece, the King's mother-in-law, he was barely able to speak to the monarch; at the second, during his mandatory presentation as Deputy Chief of the Army General Staff, he did so for an hour. Throughout the discussion Armada seemed nervous and irritated: he didn't dare reproach the King for not having appointed him Prime Minister of the government, but he did tell him he was committing a very grave error in appointing Calvo Sotelo; according to Armada, he also told him of an imminent military move involving several Captains General, among them Milans, just as he told General Gutiérrez Mellado, to whom he also paid a visit required by protocol that morning after leaving the Zarzuela. This last warning strikes me as at best improbable: General Gutiérrez Mellado at least denied it before the judge. It is certain, however, that three days later Armada opened the floodgates of the coup: on 16 February he had a meeting in his brand-new office at Army General Headquarters with Colonel Ibáñez Inglés, Milans' deputy chief of staff and habitual link between the two, and told him the political operation had failed; maybe he didn't tell him anything else, but there was no need: it was enough for Milans to know that, unless he accepted that it had all been for naught, the military operation had to go ahead.

The coup was now irrevocable. Only forty-eight hours after the meeting between Armada and Ibáñez Inglés, on the very day the debate on Calvo Sotelo's investiture as Prime Minister began in the Cortes, Tejero telephoned Ibáñez Inglés: he told him the space of time Milans had given for Operation Armada to triumph had run out, that it would be a long time before a better opportunity would present itself to carry out what they'd agreed than the sessions of the investiture debate, with the Cabinet and all the deputies together in the Cortes, assured him that he had a group of captains ready to join him, that the latest events – the offence to the King in the Basque Parliament, the murder of the Lemóniz engineer at the hands of ETA, the consequences of the death of the ETA militant Arregui – had exasperated them and he couldn't hold them back any longer, and that, in short, he was going to take the Cortes with or without Milans; Tejero's warning to Ibáñez Inglés dispelled any reservations the Captain General of Valencia was still harbouring: he couldn't stop the lieutenant colonel, Armada's political failure left him without options, he had implicated himself too far to back out at the last moment. Milans therefore gave Tejero the go-ahead, and that same day, the 18th, the lieutenant colonel organized a dinner with several trustworthy captains with whom he'd been talking vaguely of a coup d'état for a long time (he'd lied to Ibáñez Inglés: it wasn't that he couldn't hold the captains back any longer, but that he couldn't hold himself back any longer); that night he was more specific: he told them his project, got them to commit themselves to helping him carry it out, discussed with them the possibility of assaulting the Cortes during the investiture vote two days later, put off the decision of the date of the assault to the next day. The next day was 19 February. In the morning Tejero realized that preparing his sudden attack was going to take him quite a bit longer than twenty-four hours and therefore he couldn't do it on Friday, but someone – maybe one of his captains, maybe one of Milans' adjutants – brought to his attention that the parliamentary majority Calvo Sotelo had was not enough to win his election in the first vote, and that the Speaker would have to call a second vote that could not possibly be held before Monday, which would grant them a minimum of four days for their preparations; no matter what day the Speaker chose, that was the chosen day: the day of the second investiture vote.

In this way the coup was convened, and at this point my narration splits in two. Up till now I've referred to events as they've occurred or as it seems to me they occurred; given that members of CESID took part in what follows, based on the data I've exposed so far about the intelligence services, I cannot yet choose between two versions of events that clash with each other. I'll leave the choice for later on and set out both of them.

The first version is the official version; that is: the version that came out of the trial; it's also the least problematic. From the 19th onwards Tejero and Milans – one in Madrid, the other in Valencia – are working on the preparations for the coup, but from the 20th, when the Speaker fixes the date and time of the second investiture vote and inadvertently furnishes the *golpistas* with the date and time of the coup – Monday the 23rd, not before six o'clock – the work accelerates. Tejero finalizes the details of his plan, looks for the resources with which to carry it out, speaks by telephone on several occasions with Milans' adjutants (Lieutenant Colonel Mas Oliver and Colonel Ibáñez Inglés) and speaks in person with several officers of the Civil Guard, especially with his group of captains; there are at least four: Muñecas Aguilar, Gómez Iglesias, Sánchez Valiente and Bobis González. The first two are good friends of Tejero's and we know them well: Muñecas is the captain who on the evening of 23 February addressed the parliamentary hostages from the podium in the Cortes to announce the arrival of a competent military authority; Gómez Iglesias is the captain attached to AOME – the special operations unit of CESID – who has possibly been put in charge of keeping an eye on Tejero by Major Cortina and who, according to this first version of events, on 23 February acted behind his commanding officer's back, because unbeknownst to Cortina he helped the lieutenant colonel overcome the final reluctance of some of the officers who were going to accompany him on the evening of the coup and perhaps he also supplied AOME manpower and material to escort the buses to the Cortes. As for Milans, during those four days he organizes the uprising of Valencia with his two adjutants, obtains promises of support or neutrality from other Captains General, sets up at full speed the rebellion in the Brunete Armoured Division by way of Major Pardo Zancada (whom he summons to Valencia on the eve of the coup to receive instructions) and speaks by telephone on at least three occasions with Armada. The last conversation takes place on 22 February: from the office of the son of Colonel Ibáñez Inglés, Milans speaks to Armada in the presence of Ibáñez Inglés, Lieutenant Colonel Mas

Oliver and Major Pardo Zancada, and he does so repeating out loud the words of his interlocutor so the men with him can hear them, as if he didn't entirely trust Armada or as if he needed his subordinates to trust him entirely; both generals go over the plans: Tejero will take the Cortes, Milans will take Valencia, the Brunete Division will take Madrid and Armada will take the Zarzuela; fundamentally: all is being done on the King's orders. When Milans hangs up it is half past five in the afternoon. Just over twenty-four hours later the coup was triggered.

That's the first version; the second does not contradict it and only differs from it on one point: Major Cortina appears. It is a suspicious version because it is the version of the *golpistas* or, more specifically, Tejero's version: keeping to the common line of defence employed by the accused during the 23 February trial, and based on a supposed complicity between Cortina and Armada and the King, Tejero tries to exonerate himself by accusing Cortina (and with Cortina the intelligence services), accusing Armada through Cortina (and with Armada the top brass of the Army) and through Cortina and Armada accusing the King (and with the King the central institution of the state); all this does not automatically, of course, make Tejero's testimony false. In fact, during the trial's first hearing the lieutenant colonel gave some very precise details that lent credence to his version; the court, however, didn't believe him, because he erred on others and because Cortina had an impeccable alibi for each one of his accusations, obliging them to acquit him, though it hasn't kept suspicion from hanging over him: Cortina is an expert in the fabrication of alibis and, as a journalist who covered the trial sessions wrote, you don't have to be a reader of detective novels to know that an innocent man almost never has alibis, because he never even imagines he might need them one day. That in part is where the difficulty in choosing from the data I've laid out so far between the two versions of events comes from. Here is the second one:

On the evening of the 18th or the morning of the 19th, when Milans and Tejero make the decision to launch the coup, Captain Gómez Iglesias, who in effect has spent months keeping tabs on the lieutenant colonel under Cortina's orders, reports the news to his commanding officer at AOME. Cortina does not inform his superiors, does not denounce the *golpistas*; instead, he gets in contact with Armada, who

according to what Tejero has said to Gómez Iglesias is the leader of the
coup or one of the leaders of the coup or is involved in the coup and
acting on the orders of the King. Armada has known Cortina for a long
time and, because he wants to use the major or because he has no alternative, he tells him what he knows; for his part, Cortina puts himself
under Armada's orders. Next, in agreement with Armada, maybe on
Armada's orders, Cortina asks Gómez Iglesias to arrange a meeting for
him with Tejero: he seeks to find out the lieutenant colonel's plans first-
hand, remind him of the coup's objectives and reinforce the chain of
command among the conspirators. Tejero trusts Gómez Iglesias fully
and thinks that it might be a good idea to have AOME manpower and
material to assault the Cortes, so he agrees to the meeting, and on the
same night, the 19th, the two officers get together at Cortina's home, a
flat on Calle Biarritz, in the Parque de Las Avenidas neighbourhood,
where the major lives with his parents. Cortina presents himself to the
lieutenant colonel as Armada's right-hand man or spokesman; he
instructs him: he emphasizes that the operation is being carried out on
the King's orders with the aim of saving the monarchy, establishes
clearly that its political head is Armada although its military head is
Milans, he repeats the general design of the coup and its predicted
outcome (he talks of a government led by Armada, but not of a coalition or caretaker or unity government), he asks him technical questions
about how he thinks he'll carry out his part of the plan, assures him
that he can count on men and means from AOME and insists that the
assault should be bloodless and discreet and that his mission concludes
the moment an Army unit relieves him and Armada takes charge of the
occupied Cortes. That's all: the two men part company at about three
in the morning and until 23 February remain in contact through
Gómez Iglesias, but the day after the meeting Tejero calls Valencia to
make certain that Cortina is truly a component of the coup and, after
a telephone conversation between Milans and Armada, he is told from
Valencia that he can trust Cortina and to follow his instructions.
Meanwhile, at some point on that same Friday, or perhaps on Saturday
morning, Armada decides, following Cortina's advice, that he too
should meet with Tejero and, again through Gómez Iglesias, Cortina
arranges for the night of Saturday the 21st a meeting of the two men so

the general can meet the lieutenant colonel, to clarify the nature of the operation personally and give him his final orders. The meeting is held, and in it Armada gives Tejero the same instructions he received from Cortina two days earlier: the operation must be discreet and bloodless, the lieutenant colonel must enter the Cortes in the name of the King and of democracy and must leave as soon as the military authority who will take charge of everything arrives (Armada doesn't think it necessary to clarify that he himself will be this military authority, but does say he'll identify himself by using a password: 'Duque de Ahumada'); it's all being done on the orders of the King to save the monarchy and democracy by way of a government that he'll lead, but the composition of which he does not spell out. According to Tejero's statement to the court, the recurrence of the words monarchy and democracy in the general's speech makes him wary (the fact that Armada is going to lead the government doesn't make him wary: he's known this for some time and takes it for granted that this will be a military government); Tejero, however, does not ask for explanations, much less protest: Armada is a general and he is only a lieutenant colonel and, although deep down Milans is still the leader of the coup to him because he is the commanding officer he admires and to whom he feels truly linked, the Captain General of Valencia has imposed Armada as political leader and Tejero accepts him; furthermore, he is not a monarchist but is resigned to the monarchy, and he's sure that on Armada's lips the word democracy is a hollow word, a mere screen behind which to hide the stark reality of the coup. The meeting is held in a secret flat that belongs to AOME or in a flat occasionally used by the head of AOME, a place located on Calle Pintor Juan Gris to which Cortina drives Tejero after arranging to meet him at the nearby Hotel Cuzco; Armada and Tejero talk alone, but while they do so Cortina remains in the foyer, and when they finish talking the major again accompanies the lieutenant colonel back to the entrance of the Hotel Cuzco, where they say goodnight. Cortina and Armada have never admitted that this episode happened, and at the trial Tejero could not prove it: Cortina's alibi was perfect; on this occasion, Armada's was too. According to Tejero, the meeting did not last long, no more than thirty minutes between half past eight and nine o'clock. Less than forty-eight hours later the coup began.

6

These are the two versions of the immediate background to 23 February.
Let's imagine now that the second version is the true one; imagine that
Tejero is not lying and that four or five days before the coup Cortina
heard from Gómez Iglesias that the coup was going to happen and that
Armada was its ringleader or one of its ringleaders, and that he decided
to join the operation by putting himself under the general's orders. If
that's what he did, maybe it wouldn't be futile to wonder why he did it.

There is a theory that has enjoyed a certain renown, according to
which Cortina intervened in the coup as a double agent: not with the
aim of helping the coup to go well but to ensure that it should go badly,
not with the aim of destroying democracy but of protecting it. The
guardians of this theory maintain that Cortina found out the coup was
going to happen when it was already too late to deactivate it; they
maintain that he understood that it was an improvised and badly
organized operation and that he decided to precipitate it so the *golpistas*
would not have time to finish preparations and thus it would fail; they
maintain that's why he urged the coup on Tejero in their conversation
on the 19th, fixing the date for the assault on the Cortes. Nice, but
false. In the first place because Tejero didn't need anyone to urge him
to stage a coup he was already determined to stage, or anyone to fix a
date he'd already fixed or that the phases of the debate over the investiture of Calvo Sotelo in the Cortes had fixed; and in the second place
because, although he found out the coup was going to take place with
only a few days' notice, Cortina could perfectly well have deactivated
it: he would have needed only to tell his superiors what he knew, those

who in just a few hours would have been able to arrest the *golpistas* just as they'd done before with the *golpistas* of Operation Galaxia and just as they would do after 23 February with other *golpistas*.

My theory is more obvious, more prosaic and patchier. For a start I'll recall that the relationship between Cortina and Armada was real: they'd known each other since 1975, when Cortina was a frequent visitor at the Zarzuela Palace; one of Cortina's brothers, Antonio – closer than a brother, Cortina's best friend – was a friend of Armada's and a promoter of Armada's candidacy for the head of a unity government; Cortina himself approved the idea of this government and maybe Armada's candidacy. That said, my theory is that, if it's true that he was involved in the coup, Cortina was in it to make it triumph and not so it would fail: because, like Armada and Milans, he was convinced the country was ripe for a coup and because he thought it was worth running the risk of using arms to impose a political solution they hadn't been able to impose without arms; also because he thought that by joining the coup he'd be able to manage it or influence it and guide it in the most suitable direction; also because he thought that, shielded behind good alibis, the personal risk he was running was not big, and that if he acted intelligently he could benefit from the coup as much if it triumphed as if it failed (if the coup triumphed he would have been one of the architects of its triumph; if it failed he'd know how to manoeuvre in order to present himself as one of the architects of its failure); also because, although his connection to the King was not as close as the *golpistas* shouted after the coup – most likely it was no closer than that the monarch maintained with other classmates with whom he'd get together for fraternal lunches or dinners – Cortina was a firmly monarchist soldier and he thought that, whether it triumphed or failed, Armada's soft coup could work as a decompression valve, easing a political and military life strained as far as it could be in those days, ventilating with its violent shake-up the foul atmosphere and turning into a prophylactic against the ever more pressing threat of a hard coup, anti-monarchist and well enough planned to be unstoppable, and because he definitely thought that, like him, the monarchy would come out of the coup a winner whether it triumphed or failed, just as if he'd read Machiavelli and remembered that advice according to which 'a wise prince should, when he has the opportunity, astutely encourage some opposition in order that he might shine all the brighter once he has vanquished it'.

Like any of the rest of the conspirators, Cortina could argue on the eve of 23 February that there were only three ways the coup might fail: the first was a reaction by the people; the second was a reaction by the Army; the third was a reaction by the King. Like any of the rest of the conspirators, Cortina might have thought the first possibility remote (and, if he did, 23 February proved him right by a long way): in 1936 Franco's coup had failed and provoked a war because the people had taken to the streets in support of the government, with weapons in hand to defend the Republic; with the government and deputies held hostage in the Cortes, intimidated by the memory of the war, disenchanted with democracy or the functioning of democracy, lethargic and unarmed, in 1981 people didn't know whether to applaud the coup or resign themselves to it, at most they offered a weak minority resistance. Like any of the rest of the conspirators, Cortina might also have thought the second possibility equally remote (and, if he did, 23 February would again prove him right by a long way): in 1936 Franco's coup had failed and provoked a war because part of the Army had remained under the orders of the government and had joined the people in the defence of the Republic; in 1981, on the other hand, the Army was almost uniformly Francoist and therefore those in the high command who opposed a coup d'état would be the exceptions, not to mention those who would oppose a coup d'état sponsored by the King. A third possibility remained: the King. It was, in fact, the only possibility, or at least the only possibility that Cortina or any of the rest of the conspirators might have considered feasible in advance: it could be imagined – in spite of the coup not being against the King but with the King, in spite of not being a hard coup but a soft coup, in spite of not aiming in theory to destroy democracy but to rectify it, in spite of the enormous pressure the rebel officers and a large part of the Army would bring to bear on him and even in spite of the fact that the government resulting from the coup should count on the approval of the Cortes and could be presented by Armada not as a triumph of the coup but as a solution to the coup – the King might decide not to sponsor the coup and make use of his position as Franco's heir and symbolic chief of the Armed Forces to stop it, perhaps remembering the dissuasive example of his grandfather Alfonso XIII and of his brother-in-law Constantine of Greece, who accepted the help of the Army to keep themselves in power and less than a decade later were dethroned.* However, what would happen in the case of the King opposing the coup? It's true that no one could predict it, because once the coup was under way almost anything was possible, including a coup with the King captained by the two most monarchist generals in the Army turning into a coup against the King that would end up taking down the monarchy; but it's also true that, in the case of the King opposing the coup, the most likely result was that the coup would fail, because it was very unlikely that a monarchist coup would degenerate into an anti-monarchist coup, just as it's true that, if the coup failed owing to the King's intervention, he would become to all intents and purposes the saviour of democracy, which could only mean the reinforcement of the monarchy. I insist: I'm not saying that this was the only possible result of the coup for the monarchy if the King opposed it; what I'm saying is that, like any of the rest of the plotters, before joining the coup Cortina might have arrived at the conclusion that the risks the coup entailed for the monarchy were much fewer than the benefits it might bring in its wake, and that in consequence the coup was a good coup because it would triumph whether it triumphed or failed: the triumph of the coup would strengthen the Crown (that's at least what Cortina might have thought and what Armada and Milans were thinking); its failure would likewise do so. Whether or not he'd read Machiavelli and whether or not he recalled his advice, that might have been Cortina's reasoning; supposing that it was, 23 February also proved him right on this point, and proved him right by a long way.

* It is possible, however, that the monarchist *golpistas* might not have considered the example of Alfonso XIII and Constantine of Greece at all discouraging to the Crown; maybe their reasoning was the opposite of that of the King on 23 February: for them it was precisely the help of the Army that allowed the King's grandfather and brother-in-law to extend their stay in power for a few years and, if they'd known how to administer it with intelligence, could have prevented the end of the monarchy in Spain and Greece.

7

The preceding chapter is only conjecture: the main question – the main question about Cortina, the main question about the role of the intelligence services on 23 February – still stands, and that's why on the basis of the information I've set out so far we cannot yet make up our minds about either of the two alternative versions of what happened in the days before the coup. We're sure that Javier Calderón's CESID did not participate as such in the coup, but we're not sure that Cortina's AOME did participate in the coup. We're sure that a member of AOME, Captain Gómez Iglesias, collaborated with Tejero in the preparation and execution of the coup, but we're not sure he did so on Cortina's orders and not on his own initiative, out of solidarity or friendship with the lieutenant colonel; nor are we sure that other members of AOME – Sergeant Sales and Corporals Monge and Moya – participated in the coup by escorting Tejero's buses to their target, and we don't know whether, supposing that they had done, they did so on the orders of Gómez Iglesias, who, in spite of the rigorous control Cortina kept over his men, might have recruited them to the operation behind Cortina's back, or whether they did so on the orders of Cortina, who might have joined the coup with his unit or with part of his unit because he considered it a good coup no matter if it triumphed or failed. On this main point we have conjectures and we have possibilities, but we don't have certainties, we don't even have probabilities; maybe we can approach them if we try to answer two still pending questions: what exactly did Cortina do on 23 February? What exactly happened at AOME on 23 February?

In spite of the hermetic character of AOME, we have numerous first-hand testimonies of what happened in the unit that night. They are often contradictory testimonies – sometimes, violently contradictory – but they allow some facts to be established. The first is that the behaviour of the commanding officer of AOME appeared to be irreproachable; the second is that this appearance shows cracks in light of the behaviour of certain members of AOME (and in light of the light this shines on certain areas of the behaviour of the commanding officer of AOME). At the moment of the assault on the Cortes, Cortina was at the AOME academy, situated in a house on Calle Miguel Aracil. He heard the gunfire on the radio and immediately went to another of the unit's secret locations, the one on Avenida Cardenal Herrera Oria; his command post was there, the Plana Mayor, and from there, assisted by Captain García-Almenta, deputy head of AOME, he began to issue orders: given that he knew or assumed that the assault on the Cortes was the prelude to a coup d'état and might provoke tensions in the unit, Cortina ordered all his subordinates to remain at their posts and prohibited any comment in favour of or against the coup; then he ordered all the teams operating in the streets to be traced, organized the deployment of his men throughout Madrid on information-gathering missions and imposed special security measures at all their bases. Finally, around half past seven, he left for CESID central headquarters at 7 Paseo de la Castellana, where he remained until well into the early hours the coup was seen to have failed, always under Javier Calderón's orders, always in contact with the staff of his unit and always offering his bosses information he was receiving from it and which would prove decisive in blocking the coup in the capital. Up to here – and I repeat: until well into the early hours – Cortina's conduct seems to rule out his involvement in the coup, but doesn't absolutely allow us to eliminate the possibility (in reality, collaborating in the countercoup was, as the night went on and the possibility that the coup might triumph grew more distant, the best way of shielding oneself against the failure of the coup, because it was a way of shielding oneself from the accusation of having supported it); much less does what we know of some of his subordinates' conduct allow us to eliminate it. Especially that of one of them: Corporal Rafael Monge. Monge was the head of SEA (Sección

Especial de Agentes, Special Agents' Section), a secret unit within Cortina's secret unit made up of men of his utmost confidence whose principal but not exclusive mission at that time consisted of preparing agents destined to go undercover and infiltrate groups of ETA sympathizers in the Basque Country; Sergeant Miguel Sales and Corporal José Moya also belonged to this unit.* On the evening of 23 February, after arriving at the AOME academy on Miguel Aracil around seven, Monge travelled with Captain Rubio Luengo to the house where the staff officers were stationed; excited and euphoric, Monge told Rubio Luengo the following: he told him he'd escorted Tejero's buses to the Cortes, told him that he'd done so along with other members of AOME, told him he'd done so on García-Almenta's orders (Rubio Luengo immediately related Monge's triple confession to an order from García-Almenta received that very morning at the academy: they must hand over to Monge, Sales and Moya three vehicles with false number plates, walkie-talkies and low-frequency transmitters, undetectable even by the rest of the AOME teams). It was not the only time that evening Monge told of his intervention in the coup; he did so again a few minutes later, when, after talking at headquarters to García-Almenta, he ordered Sergeant Rando Parra to drive him to the vicinity of the Cortes, where the head of SEA had to pick up one of the unit's cars; on the way, Monge told Rando Parra more or less the same thing he'd told Rubio Luengo – he'd escorted Tejero in his attack, not on his own, he'd been following García-Almenta's orders – and he added that, after carrying out his mission, he'd left the car that they were now going to get on Calle Fernanflor, near the Cortes.

   That night many things happened in AOME – there were frenetic comings and goings at all their sites, there was a constant flow of information supplied by the teams deployed in Madrid and the surrounding area, there were many men demonstrating their happiness about the

---

* Among the singularities of AOME was the fact that, although it was a military unit, rank had a very relative value in it: a lieutenant could give orders to a captain, a sergeant could command a lieutenant, a corporal could command a sergeant; the essential thing in AOME wasn't the rank but the ability of each agent (or what Cortina judged to be the ability of each agent), which is how in SEA Sergeant Sales could be a subordinate of Corporal Monge's. This anomaly provoked jealousy, grievances and rivalries among the agents that undoubtedly influenced the explosion of mutual accusations within the unit as a result of the coup d'état.

coup and a few who kept their sadness quiet and at least two who went into the Cortes in the middle of the night and came out with fresh news, including that Armada was the real leader of the coup – but Monge's repeated confession to Rubio Luengo and Rando Parra is decisive. Is it also totally reliable? Of course, after 23 February Monge retracted: he said it had all been a fantasy improvised before his comrades-in-arms to boast of an invented *golpista* exploit; the explanation is not completely incredible (according to his bosses and colleagues Monge was an adventurous and swaggering soldier, and there was no better day than 23 February for boasting of *golpista* exploits, and *antigolpista* exploits as well): the fact that Monge told the story not once but at least twice makes it less credible, not only in the heat of the first moment of the coup but also in the cold of the second, when he'd already been to the unit's command post and had spoken to his superiors, at least to García-Almenta; the fact that Monge left the proof of his participation in the assault near the Cortes makes it definitively incredible.* However, if we accept that Monge's on-the-spot testimony is true – and I don't see how we can reject it – then the conduct of AOME on 23 February seems to become clearer, and Cortina's as well: the three

* In spite of everything, there are intelligence services officers from the time who still maintain that Monge's story is invented or that the participation of the Corporal was trivial, casual and strictly individual; the latter is what Cortina himself maintains, for example. According to him, on the afternoon of 23 February Monge was working on the so-called *Operación Mister*, a mission organized by AOME and carried out by SEA to keep Vincent Shields, deputy chief of the CIA in Spain, under surveillance, as he was suspected of spying, according to information CESID had received, from his own house on Calle Carlos III with powerful recording equipment, on the King's receptions at the Oriente Palace (the high risk of the operation – after all this was following a member of an allied espionage station – had obliged the use of unusual means such as low-frequency emitters); Monge had finished his surveillance work at about six in the evening and, when he was getting ready to return to the AOME base, he ran into Tejero's buses by chance in Plaza Beata María Ana de Jesús and spontaneously joined them. As hard as one tries, it's very difficult to believe this story, because it's very difficult to imagine the occupants of a bus full of Civil Guards telling a stranger like Monge, in the centre of Madrid, that they were getting ready to assault the Cortes and stage a coup d'état; the scene is no longer one by Luis García Berlanga: it's by Paco Martínez Soria (or Monty Python); the scene is no longer crazy: it's impossible. Furthermore, this does not mean Cortina's exonerating version doesn't contain a part of the truth: *Operación Mister* existed, and SEA was keeping Shields' house under surveillance for a while, but that was not the only mission SEA was involved in at the time – or even the main one – and its members never used it to carry out the exceptional measures they used that day. In short: it is reasonable to think that *Operación Mister* was used after 23 February as an alibi to hide AOME's intervention in the coup.

members of the unit – the three members of SEA: Monge, Sales and Moya – effectively collaborated in the assault on the Cortes, but they did not do so behind Cortina's back on the orders of Gómez Iglesias, with whom they had not the slightest relationship – in those days, besides, Gómez Iglesias was on temporary leave from the unit, because he was taking an opportune driving course in the very barracks from which Tejero's buses departed – but rather on the orders of García-Almenta, and it's conceivable that Gómez Iglesias recruited men and acted in favour of the coup without an order from Cortina, but it's inconceivable that García-Almenta would have done, who had no personal link with Tejero and could only have known about the coup in advance from Cortina. So, it's highly likely that on 23 February the head of AOME ordered several members of his unit – at least Gómez Iglesias, García-Almenta and the three SEA members – to support the coup.* This could explain why in the early morning of the 24th, when the failure of the attempt was already inevitable and he returned from CESID central headquarters to AOME central headquarters, Cortina met on two occasions, behind closed doors and for a long time, with Gómez Iglesias and García-Almenta, his two main accomplices, possibly to secure alibis and guard themselves against any suspicion; and it would also explain why on the 24th Cortina carried out a round of meetings in every AOME base with the aim of clearing up the rumours that were circulating in the unit – almost all proceeding from Monge's breach of confidence – establishing an official and immaculate account of what had happened within it on the 23rd and freeing it from any responsibility in General Armada's coup, whom Cortina had been praising to the skies on previous days, as if to prepare them for what should occur. Moreover, the very high probability that Cortina was in on the coup retroactively gives us other probabilities, forces us to be inclined towards one of the two versions of the immediate background

---

* According to one of the AOME members who denounced his *golpista* comrades after 23 February, Cortina had set up SEA months earlier precisely to prepare for the coup. But Cortina could not have known of the coup months ahead of time, but only days, so the hypothesis doesn't make sense; however, once he decided to participate in the coup, it does make sense that Cortina should support the assault on the Cortes with SEA, a special isolated unit, or isolatable from the rest of AOME, and made up of some of the most trustworthy men he had at his disposal.

to the coup and authorizes us to answer the main question about Cortina and about the role of the intelligence services on 23 February: it's very likely that, when he found out from Gómez Iglesias that Tejero had launched a coup led by Armada, Cortina would have got in contact with the general (if the two men were not already in contact; in any case, Cortina admits having seen Armada one unspecified day of that week, according to him to congratulate him on his appointment as Deputy Chief of the Army General Staff); it is very likely that, already under Armada's orders, Cortina would have taken care of clarifying to Tejero personally or through Gómez Iglesias the nature, objectives and hierarchy of the coup and promised the help of his men in the assault on the Cortes; it's very likely that, whether or not he arranged the meeting between Tejero and Armada and whether or not it was held, Cortina enabled Armada to transmit to Tejero the final instructions about the operation; it's very likely, in short, that in the days before the coup Cortina turned into a sort of adjutant of Armada's, into a sort of chief of staff to the coup leader. It's very likely that's what happened. That's what I believe happened.

8

23 February

Towards nine in the evening – with the Cortes held hostage, the region of Valencia occupied, the Brunete Armoured Division and the Captains General still devoured by doubts and the entire country immersed in a passive, fearful and expectant silence – Milans' and Armada's coup seemed to be blocked by the King's countercoup. The uncertainty was absolute: on one side the rebels convened, under the fraudulent shelter of the King, the Francoist heart and accumulated fury of the Army; on the other side the King, freed in principle of the temptation of accommodating the rebels – given that a hail of gunfire in the Cortes broadcast on the radio changed the façade of a soft coup with which there was the possibility of reaching a settlement into the façade of a hard coup it was obligatory to refuse – was summoning the Army's discipline and its loyalty to Franco's heir and to the head of state and of the Armed Forces. Any movement of troops, any confrontation with civilians, any incident could push the coup the *golpistas'* way, but at that point the King, Armada and Milans were perhaps those with most power to decide its triumph or failure.

The three of them were acting as if they knew it. With the aim of subduing the rebels and returning them to their barracks, but also of making clear to the country his rejection of the assault on the Cortes and his defence of constitutional order, just before ten o'clock at night the King requested a mobile team from the television studios until then held by the *golpistas* to come and film his address to the Army and the citizens; with the aim of achieving the triumph of the coup although in a different way from originally planned, more or less at the same time Milans phoned Armada at Army General Headquarters. The conversation is important. It is the first between the two generals since the beginning of the coup, but it's not a private conversation, or not entirely: Milans speaks from his office in the Captaincy General of Valencia, surrounded by the officials of his staff; in the absence of the chief of the Army General Staff, General Gabeiras (who at that moment is attending a meeting of the Joint Chiefs of Staff in another part of Madrid), Armada speaks from his superior's office in the Buenavista Palace, and does so surrounded by the generals of Army General Headquarters. Milans proposes a solution to the coup to Armada that according to him has the approval of several Captains General; it is perhaps an inevitable solution for the *golpistas*, that Armada has probably already considered in secret and amounts to an almost obligatory variation of the original plan: given that this has failed and the King is reluctant to accept the coup and Armada has not been able to get into the Zarzuela Palace and come out with express authorization from the monarch to negotiate with the parliamentary hostages, the way to arrange things is for Armada – whose behaviour has already begun to awaken some suspicions but whose precise relation to the coup no one can yet imagine – to go to the occupied Cortes from Army General Headquarters, to speak to the deputies and form with them the anticipated government of unity under his leadership in exchange for Tejero setting them free, Milans revoking the state of emergency and normality returning to the country. Although it might be much more arduous and more unpredictable than the original, Milans' improvised plan has notable advantages for Armada: if he achieves his objective and is named Prime Minister, the King's former secretary could present the triumph of the coup as a failure of the coup and his government as a prudent negotiated way out of the situation provoked by the coup, like the urgent complication – temporary, perhaps unsatisfactory but imperious – of the return to constitutional order violated by the assault on the Cortes; but, if he didn't achieve their objective, no one could accuse him of anything but having made an effort to liberate the parliamentarians by negotiating with the *golpistas*, which should dispel the suspicions that have gathered over him since the beginning of the coup. So Armada accepts Milans' proposition, but, in order not to reveal his complicity with the rebel general before the generals who surround him at Army General Headquarters – to whom he has been repeating certain chosen phrases – publicly he rejects it at first: as if the ambition to be Prime Minister had never entered his mind and he'd never spoken of it with Milans, he displays surprise at the idea and rejects it noisily, gesticulating, posing almost insuperable objections and scruples; then, slowly, sinuously, he pretends to give in to Milans' pressure, he pretends to find himself convinced by his arguments, he pretends to understand that there is no other acceptable way out for Milans and for Milans' Captains General or that this was the best way out or the only way out, and finally he ends up declaring himself ready to make this sacrifice for the King and for Spain demanded of him at this momentous hour for the nation. When Armada hangs up all the generals who've been listening to the conversation (Mendívil, Lluch, Castro San Martín, Esquivias, Sáenz Larumbe, Rodríguez Ventosa, Arrazola, Pérez Íñigo, maybe another) know or imagine Milans' proposal, but Armada repeats it to them. All the generals approve it, all agree with Armada that he should approach the Cortes with the consent of the King and, when someone wonders aloud if that formula is constitutional, Armada has a copy of the Constitution brought in, reads aloud the five points that make up article 99 and convinces his subordinates that, supposing he attains the support of a simple majority of the parliamentarians, the King can validate his appointment as Prime Minister without breaking the constitutional regulation.

Armada then telephones the Zarzuela Palace again, something he hasn't done since the King (or the King by way of Fernández Campo) prevented his entry to the Palace fifteen minutes after the beginning of the coup. The general speaks first with the King; like the one he's just had with Milans, the conversation is not entirely private either: several people listen to the monarch's words in the Zarzuela; several people listen to Armada's words at Army General Headquarters. Armada tells the King that the situation is more serious than he thinks, that things are getting worse at the Cortes with every minute that goes by, that Milans won't withdraw his troops and several military regions

are practically in revolt, that there is a risk of dividing the Army and a
serious danger of armed confrontation, perhaps of civil war; then he
says that Milans and several Captains General consider him the only
person qualified to resolve the problem, and that they've made him a
proposal that has the approval of the rest of the Captains General and
also of the generals with him there at the Buenavista. What proposal?
asks the King. Focused as intently on the generals listening to him as
on the King, instead of answering the question Armada continues playing his role of self-sacrificing servant: the idea strikes him as extravagant,
almost inappropriate, but, given that Milans, the Captains General and
the rest of the Army assure him there's no other solution, he is prepared
to sacrifice himself for the good of the Crown and of Spain and take on
the responsibility and personal costs this will entail. What proposal?
repeats the King. Armada sets out the proposal; when he finishes
the King still doesn't know that his former secretary is the leader of the
coup – probably doesn't even suspect it – but does know that he's trying
to get with the coup what he couldn't get without the coup. Perhaps
because he distrusts the influence Armada still has over him, or because
he doesn't want him to remind him of conversations in which they'd
discussed the possibility of him occupying the premiership of the
government, or because he thinks his current secretary will know how
to deal with it better than him, the King asks Armada to wait a moment
and hands the phone to Fernández Campo. The two friends speak
again, except that now they are more rivals than friends, and they both
know it: Fernández Campo suspects Armada is trying to make the
most of the coup; Armada knows Fernández Campo fears his ability to
influence the King – that's why he blames him for the fact that a few
hours ago the monarch wouldn't let him enter the Zarzuela – and he
guesses how he'll react when he tells him the only feasible way out of
the coup is a government under his leadership. Armada's guess is
confirmed or he feels it's confirmed: after talking about the risks again,
the personal sacrifices and the good of the Crown and of Spain, Armada
sets out Milans' proposal to Fernández Campo and the King's secretary
interrupts him. It's crazy, he says. I think so too, lies Armada. But if
there's no other option I'm prepared . . . Fernández Campo interrupts
him again, repeats that what he's saying is crazy. How can you think the

deputies are going to vote you in at gunpoint? he asks. How can you think the King could accept a Prime Minister elected by force? There's no other solution, answers Armada. Besides, no one will elect me by force. Tejero obeys Milans, so when I get to the Cortes I'll tell him Milans' idea and he'll take his men away and let me speak to the party leaders and make the proposal to them; they can accept it or not, no one's going to force them to do anything, but I assure you they'll accept, Sabino, including the Socialists: I've spoken to them. It's all perfectly constitutional; and even if it weren't: the important thing now is to get the deputies out of there and resolve the emergency; later there'll be time to go into legal subtleties. One thing for sure is that what's happening right now in the Cortes is not constitutional. Fernández Campo lets Armada talk, and when Armada finishes talking tells him that everything he's saying is madness; Armada insists that it's not madness, and Fernández Campo settles the argument by refusing him permission to go to the Cortes in the name of the King.

A few minutes later the argument is repeated. In the meantime news has arrived at Army General Headquarters that Tejero wants or agrees to speak to Armada, and in the Zarzuela voices rise in favour of allowing the former royal secretary's move – if he fails, it'll be him who's failed; if he succeeds, at least the danger of a bloodbath will have passed – but what makes Armada speak to the Zarzuela again is the return to the Buenavista Palace of General Gabeiras, Chief of the Army General Staff. Armada sets out Milans' plan to his immediate superior; convinced that it's a good plan and that there's nothing to lose by letting Armada try to carry it out, hoping to be more persuasive than his subordinate Gabeiras phones the Zarzuela again. He talks to the King and to Fernández Campo, and reiterates Armada's reasons to both of them, but both reject them again; then Armada gets on the phone and speaks to Fernández Campo, who tells him again that what he's proposing is crazy, and then to the King, who answers only by asking him if he's gone mad. The dispute goes on, calls from Army General Headquarters to the Zarzuela come and go and Armada insists and Gabeiras insists and perhaps voices at the Zarzuela insist and undoubtedly Milans and the Captains General and the generals who support Armada and Gabeiras at the Buenavista insist, and finally, almost at the same moment the mobile television crew arrives at the Zarzuela to record the royal message, the King and Fernández Campo end up giving in. It's madness, Fernández Campo tells Armada for the umpteenth time. But I can't prevent you from going to the Cortes; if you want to do it, do it. It has to be clear that you're going on your own account, absolutely, and only to free the government and deputies: do not invoke the King, whatever you're proposing is proposed by you and not the King, the King has nothing to do with this. Is that clear?

That's all Armada needs, and twenty minutes before midnight, accompanied only by his adjutant, Major Bonell, the general leaves the Buenavista and heads for the Cortes. Several generals, including Gabeiras, have offered to accompany him, but Armada has insisted on going alone: his double bluff allows no witnesses; he's received permission from Gabeiras to offer Tejero, in exchange for the deputies' liberty, a plane to fly to Portugal and money to finance a provisional exile; he has gone through the pantomime of asking Milans to ask Tejero for a password to allow him entrance to the Cortes (and Milans has given on Tejero's behalf the same password that Armada probably gave Tejero two days earlier: 'Duque de Ahumada'); he has gone through the pantomime of taking leave of the generals at Headquarters brandishing a copy of the Constitution (and the generals have seen him off in their turn with the certainty or hope that he'll return as Prime Minister of the government). Army General Headquarters is located just a few hundred metres from Carrera de San Jerónimo, so barely a few minutes after leaving in an official car Armada arrives outside the Cortes, enters the Hotel Palace and speaks to the group of soldiers and civilians managing the cordon round Tejero, among them Generals Aramburu Topete and Sáenz de Santamaría and the civil governor of Madrid, Mariano Nicolás: Armada offers hazy explanations about his mission, but clarifies that he's there in an individual, not institutional capacity; otherwise, the news he brings is so alarming – according to him, four Captains General are backing Milans – and his interlocutors' confidence in his prestige is so great that they all urge him to go in right away and negotiate with Tejero, who has been demanding his presence for quite some time. So he does, and at half past twelve at night, while the news that he was about to make a pact with the *golpistas* to bring the hostage-taking to an end spreads through the crowds of military officers, journalists and onlookers swarming round the Hotel Palace and vicinity, Armada arrives at the gates of the Cortes accompanied only by Major Bonell.

What happens next is one of the central episodes of 23 February; also one of the most problematic and most debated. At the entrance to the Cortes General Armada gives the password to the Civil Guards defending it: 'Duque de Ahumada'. It is a superfluous caution, because during the whole afternoon and evening numerous soldiers and civilians have gone in and out of the Cortes with almost total freedom, but the Guards advise Captain Abad and he advises Lieutenant Colonel Tejero, who immediately comes and stands to attention in front of the general, undoubtedly relieved at the arrival of the long-awaited military authority and political leader of the coup. Then, followed by Captain Abad and Major Bonell, the two men walk to the door of the old building of the Cortes, which leads to the entrance to the chamber where the deputies wait. According to Tejero, Armada apologizes for the delay, confirms that there have been certain problems that fortunately have now been resolved and, just as he'd explained on Saturday night, Tejero's mission concludes at this point: now he'll take charge of negotiating with the parliamentary leaders and get them to propose him as Prime Minister of a unity government. Tejero then asks what ministerial post General Milans will occupy in that government, and then Armada commits the biggest mistake of his life; instead of lying, instead of avoiding the question, allowing himself to be carried away by his natural arrogance and his instinct for command, he answers: None. Milans will be President of the Joint Chiefs of Staff. At this moment, on the verge of crossing the threshold of the old building, Tejero stops and grips Armada's forearm. One moment, General, says the lieutenant colonel. We have to talk about this. For the next two or three minutes Armada and Tejero remain on the patio that separates the new building and the old building of the Cortes, talking, Tejero's hand on Armada's forearm the whole time, watched from a few metres' distance by Major Bonell and Captain Abad, who don't understand what's going on. Bonell and Abad also don't understand why, after the two or three minutes, Armada and Tejero don't go into the old building, as they were about to do, but cross the patio and go into the new building and immediately appear behind the big windows of a first-floor office. Next the two men spend almost an hour shut up in there, arguing, but Bonell and Abad (and the officers and Civil Guards who observe the scene beside them from the patio) can only try to guess their words from their gestures, as if they were watching a silent film: no one can clearly distinguish the expression on their faces but they can all see them speaking, first naturally and later with emphasis, all see them get heated and gesticulate, all see them walk back and forth, at some point some of them think they see Armada taking a pair of reading glasses out of his jacket and later others think they see him take the telephone off the hook and speak into it for a few minutes before handing it to Tejero, who also speaks into the receiver and then hands it back to Armada, at least one Civil Guard remembers that towards the end he saw the two men standing still and in silence, a couple of metres apart, looking out of the windows as if they'd suddenly noticed they were being observed although actually with their gazes turned inwards, seeing nothing except their own fury and their own perplexity, like two fish gasping inside an empty fish tank. So neither Major Bonell nor Captain Abad nor any of the officials and Civil Guards watching the discussion between Armada and Tejero from the Cortes patio could pick up or deduce a single one of the words crossing between them, but they all knew that the negotiation had failed long before the two men reappeared on the patio and separated without saluting, without even looking at each other, and especially long before they heard Armada, as he passed them on his way towards Carrera de San Jerónimo and the Hotel Palace, pronounce a phrase that all who heard it would take a long time to forget: 'That man is completely mad.'

He wasn't. It's possible to reconstruct with some exactitude what happened between Armada and Tejero in the new building of the Cortes, because we have the direct and contradictory testimony of both protagonists; we also have numerous indirect testimonies. As I reconstruct it or imagine it, what happened was the following:

As soon as the two men are alone in the office, Armada explains to the lieutenant colonel again what he's just explained on the patio: his mission is complete and now he must let him in to talk with the deputies to offer them their liberty in exchange for the formation of a unity government under his premiership; he adds that, given that things haven't come out exactly as they'd anticipated and the violence and racket of the assault on the Cortes have provoked a negative reaction at the Zarzuela, the most advisable thing is that when the deputies accept his conditions the lieutenant colonel and his men should leave for Portugal in a plane that's already waiting for them at the Getafe airfield, with enough money to spend a while abroad until things calm down a little and they can return to Spain. The lieutenant colonel listens carefully; for the moment he overlooks the offer of money and exile, but not the mention of the unity government. In meetings before the coup it has been explained to him that the result of the coup would be a government of unity, but, loyal to his utopia of the nation as barracks, he has always taken as a given that this government would be a military government. He asks Armada what he means by a unity government; Armada explains: a government made up of independent public figures – military officers, businessmen, journalists – but most of all by members of all the political parties. Perplexed, Tejero asks what politicians would make up this government; Armada gets wind of the danger, digresses, tries not to answer, but ends up revealing that his government would include not only politicians from the right and the centre, but also Socialists and Communists. There are those who even claim that Armada carries a written list of his proposed government in order to be able to negotiate it with the party leaders and which, cornered by Tejero, he agrees to read to him.* Whatever the case, at this

* The existence of the list is not certain. It was made known ten years after the coup by the journalists Joaquín Prieto and José Luis Barbería. Prieto and Barbería's source was Carmen Echave, a UCD member who worked on the staff of one of the congressional vice-presidents and who, as a physician, enjoyed freedom of movement that night to attend to the deputies; as a result, Echave apparently heard one of Tejero's officers reciting Armada's list. Whether it existed or not, whether or not Armada read it to Tejero, the list is substantially plausible: there were political leaders and journalists close to Armada, such as Manuel Fraga and Luis María Anson, military officers with certain democratic credentials, such as the generals Manuel Saavedra Palmeiro and José Antonio Sáenz de Santamaría, business leaders who had publicly called for a government of national unity, such as Carlos Ferrer Salat, together with many politicians of the right, the centre and the left who had also done so or with whom Armada had kept in contact over the months before the coup or those Armada considered likely, with or without reason, to accept a solution like the one he embodied, or simply those it would have suited him to have accept. Although there are those who claim to have had news of Armada's

point the lieutenant colonel explodes: he has not assaulted the Cortes in order to hand the government over to Socialists and Communists, he has not staged a coup d'état so that the Anti-Spain could govern Spain, he is not going to get on a plane and flee like a fugitive while this ignominious scheme is organized at his expense, he will only accept a military junta headed by General Milans. Confronted with that threat of rebellion inside the rebellion, Armada tries to get the lieutenant colonel to listen to reason: a military junta is a fantasy and a mistake, the unity government is the best outcome of the coup and moreover the only one possible, Milans agrees and will not accept anything else, the King will not accept anything else, the Army will not accept anything else, the country will not accept anything else; circumstances are what they are, and Tejero must understand that the triumph of a soft coup is a thousand times better than the failure of a hard coup, because, although the forms might be different, the objectives of the hard coup are the same as those of the soft coup; he must also understand that the hard coup has no support and not the slightest possibility of triumphing and that, for him and his men, a short spell abroad as exiles living in luxury is a thousand times better than a long spell in prison as delinquents of democracy. Tejero answers that he does not even want to hear talk of exile, governments of unity and soft coups. He insists: I have not gone this far for that. Then (then or a little earlier,

---

possible plans for government in advance of 23 February, before the coup the majority of the people who figured on the list were completely unaware of it. The list is the following: Prime Minister. Alfonso Armada. Deputy Prime Minister for Political Affairs: Felipe González (Secretary General of the PSOE). Deputy Prime Minister for Economic Affairs: José María López de Letona (former governor of the Bank of Spain). Minister of Foreign Affairs: José María de Areilza (Coalición Democrática deputy). Minister of Defence: Manuel Fraga (leader of Alianza Popular and Coalición Democrática deputy). Minister of Justice: Gregorio Peces Barba (PSOE deputy). Minister of the Treasury: Pío Cabanillas (UCD deputy). Minister of the Interior: General Manuel Saavedra Palmeiro. Minister of Public Works: José Luis Alvarez (Minister of Transport and Communications and UCD deputy). Minister of Education and Science: Miguel Herrero de Miñón (UCD deputy and spokesman of their parliamentary group). Minister of Employment: Jordi Solé Tura (PCE deputy). Minister of Industry: Agustín Rodríguez Sahagún (Minister of Defence and UCD deputy). Minister of Commerce: Carlos Ferrer Salat (president of CEOE, the Confederation of Spanish Business Organizations). Minister of the Economy: Ramón Tamames (PCE deputy). Minister of Transport and Communications: Javier Solana (PSOE deputy). Minister of Autonomías and Regions: General José Antonio Sáenz de Santamaría. Minister of Health: Enrique Múgica Herzog (PSOE deputy). Minister of Information: Luis María Anson (director of EFE news agency).

or a little later: impossible to place it precisely) Armada also explodes, and the two men exchange shouts, reproaches and accusations, until Armada appeals as a last resort to discipline and Tejero replies: I obey only General Milans' orders. It is at this moment that Armada turns to Milans. Using the office telephone, tapped by the police several hours previously like all the rest of the telephones in the Cortes, Armada speaks to Milans, explains what's going on, asks him to convince Tejero that his plan is a good one and hands the receiver to the lieutenant colonel. Milans repeats Armada's arguments to Tejero: the only solution is a unity government for everyone and temporary exile for the lieutenant colonel and his men; Tejero repeats his own arguments to Milans: exile is a dishonourable way out, a government of Socialists and Communists is no solution, he'll accept no solution other than a military junta headed by General Milans himself. Who said anything about a military junta? replies Milans. I'm no politician, and neither are you: what we're doing here is putting things at His Majesty's disposition, so that he and Armada should decide what to do; now they've decided, so mission accomplished: obey Armada and let him take charge of everything. That's an order. I cannot obey that order, General, sir, answers Tejero. And you know it. Do not ask me to do what I cannot do. The conversation between the two men goes on for a few more minutes, but the coup's chain of command is now broken and Milans does not manage to get Tejero to obey him; once Milans has failed, Armada makes one last attempt, also to no avail: not even the warning that a group from special operations is preparing to take the Cortes by storm manages to overcome the stubbornness of the lieutenant colonel, who threatens Armada before he leaves with a massacre if anyone tries to end the hostage-taking by force.

This is how the meeting between Tejero and Armada finishes, or that's how I imagine it finishing. The general left the Cortes at exactly twenty-five past one in the morning; five minutes earlier the television had broadcast the message the King had recorded at the Zarzuela, a message that had been announced for several hours on various media and in which the King had proclaimed that he was on the side of the Constitution and democracy. The two events turned out to be deciding factors in the outcome of the coup, but the second was taken by most of the country as a sure sign that the coup had failed; it wasn't true: the truth is that Armada's failure in the Cortes and the broadcast of the King's televised message meant only that the coup as originally conceived had failed: the coup could no longer be Milans and Armada's coup, but it could still be Tejero's coup (and Armada and Milans could still join it); the coup could no longer be a soft coup: it had to be a hard coup; the coup could no longer be with the King or using the King as a fraudulent alibi: it had to be a coup against the King. This of course turned it into a much more dangerous coup, because it could split the Army into two opposing halves, one loyal to the King and another in rebellion; but it absolutely didn't turn it into an impossible coup, because it absolutely wasn't impossible that, seeing that the King was not with them, the most hardened Francoist officers with most accrued fury might opt to follow Tejero's example and take advantage of that perhaps unrepeatable opportunity to gather now without alibis around the coup for which they'd been calling for years. Milans and Armada's coup had died in the office of the new building of the Cortes not because Tejero was mad, as Armada thought or pretended to think, but because, drunk with power, with egomania, with renown and idealism, ready to make a grand exit from the Cortes through triumph or failure (but only a grand exit), the lieutenant colonel broke a chain of command that was too weak and tried to impose his coup on Armada and Milans: not a coup that would result in a government of unity but a coup that would result in a military junta, not a coup with the monarchy against democracy but a coup against the monarchy and against democracy; Milans and Armada's coup failed because in his talk with Armada in the Cortes Tejero gambled everything on everything and preferred the failure of the coup to the triumph of a coup different from his, but at half past one in the morning it was yet to be known how many soldiers would accept Tejero's challenge, how many would share his exclusive idea of the coup and his utopia of the country as a barracks and how many would be ready to run a real risk to achieve it, embarking on a hard coup that would present the King with the option of accepting its result or giving up the Crown.

The King's appearance on television and Armada's failure in the Cortes did not therefore mark the end of the coup, but the start of a different phase of the coup: the last one. Both things happened at almost the very same time; this simultaneity inevitably sparked off conjecture. The most persistent was devised and spread by the *golpistas* facing trial for their actions on 23 February and claims that the Zarzuela held back the royal message until they heard the result of the talk between Armada and Tejero and only authorized the broadcast once they knew the general had failed; it also claims, if Armada had not failed, if Tejero had let the general negotiate with the deputies and they had agreed to form a unity government with him as a way out of the coup, the King would have accepted the agreement, his message would not have been broadcast and the coup would have triumphed with his blessing: all things considered, with the unity government led by Armada and backed by the Cortes the King would have achieved what he wanted when he put Armada in charge of the coup. It is a tricky conjecture – one more of the many served up during the 23 February trial to attempt to blame the King and exonerate the *golpistas* – because it starts from the falsehood that the King ordered the coup and because it mixes the verifiable with the unverifiable, but in a certain sense it's not foolish. The verifiable part is false; it has been proven that the King did not wait to know the result of Armada's move before allowing the television station to broadcast his message: leaving aside the unanimous testimony denying it by the television directors and technicians, who maintain they put it on screen as soon as it was in their hands, it's a fact that Armada came out of the Cortes five minutes after the King's words were broadcast, and could not advise the Zarzuela of his failure from inside the Cortes – he would have had to do so in the presence of Tejero, who would have had the most interest in making it public during the trial – and that, when he arrived at the Hotel Palace and found out from those in charge of the cordon around the attackers that the King had just spoken on television, the general seemed surprised and displeased, in theory because the intervention of the monarch could divide the Army and provoke an armed conflict, but in practice because he was not resigned to his failure (and undoubtedly because he was beginning to feel that he had calculated badly, that he'd exposed himself too much by negotiating with Tejero, that the suspicions that hovered over him were increasingly dense and that, if

the *golpistas* were defeated, it wasn't going to be as simple as he'd originally thought to hide his actual role in the coup behind the façade of a
mere unsuccessful negotiator for the liberty of the hostaged parliamentarians). All this is verifiable; then comes the unverifiable: what would
have happened if Armada had been able to negotiate the creation of a
unity government with the parliamentarians? Would they have accepted
it? Would the King have accepted it? Armada's plan might seem implau-
sible, and perhaps it was, but history abounds in implausibilities and,
as Santiago Carrillo remembered that night as he remained locked in
the clock room of the Cortes, it wouldn't have been the first time a
democratic Parliament gave in to blackmail by its own Army and
presented a defeat as a victory or as a prudent negotiated way out –
temporary, perhaps unsatisfactory but imperious – an extreme situation:
Armada always kept in mind that, twenty years earlier, just before he
moved to Paris as a student at the École de Guerre, General de Gaulle
had reached the presidency of the French Republic in a similar way,
and he undoubtedly thought on 23 February that he could adapt de
Gaulle's model to Spain to stage a veiled coup. As for the King, one
might ask if he would have refused to sanction an agreement adopted
by the representatives of popular sovereignty, or even if he could have.
Whatever the answer one chooses to give to this question, one thing
seems beyond doubt to me: had the parliamentary leaders accepted
Armada's conditions, the royal message would not have represented
any obstacle to their being fulfilled, because not a single one of his
phrases denied that the government led by Armada could turn into the
circumstantial means for the return to the constitutional order violated
by the assault on the Cortes or because the perimeter of the King's
words had enough expanse to take on board, had it been necessary,
Armada's solution. The message was a reworking of a telex sent from
the Zarzuela Palace at half past ten that night to the Captains General
and said exactly the following: 'In addressing all the Spanish people,
briefly and concisely, in the extraordinary circumstances we are experi-
encing at this moment, I ask everyone for the greatest calm and
confidence and tell you that I have sent the following order to the
Captains General of the military regions, maritime zones and aerial
regions: "In the face of the situation created by the events unfolding in

the Cortes and of any possible confusion, I confirm that I have ordered the civil authorities and the Joint Chiefs of Staff to take all necessary measures to maintain constitutional order within existing legal frameworks. Any military measures that circumstances seem to require must have the approval of the Joint Chiefs of Staff." The Crown, symbol of the permanence and unity of the nation, cannot in any way tolerate actions or attitudes by those who would seek to intervene by force in the democratic process outlined by the Constitution ratified by the Spanish people.' These words – spoken by a monarch wearing his Captain General's uniform and with his face transfigured by the most difficult hours of his forty-three years of life – are a clear declaration of constitutional loyalty, of support for democracy and rejection of the assault on the Cortes, and that's how they were interpreted when the King spoke them and and how they've been interpreted since then; the interpretation strikes me as correct, but words have owners, and it's obvious that, if Armada had managed to forge a pact with the political leaders to agree to form the government anticipated by the *golpistas* and present as the solution to the coup what in reality was the triumph of the coup, those same words would of course have continued to mean a condemnation of those who had assaulted the Cortes, but would have been able to come to mean a recognition of those, like Armada and the political leaders, who'd agreed to form part of his government, had managed to get the parliamentary hostages released and thus restore the shattered legality and constitutional order. In short: it's not that the King's speech was written anticipating or desiring Armada to come out of the Cortes triumphant; it's that his words constitute a condemnation of Tejero's coup, not necessarily a condemnation of Armada's coup.

We'll never know whether, had Armada come out of the Cortes triumphant, the King would have rejected his triumph by refusing to sanction a unity government extracted by means of blackmail, but we know that Armada's failure shrank the perimeter of the words of the royal message until all the doors of the Zarzuela were closed to the *golpistas* and the monarch was publicly set with no turning back against Tejero's coup, against Milans' coup, against Armada's coup, against all the coups of the coup. I repeat that this does not mean that at twenty-five past one in the morning the coup had failed; Milans and Armada's soft coup had failed, but not Tejero's hard coup: the lieutenant colonel was still occupying the Cortes, Milans was still occupying Valencia and part of the Army was still lying in wait, indifferent to the King's message or irritated or disconcerted by it, awaiting the slightest troop movements to dispel their doubts, gathering the fury accumulated in their Francoist hearts to hand the victory to the supporters of the coup. And it was at that moment when the excuse appeared that so many had spent the evening waiting for, the tiny movement that could predict a rebel avalanche: at thirty-five minutes past one in the morning, ten minutes after the defeat of the former royal secretary had been consummated, a column sent by a major of the Brunete Armoured Division and made up of fourteen light vehicles and more than a hundred soldiers tried to break the balance of the coup by joining the several hundred Civil Guards who were holding the Cortes hostage. And in this way the coup began to enter its final phase.

PART FIVE

VIVA ITALIA!

The frozen image shows the right wing of the chamber of the Congress of Deputies on the evening of 23 February. Almost a quarter of an hour has gone by since the rebel Civil Guards burst in and Captain Jesús Muñecas has just announced from the speakers' rostrum the arrival of a competent military authority to take charge of the coup. At this precise moment the camera – the only camera still in operation – shows a fixed and frontal shot of that area of the chamber, with the figure of Adolfo Suárez almost in the exact centre of the image, monopolizing the spectator's attention as if they were filming a historical drama in the hall and the Prime Minister were playing the starring role.

Nothing belies the similarity when the image unfreezes; nothing will contradict it to the end of the recorded film. After Captain Muñecas' speech the atmosphere in the chamber relaxes, the deputies give each other lights and cigarettes and weak glances and Adolfo Suárez asks an usher for a cigarette with gestures and then stands up, walks over to the usher, takes the offered cigarette and goes back and sits down again. Suárez is an incorrigible smoker, he always has tobacco with him and this evening is no exception (in fact, he has already smoked several cigarettes since the beginning of the incursion), so his gesture is a way of sounding out the assailants, testing their level of permissiveness with the hostages and investigating a way of acquiring information about what is going on. He soon finds out. He hasn't smoked half the cigarette yet when a man in civilian clothes enters through the right-hand door; behind him appears Lieutenant Colonel Tejero, who motions to his men to let the recent arrival take a seat next to the Prime Minister, on the staircase running up beside the benches. The man (thin

*and tall and swarthy, with a white handkerchief sticking out of the pocket
of his dark jacket) sits in the indicated spot and he and Suárez begin a
dialogue that goes on almost without interruption for the next several
minutes; the word dialogue is excessive: Suárez just listens to the words of
the recent arrival and occasionally offers comments or questions, or what
look to be comments or questions. Who is the recent arrival? Why has he
been allowed into the chamber? What is he talking about with Suárez? The
recent arrival is Cavalry Major José Luis Goróstegui, General Gutiérrez
Mellado's adjutant; credibly, the assault on the Cortes has caught him by
surprise in the vicinity of the building or in some office in the building; also
credibly, he has made use of his position as a military officer, friend or
acquaintance of Captain Muñecas and acquaintance of Tejero to get them
to let him sit next to the Prime Minister and tell him what he knows. To
judge by the distracted attention the ministers and deputies around Suárez
pay him, Goróstegui must have very little and not very important news to
impart; to judge by the undivided attention Suárez pays him, it must be
abundant and of enormous importance. The news is most likely all four
things at once, and Tejero has most likely allowed Goróstegui to talk to
Suárez to undermine his morale, so that he'll understand that everything in
the Cortes is under control and that the coup has triumphed.*

*Several identical minutes pass in this way, after which a knife-like voice
cuts the silence filled with coughs and murmurs that seems to shroud the
chamber. 'Doctor Petinto, please come here. This gentleman appears to be
slightly injured.' The voice belongs to one of the* golpista *officers or an NCO
who summons the parliamentary doctor to attend to Fernando Sagaseta,
deputy from the Canary Islands, who's been hit by some pieces of the ceiling
that have fallen after the shooting. All the parliamentarians have turned at
the same time towards the upper area of the chamber, where the voice came
from, though they soon go back to their positions on the bench; Adolfo
Suárez does so as well, and seconds later resumes his discussion with Major
Goróstegui. At a certain moment, however, the two men fall silent and
stare at the left-hand entrance to the chamber: there, after a few seconds,
almost imperceptible in the bottom corner of the screen, Lieutenant Colonel
Tejero's back appears, then he turns right round to look over the whole
chamber, as if making sure that all is in order; the lieutenant colonel disappears and a moment later appears again and then disappears once more,*

and his coming and going is a mirror image of other comings and goings that animate the image: a deputy – Donato Fuejo, doctor and Socialist – goes up to Fernando Sagaseta's seat, two ushers take glasses of water to the stenographers and finally take the stenographers out of the chamber, a journalist with his accreditation visible on the front of his pullover goes up one of the side stairways followed by a Civil Guard. These movements have not interrupted Adolfo Suárez and Major Goróstegui's speculations and commentaries and, just after Antonio Jiménez Blanco (UCD member and president of the Council of State, who has heard the news of the assault on the radio and has managed to get the assailants to authorize him to enter the Cortes to share his colleagues' fate) comes into the chamber and sits behind Goróstegui, Suárez gets up from his bench and says to the two Civil Guards watching the entrance to the chamber: 'I want to talk to the commander of the force'; then he walks down the stairs and takes a few steps towards the Guards. What happens next is not registered by the camera, because, although unaware that it's still recording, a Civil Guard has just bumped into its viewfinder and made it present a confusing close-up of the press box; the sound of the chamber, however, can still be heard clearly. We can hear Suárez's voice, unintelligible, in the midst of a commotion; we hear harsh military voices trying to impose silence (one says: 'Calm down, gentlemen!'; another says: 'The next time someone moves their hands this is going to move, got it?'; another says: 'Hands still. That's for when you're alone. Here it's over.'); harsher, louder and more contemptuous than the others, one voice ends up dominating ('Mr Suárez, stay in your seat!') and that's when the Prime Minister manages to make himself heard amid the uproar ('I have the authority as Prime Minister of the government . . .') until his voice is drowned out in a hail of shouts, insults and threats that seem to quieten the hall and return it to the simulacrum of normality it has been for half an hour. From that moment on the earlier mortuary silence reigns in the chamber again, while the camera, abandoned, continues offering a static shot of the press box; there, in the minutes that follow, a disorder of unconnected fragments crosses in chiaroscuro: the fleeting face of a woman wearing glasses, jackets with illegible journalists' accreditations, tense hands that vent their nervousness or fear by twirling cheap ballpoint pens or holding shaking cigarettes, a bundle of papers with Cortes letterhead lying on a step, the wrought-iron railing of a stairway, ties with rhomboids and white shirts and white fists and violet dresses and pleated skirts and grey sweaters and trousers and hands gripping folders bursting with papers and briefcases. And finally, almost thirty-five minutes after the beginning, the film finishes with a whirlwind of snow.

I

That's how the film ends: in a perfectly meaningless chaos, just as if the essential document about 23 February was not the chance result of a camera left running during the first minutes of the seizure, but the result of the guiding mind of a producer who decides to conclude his work with a plausible metaphor of the coup d'état; also, with a vindication of Adolfo Suárez as Prime Minister. Suárez was not a good Prime Minister during his last years in power, when democracy seemed to begin to establish itself in Spain, but maybe he was the best Prime Minister to confront a coup d'état, because no other Spanish politician of the time knew better than he did how to conduct himself in extreme circumstances or possessed his sense of the dramatic, his convert's faith in the value of democracy, his mythologized concept of the dignity of a prime minister, his knowledge of the Army and his bravery in opposing the rebel military officers. 'We must make very clear that in Spain there is no such thing as a civilian power and a military power,' wrote Suárez in June 1982, in an article where he protested the benevolence of the sentences handed down to those prosecuted for the 23 February coup. 'Power is only civilian.' That was one of his obsessions during his five years at the head of the government: he was the Prime Minister of the country and the military officers' only obligation was to obey his orders. Until the last moment of his mandate he got them to obey, until the last moment of his mandate he thought he'd subdued the military, but in the very last moment of his mandate on 23 February that belief was thwarted; maybe he'd lost his touch, or maybe it was impossible to subdue them. In any case, Suárez was not unaware of how to handle them, but he didn't always think he should have to handle the military with kid gloves, and from the very day he became Prime Minister and especially as he established himself in the post he had a tendency abruptly to remind them of their obligations with orders or rudeness: he liked to take generals down a peg or two by making them wait outside his office door and never hesitated to confront any soldier who questioned his authority or showed him a lack of respect (or threatened him: in September 1976, during a very heated argument in Suárez's office, having just accepted or demanded his resignation as Deputy Prime Minister, he was told by General de Santiago: 'Let me remind you, Prime Minister, that this country has seen more than one coup d'état.' 'And let me remind you, General,' answered Suárez, 'that this country still has the death penalty'); he was brave enough to make vital decisions like the legalization of the Communist Party without the approval of the Armed Forces and against their almost unanimous view; and therefore the store of 23 February anecdotes is overflowing with examples of his outright refusal to be intimidated by the rebels or to cede a single centimetre of his power as Prime Minister. Some of these examples are inventions of Suárez's hagiographers; two of them are undoubtedly true. The first happened in the early hours, in the tiny room near the chamber where Suárez was shut away after his first attempt to parley with the *golpistas*. According to the testimony of the Civil Guards keeping watch, at a certain moment Lieutenant Colonel Tejero burst into the room and without a word drew his pistol and aimed it at the Prime Minister's chest; Suárez's response was to stand up and twice shout in the face of the rebel officer the same emphatic order: 'Stand at attention!' The second happened on the evening of the 24th, once the coup had failed, during a meeting of the National Defence Council at the Zarzuela, chaired by the King; that was when Suárez understood that Armada had been the main ringleader of the coup and, after hearing the evidence that incriminated the King's former secretary, among which were the recordings of the telephone conversations between the occupiers of the Cortes, the Prime Minister ordered General Gabeiras to arrest him immediately. Gabeiras seemed to hesitate – he was Armada's immediate superior at Army General Headquarters, he had hardly been apart from him all night and the measure must have struck him as premature and disproportionate – then the general looked at the King for a ratification or a contradiction of the order he'd been given by Suárez, who, because he knew very well who the authentic chief of the Army was, hurled two furious phrases at the general: 'Don't look at the King. Look at me.'

That was Adolfo Suárez deep down or what he liked to imagine he was: a cocky provincial risen to the top of the government and completely immersed in his role of Prime Minister. That's how he tried to behave during the almost five years he was in power and that's how he behaved on 23 February. His gesture of standing up and trying to parley with the *golpistas* is basically no different from his gesture of confronting Tejero or Gabeiras: all three are attempts to assert himself as Prime Minister; nor is it basically any different from his gesture of remaining seated while the bullets whizzed around him in the chamber: this is a gesture of courage and grace and rebellion, a histrionic gesture and an entirely free gesture and a posthumous gesture, the gesture of a washed-up man who conceives of politics as an adventure and who tries agonizingly to legitimize himself and for one moment seems fully to embody democracy, but it is also a gesture of authority. That's to say: a gesture of violence. That is: the gesture of a pure politician.

2

What is a pure politician? Is a pure politician the same as a great politician, or an exceptional politician? Is an exceptional politician the same as an exceptional man, or an ethically irreproachable man, or simply a decent man? It's very likely that Adolfo Suárez was a decent man, but not an ethically irreproachable man, or even an exceptional man, or at least not the kind of man usually thought of as exceptional; he was however, all things considered, the most forceful and decisive Spanish politician of the last century.

Around 1927 Ortega y Gasset tried to describe the exceptional politician and perhaps ended up describing the pure politician. For Ortega, this is not an ethically irreproachable man, nor does he have any reason to be (Ortega considers it insufficient or paltry to judge a politician ethically: he must be judged politically); some qualities that in the abstract tend to be considered virtues coexist in his nature with others that in the abstract tend to be considered defects, but the latter are no less essential than the former. Here are some virtues: natural intelligence, courage, serenity, fighting spirit, astuteness, stamina, healthy instincts, the ability to reconcile the irreconcilable. Here are some defects: impulsiveness, constant preoccupation, lack of scruples, talent to deceive, vulgarity or absence of refinement in one's ideas and tastes; also, the absence of an inner life or a defined personality, which turns him into a chameleon-like actor and a transparent being whose deepest secret is that he lacks any secrets. The pure politician is the opposite of an ideologue, but he is not only a man of action; nor is he exactly the opposite of an intellectual: he possesses an intellectual's enthusiasm for knowledge, but he has invested it entirely in detecting the dead in what appears to be alive and in refining the essential ingredient of his trade: historical intuition. That's what Ortega called it; Isaiah Berlin would have given it another name: he would have called it a sense of reality, a transitory gift not learned in universities or in books, that assumes a certain familiarity with the relevant facts that allows certain politicians at certain moments to know 'what fits with what: what can be done in given circumstances and what cannot, what means will work in what situations and how far, without necessarily being able to explain how they know this or even what they know'. The Ortegan handbook of the pure politician is not unassailable; that's not why I've summarized it here, but because it proposes an exact portrait of the future Adolfo Suárez. It's true that among the qualities of the pure politician Ortega barely mentions in passing the one for which Suárez was reproached most insistently in his day: ambition; but that's because Ortega knows that for a politician, as for an artist or a scientist, ambition is not a quality – a virtue or a defect – but a basic premise.

Suárez complied with it comfortably. The feature that best defined him until he arrived in power was an outrageous hunger for power: like one of those wild young men of nineteenth-century novels who set out from the provinces to conquer the capital – like Stendhal's Julien Sorel, like Balzac's Lucien Rubempré, like Flaubert's Frédéric Moreau – Suárez was ambition incarnate and was never ashamed of that, because he never accepted there was anything reprehensible about the desire for power; on the contrary: he thought that without power there was no politics and without politics for him there was not the slightest possibility of fulfilment. He was a pure politician because he never thought of being anything else, because he never dreamt of being anything else, because he was an ascetic of power ready to sacrifice everything to acquire it and because he would have made a pact with the devil without a second thought in exchange for getting to be what he got to be. 'What is power for you?' a *Paris Match* journalist asked him days after he was named Prime Minister, and Suárez only managed to respond with his dazzling winner's smile and a few words that explained nothing and explained everything: 'Power? I love it.' During his best years this jubilant brazenness gave him an unbeatable superiority over his adversaries, who saw insatiable greed in his eyes and were nevertheless unable to stare him down and kept feeding it to their own cost. Political power turned into his instrument of personal growth, but only because before it had been a free-standing, voracious passion, and if he had an idealized vision of the dignity of a prime minister to the point of myth it was because the position of Prime Minister constituted for him the highest expression of power and because for his whole life he hadn't wanted anything other than to be Prime Minister.

It's true: he was an uneducated rogue, he was a little provincial Falangist, he was a Francoist upstart, he was the King's messenger boy; his detractors were right, except that his life story demonstrates that being right isn't the whole story. He possessed an actor's talent for deceit, but the first time he saw Santiago Carrillo he didn't deceive him: he did belong to a family of defeated Republicans, several of whom had seen the inside of Franco's prisons during the war; no one in his house, however, instilled in him the slightest political conviction, and it's quite possible that no one ever talked to him about the war except as a natural catastrophe; it's likely, however, that he learned from childhood to hate defeat the way one hates a family affliction. He was born in 1932 in Cebreros, a wine-producing town in the province of Ávila. His mother's family had a small business, and she was a tough, religious and headstrong woman; his father was the son of the court secretary and also a likeable, cocky, vain, swindling, skirt-chasing gambler. Although he never really got on well with his father – or perhaps for this very reason – it might be that deep down he was just like his father, except for the fact that in his case the exercise of these inclinations and features of his character was entirely subordinate to the satisfaction of his only true appetite. He was a terrible student, who went from one school to the next and rarely set foot inside the university except to take exams for courses he'd often memorized without understanding; he never acquired the sedentary habit of reading, and till the end of his days he was pursued by a rumour, only initially encouraged by him, according to which he'd never gathered enough patience to read a book from the first page to the last. He was interested in other things: girls, dancing, football, tennis, cinema and cards. He was hyperactive, vital and compulsively sociable, a neighbourhood leader with a spontaneous kindness and indisputable success with women, but he flipped easily from euphoria to dejection and, although he probably never visited a psychiatrist, some of his close friends always considered him a prime candidate for psychiatry. The balm against his psychological fragilities was a solid religiosity that threw him into the arms of Acción Católica and channelled his vocation for prominence from adolescence by allowing him to found and preside over pious associations with innocuous political pretensions. At the end of the 1940s or beginning of the 1950s, in a city like Ávila, fortified by the provincial sanctimoniousness of Spanish Catholicism, Adolfo Suárez personified to perfection the ideal youth of the dictatorship: a neat, handsome, cheerful, sporty, Catholic, bold and enterprising young man, whose political ambitions were bound up with his social and economic ambitions and whose mentality of obedience and the sacristy could not even imagine that anybody might question the foundations and mechanisms of the regime, but only make use of them.

Everything seemed to augur a radiant future, but from one day to the next it all seemed to collapse. At the beginning of 1955, when he'd just turned twenty-three, finished his law degree with great difficulty and secured his first paying job at the Beneficencia de Ávila (a local welfare charity), his father fled from the city shrouded in a business scandal, abandoning the family. Suárez bore this desertion like a cataclysm: as well as the emotional wrench, his father's flight meant social dishonour and economic poverty for a large family whose shortage of money did not correspond with their high social standing in the city; it's likely that, prey to hypochondria and unable to meet the needs of his mother and four younger brothers on his trainee's salary, Suárez seriously considered the escape route of entering a seminary. A stroke of luck freed him from his tribulations. In the month of August Suárez met Fernando Herrero Tejedor, a young Falangist prosecuting attorney and member of Opus Dei who had just been named civil governor and provincial chief of the Movimiento in Ávila and who, thanks to the recommendation of one of his private teachers, gave Suárez a job in the civil government, which allowed him to supplement his Beneficencia salary, enter the structure of the single party and cultivate the friendship of a powerful and well-connected person who over the years would

298 THE ANATOMY OF A MOMENT

become his political mentor. His joy, however, was short-lived: in 1956 Herrero Tejedor was transferred to Logroño, Suárez lost his job and the following year, with no money or hope of prosperity in the province, he decided to try his luck in Madrid. There he was reunited with his father, there he set up an office with him to practise as a legal agent (a line of work his father had practised irregularly in Ávila), there he managed to reunite under the same roof his father, his mother and one of his brothers in a flat on Calle Hermanos Miralles. But after only a few months things went off the rails again: his father got the family involved in shady financial business again and Suárez broke with him, left the office and went to live on his own in a boarding house. Perhaps at that stage he hit rock bottom, although we know little about it for sure: people say he barely knew anyone in Madrid, that he saw his mother occasionally and made his living with sporadic jobs, carrying luggage at the Príncipe Pío railway station or selling electrical appliances door to door; they say he suffered hardships, that he went hungry, that he spent a lot of time wandering the streets. Some of Suárez's apologists appeal to the real predicaments of those days to depict a 'self-made man' who'd known misery and not the privileges the politicians of Francoism grew up with; the depiction is not false, as long as we don't forget that the period was very brief and that, while it lasted, Suárez was just a young provincial fallen on hard times, exiled in the capital awaiting an opportunity worthy of his ambition. The one to provide it was again Herrero Tejedor, who then held the post of national provincial delegate in the secretary generalship of the Movimiento and who, as soon as the father of one of Suárez's friends told him the situation he was in and asked for a job for him, hastened to appoint him as his personal secretary. That happened in the autumn of 1958. From that time on, and until the death of Herrero Tejedor in 1975, Suárez was hardly ever apart from his mentor; from that time on, and until he himself ended up destroying it, Suárez was hardly ever apart from Francoist power, because that was the ever so modest start of his step-by-step ascent of the Movimiento hierarchy. Before he began it, however, something else had happened: in Ávila Suárez had met Amparo Illana, a beautiful, rich, classy young woman with whom he fell immediately in love and whom he would take another four years to marry; by then he was about to leave for Madrid with nothing in his pockets but his hands, and the first time he visited the house of his future wife her father – a military lawyer with the rank of colonel and treasurer of the Press Association of Madrid – interrogated him about how he was earning his living. 'Badly,' he answered, with his cocky Ávila charm intact. 'But don't worry: before I'm thirty I'll be civil governor; before forty, undersecretary; and before fifty, a minister in the government and then Prime Minister.'

It might be that the above-mentioned anecdote is false – one more of the legends that surround his youth – although Suárez did fulfil that programme point for point. In the closed and pyramidal order of Francoist power, where servility was an indispensable tool of political promotion, doing so demanded from the start that he thoroughly employ all his flair for congeniality and all his capacity for adulation. As Herrero Tejedor's secretary his job consisted of taking care of correspondence, arranging appointments and attending to visitors, many of whom were Party leaders or civil governors passing through Madrid, none of whom would forget the handsome, diligent and enthusiastic Falangist who greeted them with a raised arm in an imitation of the fascist salute (At your service, chief!) and saw them off with an imitation of a military click of his heels (May I be of any further service?). This is how he began to carve out his prestige as a Falangist cub and scale the promotion ladder of two strategic enclaves of the regime: the secretary generalship of the Movimiento and the Prime Minister's Office; and this was how, without giving up his loyalty to Herrero Tejedor, he began to win the confidence of the dictator's subordinates who in the mid-1960s held most of the effective power in Spain and represented the most viable possibility of a future Francoism without Franco: Admiral Luis Carrero Blanco, Minister of the Presidency, and Laureano López Rodó, Minister for the Development Plan. By that time Suárez already knew better than most all the nooks and crannies of the corridors of power, had developed a sixth sense for capturing the slightest tremor in the delicate tectonics that sustained it and had a doctorate with full honours in the extremely refined discipline of circulating among the conflicting families of the regime without making unmanageable enemies for himself, and persuading them all, from the

Falangists to the members of Opus Dei, that he was one of their own. The time was still distant when he would consider the Madrid political village to be a great sewer: now that same city held him spellbound with the supernatural gleam of an exquisite jewel; his least indulgent biographer, Gregorio Morán, has described in detail the ambitious strategies he used in his desire to conquer. According to Morán, Suárez heaped attention on those he needed to captivate, he took advantage of any excuse to visit their houses and offices, he did everything possible to win over their relatives and, wielding first-hand information about the interiorities of power and of the abuses and weaknesses of those who exercised it, he came and went with news, gossip and rumours that made him a very valuable informer and opened the way for his climb. He took no notice of methods, didn't skimp on resources. In 1965 he was appointed programme director of Radiotelevisión Española (RTVE); his boss was Juan José Rosón, a sombre Galician insensible to his talent and charm with whom he maintained not very cordial relations: he managed to improve them by moving with his family into a flat in the same building where he lived. Around about the same time he decided that his next objective should be to become a civil governor; it was a very attractive post because in those years a civil governor possessed enormous power in his province and, in order to win over the Minister of the Interior, Camilo Alonso Vega – close friend of Franco's and responsible to a great extent for the appointment of civil governors – for three consecutive summers he rented an apartment next door to the one occupied every year by the minister in a development in Alicante and subjected him to a non-stop siege that began with the daily Mass first thing in the morning and ended with the last drink in the early hours. In 1973, when he was starting to harbour well-founded hopes of becoming a minister, he conceived the brilliant idea of renting a summer villa just a few metres from La Granja Palace in Segovia, in the gardens of which a celebration was held each year for an entire day to mark the anniversary of the outbreak of the Civil War in the presence of Franco and all the bigwigs of Francoism; Suárez invited a select few to the villa, who, before and after the endless reception, the tedious lunch and the spectacle the Minister of Information and Tourism inflicted on those who attended, enjoyed the privilege of relief from the heartless heat of every 18 July, freedom from the torture of travelling the eighty kilometres that separated the palace from Madrid with their evening dresses and tuxedos stuck to their bodies with sweat, and being fêted by the host, whose sympathy and hospitality generated feelings of lasting gratitude.

He won the friendship of Camilo Alonso Vega, and in 1968 was named civil governor of Segovia; he won the friendship of Rosón – or at least managed to reduce the mistrust he inspired – and in 1969 was named director general of RTVE; he won the friendship of many of Francoism's bigwigs, and in 1975 was named minister. He was irresistible, but these purely picaresque episodes not only constitute part of his real reputation, but also a demonstration that few politicians mastered as well as he did the degraded inbreeding of Francoist power and that few were willing to go as far as he was to make the most of it. That's why the person who in certain respects best portrayed Suárez at this time was Francisco Franco, who was the person who knew better than anyone the logic of Francoist power because he was the one who'd created it. The two men hardly ever coincided in their lives outside of ceremonial occasions, on one of which, however, the young politician drew attention with some discordant declaration; maybe because of that, and undoubtedly using the psychological gifts that had served him so well in his occupation of the leadership of the state for forty years, Franco thought he recognized in Suárez the disposition of a blossoming traitor, and on one occasion, when Suárez was head of RTVE, after the two had been chatting for a while in El Pardo Palace the dictator commented to his personal physician: 'That man's ambition is dangerous. He has no scruples.'*

Franco was right: Suárez's ambition ended up being lethal for Francoism; his lack of scruples as well. These two things alone, however,

---

* Suárez had gone to El Pardo that day to record Franco's Christmas message; we don't know what they talked about, but we do know that at some official reception held around the same time Suárez spoke to Franco – this is what I was referring to above when I mentioned a discordant declaration – of the inevitable democratic future awaiting the country after his death. For any of us this nerve means only that Suárez was a Francoist so sure of his impeccable Francoist record and of his loyalty to Franco that he allowed himself to cast doubt on the continuity of the regime without fear of unleashing the wrath of its founder; it's possible that for Franco it might have meant the same thing, but that precisely for this reason he might have considered the comment even more insidious, and did not forget it.

do not suffice to explain his stunning ascent in the 1960s and 1970s. Suárez was always working, and his political talent was beyond doubt: he had curiosity, listened more than he spoke, learned quickly, solved problems by the simplest and most direct routes, cleared out the teams of politicians he inherited without a second thought, knew how to bring opposing wills together, reconcile the irreconcilable and detect the dead in what appeared to be still alive; furthermore, he never let a single opportunity slip by to prove his worth: as if he really had sealed a pact with the devil, he didn't even waste opportunities that could have ruined the career of any other politician. On 15 June 1969, when he was still civil governor of Segovia, fifty-eight people died under the rubble of a collapsed restaurant in the residential development of Los Ángeles de San Rafael; the tragedy was the result of the proprietor's greed, but normally such a scandal would have spattered Suárez politically, especially at a time when the battle Falangists and Opus Dei were waging for control of the regime was reaching its decisive point; Suárez nevertheless managed to come out of the catastrophe reinforced: for weeks the newspapers were constantly praising the serenity and courage of the civil governor, who as the accounts kept repeating arrived at the scene of events shortly after the collapse, took charge of the situation and began pulling the wounded out of the debris with his own hands, and whom the government decorated a short time later for his conduct with the Great Cross of Civil Merit.

Months after the disaster of Los Ángeles de San Rafael an event that changed the future Prime Minister's life occurred: he met the future King. By that time Suárez already had the conviction that Prince Juan Carlos was the winning horse in the imminent race of post-Francoism – he had it from Herrero Tejedor, from Admiral Carrero, from López Rodó, he had it especially from a reasoning and a political instinct that were in him the same thing – so he bet all his capital on the Prince, who, for his part, also bet on Suárez, in need as he was of the loyalty of young politicians prepared to do battle at his side against the powerful sector of old inflexible Francoists doubtful of his capacity to succeed Franco. That was the task to which Suárez devoted himself almost exclusively over the next six years, because he knew that doing battle to make the Prince King was doing battle for power, though also because, just as he knew how to detect what was dead in what appeared still alive, he knew how to detect what was still alive in what appeared dead. As for the King, from the beginning he felt enormous sympathy for Suárez, but never deceived himself about him: 'Adolfo is neither for Opus Dei nor for the Falange,' he said on some occasion. 'Adolfo is for Adolfo.' Shortly after meeting the Prince – and partly owing to his insistence – he was named director general of RTVE; he stayed in this post for four years during which he served the cause of the monarchy with belligerent fidelity, but this was also an important phase in his political life because this was when he discovered the brand-new potential of television to configure reality and because he began to feel the proximity and the actual breath of power and to prepare his assault on government: he visited the Zarzuela very frequently, where he gave the Prince recordings of his travels and ceremonial acts regularly broadcast on the news bulletin of the main channel, consulted with Admiral Carrero every week in the headquarters of the Prime Minister's Office, at Castellana 3, where he was welcomed affectionately and where he received ideological orientation and concrete instructions he applied without hesitation, pampered military officers – who celebrated him for the generosity with which he received any proposal from the Army – and even the intelligence services, with whose chief, the future *golpista* Colonel José Ignacio San Martín, he struck up a certain friendship. It was also during that time, towards the end of his term at RTVE, that Suárez's sixth sense registered an almost invisible shift of the centre of power which in a very short time would turn out to be decisive: although Carrero Blanco continued symbolizing the assurance that Francoism would continue after the death of Franco, López Rodó began to lose influence and instead Torcuato Fernández Miranda emerged as the new key politician, then Minister Secretary General of the Movimiento, a cold, cultured, fox-like and silent man whose haughty independence of mind provoked the suspicions of all the families of the regime and the partiality of the Prince, who had adopted that professor of constitutional law as his first political adviser. Suárez took note of the change: saw less of López Rodó and more of Fernández Miranda, who, although perhaps secretly despising him, publicly allowed himself to be befriended, undoubtedly because he was sure of being able to manage that young Falangist hungry for glory. Suárez's hunch turned out to be right, and in June of 1973 Carrero was named Prime Minister – the first named by Franco who still kept the powers of head of state for himself – and Fernández Miranda added the leadership of the Movimiento to the vice-presidency of the Cabinet, but Suárez did not obtain the post of minister he thought he already deserved, and didn't even convince Fernández Miranda to console him with the post of deputy Secretary General of the Movimiento. The disappointment was enormous: Suárez resigned from his post at RTVE because of it, taking refuge in the directorship of a state company and of the YMCA.

For the next two and a half years Suárez remained far from power, and his political career seemed stagnant; at some point it even seemed to have reached its end. Two violent deaths contributed to this fleeting impression: in December 1973 Admiral Carrero died in an ETA attack; in June 1975 Herrero Tejedor died in a car accident. The murder of Carrero was providential for the country because the disappearance of the Prime Minister who was to have preserved Francoism facilitated the change from dictatorship to democracy, but, given that with Carrero he lost a powerful protector, for Suárez it could have been catastrophic; Herrero Tejedor's death could have been even worse: with it Suárez might have been said to have been left definitively out in the open, deprived as well of the shelter of the man in whose shadow most of his political career had been played out and who just three months before the accident had appointed him deputy Secretary General of the Movimiento. Suárez overcame that double setback because by the time it happened he was too sure of himself and of the Prince's confidence to allow himself to be defeated by adversity, so he devoted that parenthesis in his political ascent to making money in shady business, convinced with reason that it was impossible to prosper politically in Francoism without the benefit of some personal fortune ('I'm not a minister because I don't live in Puerta de Hierro and I didn't study at the Pilar,' he once said during those years); he also devoted it to strengthening his relations with Fernández Miranda – and, through him, with the Prince – and to organizing the Union of the Spanish People (Unión del Pueblo Español, UDPE), a political association

created in the wake of the tiny liberalizing impulse promoted by
Admiral Carrero's replacement at the head of the government, Carlos
Arias Navarro, and made up of former ministers under Franco and
young officials of the regime like Suárez himself. Otherwise, at a time
when the death of Franco after forty years of absolute government
appeared at once as an imminent and marvellous event and when every
health crisis of the octogenarian dictator left the country trembling
with uncertainty, Suárez cultivated masterfully the necessary ambiguity
to prepare his future no matter what the future of Spain: on one hand,
he let no opportunity slip by to proclaim his fidelity to Franco and to
his regime, and on 1 October 1975, accompanied by other members of
the UDPE, he attended a huge demonstration in the Plaza de Oriente
in support of the general, hounded by the protests of the international
community owing to his decision to execute several ETA and FRAP
members; on the other hand, however, he went around saying in public
and in private that he was in favour of opening up the political game and
creating channels of expression for the different sensibilities present in
society, commonplaces of the political soup of the time that sounded
to Francoists like inoffensive impudence or naive ruses and to those in
favour of ending Francoism could sound like still repressed affirma-
tions of the desire for a democratic future for Spain. It is likely that
neither on one hand nor the other – not when he declared himself
unquestionably Francoist or when he declared himself an incipient
democrat – was Suárez telling the truth, but it's almost certain that, like
a transparent being whose deepest secret consists of not having secrets
or like a virtuoso actor declaiming his part on a stage, he always believed
what he was saying, and that's why everyone who heard him ended up
believing in him.

The death of Franco – whose funeral chapel he visited in the company
of the top brass of the UDPE after waiting for hours along with thousands of Francoists bathed in tears – relaunched his political career for
good. After being proclaimed King, Juan Carlos ceded to the pressure
of the most hard-line band of Francoism and kept a firm Francoist like
Arias Navarro at the head of the government, but he managed to get
Fernández Miranda to be both President of the Cortes and of the
Council of the Kingdom – the other two principal organs of power

– and also, thanks to Fernández Miranda, got Arias Navarro to appoint Suárez Minister Secretary General of the Movimiento. It was a post he'd been coveting for years, fit to satisfy the most ambitious ambition, but Suárez was more ambitious than the most ambitious, and did not settle for that. In theory his mission in that government that was to guide post-Francoism was almost ornamental (the substantial ministries were taken by older men with much more presence, prestige and political experience, like Manuel Fraga and José María de Areilza): Suárez was not unaware that he'd been placed there as the King's valet or messenger boy; however, he was again quick to seize any opportunity that presented itself and, especially as Arias proved himself to be a clumsy and hesitant prime minister incapable of shrugging off his colossal Francoist debts, took advantage of the disunity and inefficiency of a government overtaken by a wave of social conflicts that were actually political actions to steal the limelight from his Cabinet colleagues: in March 1976, in the absence of Manuel Fraga, Minister of the Interior, Suárez skilfully managed the crisis provoked in Vitoria by the death of three workers at the hands of the police, preventing Prime Minister Arias from decreeing a state of emergency in order to suppress what in the eyes of the government seemed about to degenerate into a revolutionary outbreak; in June of the same year he defended in the Cortes, with a brilliant speech in which he advocated political pluralism, a timid attempt at reform sponsored by the government, as a way of achieving reconciliation among Spaniards. The attempt failed, but its failure meant a much greater success for Suárez than its success would have. It's not a contradiction: at that moment, six months after the proclamation of the monarchy, the King and his political mentor, Fernández Miranda, had already understood that in order to conserve the throne he'd have to renounce the powers or a large part of the powers he'd inherited from Franco, converting the Francoist monarchy into a parliamentary monarchy; they'd also conceived a project of more profound and ambitious reform than that supported by the government, they knew that Arias Navarro could not and did not want to put it into practice and Suárez's speech in the Cortes finished persuading them that the young politician was the right person to do it. Or rather finished persuading the King, because Fernández Miranda had been persuaded of it for some time by then, while the monarch had not yet clearly seen that this obliging and ambitious nonentity, that this affable, crooked, uncultured and cocky little Falangist – so useful to him as a valet or messenger boy – was the ideal character to carry out the extremely subtle task of dismantling Francoism without disasters and erecting some form of democracy on top of it that would assure the future of the monarchy. It was Fernández Miranda who, with his rhetoric of a reader of Machiavelli and his intellectual influence over him, convinced the King that at least for his purposes at the time those personal characteristics of Suárez's were not defects but virtues: they needed an obliging and ambitious nonentity because his obligingness and ambition guaranteed an absolute loyalty, and because his lack of relevance and of a definite political project or ideas of his own guaranteed that he would apply those they dictated to him without deviating and that, once his mission was completed, they could get rid of him after thanking him for services rendered; they needed a cocky Falangist with his spirit because only a cocky, young, quick, tough, flexible, resolute, tenacious, spirited Falangist would be able to put up with the ferocious attacks of the Falangists and military officers first and keep them at bay afterwards; they needed an affable guy because he would need to seduce half the world and a crooked guy because he would need to fool the other half; and as for his lack of culture, Fernández Miranda was cultured enough to know that one doesn't learn politics in books and for that endeavour culture could be a hindrance, and perceptive enough to have noticed already that Suárez possessed more than any other politician of his generation that transitory gift or that exact and inexplicable comprehension of what at that moment was dead and what was alive and that familiarity with significant events   with what fits and what doesn't fit, with what can and cannot be done, with how and with whom and at what cost it can be done – that Ortega called historical intuition and Berlin called a sense of reality.

Resolved to make Suárez the Prime Minister who would carry out the reform, on 1 July 1976 the King secured Arias Navarro's resignation; he did not have, however, a free hand in naming his replacement: according to Francoist legislation, he had to choose between a shortlist of three candidates presented to him by the Council of the Kingdom, a consultative body on which sat some of the most conspicuous members of orthodox Francoism. But, thanks to the guile and ability of Fernández Miranda, who chaired the Council and had been preparing this for months, at midday on 3 July the King received a shortlist that included the name of the chosen one. Suárez knew it; or rather: he knew he was on the shortlist, but he didn't know he was the chosen one; or rather: he didn't know it but he guessed, and that Saturday afternoon, while waiting for the King's phone call in his house in Puerta de Hierro – he was finally living in Puerta de Hierro and that's why he was a minister and could be Prime Minister – he was consumed by doubts. In his last years of lucidity Suárez remembered the scene publicly a few times, at least once on television, old, grey and with the same melancholy smile of triumph with which Julien Sorel or Lucien Rubempré or Frédéric Moreau would have remembered at the end of their lives their supreme moment, or with the same ironic smile of failure with which a man who'd sold his soul to the devil remembers many years later the moment when the devil finally fulfilled his part of the bargain. Suárez knew of the King's and Fernández Miranda's calculations, of Fernández Miranda's certainties and the King's doubts, knew the King appreciated his fidelity, his personal charm and the efficiency he'd demonstrated in government, but he wasn't sure that at the last moment prudence or fear or conformity wouldn't advise him to forget the audacity of appointing a secondary politician like him almost unknown to the public and opt for the long-serving Federico Silva Muñoz or Gregorio López Bravo, the two others on the shortlist. He'd never wanted to be anything else, never dreamt of being anything else, he'd always been an ascetic of power, and now everything seemed prepared to allow him to sate his hunger in real life and his ambition for plenitude sensed that if he didn't get it now he would never get it. He felt impatient beside the telephone and finally, at some point in the afternoon, the telephone rang. It was the King; he asked him what he was doing. Nothing, he answered. I was getting some papers in order. Ah, said the King, and then he asked him how his family was. They're on holiday, he explained. In Ibiza. I've stayed home alone with Mariam. He knew the King knew that he knew, but he didn't say anything else and, after a very short silence that seemed eternal to him, he decided to ask the King if he wanted anything. Nothing, said the King. Just wanted to know how you were. Then the King said goodbye and Suárez hung up the phone with the certainty that the monarch had been unnerved and had appointed Silva or López Bravo and hadn't had the courage to tell him. A short time later the phone rang again: it was the King again. Hey, Adolfo, he said. Why don't you come over here? I want to talk to you about something. He tried to control the euphoria and, while he was getting dressed and driving his wife's Seat 127 to the Zarzuela through the light traffic of a summer weekend, in order to protect himself from disappointment against which he was defenceless he kept telling himself over and over again that the King only called him to apologize for not having chosen him, to explain his decision, to assure him he was still counting on him, to wrap him in protestations of friendship and affection. At the Zarzuela he was received by an aide-de-camp, who made him wait a few minutes and then invited him to enter the King's office. He went in, but he didn't see anyone, and at that moment he experienced a sharp sense of unreality, as if he were about to conclude abruptly a theatrical performance he'd spent many years acting without knowing it. A loud laugh pulled him out of that second of panic or bewilderment; he turned around: the King had hidden behind his office door. I have to ask you a favour, Adolfo, he told him point-blank. I want you to be Prime Minister of the government. He didn't yell in jubilation; all he managed to articulate was: Shit, Your Majesty, I thought you'd never ask.

3

On 18 February 1981, five days before the coup d'état, the newspaper *El País* published an editorial comparing Adolfo Suárez to General Della Rovere. It was another cliché, or almost: in the Madrid political village at the beginning of the 1980s – in certain circles of the left of this village – comparing Suárez to the Italian who collaborated with the Nazis turned hero of the resistance, the protagonist of an old Roberto Rossellini film, was almost as common as mentioning the name of General Pavía every time there was a mention of the threat of a coup d'état. But, although Suárez had resigned from his post as Prime Minister three weeks before and this fact perhaps might have been an invitation to leave behind the errors and recall the successes of the maker of democracy, the newspaper was not resorting to the comparison to praise the figure of Suárez, but to denigrate him. The editorial was extremely harsh. It was titled '*Adiós, Suárez, Adiós*' and contained not only implacable reproaches of his passivity as acting Prime Minister, but also especially a global rejection of his management at the head of the government; the only merit they seemed to admit consisted in 'having conferred the dignity of a democratic prime minister on curbing the remains of Francoism for years, like a convinced General Della Rovere transmuted into his role as defender of democracy'. But the newspaper soon denied Suárez this consolation honour and accused him of having given in to right-wing blackmail with his resignation. 'General Della Rovere died in front of a firing squad,' it concluded, 'and Suárez is running away in a hurry, with no end of bitterness and not a lot of guts.'

Did Suárez know Rossellini's film? Had he read the editorial in *El País*? Suárez was very fond of the cinema: as a young man he'd been a regular at double features, and as Prime Minister rarely would a week go by that he wouldn't watch at least one of the 16-mm films his butler Pepe Higueras obtained from Televisión Española and projected in a room in Moncloa (sometimes he watched these films with his family or with the family's guests; he often watched them alone, in the early hours: Suárez slept little and ate badly, a diet based on black coffee, cigarettes and omelettes); his taste in movies was not sophisticated – he mostly enjoyed adventure films and American comedies – but it's not impossible that he might have seen Rossellini's film in 1960 when it was released in Spain, or even that he might have seen it years later in Moncloa, curious about the character the great sewer of Madrid was comparing him to. As for the editorial in *El País*, he probably read it; although in the months of political siege and personal collapse that preceded the coup he didn't allow the newspapers into the family's living quarters without being expurgated, to spare his wife and children the daily broadsides against him, Suárez continued to read them, or at least he continued to read *El País*: from the very day of his appointment until that of his resignation, the newspaper had been a very severe critic of his mandate, but, because it represented the intellectual, modern and democratic left that his unredeemed guilty conscience of a former Falangist envied and for years dreamt of representing, not for a single instant had he not kept it in mind and maybe even secretly sought its approval, and that's why so many people in his party and outside it accused him of governing with one eye on its pages. I don't actually know if Suárez read the editorial in *El País* on 18 February; if he did, he must have felt a profound humiliation, because nothing could humiliate the cocky old Falangist as much as being called a coward, and few things could have pleased him more than demonstrating five days later that the accusation was false. I don't actually know if Suárez had a capricious urge or the curiosity to watch Rossellini's film when he was still Prime Minister and so many were identifying him with its protagonist; but if he did, maybe he would have felt the same profound emotion that strikes when we see outside ourselves what we carry inside ourselves, if he'd remembered it after 23 February, maybe he would have thought of reality's strange propensity to allow itself to be colonized by clichés, to demonstrate that, despite their being fossilized truths, that doesn't mean they're not the truth, or that they don't foreshadow it.

General Della Rovere tells a fable set in the tattered ruins of an Italian city occupied by the Nazis. The protagonist is Emmanuele Bardone, a handsome, affable, skirt-chasing, lying, swindling, gambling nonentity, an unscrupulous rogue who extorts money from the families of anti-fascist prisoners with the lie that he's using it to alleviate the captivity of their relatives. Bardone is also a chameleon: to the Germans he is an enthusiastic supporter of the Reich; to the Italians, an undercover adversary of the Reich; he employs all his seductive gifts on both sides, manages to convince both that there's no one more important than them and that he is ready to do anything for their cause. Bardone's destiny begins to change when, at a routine roadblock, the Germans kill General Della Rovere, an aristocratic and heroic Italian soldier recently returned to the country to coordinate the resistance against the invader; for Colonel Müller – the commanding officer of the occupying forces in the city – this is terrible news: had he been taken prisoner, Della Rovere could have been of some use; dead, he has none. Müller then decides to spread the news that Della Rovere has been taken prisoner, and very soon Bardone, whose acting talent the colonel has come to know not long before and whose shady dealings with a corrupt official he soon unmasks, offers him the chance to take advantage of this hoax: Müller proposes to save him from the firing squad and offers him freedom and money if he agrees to pass for General Della Rovere in jail, trusting he'll be able to use his presence there in the future.

Bardone accepts the deal and is taken to a prison crowded with anti-fascist prisoners. From the first moment the unscrupulous rogue plays the part of the left-wing aristocrat with aplomb, and everything he sees or feels in prison seems to help his interpretation, shaking his conscience: the very day he arrives he reads the posthumous messages of executed partisans on the walls of his cell; the prisoners place themselves under his orders and treat him with the respect the man who for them personifies the promise of a liberated Italy deserves, ask him about relatives and friends who fought in units under his command, joke about the unhappy fate awaiting them, beg him wordlessly to instil them with courage; one of the prisoners who frequents Bardone commits suicide rather than turn informer; later, to establish Della Rovere in his role, the Germans torture Bardone himself, which almost sets off a riot among his fellow prisoners; later still Bardone receives a letter from the Contessa Della Rovere in which the general's wife tries to comfort her husband by assuring him that she and his children are well and think only of being worthy of his courage and patriotism. This continuous series of impressions begins to cause a subtle, almost invisible metamorphosis in Bardone, and one night something unexpected happens: during an allied bombing raid that provokes cries of panic in the prison Bardone demands to leave his cell; he is trembling with fear, but, as if the general's character had momentarily taken over his person, standing in the corridor of the political prisoners' wing and, invested with the grandeur of Della Rovere, Bardone calms his comrades' fear by raising his voice in the midst of the thunder of battle: 'Friends, this is General Della Rovere,' he says. 'Show some dignity and self-control. Be men. Show these scoundrels you're not afraid of dying. They're the ones who should tremble. Every bomb that falls brings them closer to the end, and brings us closer to freedom.'

Shortly after this episode fate offers Colonel Müller the opportunity he's been waiting for. A group of nine partisans captured in a raid are sent to the prison; one of them is Fabrizio, the leader of the resistance, but the Germans do not know which one: Müller asks Bardone first to identify him and then betray him. For a moment Bardone hesitates, as if Bardone and Della Rovere are fighting it out within him; but Müller reminds him of the promised money and liberty and adds the bribe of a safe conduct with which to escape to Switzerland, and finally breaks Bardone. He hasn't yet managed to identify Fabrizio when a high-ranking fascist authority dies at the hands of the resistance; in reprisal, Müller must shoot ten partisans, and the colonel understands that this is the moment to facilitate Bardone's task. The night before the execution Müller locks twenty men in a cell, ten of whom will be the expiatory victims; sure that at death's door Fabrizio will make himself known to Della Rovere, Müller includes Bardone and the nine prisoners caught in the raid. Müller is not mistaken: over the long night awaiting execution, while the prisoners look for strength or consolation in the valiant company of the false General Della Rovere, Fabrizio reveals himself. Finally, at dawn, when the men come out of the cell, Bardone is one of them, but Fabrizio is not. They walk out to the firing squad formed on the patio of the prison, Müller stops Bardone, separates him from the line of the condemned, asks him if he's managed to find out who Fabrizio is. Bardone stares at Müller, but says nothing; he needs only to say one word in order to be set free, with enough money to carry on his interrupted life of gambling and women, but he says nothing. Perplexed, Müller insists: he's sure that Bardone knows who Fabrizio is, sure that on a night like that Fabrizio would have told him who he is. Bardone does not take his eyes off Müller. 'And, what do you know?' he finally says. 'Have you ever spent a night like this?' 'Answer me!' shouts Müller furiously. 'Do you know who he is?' In response, Bardone asks Müller for a pencil and paper, scribbles a few lines, hands them to him and, before the colonel can see whether they contain the real name of Fabrizio, he asks him to see that they get to Contessa Della Rovere. While Bardone orders a jailer to open the gates to the patio, Müller reads the paper: 'My last thoughts are with you all,' it says. '*Viva Italia!*' The patio is covered with snow; tied to posts, ten blindfolded men wait for death. Bardone – who is no longer Bardone but Della Rovere, as if somehow Della Rovere had always been within him – takes his place beside his comrades and, just before falling under the bullets of the firing squad, speaks to them. 'Gentlemen,' he says. 'In these final moments let us dedicate our thoughts to our families, our nation and His Majesty the King.' And he adds: '*Viva Italia!*'

4

It's likely that the metamorphosis of Adolfo Suárez into the man who had somehow always been in him and who scarcely bore any relation to the former provincial Falangist upstart began the very day the King named him Prime Minister, but the reality is that it only started to become visible many months later. The reception afforded his appointment by public opinion was devastating. No one summed it up better than a cartoonist. In a Forges cartoon two Franco devotees in a bunker were commenting on the news; one of them said: 'Isn't it wonderful? He's called Adolfo'; the other answered: 'Indeed.' That's how it was: apart from rare exceptions, only the far right – from the old shirts of the Falange to the soldiers and technocrats of Opus Dei, along with the Guerrilleros de Cristo Rey – celebrated Suárez's ascent to the premiership, convinced that the young, obsequious and disciplined Falangist represented new wine in old barrels, the palpable demonstration that the ideals of 18 July still prevailed and the best guarantee that Francoism, with all the cosmetic changes that circumstances demanded, wasn't going to die along with Franco. Beyond the far right, however, there was only pessimism and fright: for the immense majority of the democratic opposition and the regime's reformers, Suárez was just going to be, as *Le Figaro* wrote, 'the executor of the low manoeuvrings of the far right, determined to torpedo democratization by any means', or, as *El País* insinuated, the spearhead of 'a machine that turns out to be the authentic immovable bunker of the country', and which 'embodies the traditional way of being Spanish according to its darkest and most irascible legend: economic and political power allied in perfect symbiosis with ecclesiastical fundamentalism'.

Suárez was not daunted: that was undoubtedly the reception he expected – given his trajectory, he couldn't have expected any other – and it was also the reception that best suited him. Because if the King had charged him with dismantling Francoism to set up a parliamentary monarchy with its pieces, liquidating the dead that still seemed alive and bringing to life what seemed dead, the first thing he needed to count on was the complicity (or at least the confidence, or at least the passivity) of Francoist orthodoxy; the second thing he needed to count on was the comprehension (or at least the tolerance, or at least the patience) of the clandestine opposition. He embarked on this double, self-evidently impossible task from the first moment. Machiavelli recommends the politician 'keep the minds of his subjects in suspense and admiration', and link his actions with the object of not allowing his adversaries 'the time to work steadily against him'. Perhaps Suárez had not read Machiavelli, but he followed his advice to the letter, and as soon as he was named Prime Minister began a sprint of coups de théâtre of such speed and confidence that no one could muster the reasons, resources or enthusiasm to stop him: the day after he took office he read a televised message in which, with a political language, tone and form incompatible with the tattered starch of Francoism, promised concord and reconciliation by way of a democracy in which governments would be 'the result of the will of the majority of the Spanish people', and the next day he formed with the help of his Deputy Prime Minister Alfonso Osorio an extremely youthful cabinet composed of Falangists and Christian Democrats who had good relations with the democratic opposition and the economic powers; one day he presented a programmatic declaration, virtually breaking with Francoism, in which the government committed itself to 'the devolution of sovereignty to the Spanish people', and announced a general election before 30 June of the coming year, the next day he reformed by decree the Penal Code that prevented the legalization of the parties and the day after that he decreed an amnesty for political crimes; one day he granted the heretofore banned Catalan language equal official status and the next he declared the banned Basque flag legal; one day he announced a law that authorized the repeal of the Fundamental Laws of Francoism and the next day he got the Francoist Cortes to pass it

and the following day he called a referendum to approve it and the day
after that he won it; one day he abolished by decree the Movimiento
Nacional and the next day he ordered all the Falangist symbols to be
removed secretly overnight from all the façades of all the Movimiento
buildings and the following day he legalized the Communist Party by
surprise and the day after that he called the first free elections in forty
years. That was his way of proceeding during his first eleven-month
term of government: he made an unusual decision and, as the country
was still trying to take it in, he made another more unusual decision,
and then another even more unusual, and then one more; he was
constantly improvising; he swept events along, but also allowed himself
to be swept along by them; he allowed no time to react, or to work
against him, or to notice the disparity between what he did and what
he said, no time even for admiration, or no more than he gave himself:
all his adversaries could do was remain in suspense, attempt to understand what he was doing and try to keep up.

At the beginning of his mandate his main objective was to convince
the Francoists and the democratic opposition that the reform he was
going to carry out was the only way they would both achieve their
conflicting purposes. He assured the Francoists that they'd have to
renounce certain elements of Francoism in order to ensure the survival
of Francoism; he assured the democratic opposition that they'd have
to renounce certain elements of the break with Francoism in order to
ensure the break with Francoism. To everyone's surprise, he convinced
them all. First he convinced the Francoists and, when he'd convinced
them, he convinced the opposition: he completely deceived the
Francoists, but not the opposition, or not entirely, or no more than he
deceived himself, but he did as he pleased with them, obliged them to
play on the field that he chose and by the rules he devised and, once
he'd won the match, put them to work in his service. How did he
achieve it? In a certain sense, with the same histrionic methods of
seduction with which Emmanuele Bardone persuaded Italians and
Germans alike that there was no one in the world more important than
them and that he was ready to do anything for their cause, and with the
same chameleon-like gifts with which Bardone convinced the Germans
that he was a fervent supporter of the Reich and the Italians that he was

an undercover adversary of the Reich. If he was almost always unbeatable on television, because he mastered it better than any other politician, face to face he was even better: he could sit down alone with a Falangist, with an Opus Dei technocrat or with a Guerrillero de Cristo Rey and the Falangist, technocrat or paramilitary would say goodbye to him with the certainty that deep down he was a paramilitary, a Falangist or a defender of Opus; he could sit down with a soldier and, remembering his time as a reserve second lieutenant, say: Don't worry, deep down I'm still a soldier; he could sit with a monarchist and say: I am first and foremost a monarchist; he could sit down with a Christian Democrat and say: In reality, I've always been a Christian Democrat; he could sit with a Social Democrat and say: What I am, deep down, is a Social Democrat; he could sit with a Socialist or a Communist and say: I'm no Communist (or Socialist), but I am one of you, because my family was Republican and deep down I've never stopped being one. He'd say to the Francoists: Power must be ceded to win legitimacy and conserve power; to the democratic opposition he'd say: I have power and you have legitimacy: we have to understand each other. Everyone heard from Suárez what they needed to hear and everyone came out of those interviews enchanted by his kind-heartedness, his modesty, seriousness and receptiveness, his excellent intentions and his will to convert them into deeds; as for him, he wasn't yet Prime Minister of a democratic government, but, just as Bardone tried to act the way he thought General Della Rovere would have acted from the moment he entered the prison, from the moment of his appointment as Prime Minister he tried to act the way he thought a prime minister of a democratic government would act: like Bardone, everything he saw and felt helped him to perfect his interpretation; like Bardone, he soon began to steep himself in the political and moral cause of the democratic parties; like Bardone, he deceived with such sincerity that not even he knew he was deceiving.

That was how over the course of that short first year in government Suárez constructed the foundations of a democracy out of the materials of a dictatorship by successfully carrying out unusual operations, the most unusual of which – and perhaps the most essential – entailed the liquidation of Francoism at the hands of the Francoists themselves. The idea he owed to Fernández Miranda, but Suárez was much more than simply its executor: he studied it, he got it ready and he put it into practice. It was almost about achieving the squaring of a circle, and in any case reconciling the irreconcilable to eliminate what was dead and seemed alive; at heart it was about a legal ruse based on the following reasoning: Franco's Spain was ruled by an ensemble of Fundamental Laws that, as the dictator himself had often stressed, were perfect and offered perfect solutions for any eventuality; however, the Fundamental Laws could be perfect only if they could be modified – otherwise they wouldn't have been perfect, because they wouldn't have been capable of adapting to any eventuality – the plan conceived by Fernández Miranda and deployed by Suárez consisted of devising a new Fundamental Law, the Law for Political Reform, which would be added to the rest, apparently modifying them though actually repealing them or authorizing them to be repealed, which allowed the change of a dictatorial regime for a democratic regime respecting the legal procedures of the first. The sophistry was brilliant, but needed to be approved by the Francoist Cortes in an unprecedented act of collective immolation; its implementation was vertiginous: by the end of August 1976 a draft of the law was already prepared, at the beginning of September Suárez announced it on television and over the next two months threw himself into battle on all fronts to convince the Francoist representatives to accept their suicide. The strategy he devised to achieve it was a wonder of precision and swindle: while from his position as President of the Cortes Fernández Miranda threw spanners in the works of the law's detractors, they put in charge of its presentation and defence the nephew of the founder of the Falange and member of the Council of the Kingdom, Miguel Primo de Rivera, who would ask them to vote in favour 'in memory of Franco'; in the weeks before the plenary session, Suárez, his ministers and top government officials, after dividing up the *procuradores*, as the Francoist Cortes members were called, opposed to or reluctant to support the project, breakfasted, had aperitifs, lunched and dined with them, flattering them with brimming promises and tangling them in traps for the gullible; only in a few cases did they have to resort to unveiled threats, but with one group of recalcitrant members there was nothing for it but to pack them off on a Caribbean cruise on a junket to Panama. Finally, on 18 November, after three consecutive days of debate during which on more than one occasion it seemed like everything was going to fall through, the Cortes voted on the law; the result was unequivocal: 425 votes in favour, 59 against and 13 abstentions. The reform was approved. The television cameras captured the moment, and it's since been reproduced on a multitude of occasions. The members of the Francoist Cortes stand and applaud; standing up, Suárez applauds the Francoist *procuradores*. He looks emotional; he looks like he's on the verge of tears; there is no reason to think he's pretending or, like the consummate actor he is, if he is pretending, that he's not feeling what he's pretending to feel. The truth is he might as well have been laughing inside and crying his eyes out for the bunch of fools who've just signed their own death sentence amid the embraces and congratulations of a tremendous Francoist fiesta.

It was a spectacular sleight of hand, and the greatest success of his life. In Spain the democratic opposition rubbed their eyes; outside Spain the incredulity was total: 'STUNNING VICTORY FOR SUÁREZ', ran the headline in the *New York Times*; 'CORTES APPOINTED BY DICTATOR HAVE BURIED FRANCOISM', said *Le Monde*. A few days later, allowing himself not an instant's respite or his adversaries any time to recover from their stupor, he called a referendum on the recently approved law; it was held on 15 December and he won it with almost 80 per cent participation and almost 95 per cent of the votes in favour. For the Francoists and for the democratic opposition, who had advocated voting against or abstaining, the setback was conclusive; much more so for the former than for the latter, of course: from that moment on the Francoists could resort only to violence, and the week of 23 to 28 January – in which far-right groups murdered nine people in a prewar atmosphere and Suárez was certain someone would attempt a coup d'état – was the first notice that they were ready to employ it; as for the democratic opposition, they found themselves obliged to discard the chimera of imposing their outright clean break with Francoism to accept the unexpected and tricky reforming break imposed by Suárez and began to negotiate with him, divided, messed up and weakened, under terms he had chosen and that best suited him. Furthermore, by then, around February 1977, it was already clear to everyone that Suárez

was going to fulfil the task the King and Fernández Miranda had
entrusted to him in record time; in fact, once the Rubicon of the Law
for Political Reform was crossed, Suárez had only to finalize the dismantling of the legal and institutional framework of Francoism and call free
elections after agreeing with the political parties the requisites of their
legalization and participation in the elections. In theory his job ended
there, that in theory was the end of the show, but by then Suárez already
believed in his character and was elated, riding the biggest wave of the
tsunami of his success, so nothing would have seemed more absurd to
him than giving up the position he'd always dreamt of; it may be,
however, that this was the King's and Fernández Miranda's intention
when they gave him the starring role in that drama of seductions, half-
truths and deceits, sure as they were perhaps that the charming and
smooth nonentity would burn out on stage, sure as they were in any
case that he would be incapable of managing the complexities of the
state in normal conditions, and even more so after democratic elections: once these were called and his task concluded, Suárez should
retire behind the curtain, amid applause and tokens of gratitude, to
cede the favour of the spotlight to a real statesman, perhaps Fernández
Miranda himself, perhaps the eternally prime ministerial Fraga, perhaps
the Deputy Prime Minister Alfonso Osorio, perhaps the cultivated,
elegant and aristocratic José María de Areilza. Of course, Suárez could
have ignored the King's intention, forced his hand and stood for election without his consent, but he was the Prime Minister appointed by
the King and he wanted to be the King's candidate and then the King's
Prime Minister-elect, and during those brilliant months, while he
gradually freed himself of Fernández Miranda's tutelage and paid less
and less attention to Osorio, he worked hard at demonstrating to the
King that he was the Prime Minister he needed because he was the only
politician able to establish the monarchy by assembling a democracy
just as he'd dismantled Francoism; he also worked at demonstrating
that by contrast Fernández Miranda was just a spineless, old, unreal
jurist, Fraga an indiscriminate bulldozer, Osorio a politician as pomp-
ous as he was inane and Areilza a well-dressed dead loss.

All this would become clear to the King at the beginning of April
when Suárez pulled the most audacious move of his career, another

death-defying political leap, but this time with no net: the legalization of the Communist Party. That measure was the limit the military had placed on the reform and which Suárez had seemed to accept or had made them believe he accepted; perhaps at first he really did accept it, but, as he became steeped in his character of democratic Prime Minister without democracy and he absorbed the reasons of an opposition pushing him from the street with popular demonstrations and forcing him to go much further than he had planned on the path of reform, Suárez understood he needed the Communist Party as much as the Communist Party needed him. Towards the end of February he'd already made one decision and had come up with an idea for a high-wire juggling act like the one that let Franco's Cortes sacrifice themselves, except this time he chose to carry it out practically alone and practically in secret: first, with the disagreement of Fernández Miranda and Osorio but the agreement of the King, he held a secret meeting with Santiago Carrillo and sealed with him a pact of steel; then he sought to cover his back with a legal opinion from the Supreme Court favourable to the legalization and, when they refused him, he manoeuvred to get it out of the Attorney General's Office; then he sounded out the military ministers and sowed confusion among them, ordering General Gutiérrez Mellado to warn them that the PCE could be legalized (they were waiting for a judicial proceeding, Gutiérrez Mellado told them, and also if they wanted some clarification the Prime Minister was prepared to provide it), although he didn't tell them when or how or even if it was effectively going to be legalized, a juggling act within the juggling act with which he intended to avoid the charge from the military ministers that he hadn't informed them and at the same time to prevent them from reacting against his decision before it was announced; then he waited for the Easter holidays, sent the King and Queen on a trip to France, Carrillo to Cannes, his ministers on vacation and, with the streets of the big cities deserted and the barracks deserted and the editorial offices of the newspapers and radio and television stations deserted, he stayed alone in Madrid, playing cards with General Gutiérrez Mellado. Finally, again with the King's support and Osorio's opposition and without even consulting Fernández Miranda, on Easter Saturday – the most deserted day of those deserted days – he legalized the PCE. It was a bombshell, and it very nearly blew up in his hands: he'd made that wild decision because triumphs had given him an absolute confidence in himself and, although he expected the shock to the Army would be brutal and that there would be protests and threats and perhaps outbreaks of rebellion, reality outdid his worst predictions, and at some moments during the four insane days that followed Easter Saturday, maybe Suárez thought more than once that he'd overestimated his strengths and that a coup d'état was inevitable, until on the fifth day he once again translated the imminent catastrophe into his own gain: he kept the utmost pressure on Carrillo until he managed to persuade the Party publicly to renounce some of its symbols and accept all those the Army considered threatened by their legalization: the monarchy, the unity of the nation and the red-and-yellow flag. At this point it all stopped. The soldiers stayed in their barracks, the whole country must have held its breath and Suárez scored a double victory: on the one hand he managed to tame the military – or at least tame them for the moment – forcing them to swallow what was for them an indigestible decision and for him (and for democracy) an indispensable one; on the other hand he managed to tame the Communist Party – and with the Communist Party, not much later, the whole democratic opposition – forcing them to join the project of the parliamentary monarchy unreservedly, turning the eternal adversary into the principal support of the system. To finish off the fluke, Suárez had converted Fernández Miranda and Osorio into two suddenly antiquated politicians, ready for retirement, and everything was ready to call the first democratic elections in forty years and win them by capitalizing on the success of his reforms.

He called them and won them, and along the way also eliminated Fraga and Areilza, his last two rivals. The first he shelved away in an antediluvian party where they flailed at the fugitive glories of the Francoist exodus; on the second he took no pity. Suárez had no party of his own with which to stand for election, so for months, crouched down, plotting from a distance and playing along with the bluff that he wasn't even going to stand as a candidate, he waited while a huge coalition of centrist parties formed around a party led by Areilza; once the coalition was formed, he pounced on it and, strengthened by the generalized certainty that the electoral list headed by his prestige as midwife of the reform would be the winner of the elections, he placed before the leaders of the new formation a clear dilemma: either Areilza or him. There was no need to answer: Areilza had to withdraw, Suárez remodelled the coalition to suit himself and on 3 May 1977, the same day the UCD was founded, announced his candidacy in the elections. Less than a month and a half later he won. Perhaps Suárez rightly thought that he, not the UCD, had won, that without him the UCD was nothing; but, rightly or wrongly, perhaps he also began to think other things. Perhaps he thought that without him not only would the UCD not exist: the rest of the parties wouldn't exist either. Perhaps he thought that without him not only would the rest of the parties not exist: democracy wouldn't exist either. Perhaps he thought that he was his party, that he was the government, that he was democracy, because he was the charismatic leader who had brought forty years of dictatorship to an end in eleven months, peacefully with an unprecedented operation. Perhaps he thought he was going to govern for decades. Perhaps he thought, therefore, that he wasn't going to govern just with a view to the right and to the centre – where his voters were, the ones who had put him in power – but also with a view to the left: after all, he would think, a true leader does not govern for the few, but for all; after all, he would think, he also needed the left to be able to govern; after all, he would think, deep down he was a Social Democrat, almost a Socialist; after all, he would think, he was no longer a Falangist but he had been one and Falangism and the left shared the same anti-capitalist rhetoric, the same social concern, the same contempt for the tycoons; after all, he would think, he was anything but a tycoon, he'd risen from the ranks in politics and in life, he knew the forsakenness of the street and miserable boarding houses and starvation wages and there was no way he was going to accept being described as a right-wing politician, he belonged to the centre left, increasingly more to the left and less to the centre although the centre and the right voted for him, he was light years away from Fraga and his Francoist pachyderms, to be on the right was to be old in body and spirit, to be against history and against the oppressed, carrying the guilt and the shame of forty years of Francoism, while to be progressive was the fairest, most modern and most audacious thing to be and he always – always: since he ruled his adolescent crew in Ávila and embodied to perfection the ideal youth of the dictatorship – had been the fairest, most modern and most audacious, his Francoist past was at once very far away and too close and humiliated him with its proximity, he was not who he had once been, he was now not only the maker of democracy but also its champion, the main bastion of its defence, he had constructed it with his own hands and he was going to defend it from the military and from the terrorists, from the far right and from the far left, the bankers and the businessmen, politicians and journalists and adventurers, Rome and Washington.

Perhaps that was what Adolfo Suárez felt as the years went by; that or part of it or something very similar to it, a feeling that started to come over him gradually as soon as he was elected Prime Minister in the first democratic elections and from that moment on began to cause him to undergo a radical metamorphosis: the former provincial Falangist, the former Francoist upstart, the Julien Sorel or Lucien Rubempré or Frédéric Moreau of the 1960s ended up investing himself with the dignity of a hero of democracy, Emmanuele Bardone believed himself to be General Della Rovere and the plebeian fascist dreamt of himself converted into a left-wing aristocrat. Like Bardone, he didn't do it out of haughtiness, because there was no haughtiness in his nature, but because an aesthetic and political instinct surpassed him and pushed him to interpret with a fidelity deeper than reason the role history had assigned him or that he felt it had assigned him. I've said over the years, I've said gradually: like that of Bardone, Suárez's mutation was not, it almost goes without saying, an instantaneous epiphany, but a slow, zigzagging process, often secret from everybody or almost everybody, but maybe especially from Suárez himself. Although it would be reasonable to date the origin of it all to the very day the King appointed him Prime Minister and, ennobled by the position, he proposed to act as if he were a prime minister appointed by the citizens, opening himself to the political and moral reason of the democratic opposition, the truth is that his new character didn't show signs of life until, in order to disassociate himself from the right, shortly before the elections Suárez insisted on conceding a disproportionate weight in the UCD to the small Social Democratic Party in the coalition, and when, just afterwards – while his parliamentary group discussed the possibility that their deputies might occupy the left wing of the chamber in the Cortes, symbolically reserved for the parties of the left – he declared himself a Social Democrat to his former Deputy Prime Minister and announced the formation of a centre-left government. These postures anticipate the drift Suárez experienced during the four years he was still in government. They were years of decline: he was never again the explosive politician he'd been during the first eleven months of his mandate, but until March 1979, when he won his second general election, he was still a bold and efficient politician; from then until 1981 he was a mediocre, sometimes disastrous politician. Three projects monopolized the first period; three collective projects, which Suárez steered but in which the main political parties all took part: the Moncloa Pact, the drawing up of the Constitution and the designing of the so-called *Estado de las Autonomías*. They weren't the epic undertakings that had spurred his imagination and multiplied his talent during his first year in the premiership, deeds that demanded juridical con-tricks, magic feints never before seen, false duels against false enemies, secret meetings, life-or-death decisions and stages set for a champion facing danger alone with his squire; they were not these sorts of undertakings, but they were matters of historical magnitude; he did not set upon them with the predatory momentum he'd shown up till then, but at least he did so with the conviction gained by the strength of his triumphs and the authority of the voters; he also did so while little by little General Della Rovere displaced Emmanuele Bardone inside him. Thus, the Moncloa Pact was a largely successful attempt to pacify a society on a war footing since the death rattles of Francoism and convulsed by the devastating consequences of the first oil crisis; but the pact was most of all an agreement between the government and the left and, although signed by all the main political parties, it received harsh criticism from the business sector, from the right and from certain sectors of the UCD, which accused the Prime Minister of having surrendered to the unions and the Communists. Thus as well, the Constitution was a successful attempt to give democracy a lasting legal framework; but Suárez most likely only agreed to draw it up owing to the demands pressed on him by the left, and it is certain that, despite at first doing everything possible to make the text conform to his interests down to the last letter, when he understood that this aspiration was useless and pernicious he endeavoured more than anyone to make sure the result was the work of the accord of all the parties, and not, as all or almost all the previous constitutions had been, a constant cause for discord and eventually a burden for democracy, just as it's true that in order to achieve it he always sought alliances with the left and not with the right, which produced more resentment in his own party. These two great projects – the first approved in the Cortes in October 1977 and the second approved by a referendum in December 1978 – represented two successes for Suárez (and for democracy); with the third it's again impossible not to imagine General Della Rovere fighting to supplant Emmanuele Bardone: the difference is that on this occasion Suárez lost his grip on the project and it ended up turning into one of the main causes of the political disorder that led to his leaving power and to the 23 February coup.

It shouldn't have happened, because the idea of the *Estado de las Autonomías* was at least as valid as that of the Moncloa Pact and almost as necessary as that of drawing up a Constitution. Perhaps Suárez didn't know a single word of history, as his detractors repeated, but what he did know is that democracy was not going to function in Spain if it didn't satisfy the aspirations of the Basque Country, Catalonia and Galicia to see their historical and linguistic singularities recognized and to enjoy a certain amount of political autonomy. Title VIII of the Constitution, where the territorial organization of the state is defined, attempted to respond to these ancient demands; predictably, its writing ignited a battle between the political parties the result of which was a hybrid, confusing and ambiguous text that left almost all the doors open and which, to be applied with immediate success, would have called for guile, subtlety, a capacity to reconcile the irreconcilable and a historical intuition or sense of reality that from the beginning of 1979 Suárez was rapidly losing.

It all started long before the approval of the Constitution and it started well, or at least it started well for Suárez, who carried off another magic trick in Catalonia: in order to avert the danger of the left, which had won the general election there, forming an autonomous left-wing government, Suárez pulled out of his sleeve Josep Tarradellas, the last Prime Minister of the Catalan government in exile, a pragmatic old politician who at once guaranteed the support of all the Catalan parties and respect for the Crown, the Army and the unity of Spain, so his return in October 1977 meant turning the re-establishment after forty years of a Republican institution into a legitimizing tool of the parliamentary monarchy and into a victory for the government in Madrid. In Galicia things didn't go so well, and in the Basque Country even less so. Many in the military took the announcement of the autonomy of these three territories to be an announcement of the dismembering of Spain, but the real problems arose later; later and in more than one sense through Suárez's own fault or that of the General Della Rovere inside Suárez rushing to expel Emmanuele Bardone: given that with manifest incongruence in the Spain of those years nationalism was identified with the left, given that with manifest congruence the left was identified with the decentralization of the state, in part to move closer to the left and in any case so nobody could accuse him of discriminating against anybody – to continue being the fairest, most modern and most audacious – Suárez hurried to concede autonomy to all the territories, including those that had never asked for it because they lacked a consciousness or ambition of singularity, with the corollary that even before the constitutional referendum was held fourteen preautonomous governments appeared almost overnight and began to discuss fourteen statutes of autonomy, the approval of which would have required holding in a great rush dozens and dozens of referenda and regional elections in the midst of an improvised blooming of vernacular particularisms and of a latent war of suspicion and comparative injuries between communities. It was more than a secularly centralist state could bear in a few months without threatening to lose its mast, and even the nationalists and the most enthusiastic supporters of decentralization began to sound the alarm at a flight forward in which nobody could glimpse the finishing line and the consequences of which almost everybody began to fear. Towards the end of 1979 Suárez himself seemed to notice that the galloping disorder of the decentralization of the democratic state entailed a threat to democracy

and to the state, so he tried to put it into reverse, rationalize it or slow
it down, but by then he had already turned into an awkward, no longer
resourceful politician, and the attempt to put the brakes on only
managed to divide the government and his party and earn him unpop-
ularity that at the beginning of the following year led him to lose in less
than a month, successively and spectacularly, a referendum in Andalusia,
one election in the Basque Country and another in Catalonia. It's true
that no one helped him fix the mess: by the spring and summer of 1980
it seemed anything was valid against him: instead of trying to prop him
up as they had done during the first years of his mandate – because
they understood that propping him up meant propping up democracy
– the political parties became obsessed with toppling him at any price,
not understanding that toppling him at any price meant contributing
to toppling democracy; but it was not just that obsession: to articulate
the state territorially was perhaps the central problem of the moment,
and no other matter laid bare the indigence and frightful frivolity of a
political class, which to its cost got embroiled over the course of 1980
in delirious quarrels, unscrupulously chased advantageous positions,
encouraged an appearance of universal chaos and won an accelerated
disrepute, placing the country in an increasingly precarious frame of
mind while the second oil crisis dissipated the fleeting bonanza won by
the Moncloa Pact, strangled the economy and left half the workers
unemployed, and while ETA tried to bring on a coup d'état by murder-
ing soldiers in the most merciless terrorist campaign of their history.
That was the omnivorous soil in which 23 February was born and grew,
and Suárez's clumsiness in managing the start-up of the *Estado de las
Autonomías* fed its voraciousness more than any of the other clumsi-
nesses he committed at that time. Seen in hindsight, however, it is at
least an exaggeration to claim that in those days the situation was
objectively catastrophic and that the country was rushing uncontrol-
lably towards its disintegration, but that seems to be what everyone was
thinking on the eve of the coup d'état; not just the *golpista* soldiers:
everyone, including some of the few who on 23 February had the courage to come to the defence of democracy from the first moment. On
the penultimate day of December 1980 *El País* depicted an end-of-the-
world scenario in which the territorial chaos augured a violent solution;

after accusing all the political parties without exception of irresponsibility and reproaching them for their culpable ignorance of the point of arrival of the *Estado de las Autonomías*, or their interested lack of interest in defining it, the editorial ended by saying: 'A less serious political decomposition than this one [. . .] led Companys to rebel, on 6 October 1934, against a right-wing coalition government, and a Socialist faction to provoke the desperate rising in Asturias.' Since this was the pre-revolutionary diagnosis of the newspaper that best represented the Spanish left, perhaps we might wonder whether a large part of democratic society was not providing the *golpistas* with daily excuses to reaffirm their certainty that the country was in a situation of maximum emergency that demanded maximum emergency solutions; perhaps we might even wonder – it's only a more uncomfortable way of formulating the same question – if a large part of democratic society was not conspiring in spite of themselves to involuntarily facilitate the task of the enemies of democracy.

The Suárez of those days could be accused of passivity and incapacity, and also of political poverty, but not of being irresponsible or frivolous or an unscrupulous opportunist: Suárez was still Suárez but he was no longer a Julien Sorel or a Lucien Rubempré or a Frédéric Moreau, or an Emmanuele Bardone about to definitively transmute into General Della Rovere. Maybe the final occasion Suárez played Bardone was just before being elected Prime Minister for the second time, in March 1979; fearing a PSOE victory, he tried out his last conjurer's trick, the final great swindle of the provincial rogue: he appeared on television the night before the election clamouring against the danger of the revolutionary left winning and destroying the family and the state; he knew very well that this clamour was nothing but a way of frightening old ladies, but perhaps he suspected that only by risking a demagogic prank could he win the election, and he did not hesitate to risk it. The ruse worked, he won the election, and after winning he held more power than he had ever had before. After a very short space of time, however, he went into free fall; we know the rest of the story: 1979 was a bad year for him; 1980 was worse. In spite of that, it's likely that during this era of disasters – while the moment he would give up the job of Prime Minister and the moment of the military coup approached and he imagined himself in the centre of the ring, blind and staggering and sobbing amid the howling of the spectators and the heat of the lights, politically sunk and personally broken – Suárez would have been filling his aristocratic role of progressive statesman more than ever, increasingly convinced he was the final bastion of democracy when all democracy's defences were tumbling down, increasingly sure that the innumerable political manoeuvres under-taken against him were pushing open the doors of democracy to the enemies of democracy, ever more profoundly invested with the dignity of his position as the Prime Minister of democracy and his responsibil-ity as the maker of democracy, the character ever more incorporated in his person, like an invented Suárez but more real than the real Suárez because he was superimposed on the real one, transcending him, like an actor about to interpret the scene that will justify him to history hidden behind a mask which rather than covering reveals his authentic face, like an Emmanuele Bardone now converted once and for all into General Della Rovere who on the evening of 23 February, at the moment of truth, while the bullets whizzed around him in the cham-ber of the Cortes and the deputies sought shelter under their benches, would have remained in his amid the roar of battle to calm the fear of his comrades and help them to face up to the misfortune with these words: 'Friends, this is your Prime Minister speaking. Show some dignity and self-control. Be men.' And also with these words: 'Show these scoundrels that you're not afraid of dying.' And also with these: 'In these final moments let us dedicate our thoughts to our families, our nation and to His Majesty the King.' And finally with these: '*Viva Italia!*'

5

Rossellini wasn't particularly proud of *General Della Rovere*, but an artist is not always the best judge of his own work, and I think he was mistaken: the film is traditional in form, sometimes even conventional, but the fable it tells of the destiny of Emmanuele Bardone – a collaborator with fascism converted into a hero of anti-fascist Italy – is one of extraordinary richness and complexity; even richer and more complex, perhaps, is the parallel fable of the destiny of Adolfo Suárez – a collaborator with Francoism converted into a hero of democratic Spain – because Suárez was a politician and his journey suggests that in a politician private vices can be public virtues or that in politics it's possible to arrive at good through evil or that it's not enough to judge a politician ethically and first he must be judged politically or that ethics and politics are incompatible and the expression political ethics is an oxymoron or perhaps that vices and virtues don't exist in the abstract, but only in relation to the circumstances in which they're practised: Suárez was not an ethically irreproachable man, but it's very possible that he would never have been able to do what he did for years if he hadn't been a rogue with the morality of a survivor and a gift for deceit, an upstart without much culture or firm political ideas, a cocky, fawning, swindling Falangist. It is reasonable to surmise that any of the young Francoist politicians who at the death of Franco knew or guessed like he did that Francoism had no future and would have to be expanded or transformed could have done what Suárez did; it's reasonable, but the reality is that while almost all of them shared his private vices none of them combined his courage, his audacity, his strength, his

toughness, his exclusive political vocation, his acting talent, his seriousness, his charm, his modesty, his natural intelligence, his aptitude for
reconciling the irreconcilable and most of all a sense of reality and a
historical intuition that allowed him to understand very early, pushed
by the democratic opposition, that rather than trying to impose himself
on reality he should allow it to mould him, that expanding or trans-
forming Francoism would only give rise to misfortune and the only
thing to do with it was to kill it once and for all, betraying the past in
order not to betray the future. Be that as it may, we don't need to
exhaust the parallels between Bardone and Suárez: Bardone was a
morally abject individual who committed atrocious sins in an atrocious
time; Suárez was instead a basically honest man: while he occupied the
leadership of the government his sins were not mortal ones – or they
were only the mortal sins involved in the exercise of power – and before
occupying the leadership of the government his sins were the usual sins
of a rotten time. As well as the political successes he harvested, this
perhaps explains why for so many years so many people admired him
and kept voting for him; I mean that it's not true that people voted for
Suárez because they were deceived about his defects and limitations,
or because Suárez managed to deceive them: they voted for him in part
because he was like they would have liked to be, but most of all they
voted for him because, less in his virtues than in his defects, he was just
like them. That's more or less what Spain in the 1970s was like: a country full of vulgar, uncultivated, swindling, womanizing, gambling men
without many scruples, provincials with the morality of survivors
brought up between Acción Católica and the Falange who had lived
comfortably under Francoism, collaborators who wouldn't even have
admitted their collaboration but were secretly increasingly ashamed of
it and trusted Suárez because they knew that, although he might have
wanted to be the fairest and the most modern and most audacious – or
precisely because he wanted to be – he would always be one of theirs
and would never take them where they didn't want to go. Suárez didn't
let them down: he constructed a future for them, and by constructing
it he cleansed his past, or tried to cleanse it. If you look closely, at this
point Suárez's strange fate also resembles that of Bardone: by shouting
'*Viva Italia!*' at the firing squad on a snowy dawn, Bardone not only

redeems himself, but in a way redeems his whole country for having collaborated massively with fascism; by remaining on his bench while the bullets whizz around him in the chamber on the evening of 23 February, Suárez not only redeems himself, but in a way redeems his whole country for having collaborated massively with Francoism. Who knows: maybe that's why – maybe that's also why – Suárez didn't duck.

6

Are a politician's private vices public virtues? Is it possible to arrive at good by way of evil? Is it insufficient or ungenerous to judge a politician ethically and should he only be judged politically? Are ethics and politics incompatible and is the expression political ethics an oxymoron? At least since Plato philosophy has discussed the problem of the tension between means and ends, and there is no such thing as a serious code of ethics that has not wondered whether or not it is permissible to use dubious, or dangerous, or simply evil means to achieve good ends. Machiavelli had no doubt that it was possible to arrive at good by way of evil, but a near contemporary of his, Michel de Montaigne, was even more explicit: 'The public weal requires that men should betray, and lie, and massacre'; that's why both thought politics should be left in the hands of 'the strongest and boldest citizens, who sacrifice their honour and conscience for the good of their country'. Max Weber put the question in similar terms. Weber doesn't think that ethics and politics are exactly incompatible, but he does think that political ethics are a specific type of ethics, with lethal secondary effects: against absolute ethics, which he calls the 'ethics of conviction' and which are concerned with the goodness of actions without regard to their consequences – *Fiat justitia et pereat mundus* – the politician practises relative ethics, which Weber calls 'ethics of responsibility', which instead of being concerned only with the goodness of actions are concerned most of all with the goodness of the consequences of the actions. However, if the essential means of politics is violence, as Weber thinks, then the politician's calling consists of using perverse means, abiding by the ethics of

responsibility, to achieve beneficial ends: from there it follows that for
Weber a politician is a lost man because he cannot aspire to the salvation of his soul, because he made a pact with the devil when he made a
pact with the forces of power and he's condemned to suffer the consequences of that abominable pact. From there as well, I would add,
power resembles an abrasive substance that leaves behind a wasteland,
the more power accumulated the bigger the wasteland, and from there
it follows that every pure politician sooner or later ends up thinking
he's sacrificed his honour and his conscience for the salvation of his
country, because sooner or later he understands he's sold his soul, and
that he won't be saved.

Suárez didn't understand it immediately. After leaving power following the coup d'état he remained involved in politics for exactly ten
years, but during that time he became a different politician; he didn't
stop being a pure politician, but he barely acted like one any more, and
he began to be a politician with fewer responsibilities and more convictions – he, who as a young man had barely had any – as if he thought
this last-minute change could prevent the devil from extracting his part
of the deal. Around the time he presented his resignation as Prime
Minister the King promised to grant him a dukedom as a reward for
services rendered to the country; few people around the Zarzuela were
in favour of ennobling that upstart who many thought had rebelled
against the King and endangered the Crown, so the concession was
postponed and, in a gesture more poignant than embarrassing – because
it reveals the plebeian provincial arriviste still fighting for legitimacy
and to atone for his past – Suárez demanded what he'd been promised
and just two days after 23 February the monarch finally made Suárez a
duke on the condition that he stayed away from politics for a while.
Suárez wasted no time in accepting this degrading arrangement, having
his shirts embroidered with a ducal crown and starting to use his title;
these were the external signs that allowed him to nail down his interpretation of the character he'd aspired to be for some time and in a way
already was: a progressive aristocrat, exactly like General Della Rovere.
Perhaps less intent on his political future than on putting finishing
touches to his historical figure, set on the futile proposal of merging the
ethics of conviction with the ethics of responsibility, he tried to be

faithful to this only partly unreal image for the rest of his political life: the image of a statesman with no ambition for power, devoted to what he then called 'bringing ethics into politics', preserving democracy, encouraging concord, expanding liberty and combating inequality and injustice. He didn't always achieve his objective, sometimes through thoughtlessness, other times through spite, often through his difficulty in restraining the pure politician still inside him. Three days after the coup d'état he left for a long holiday in the United States and the Caribbean with his wife and a group of friends; it was the understandable bolting of a man undone and weary to the core, but it was also a bad way to leave the premiership, because it meant abandoning his successor: he did not hand over his powers, didn't leave him a single suggestion or a single piece of advice, and all Leopoldo Calvo Sotelo found in his office in Moncloa was a locked safe of the ruler's secrets but whose only contents turned out to be, as he found out after a locksmith forced it open, a piece of paper folded in four on which Suárez had written down the combination to the safe, as if he'd wanted to play a joke on his replacement or as if he'd wanted to give him a lesson on the true essence of power or as if he'd wanted to reveal that in reality he was only a chameleon-like actor without an inner life or distinct personality and a transparent being whose deepest secret was that he had no secrets.

But he didn't just abandon his successor; he also abandoned his party. On his return from the holiday, Suárez set up a legal office with a handful of faithful from his cabinet, and for some time he made an effort to stay away from politics; the political village of Madrid facilitated his efforts: the calamity of the final months of his government and the trauma of his resignation and 23 February had made him just short of undesirable, and anybody who harboured the slightest ambition – and almost everybody who harboured none – endeavoured to keep him at a distance. His vocation, however, was much stronger than his insolvency and, in spite of the promise he'd made to the King, that period out of politics was brief and his distancing from power relative; after all he still maintained a certain control of UCD through some of his men, which didn't prevent the Party from continuing to unhinge itself or him from watching this unhinging with a disgust mixed with vindictive rage: contrary to what so many of his fellow Party members had been predicting for a long time, it proved that his leadership had not been the cause of all the UCD's woes; with his successor, on the other hand, the disgust was not mixed: as soon as he became Prime Minister Calvo Sotelo began to adopt measures that would root out Suárez's policies and which he interpreted as an intolerable swing to the right. As a result of all this, within a few months of his retirement from politics Suárez began to prepare his return. By then Calvo Sotelo had removed Suárez's supporters from the leadership of the UCD and he was feeling increasingly ill at ease in a party that rightly blamed him for its fall, so, although there were offers made for him to retake the wheel of the UCD to keep it from crashing, Suárez turned them down, and in the last days of June 1982, just three months before the general election, he announced the creation of a new party: the Centro Democrático y Social (CDS, Democratic and Social Centre).

It was his last political adventure. It was guided by a double purpose: on the one hand, to create a real party, organizationally and ideologically cohesive, as the UCD had never been; on the other hand, to promote his new principles of a progressive statesman of concord, his new political ethic of a left or centre-left aristocrat. He set up the party with hardly any resources, hardly any men, without anyone's backing or hardly anyone's, and less than none of the so-called powers that be, who had done everything they could to throw him out of power and contemplated the possibility of his return with horror. Far from disheartened, he was excited by this abandonment, maybe because he felt that it returned to politics an epic and aesthetic spirit that he hadn't felt since his first months in government and had almost forgotten, authorizing him as well to present himself as a victim of the powerful and as a solitary fighter against injustice and adversity or, as he told the journalists at the presentation of the new party, as a Quixote coming out lance at the ready to take on all comers in the wind and the weather out on the road. Around that time a story was widely circulated that many consider apocryphal. The story goes that shortly before the election one of his collaborators recommended he hire an American adviser for the campaign; Suárez accepted the suggestion. Do you want to win the election? was the question the adviser asked Suárez straight away when they met. Naturally, Suárez said yes. Then let me use the film of the coup d'état, said the adviser. Show the people the empty chamber and you sitting on your bench and you'll get an absolute majority. Suárez burst out laughing, thanked the adviser and dismissed him then and there. The anecdote resembles a vignette invented by one of Suárez's hagiographers – to use the most devastating images of the democracy in an electoral campaign was not doing any favours to democracy, and the great man chose to wage a clean fight even at the cost of losing the election – I don't know whether it is or not, but, if it's true that some adviser made such a proposal to Suárez, I would bet that was his reaction: first, because he knew the adviser was mistaken and, although the image of the chamber on the evening of 23 February could have won him thousands of votes, it would never have won the election for him; and second – and especially – because, even supposing that the electoral use of those images would have won him the election, it would have ruined irredeemably the role he needed to play in order to definitively exorcize his past and fix his place in history; or to put it another way: perhaps Emmanuele Bardone would have accepted the adviser's suggestions, but not General Della Rovere, and Suárez didn't want anything to do with Emmanuele Bardone anymore and hadn't for a long time.

In that election he won two seats. It was a very poor result, not even enough to form his own parliamentary group in the Cortes, and relegated him to the benches reserved for the mixed group beside his eternal buddy Santiago Carrillo, who by then was prolonging his agony at the head of the PCE and never tired of laughingly repeating to him that this was how the country was paying them back for their gesture of keeping their composure on the evening of 23 February; but it was also enough of a result to allow him to play the left-wing or centre-left aristocrat and statesman of concord. He began to do so at the first opportunity: during the session of investiture for the new Prime Minister he cast his vote for Felipe González, who had been his fiercest adversary while he led the government and who didn't even thank him for the support, undoubtedly because the absolute majority obtained by the PSOE in the elections made it superfluous. 'We mustn't contribute to disillusion,' Suárez said that day from the speakers' rostrum in the Cortes. 'We shall not cheer this government's possible errors. We shall not participate, neither in this chamber nor outside of it, in destabilizing operations against the government. We are not supporters of the irresponsible and dangerous game of capitalizing on the difficulties of those who hold the honourable charge of governing Spain.' These words were met with the sonorous indifference or silent disdain of an almost empty chamber, but contained a declaration of principles and a lesson in political ethics that over the next four years he did not tire of imparting: he was not prepared to do to others what they'd done to him at the price of provoking a crisis of state like the one that had led to his resignation and to 23 February. It was a retroactive form of defence and, although nobody recognized his authority to give anybody lessons in political ethics, Suárez continued doggedly preaching his new gospel. The truth is he abided by it, in part because his parliamentary insignificance permitted it, but above all because he wanted more than anything else to be true to the idiosyncrasies of his new character. That's how he began to forge his resurrection: little by little people began to bury the disoriented politician of the last years of his mandate and dig up the vibrant maker of democracy, and little by little, and especially as some grew disappointed with the Socialist illusion, his statesman's gestures and rhetoric, his ethical regenerationism began to catch on and a confusing progressive discourse that allowed him to flirt with the intellectual left in the capitals, to which he always wanted to belong, as well as recover part of his attraction for the traditional right of the provinces, to which he always had belonged.

Four years after his first speech in the Cortes as an ordinary deputy he felt that the general elections were again placing him at the gates of government. They were held in June 1986 and he stood again with hardly any money or media backing, but with a radical message that undermined his adversaries and handed him millions of votes and almost twenty parliamentarians. That enlarged and unexpected triumph plunged the right into sorrow ('If this country gives nineteen seats to Suárez there's no hope for it,' declared Fraga, who would give up the leadership of his party a short time later) and the left into uncertainty, finding themselves forced to take Suárez's rise seriously, from that moment on they kept asking him to stop trying to steal their voters and to go back to his old rhetoric and his proper place on the right. If his only purpose had been to reconquer the premiership, he should have done so: with Fraga out of the picture and the so-called powers that be resigned to his return to politics, Suárez was for almost everyone the natural leader of the centre right, and therefore Fraga's successor offered him over and over again the chance to lead the electoral ticket of a big coalition capable of defeating the Socialists. He should have done it, but he didn't: he'd lost his youthful pure politician's ferocity and was no longer prepared to return to government by trampling on the ideas he'd made his own; he was a conviction politician and not a piranha of power; he felt closer to the generous left that looked after the disadvantaged than to the miserly right jealous of its privileges; in short: he'd resolved to play his character to the end. Besides, after five years of political hardships, success drove him to a euphoria that at times seemed to repay the agonies of his last years in Moncloa: flourishing the idealism of his values and his real achievements against what he considered the Socialists' wingless pragmatism and the right's futureless impotence, as if he'd never lost his old charisma and his capacity to reconcile the irreconcilable and his historical intuition, Suárez stirred his former supporters again over the following months and attracted politicians, professionals and intellectuals of the left or the centre left, and in a very short time had established a party, with no guarantees other than the stubbornness and record of its leader, across the whole of Spain, and some could imagine him setting up a serious alternative power to Socialist power.

It's not impossible that some symbolic triumphs of this little return to the big stage meant in secret almost more than the electoral triumphs to him. In October 1989 he was named president of the Liberal International, an organization that on his insistence changed its name to the Liberal and Progressive International: it was a recognition that the Falangist from Ávila who had been Secretary General of Franco's single party had turned into a benchmark politician for international progressiveness, and the definitive certificate that for the world as well Emmanuele Bardone was now General Della Rovere. A tiny thing that happened in the Cortes two years earlier must have made him privately happier still. During a parliamentary debate the new leader of the right,

Antonio Hernández Mancha, whose requests for support Suárez had repeatedly rejected, dedicated with the haughty irony of a state lawyer some lines of verse reworked for the occasion that he attributed to St Teresa of Ávila: 'What have I, Adolfo, that my enmity you should seek? / What wealth from it, my Adolfo, / that before my door, covered in dew, / you spend dark winter nights in snow and sleet?' As soon as his adversary had finished speaking, Suárez jumped up from his bench and asked for the floor: he assured the chamber that Hernández Mancha had got each and every line of the quatrain wrong, then recited them correctly to finish by saying that the author was not St Teresa but Lope de Vega; then, without another word, he sat back down. It was the scene dreamt of by any cocky provincial with a desire for revenge: he'd always been a reserved and pedestrian parliamentarian, but he'd just shamed his most direct competitor before the television cameras and in a full session of the Cortes, reminding those who for years had considered him an uneducated nonentity that perhaps he hadn't read as much as they had but he'd read enough to do much more for the country than they'd done, and reminding them in passing that Hernández Mancha was just one more of the many good-for-nothings adorned with honorary degrees he'd measured up to in his political career and who, because they thought they knew everything, would never understand anything.

All this was a mirage, the posthumous glow of an extinguished star, the hundred days of glory of a dethroned emperor. I refuse to believe that Suárez didn't know it; I refuse to believe that he'd returned to politics unaware that he would not be returning to power: after all very few knew as well as he did that it was perhaps impossible to bring ethics into politics without renouncing politics, because very few knew as well as he did that perhaps nobody comes to power without using dubious or dangerous or simply evil means, playing fair or trying as hard as he could to play fair to make himself an honourable place in history; I even wonder if he didn't know more, if he didn't at least guess, supposing that we can truly admire heroes and that they don't make us uncomfortable or offend us by diminishing us with the emphatic anomaly of their actions, maybe we cannot admire heroes of the retreat, or not fully, and that's why we don't want them to govern us again once their job is completed: because we suspect that they have sacrificed their honour and their conscience, and because we have an ethic of loyalty, but we do not have an ethic of betrayal. The mirage, in any case, barely lasted a couple of years: by the third the certainty had already begun to invade the Cortes and public opinion that what Suárez called politics of state was in reality ambiguous, tricky, populist politics, seeking left-wing votes in Madrid and right-wing ones in Ávila, and which allowed him to make pacts with the left in the Cortes and with the right in the municipalities; by the fourth, after disappointing results in the general and European elections, problems arose in the Party, internal divisions, expulsions of unruly members, and the right and the left saw the long-awaited occasion to kill off a common adversary and pounced on him at the same time in pursuit of their left-wing and right-wing voters; in the fifth year came the collapse: in the regional elections of 26 May 1991 the CDS lost more than half its votes and was left out of almost all the parliaments of the autonomous regions, and that same night Suárez announced his resignation as Party leader and relinquished his seat in the Cortes. It was the end: a mediocre ending, with no grandeur or brilliance. He had no more to give: he was exhausted and disappointed, powerless to battle on inside and out of his party. He didn't retire: they retired him. He left nothing behind: the UCD had disappeared years before, and the CDS would soon disappear. Politics is a slaughterhouse: many sighs of relief were heard, but not a single lament for his withdrawal.

Over the next year Suárez began to familiarize himself with his future as a precociously retired politician, father of a nation on the dole, intermediary in occasional business deals, high-priced speaker in Latin America and player of prolonged games of golf. It was a long, peaceful and slightly insipid future, or that's how he must've imagined it, perhaps with a certain unexpected dose of happiness. The first time he left power, after his resignation and the coup d'état, Suárez undoubtedly felt the chill of a heroin addict without heroin; it's very possible that now he felt nothing of the sort, or that he felt only something very similar to the joyful astonishment of one who throws off an impediment he hadn't been aware he was carrying. He forgot politics; politics forgot him. He continued to be profoundly religious and I don't think

he would have read Max Weber, so he had no reason to doubt he would
be saved and that, although power was an abrasive substance and he
had signed a pact with the devil, no one was going to come and collect
on it; he continued to be a compulsive optimist, so he must have been
sure that now all he had to do was let time go placidly by in the hope
that the country would be grateful for his contribution to the victory
of democracy. 'The hero of retreat can only be sure of one thing,' wrote
Hans Magnus Enzensberger of Suárez shortly before he gave up politics, 'the ingratitude of the fatherland.' It appears that Enzensberger
was mistaken, or at least he was partly mistaken, but Suárez was entirely
mistaken, and a little while later a final metamorphosis began to work
on him, as if, after having played a young arriviste from a nineteenth-
century French novel and a grown-up rogue converted into an
aristocratic hero of a neorealist Italian film, a demiurge had reserved for
the last plot of his life the tragic role of a pious, old, devastated prince
from a Russian novel.

Suárez received the first warning that a placid retirement was not
what awaited him just a year and a half after leaving politics, when in
the month of November 1992 he learned that his daughter Mariam had
breast cancer and the doctors thought she had less than three months
to live. The news left him stunned, but it did not paralyse him and
without a minute to lose he devoted himself to stopping his daughter's
illness. Two years later, once he thought they'd managed it, they diag-
nosed an identical cancer in Amparo, his wife. On this occasion the
blow was harder, because it came on top of the previous one, and this
time he didn't recover. It may be that, Catholic to the end, weakened
by age and misfortune, he ended up being defeated not by that double
mortal disease, but by guilt. In the year 2000, when his wife and daughter were still alive, Suárez wrote a prologue for a book his daughter
wrote about her illness. 'Why them? Why us?' he lamented. 'What
have they done? What have we done?' Suárez understands that such
questions are absurd, 'the logical attribute of an instinctive egomania',
but in spite of that it proves he posed them many times and that,
although he hadn't read Max Weber, remorse mortified him many
times with the illusory reproach that the devil had come to collect his
part of the bargain and that the burnt wasteland that surrounded him

was the result of the instinctive egomania that had allowed him to get to be who he'd always wanted to be. And it was just then that it happened. It was just then, at perhaps the darkest moment of his life, that the inevitable arrived, the longed-for moment of public recognition, the opportunity for all to show their gratitude for the sacrifice of his honour and his conscience for the country, the humiliating national din of compassion, he was the great man cut down by misfortune who no longer bothered anyone, was no longer able to overshadow anyone, who was never going to return to politics and could be used by this side and that and converted into the perfect paladin of concord, into the unbeaten ace of reconciliation, into the immaculate enabler of democratic change, into a living statue suitable for hiding behind and cleansing consciences and securing shaky institutions and shamelessly exhibiting the satisfaction of the country with its immediate past and, in Wagnerian scenes of gratitude for the fallen leader, homages, awards, honorific distinctions began to rain down on him, he recovered the King's friendship, the confidence of the Prime Ministers who followed him, popular favour, he achieved everything he'd wanted and anticipated although it was all a little false and forced and hurried and most of all late, because by then he was going or had gone and could barely contemplate his final collapse without understanding it too well and begging everyone who crossed his path to pray for his wife and for his daughter, as if his soul had got definitively lost in a labyrinth of self-pitying contrition and tormented meditations on the guilty fruits of egomania and he had become definitively transformed into the old repentant sinner prince of a novel by Dostoevsky.

In May 2001 his wife died; three years later his daughter died. By then his mind had abdicated and he was in another place, far from himself. The illness had begun to appear long before, taking him back and forth from memory to forgetfulness, but towards 2003 his deterioration could no longer be hidden. His last political speech dates from that time, although it wasn't exactly a political speech; a fragment was shown on television. The party of the right had offered his son Adolfo the candidacy for premier of the autonomous community of Castilla-La Mancha; because he was not unaware that the intention of the offer was to cash in on the prestige of his surname, Suárez advised his son not to accept, but the yearning to emulate his father was stronger than his lack of vocation and the son stood as candidate and the father felt obliged to defend him. On 3 May the two of them held a rally in Albacete. Standing in front of the crowd facing a lectern, Suárez is wearing a dark suit, white shirt and a polka-dot tie; he is seventy years old and, though his body still has vestiges of his poise on the tennis court and dance floor, he looks it, his hair flecked with white, receding sharply, his skin mottled with age spots. He doesn't talk of politics; he talks of his son, he mentions the fact that he studied at Harvard and then he stops dead. 'My God,' he says, barely smiling and shuffling the papers he's prepared. 'I think I've got myself in a terrible mess.' The audience applauds, encourages him to go on, and he looks up from his papers, bites his lower lip with a faded flirtatiousness and smiles for a long time; for those who've known him for years, it's an unmistakable smile: it's the same smile of the beau sure of his charms with which in other times he could convince a Falangist, an Opus Dei technocrat or a Guerrillero de Cristo Rey that deep down he was a paramilitary, a Falangist or an admirer of Opus; it's the same smile with which he could say: I'm no Communist (or Socialist), no, but I am one of you, because my family was always Republican and deep down I've always been one; it's the same smile with which he said: I have power and you have legitimacy: we have to understand each other. It's the same smile, perhaps a little less natural or more vague, but deep down it's the same. He looks back at the papers, he says again that his son studied at Harvard, he stops dead again. 'I don't know if I'm repeating myself,' he says. An urgent round of applause breaks out. 'I'm in a terrible mess with these papers,' he repeats. The music starts up, people stand to drown out his muttering with applause, he forgets about the papers and tries to improvise a closing, but amid all the uproar all that can be heard of what he says is the following phrase: 'My son will not let you down.'

They were the last words he pronounced in public. There it all ended. Then, for some years, he disappeared, shut up in his house in La Florida, and it was as if he had died. In fact, everyone began to speak of him as if he were dead. I myself have written this book as if he were dead. One day, however, he appeared again: it was 18 July 2008. That morning all the Spanish newspapers had his latest photograph on the front cover. His son Adolfo had taken it the day before, and in it Suárez appears with the King in the garden of his house in La Florida. The two men have their backs to the camera, walking beneath the sun on a recently mown lawn towards a leafy tree. The King is wearing a grey suit and his right hand is resting on Suárez's right shoulder, with a friendly or protective air; Suárez is wearing a light-blue shirt with the sleeves rolled up, beige trousers and tan shoes. The photograph captures a moment of a visit by the King to give Suárez the chain of the Order of the Golden Fleece, the highest honour granted by the Spanish Royal Family; according to the articles, the King has also granted it to other significant figures in Spain's recent past – among them Grand Duke Juan I of Luxembourg, Beatriz I of the Netherlands or Margarita II of Denmark – although he's only granted it a little more than a year ago to the nonentity who helped him more than anyone to conserve the Crown, and until that day he hadn't had time to bring it to him. The gratitude of the nation.

7

We know what happened in the intelligence services before 23 February and on 23 February, but what happened afterwards? What happened afterwards presents very few doubts, and can be told briefly.

There was much nervousness in CESID during the days following the coup. Rumours circulated around the organization's headquarters about the participation of members of Major Cortina's unit in the coup attempt; many of them pointed to the three members of the SEA (Sección Especial de Agentes) – Sergeant Sales, Corporals Monge and Moya – to Captain Gómez Iglesias, Captain García-Almenta, Major Cortina's second-in-command, and Cortina himself; all or almost all of them came from the same source: Captain Rubio Luengo and Sergeant Rando Parra, whom on the afternoon of the coup Monge had told of his adventures as a guide for Tejero's buses to the Cortes, seconded by Moya and Sales, on the orders of García-Almenta and, according to general inference, of Cortina. The major might have been sure of having created during his five years in command of AOME an organization as elitist, hermetic, loyal and disciplined as an order of sworn knights, but at that time he found out that some of his men had unresolved grievances against him and had decided to take advantage of the opportunity to settle them. They were the ones who went to Calderón, the service's strongman, to denounce Cortina and the rest of the *golpistas* of his unit. For obvious reasons, Calderón was terrified by the idea that responsibility for what had happened on 23 February might even graze CESID (the accusations of negligence and lack of foresight were enough to deal with), so he spoke to Cortina and, after being assured that AOME had not taken part in the coup, demanded he speak to his men and tackle the rumours. Over the following days Cortina held meetings with Rubio Luengo and Rando Parra: according to Cortina, he tried to prove to them that their accusations were false; according to Rubio Luengo and Rando Parra, he tried to buy their silence, blackmail and bribe them, and threatened them in a veiled way (the threats from some of their colleagues in the unit they'd informed on were more direct according to Rando Parra, and included insults, death threats and the destruction of a motorcycle). In the middle of March an AOME officer told the leader of the Congressional Defence Committee that the leadership of CESID was trying to cover up the participation of some of his colleagues in the coup, and at the end of the month, pressured from outside and from within – perhaps especially from within – Calderón ordered an investigation under the auspices of Lieutenant Colonel Juan Jáudenes, chief of the Interior Division, who, after several weeks of interrogations of accusers and accused, submitted a report that not unexpectedly absolved CESID in general and Major Cortina and his subordinates in particular of any link whatsoever to the coup.

It was all in vain. A few days after a new director of CESID took possession of his post at the beginning of May and sent the Jáudenes Report to the judge appointed by the government to try the case of those involved in the 23 February coup, Major Cortina was charged. He was not charged because of the report, although it's likely that some of the information it contained contributed to convincing the judge of his implication in the coup; it was Lieutenant Colonel Tejero's fault that he was prosecuted. In his first two declarations before the judge, he mentioned neither Cortina nor his friend Gómez Iglesias, according to Tejero because both of them sent him an identical message through his lawyer: the only thing he'd achieve by giving them away would be to deprive himself of their protection and that of CESID when he needed it most; however, in his third declaration, made at the beginning of April in the Castle of La Palma in Ferrol, the lieutenant colonel claimed that Cortina had been the real instigator of the coup. I've already noted the reasons for this change: during the two months since 23 February the defence counsels of almost all the accused had elaborated a joint strategy, cheered by the far-right press, consisting of maintaining the defendants were innocent of the crime of rebellion because they'd simply been obeying the orders of their superior officers, who were obeying the orders of Milans and of Armada, who were in their turn obeying the orders of the King; that was their principal line of argument before the trial and during the trial, and implicating Cortina was not only a way of implicating an essential organization of the state in the coup, but especially, because it could relate the major to Armada and to the King, a way of implicating the upper echelons of the Army and the Crown in the coup. So the third time he testified before the examining magistrate Lieutenant Colonel Tejero decided to forgo the promised shelter of CESID, and told or invented his two encounters with Cortina, accusing him of having spurred on the coup and of being his link to Armada, and on 21 May, after being interrogated by the examining magistrate, Major Cortina went to jail accused of having participated in the coup. Some days later, on 13 June, Captain Gómez Iglesias was charged. No other member of AOME underwent the same fate.

8

23 February

In a way, it was the most dangerous moment of the night. It was half past one in the morning and, after the King's televised speech condemning the assault on the Cortes and demanding respect for the Constitution, many people all over the country who had been on tenterhooks until then, glued to the radio and the television, went to bed, and almost everyone felt that the appearance of the monarch marked the end of the coup or the beginning of the end of the coup. It was a feeling that was only partly accurate. After Armada's failure in the Cortes the soft coup of Armada and Milans had failed, but not Tejero's hard coup, a coup intended to finish with democracy even at the cost of finishing with the monarchy and which – with the lieutenant colonel still occupying the Cortes, Milans' tanks still on the streets of Valencia, the reactions of the Captains General still pending and many generals, commanders and officers still tempted to act – was still waiting for a minimum movement of troops that might spark off a chain reaction in the Army. The problem was that at that point, with the King now standing firm against the *golpistas*, such a reaction would have entailed almost necessarily an armed confrontation between those loyal to the Crown and those in rebellion, something that had been a possibility since the beginning of the coup but that had perhaps never been as close to happening as then, when the King's orders were only just beginning to erode the rebels' morale and the certainty had not yet spread throughout the Army that the coup was now not going to triumph.

At that time, fifteen minutes after the King appeared on television, ten minutes after Armada left the Cortes without having been able to make his proposal for a unity government to the parliamentarians, the minimal troop movement the *golpistas* were hoping for occurred: a column of fifteen Land-Rovers occupied by a major, four captains, two lieutenants, five NCOs and a hundred and nine conscripts appeared in the centre of Madrid, got as far as Carrera de San Jerónimo, broke through the double security cordon of Civil Guards and national police surrounding the Cortes and, while the crowd milling around the Hotel Palace tried to discern whether the objective of the recent arrivals was to dislodge the rebels or support them, they joined Lieutenant Colonel Tejero's forces. The column came from the headquarters of the Brunete Armoured Division on the outskirts of the capital and was under the command of Ricardo Pardo Zancada, the same major who on the eve of the coup, during a return trip to Valencia, received from Milans the mission to incite his division to rebellion with the help of General Torres Rojas and Colonel San Martín. Over the course of the whole evening and night Pardo Zancada had watched perplexed, irate and powerless as the rebellion failed at the Brunete once General Juste, the commanding officer, revoked the departure order issued to all the regiments minutes before the assault on the Cortes; embarrassed by the fleeing of Torres Rojas, who shortly after eight had flown back to La Coruña without carrying out his mission, and by the paralysis of San Martín and the rest of the commanders and officers of the unit, so often ardent enthusiasts of a coup, just before one in the morning Pardo Zancada changed out of his standard uniform and into battle-dress, improvised his column of light vehicles with the collaboration of several young captains and the only two companies stationed at headquarters and, after waiting in formation for more than a quarter of an hour at the exit barrier as a show of defiance or invitation to his comrades, left for the Cortes after verifying that no one was going to swell their ranks and threatening to shoot in the head any soldier who disobeyed his orders.

It was not a quixotic act. Given that Pardo Zancada joined Tejero when for many the coup had already practically been neutralized, many thought that his was a quixotic act or what is often designated a quixotic act: a noble gesture of loyalty to a lost cause. It was not: it's true that, unlike many of his comrades, Pardo Zancada demonstrated he was no coward, just as it is true that he was an idealist with his imagination too inflamed by the reverence for the crock of Francoist heroism and a radical too soaked in the ideological concoction of the far right to be intimidated at the last moment, but it's not true that his action was a quixotic act. It was an act of war: strictly speaking, the only act of war that had occurred since Tejero occupied the Cortes and Milans the streets of Valencia, and therefore the necessary pinprick to incite the military and let loose those repressed *golpista* outbursts that had been agitating the barracks for many hours, the spark that could ignite the powder keg of the Brunete Division and, with it, that of the whole Army. For this reason Pardo Zancada's move was dangerous; for this reason and perhaps for another. Although on 23 February he was acting under the orders of Milans, it's possible that Pardo Zancada was connected more or less closely to a group of colonels connected in turn to San Martín or captained by San Martín, a group that, as was explained in November of the previous year in Manuel Fernández-Monzón Altolaguirre's report entitled 'Panorama of Operations Under Way', had spent months planning a hard coup the aim of which was the establishment of a presidential republic or a military directorate; San Martín and Pardo Zancada had climbed aboard Milans and Armada's monarchist coup at the last moment, but, this having failed, the colonels' coup was perhaps the only visible alternative for the *golpistas* in the midst of the reigning nervousness, confusion and chaos, and Pardo Zancada's action could be a means, although perhaps not to activate that operation, to activate its organizers, accomplices and sympathizers of its organizers, incorporating them into the attempted coup and dragging Milans and other Captains General by force into a coup that could no longer be staged with the King, but only against the King.

In spite of the fact that at half past one in the morning perhaps few people feared that contingency might be enough of a counterirritant to hand triumph to the *golpistas*, Pardo Zancada's first moments in the Cortes seemed to confirm these dark predictions. His column's arrival lifted the spirits of the rebel Civil Guards, who were beginning to fall victim to fatigue and discouragement, aware that the failure of the negotiation between Armada and Tejero had impeded a favourable outcome of the hostage-taking and every moment that passed made it less likely that the Army would come to its assistance; but, as well as briefly boosting the rebels' morale – allowing them to believe that the Brunete Division had finally joined the coup and this detachment was just the bridgehead of the expected general movement – as soon as he put himself at Tejero's orders Pardo Zancada concentrated on the task of rousing other units to rebellion: armed with a division telephone book that he'd got from headquarters and jumping from one phone to another as those directing the siege of the Cortes cut his communications with the exterior until leaving only four or five phones working of the eighty in the building, Pardo Zancada spoke (from an office on the ground floor of the new building, from the switchboard, from the press box) with several officers at Brunete with troops at their command; after reporting to San Martín at headquarters, he spoke to Colonel Centeno Estévez, of the 11th Mechanized Brigade, to Lieutenant Colonel Fernando Pardo de Santayana, of the Anti-aircraft Artillery Group, to Colonel Pontijas, of the XII Armoured Brigade, to Lieutenant Colonel Santa Pau Corzán, of the 14th Villaviciosa Cavalry Regiment. The conversation with each of them was similar: Pardo Zancada informed them of what he'd done and then urged them to follow his example, assuring them that many others were getting ready to imitate his gesture and all they had to do was get a tank on Carrera de San Jerónimo for the coup to be irreversible. The reactions to his telephonic harangues oscillated between Pardo de Santayana's defeatism and Santa Pau Corzán's enthusiasm ('Don't worry, Ricardo, we won't leave you there with your ass hanging out! We're coming with you!'), and by half past three in the morning his efforts seemed to be bearing fruit when one of Milans' adjutants phoned the Cortes to announce that the Villaviciosa and Pavía Cavalry Regiments had just rebelled and were on their way to Carrera de San Jerónimo. It wasn't true, but – thanks to Lieutenant Colonel De Meer and Colonel Valencia Remón, who until well into the early hours were on the brink of sending the tanks out of the barracks – it was very close to being so; at least two or three other units from the Brunete were also very close to imitating Pardo Zancada.

He also failed when he wanted to disseminate a manifesto outlining the *golpistas*' reasons: the newspaper *El Alcázar* refused to publish it in its pages; the radio station La Voz de Madrid claimed to have technical problems in order not to broadcast it: both thus deprived the major of a means of propaganda directed at overcoming the indecision of his comrades-in-arms all over the country.

Shortly after receiving the news of this double setback Pardo Zancada called Valencia and spoke to Milans. It was the last time he did so that night; although the major didn't know it, by then Milans had understood for several hours that the coup was drawing to a close. Minutes after the King's televised address and Tejero's refusal to obey him from the office in the new building of the Cortes, sealing the failure of his soft coup, Milans received a telex from the Zarzuela in which he was urged dramatically to put a stop to his uprising. In it, after reiterating his decision to defend constitutional order, the King said: 'Any coup d'état cannot hide behind the King, it is against the King.' And he also said: 'I order you to withdraw all the units that you have mobilized.' And also: 'I order you to tell Tejero to desist immediately.' And finally: 'I swear that I will neither abdicate the Crown nor abandon Spain. Whoever rebels is ready to provoke a new civil war and will bear responsibility for doing so.' This ultimatum appears to have overcome the resistance of Milans, who as soon as he received it dispatched to all his tactical groups the order to return to quarters, but the tension at the Captaincy General of Valencia would be prolonged for another several hours yet, and not only because of the failed attempts to arrest its incumbent directed from Army General Headquarters by General Gabeiras, but most of all because Milans was still tormented by doubts and not entirely ready to let his arm be twisted, as if he were relying on some straggling support that might still afford victory to the *golpistas*, or perhaps as if he were ashamed of abandoning the occupiers of the Cortes to their fate, having sent them there himself. There was no more support, no one dared to disobey the King, the colonels led by San Martín or linked to San Martín decided to keep waiting in the hope that a more auspicious occasion would arise and, after convincing themselves that nothing could be done for Tejero and Pardo Zancada either (or that the best thing they could do for them was precisely to

abandon them, to provoke their surrender and end the occupation),
Milans admitted his defeat. That's what he eventually said to Pardo
Zancada the last time they spoke by telephone that night: that no
Captaincy General was backing the coup and that he'd returned his
troops to quarters and rescinded the edict proclaiming a state of emergency; to this he added only that Pardo Zancada should try to persuade
Tejero to accept the agreement that Armada had offered him and
the lieutenant colonel had rejected hours before. At that moment the
request was absurd, as well as futile, and they both knew it was futile
and absurd. General, sir, said Pardo Zancada. Wouldn't you like to
speak to the lieutenant colonel yourself? No, answered Milans. You
speak to him. Yes, sir, General, said Pardo Zancada. Is there anything
else I can do for you, sir? No, nothing, said Milans. Take care, Pardo.

It was half past four on the morning of the 24th and the coup had
still not ended, but its nature had definitively changed: until then it
had been a political and military problem; from then on, once Milans
and Armada's soft coup had failed and so had the attempt at conversion
there and then into Tejero's hard coup, it was now just a problem of
public order: everything consisted of finding a non-violent way to get
the hostages released. And the reality was that by that time in the morning – after the King's appearance on television as cascades of
condemnations of the coup poured forth from political and professional organizations, trade unions, regional governments, municipalities,
county councils, the press and from a whole country that had remained
silent until it glimpsed the failure of the *golpistas* – the interior of the
Cortes began to be ripe for capitulation, or that was at least what those
who were directing the blockade were thinking now that they'd abandoned the idea of assaulting the building with groups from special
operations out of fear of a massacre and had concluded that they just
needed to allow time to go by so the lack of external support would
make the occupiers succumb: except for the party leaders, isolated for
the whole night in other rooms of the Cortes, the parliamentarians
were still in the chamber, smoking and dozing and exchanging contradictory bits of news in low voices, more sure with each minute that
passed of the defeat of the coup, watched over by Civil Guards who
tried to make them forget the outrages of the first moments of the

occupation, treating them with more and more consideration because they were more and more demoralized by the evidence of their solitude, more decimated by drowsiness, fatigue and discouragement, more repentant of having embarked on, having let themselves be embarked on, that odyssey with no way out, more frightened of the future awaiting them and more impatient for it all to be over as soon as possible.

Towards dawn the first attempts to negotiate the surrender of the rebels began. The first came from the Captaincy General of Madrid (or perhaps from the Zarzuela) and the one in charge of carrying it out was Colonel San Martín; the second came from Army General Headquarters and in charge of carrying it out was Lieutenant Colonel Eduardo Fuentes Gómez de Salazar. Both attempts sought to get Pardo Zancada out of the Cortes (the theory was that, if Pardo Zancada left, Tejero would soon follow), but, although San Martín seemed to be the ideal person to achieve it, since he was Pardo Zancada's friend and immediate superior and because many might have suspected that he was somehow involved in the coup, the first attempt failed; not the second. Lieutenant Colonel Fuentes was an officer stationed in the Exterior Intelligence Division of Army General Headquarters and an old friend of Pardo Zancada's: both had worked under San Martín's orders in Admiral Carrero Blanco's intelligence service, both were on the editorial board of the military magazine *Reconquista* and both shared radical ideas; that night Pardo Zancada and he had spoken by telephone on several occasions, haranguing each other, but towards eight in the morning Fuentes had accepted that his friend's remaining in the Cortes no longer made sense and he decided to request his superiors' permission to speak to him and try to get him to desist. His idea was well received at Headquarters, they granted him permission and, after passing through the command post of the blockade at the Hotel Palace – where Generals Aramburu Topete and Sáenz de Santamaría demanded he accept only surrender conditions he judged absolutely reasonable – shortly after nine he approached the Civil Guards watching over the access gate to the Cortes and asked to speak to Pardo Zancada.

Thus opened the epilogue of the coup. By then it had been several hours since the country had awoken to a rather belated *antigolpista* fervour, the newspapers were selling out of their special editions with front pages crackling with enthusiasm for the King and the Constitution and invective against the rebels and, although all the cities recovered the hustle and bustle of any winter morning following calls for normality sent out by the Zarzuela and by the provisional government, in Madrid more than four thousand people thronged the area around Carrera de San Jerónimo, disturbed during the night by far-right gangs, cheering for liberty and democracy; by then the occupiers were barely dominating the situation inside the Cortes any more: around eight in the morning the parliamentarians had refused amid shouts of protest to eat the provisions they offered them for breakfast – milk, cheese, sliced ham – around nine the Civil Guards had to put down with the threat of arms the beginnings of a riot led by Manuel Fraga and seconded by several of his associates, and there was still a little more than an hour to go before Tejero would allow the deputies to leave and several dozen Civil Guards would hand themselves over to the loyal forces by jumping out the window of the press room of the new building of the Cortes on to Carrera de San Jerónimo. These symptoms of stampede explain how, unlike Colonel San Martín a few hours earlier, Lieutenant Colonel Fuentes would find a Pardo Zancada predisposed to agree a finale. The negotiation, however, was long and laborious. Pardo Zancada asked to leave the Cortes at the same time as Tejero, he asked to do so at the command of his unit and to be able to hand it over at Brunete headquarters, he asked that only he and none of his men be held responsible, he asked that there be no photographers or television cameras allowed to film the moment of leaving. Fuentes considered all the conditions acceptable except for one. They won't allow the captains to remain at liberty, he objected. All right, answered Pardo. Then from the lieutenants down. Fuentes left for the Hotel Palace, where they hurried to approve what he'd agreed, as did General Gabeiras from Army General Headquarters, and the lieutenant colonel went straight back to the Cortes to try to convince Tejero as well. After meeting with his officers and guards, Tejero endorsed Pardo Zancada's demands, but qualified some and added others, among them that it should be General Armada who vouched for the accord with his presence. Fuentes wrote it all down on a sheet of paper, and as he left for the Hotel Palace again he met General Aramburu Topete a few metres from the entrance gate accompanied by General Armada, whom he'd summoned to reinforce the negotiations. There were more secret discussions, more comings and goings between the Cortes and the Hotel Palace, and by about half past one the surrender was complete: on the patio that separates the new building and the old building, on the roof of one of Pardo Zancada's Land-Rovers, in the presence of him, Tejero, Fuentes and Aramburu Topete, General Armada guaranteed the fulfilment of the points of the pact by signing the sheet of paper where Fuentes had written them down. Half an hour later the evacuation of the Cortes began. It was carried out in an orderly fashion: the Speaker closed the session in due form and the parliamentarians began to file out; a final humiliation awaited them on the patio, however, where Pardo Zancada had lined up his column of soldiers three deep to force them to pass in front of it, ravaged by the anxiety of the sleepless night and observed from afar by the crowd waiting outside the doors of the Hotel Palace, before walking out into freedom on Carrera de San Jerónimo.

One of the first parliamentarians to leave was Adolfo Suárez. He did so alone, urgently, ignoring the soldiers lined up on the patio, but as he crossed the entrance gates and headed for his official car he noticed the presence of General Armada and, because at some point during his long hours locked up alone in the ushers' room he'd heard that the King's former secretary was negotiating a solution to the hostage-taking, Suárez changed direction and went over and greeted him warmly, almost embracing him, convinced that the man he'd always considered a potential *golpista* and in recent times the promoter of slippery political operations against the government had turned out to be the one responsible for his liberation and the failure of the coup. Other deputies copied Suárez's gesture, among them General Gutiérrez Mellado, but almost all of them would remember many times the cadaverous look on General Armada's face while he coped with their effusions. It was exactly twelve noon on a freezing foggy Tuesday, the most confusing and most decisive seventeen and a half hours of the last half-century of Spanish history had just gone by and the 23 February coup had ended.

EPILOGUE

PROLOGUE TO A NOVEL

I

The trial of those involved in the 23 February coup d'état was held between 19 February and 3 June 1982 in the paper warehouse of the Army's Geographical Service, in Campamento, a compound of military installations near Madrid, under strict security measures and over the course of interminable morning and afternoon sessions, in a courtroom crammed with relatives, lawyers, journalists, military committees, invited guests and observers. The tribunal was composed of thirty-two general officers of the Supreme Court of Military Justice, the highest branch of military jurisdiction, and thirty-three people were tried, all military officers except for one civilian. It is a ridiculous figure compared with the real number of those involved in the coup; the reason for this disparity is clear: three days after the attempted coup a special judge was appointed to investigate the case, and from that point on, over the course of the four full months the legal proceedings lasted, Leopoldo Calvo Sotelo's government did everything it could to limit to the utmost the number of those charged because he thought the shaky post-coup democracy would not withstand a procession of hundreds of top-ranking military officers through the courtroom and the rigorous examination of their civilian accomplices, an examination liable to splatter many members of the ruling class who knowingly or unknowingly prepared the placenta of the coup. In fact, between the time of the coup and that of the hearing, while a campaign in the barracks and the far-right newspapers designed to blame the King in order to exonerate the *golpistas* was growing stronger, some of the defendants nurtured the hope that the trial would not take place, and shortly before the sessions began the Prime Minister himself met with the editorial directors of the main national newspapers and asked them to avoid publishing news the military would find hurtful, not to turn their pages into involuntary loudspeakers for the *golpistas'* propaganda and therefore to report what happened in the courtroom of the Army's Geographical Service in a minor key, almost on the quiet. There was a trial, the accuseds' hopes of impunity were dashed, but the newspapers refused the kind of self-censorship the government requested of them, and over more than three months of public interrogations the Spanish people had daily and exhaustive news of the coup and the *golpistas* had at their disposal a potent amplifier for each of their words, something that contrary to what the government feared contributed to discrediting them before the majority of the population, although providing them with extra prestige in the eyes of their unconditional supporters.

It was the longest trial in Spanish history. Since the judges and the defendants were military officers and the Army a meticulously inbred institution, it was basically an almost impossible trial: judges and defendants had shared military destinations and quarters, their wives were friends and shopped at the same stores, their children were friends and went to the same schools; some of the judges could have been in the defendants' position and some of the defendants could have been in the judges' position. From the first moment the *golpistas*, their families and their defence lawyers tried to transform the hearing room and surroundings into the stage for a sordid carnival, and up to a certain point they succeeded: barely a day went by without stoppages, protests, shouts, applause, insults, threats, expulsions, interruptions or provocations, to such an extent that as the days went on the accused and their defenders became bolder and bolder until they managed to intimidate the tribunal, which explains why before the preliminary deliberations on the verdict the presiding general, too weak to bear the pressure to which he was being subjected and keep the *golpistas'* bullying under control, was replaced. From the first moment it was also clear that the defence strategy was dividing the accused into two antagonistic groups: one was made up of General Armada, Major Cortina and Captain Gómez Iglesias, Cortina's subordinate in AOME; the other was made up of the rest, with General Milans and Lieutenant Colonel Tejero at its head. The first kept to defending themselves for better or for worse against the crime of military rebellion and trying to dissociate themselves from the coup and from the rest of the accused; whereas the second group – with the exception of Major Pardo Zancada, who openly accepted responsibility for his part in the events – tried to associate themselves with the first group and, through them, with the King, seeking to convert the court martial into a political trial and presenting themselves as a group of honourable men who had acted under the orders of Armada, who in his turn had acted on the orders of the King, with the aim of saving a country corrupted by a corrupt political regime and a corrupt political class, and in accordance with the military grounds for acquittal of due obedience and the political grounds for acquittal of state of necessity. Legally this line of defence was apparently logical: either Armada had told Milans the truth in their conspiratorial meetings and the coup d'état was an operation desired by the King, therefore according to their defence lawyers the accused were not guilty because they had merely been obeying the King through Armada and Milans, or Armada had lied to Milans and the King did not want a coup and therefore the only one guilty of everything was Armada; in reality it was a contradictory and ludicrous line of defence: contradictory because the due-obedience grounds for acquittal negated the state-of-necessity grounds for acquittal, given that if the *golpistas* considered a *golpe de estado* necessary or indispensable it was because they knew the situation the country was in and could therefore not have been acting ingenuously and blindly on the orders of the King; ludicrous because it was ludicrous to pretend that the judicial concept of due obedience should cover outrages like the assault on the Parliament or the invasion of Valencia with tanks. That was how on the basis of contradictions and nonsense the trial deteriorated into a festival of lies in which, except for Pardo Zancada, none of the defendants said what they should have said: that they'd done what they'd done because they believed it was what had to be done, availing themselves of the fact that Milans said that Armada said that the King said that it was what had to be done, and in any case what they would have done sooner or later, because it was exactly what so many of their comrades had been wanting to do for such a long time.

During the hearing the principal protagonists of the coup behaved like what they were: Tejero, like a brutalized lout with a clear conscience; Milans, like a uniformed and defiant filibusterer; Armada, like a millionaire, double-dealing courtier: isolated, despised and insulted by almost all the others in the dock with him, who demanded he inform on the King or admit that he'd lied, Armada on the one hand refused to implicate the monarch, but on the other insinuated with his proclamations of loyalty to the Crown and even more with his silences, which suggested he was keeping quiet to protect the King; as for Major Cortina, he proved to be by far the most intelligent of the defendants: he dismantled all the accusations hanging over his head, dodged all the traps laid for him by the prosecutor and the defence attorneys and, according to Martín Prieto – court reporter for *El País* during the trial – subjected his interrogators to 'greater suffering than humans are able to bear'. The final days were difficult for Armada, Cortina and Gómez Iglesias; although for months they had coexisted without too many problems with the rest of the accused in the Geographical Service's quarters, as the time of the verdict approached and it was obvious that all or almost all of them were going to be found guilty, relations between the two groups became untenable, and the same day that Tejero tried to lay into Cortina at the end of the morning session the tribunal decided to confine the three dissidents to a separate wing of the quarters for their protection. Finally, on 3 June, the tribunal delivered its judgement: Tejero and Milans were condemned to thirty years in prison – the maximum sentence – but Armada received only six, as did Torres Rojas and Pardo Zancada, and all the rest of the commanders and officers got off with sentences of between one and five years; all except Cortina, who was acquitted, as were one Brunete captain and one of the captains and nine of the lieutenants who had accompanied Tejero into the Parliament. It was not just an indulgent sentence, but practically an invitation to repeat the coup, and the government appealed it before the civilian magistrates of the Supreme Court. Less than a year later the final court passed the definitive sentence; the majority of the accused saw their sentences at least doubled: Armada went from six years to thirty, Torres Rojas and Pardo Zancada from six to twelve, Ibáñez Inglés from five to ten, San Martín from three to ten, and so on, and even the lieutenants who stormed the Parliament and had been declared innocent by the first court were also found guilty. The government did not appeal Cortina's acquittal or that of the two captains, and the Supreme Court simply confirmed the thirty years handed down to Milans and Tejero.

Perhaps the punishment was still benevolent, but there were no more courts to turn to and the *golpistas* began to leave prison shortly after their final sentences were handed down. Some were forced out of the Army, but almost all of them had the opportunity to remain, even of course the Civil Guards and NCOs who, in spite of having fired shots inside the chamber of the Cortes and roughed up General Gutiérrez Mellado, were not even tried. There were officers who had notable military careers after the coup: Manuel Boza – a lieutenant shown in the footage of the assault on the Cortes face to face with Adolfo Suárez, probably berating or insulting him – was reinstated in the Civil Guard after serving a twelve-month prison sentence, and in subsequent years received the following decorations for his exceptional merits and impeccable conduct: Civil Guard Cross of Merit with White Emblem, Royal Order of St Hermenegildo, Plaque of St Hermenegildo and Command of St Hermenegildo; Juan Pérez de la Lastra – a captain whose enthusiasm for the coup did not prevent him from leaving his men in the Cortes on the night of 23 February to go home for a few hours' sleep and come back without anyone noticing his absence – also returned to the Civil Guard once he'd served his sentence, and in 1996 retired with the rank of colonel and with the following decorations granted since the coup: Cross of St Hermenegildo, Command of St Hermenegildo and Plaque of St Hermenegildo. The gratitude of the nation.

Those mainly responsible for 23 February took longer to get out of prison; some of them have died. The last to obtain his liberty was Lieutenant Colonel Tejero, who a year after the coup tried in vain to stand for election with an ephemeral party called Spanish Solidarity whose campaign slogan went: 'Put Tejero in the Cortes with your vote'; like many of his comrades, during his years of imprisonment he led a comfortable life, guest of honour to some of the wardens of the jails where he served his sentence and converted into an icon of the far right, but when he left prison in 1996 he was no longer an icon of anything or he was just a pop icon, and his only known activities since then are painting pictures nobody buys and sending letters to newspaper editors that nobody reads, as well as celebrating the anniversary of his exploit every February. Milans died in July 1997 in Madrid; he was buried in the crypt of the Alcázar in Toledo, where he had begun his record as a Francoist war hero; like Tejero, he never repented of having organized 23 February, but after that date he abandoned his lifelong monarchism, and over the years he spent in prison spurred on or gave his blessing to almost every new attempted coup d'état, including the one on 2 June 1985 that planned to assassinate the upper echelons of the Army, the Prime Minister and the entire Royal Family during a military parade. Armada, on the other hand, did continue to be a monarchist, or at least he claims to be, even if in none of his numerous public declarations – or of course in his mellifluous and tricky memoirs – has he stopped nurturing the ambiguity about the King's role in the coup; he was pardoned by a Socialist government at the end of 1988, and since then he has divided his time between his house in Madrid and his country estate in Santa Cruz de Rivadulla, in La Coruña, a baroque aristocratic mansion where until recently he personally looked after a nursery that produced a hundred thousand camellias. As for Cortina, what happened to him after the coup deserves a less succinct explanation.

In the early hours of 14 June 1982, just over a month after the sentence of the Court of Military Justice absolved the intelligence service major, four powerful explosive charges blew up four secret AOME headquarters. The bombs exploded almost at the same time, in a synchronized operation that produced no victims, and the next day the media attributed the attack to a new terrorist offensive on the part of ETA. This was false: ETA never claimed responsibility for the action, which had the Civil Guard's signature written all over it and could only have been carried out with information from AOME members. Still under the effect of the tremendous military tension provoked by the mass court martial and the sentencing of some of the most prestigious leaders of the Army, there were those who interpreted the quadruple attack as a sign that a new military coup was under way and as a warning to

CESID not to get in its organizers' way this time; it was most likely a more personal warning: many in the military and the Civil Guard were furious with CESID for not having been on the side of the coup on 23 February and for having done everything possible to stop it, but they were even more furious with Cortina, who according to them had launched the *golpistas* on the adventure, left them in the lurch and then managed to come through the trial unscathed. This ominous precedent and certain coincidences of dates and locations explain the doubts aroused by an episode that happened a year later, 27 July 1983. That day, just months after the Supreme Court passed their definitive ruling at least doubling the length of the sentences of most of those found guilty of the 23 February coup, Cortina's father burned to death in a fire at his home; the fact that the location was, according to Tejero, where his interview with the major had taken place in the days leading up to the coup, not to mention the circumstances of the calamity – at four o'clock in the afternoon while Cortina's father was taking his siesta – reinforced the hypothesis of revenge. Cortina and the investigators attributed the fire to an electrical short-circuit; the explanation convinced almost no one, but the truth is not always convincing. Be that as it may, after the trial Cortina was reinstated in the Army; although he never returned to the intelligence services – all his assignments from then on were related to logistics – he did not manage to dispel the suspicions that hung over him, his equivocal reputation followed him everywhere and in recent years the Army has hardly had a single scandal not somehow associated with his name. In 1991, by then promoted to colonel, he was relieved of his command for facilitating a leak to the press of secret plans of military operations, but, in spite of being finally absolved of the accusation of negligence, by then he'd already requested a transfer to the reserves. Later, for a time, he served as adviser to a deputy prime minister in José María Aznar's government, and at present he runs a logistics firm called I2V and participates in a family security business. As I complete this book he is an athletic old man, with sparse white hair, freckle-spattered scalp, gold-rimmed glasses and a boxer's nose, an affable, ironic and cheerful man, who has an autographed portrait of the King in his office and for many years has not wanted to hear a word about 23 February.

2

During the months that followed the failure of the coup d'état some democratic politicians and journalists frequently repeated that the coup had triumphed, or at least that it hadn't entirely failed. It was a figure of speech, a way of pointing up what they considered a shrinking of democracy after 23 February. The coup did not triumph, it didn't even triumph in part, but in the short term some of the *golpistas'* political objectives seemed to be fulfilled.

What in theory was the *golpistas'* fundamental political objective? For Armada, for Cortina, for those who thought like Armada and Cortina – not for Milans or for Tejero or for those who thought like Milans and Tejero, who were undoubtedly the majority of the *golpistas* – the fundamental political objective of 23 February consisted of protecting the monarchy, rooting it in Spain and correcting or trimming or shrinking a democracy that in their judgement constituted a threat to it. To achieve this fundamental objective they had to achieve another fundamental objective: put a stop to the political career of Adolfo Suárez, who was mainly responsible for the state of affairs; then they had to put a stop to that state of affairs: they had to put a stop to the risk of a hard-core, anti-monarchist coup, had to put a stop to terrorism, had to put a stop to the *Estado de las Autonomías* or put it in brackets or humble its pretensions and consolidate national feelings, had to put a stop to the economic crisis, had to put a stop to international policies that irritated the United States because they were distancing Spain from the Western bloc, had to narrow the space for tolerance in all areas, had to teach the political class a lesson and had to give the country back its lost confidence. Those were in theory, I insist, the objectives of 23 February. In the months after the coup – while the country tried to take in what had happened, awaiting the *golpistas'* trial with more scepticism than fear, and while the government and the opposition practised the politics of pacification with the military and certain politicians and many journalists denounced the reality of a democracy watched over by the Army – some of them were immediately fulfilled. Adolfo Suárez's political career ended on 23 February, just as he carried out his last truly political act by remaining seated while the bullets whizzed around the chamber of the Cortes: without the coup Suárez might have had some chance to return to power; with the coup he had none: perhaps we can admire heroes, perhaps we can even admire heroes of the retreat, but we don't want them to govern us, so after 23 February Suárez was nothing more than a survivor of himself, a posthumous politician. After the coup d'état all official offices, every municipal balcony, all the party headquarters and all the autonomous-government assemblies suddenly bloomed with national flags, and all the jails filled with common criminals. The coup d'état, it has often been said, was the most efficient vaccination against another coup d'état, and it's true: after 23 February Leopoldo Calvo Sotelo's government invested billions in modernizing the Armed Forces and carried out a far-reaching purge – replaced the Joint Chiefs of Staff en masse, retired the most Francoist generals, rejuvenated the command structure, strictly controlled promotions and remodelled the intelligence services – and, although after 1981 there were still several attempts at military rebellion, the truth is they were organized by an ever more eccentric and isolated minority, because 23 February not only discredited the *golpistas* in the eyes of society, but also in the eyes of their own comrades-in-arms, thus hastening the end of a two-century tradition of military coups. Barely three months after 23 February, the government signed the NATO accession treaty that Suárez refused to sign for years, which reassured the United States, contributed to civilizing the Army by putting it in contact with democratic armies and embedded the country firmly in the Western bloc. A short time later, at the beginning of June, the government, businessmen and trade unions, with the support of politicians from the other parties and a similar intention to that behind the Moncloa Pact, signed a National Employment Accord, which halted the daily destruction of thousands of jobs, reduced inflation and meant the start of a series of changes that heralded the beginning of the economic recovery of the mid-1980s. And a month and a half later the government and the opposition, amid howls of protests from the nationalists, signed the so-called LOAPA, an organic law defending the need to rationalize the autonomous powers of the regions that tried to put the brakes on the decentralization of the state. The terrorists did not stop killing, of course, but it's a fact that after the coup the attitude of the country changed towards them, the left did its best to wrest away the alibis it'd allowed them, the Armed Forces began to notice the solidarity of civil society and the governments began to fight against ETA with instruments Suárez never dared use: in March 1981 Calvo Sotelo authorized the Army's intervention in the anti-terrorist struggle on land and maritime borders, and just two years later, recently arrived in power, the Socialists created GAL, a group of state-financed mercenaries who began a campaign of kidnapping and assassinating terrorists in the south of France. The greater social belligerence against terrorism was just one aspect of a wider social change. Seventeen and a half hours of humiliation in the chamber of Parliament amounted to a sufficient corrective for the political class, who seemed to find a sudden forced maturity, shelved for a time their furious inter-party rows and the furious greed for power that had served to create the placenta of the coup, stopped speculating with shady operations of constitutional engineering and did not mention again caretaker or interim or salvation or unity governments or involving the Army in any way; no less tough was the lesson for the majority of the country, which had passively accepted Francoism, had been excited at first by democracy and then seemed disillusioned: the disenchantment vanished overnight and everyone seemed to rediscover with enthusiasm how good liberty was, and maybe the best proof is that a year and a half after the coup an unknown majority of Spaniards decided there would be no real reconciliation until the heirs of the losers of the war governed again, permitting a rotation of power that ended up consolidating democracy and the monarchy. This is another secondary effect difficult not to credit, at least partially, to 23 February's account: at the beginning of 1981 it was still difficult to imagine the Socialist Party governing Spain, but in October of the following year it came to power with ten million votes and all the congratulations of the monarchy, the Army, businessmen and bankers, journalists, Rome and Washington.

It's true: none of the preceding happened thanks to the coup, but in spite of the coup; it didn't happen because the coup triumphed, but because it failed and because its failure convulsed the country and seemed to change it completely. But without the coup this convulsion would not have happened, nor would this change, or not the way it happened and with the speed it happened, and most of all, the most important thing would not have happened, and that is the Crown accumulated a power and legitimacy it could only have dreamt of before the coup. The King's power came from Franco, and his legitimacy from having renounced Franco's powers or part of his powers to cede them to popular sovereignty and become a constitutional monarch; but this was a precarious legitimacy, which deducted effective power from the King and left him exposed to the risk of the swings of fortune of a history that had expelled from the throne many of those who'd preceded him. The coup d'état reinforced the Crown: acting apart from the Constitution, using a powerless King's last trick of power – which he held as symbolic commander-in-chief of the Army and Franco's heir – the King stopped the coup and became democracy's saviour, which lavished legitimacy upon the monarchy and turned it into the most solid, most appreciated, most popular, most safeguarded from criticism and, deep down, most powerful institution in the country. That's what it still is today, to the incredulity from beyond the grave of the King's ancestors and the envy of all the Continent's monarchies. Or to put it another way: if before 23 February the *golpistas* had calculated the risks and benefits they would have reached the conclusion that it was less dangerous for the parliamentary monarchy to stage a coup or allow one than not to stage one, or if they'd designed the coup not to destroy democracy but to shrink it for a time and thus safeguard the monarchy in a moment of anxiety and consolidate it in the country, then there would be reasons to maintain that the 23 February coup triumphed, or at least didn't completely fail. But it's better to put it like this: the coup d'état failed completely and it was its complete failure that turned the democratic system in the form of a parliamentary monarchy into the only viable system of government in Spain, and for that reason it's also possible to say, as if I'd wanted to insinuate that violence is history's essence, the material of which it is made, and that only an act of war can revoke another act of war – as if I'd wanted to insinuate that only a coup d'état can revoke another coup d'état, that only a coup d'état could revoke the coup d'état that on 18 July 1936 engendered the war and the prolongation of the war by other means that was Franco's regime – 23 February not only brought an end to the transition and to Franco's post-war regime: 23 February brought an end to the war.

3

Is Borges right and is it true that every destiny, however long and complicated, essentially boils down to a single moment, the moment a man knows once and for all who he is? I look again at the image of Adolfo Suárez on the evening of 23 February and, as if I hadn't seen it hundreds of times, it strikes me again as a radiant, hypnotic image, real and unreal at the same time, meticulously stuffed with meaning: the Civil Guards shooting over the chamber, General Gutiérrez Mellado standing beside him, the depopulated Parliament, the stenographers and ushers lying on the floor, the parliamentarians lying on the floor and Suárez leaning back against the blue leather of his prime ministerial bench while the bullets whizz around him, solitary, statuesque and spectral in a desert of empty benches.

It's a slippery image. If I'm not mistaken, there is in the parallel gestures of Gutiérrez Mellado and Santiago Carrillo a logic we sense straight away, with instinct rather than intelligence, as if they were two gestures necessary for those who had been programmed by history and by their two counterpoised biographies of old wartime enemies. Suárez's gesture is almost identical to theirs, but at the same time we sense that it's different and more complex, or at least I sense this, undoubtedly because I also sense that its complete significance escapes me. It's true that it's a courageous gesture and a graceful gesture and a rebellious gesture, a supreme gesture of liberty and a histrionic gesture, the gesture of a man who's finished and who conceives of politics as an adventure and is trying for deathbed legitimacy and for a moment seems fully to embody democracy, a gesture of authority and a gesture of individual and perhaps collective redemption, the final purely political gesture of a pure politician, and for that reason the most violent; all this is true, but it's also true that for some reason that inventory of definitions does not satisfy the emotions, the instinct or the intelligence, as if Suárez's gesture were an inexhaustible or inexplicable or absurd gesture, or as if it contained an infinity of gestures. A few days ago, for example, I thought Suárez's gesture wasn't really a gesture of courage, but a gesture of fear: I remembered a bullfighter who said the only thing that moved him to tears was fighting bulls, not by how well he did it, but because fear made him overcome fear, and I remembered at the same time a poet saying a bullfighter walked into the ring scared to death and that, since he was already dead, he was no longer scared of the bull and was invulnerable, and then I thought that in that moment Suárez was so still on his bench because he was moved to tears, bathed in tears inside, scared to death. The night before last I thought that Suárez's gesture was the gesture of a neurotic, the gesture of a man who crumbles in the face of good fortune and comes into his own in adversity. Last night I thought something else: I thought I had written many pages about Suárez and I still hadn't said that Suárez was anything but a nonentity, that he was a serious character, a fellow who was responsible for his words and his actions, a guy who had put together democracy or felt that he had put it together and on the evening of 23 February he understood that democracy was in his care and he did not hide and remained still on his bench while the bullets whizzed around him in the chamber like a captain who remains at the helm of his sinking ship. And a while ago, after writing Borges' sentence that opens this fragment, I thought that Suárez's gesture was a Borgesian gesture and that scene a Borgesian scene, because I remembered Alan Pauls, who in an essay on Borges claims that the duel is the DNA of Borges' short stories, their fingerprint, and I said to myself, instead of the false duel Adolfo Suárez and Santiago Carrillo once pretended to engage in, that scene was a real duel, a duel between armed men and unarmed men, a state of ecstasy, a vertiginous juncture, a hallucination, a second extirpated from the current of time, 'a suspension of the world', says Pauls, 'a block of life torn out of the context of life', a tiny dazzling hole that repels all explanations or perhaps contains them all, as if it would be enough effectively to know how to look in order to see in that eternal moment the exact code of 23 February, or as if mysteriously, in that eternal moment, not just Suárez but everyone in the country had known once and for all who they were.

I don't know: maybe I could prolong this book indefinitely and extract different meanings from Suárez's gesture indefinitely without exhausting its meaning or grazing or discerning its real meaning. I don't know. Sometimes I tell myself that this is all a mistake, one more fantasy added to the incalculable fantasies that surround 23 February, the last and most insidious: although the truly enigmatic is not what nobody's seen, but what everyone has seen and nobody has managed entirely to understand, maybe Suárez's gesture holds no secret or real meaning, or no more than any other gesture holds, all inexhaustible or inexplicable or absurd, all arrows flying off in countless directions. But other times, most of the time, I tell myself that it's not like that: the gestures of Gutiérrez Mellado and Santiago Carrillo are translucent, exhaustible, explicable, intelligible, or that's what we feel; Suárez's gesture is not: if you don't wonder what it means then you understand what it means; but if you wonder what it means then you don't understand what it means. That's why Suárez's gesture is not a translucent gesture but a transparent gesture: a meaningful gesture because in itself it doesn't mean anything, a gesture that contains nothing but through which, as through a window, we feel we could see everything – we could see Adolfo Suárez, 23 February, the recent history of Spain, perhaps a face that might be our own true face – a gesture all the more disconcerting because its deepest secret lies in its having no secret. Unless, of course, that rather than a mistake or a correct answer all this is a misunderstanding, and that examining the meaning of Suárez's gesture doesn't amount to the same thing as coming up with a correct question or a mistaken question or an unanswerable question, but just coming up with an essentially ironic question, whose true answer lies in the question itself. Unless, I mean, that the challenge I set myself in writing this book, trying to respond by way of reality to what I didn't know and didn't want to respond to by way of fiction, was an unmeetable challenge, and that the answer to that question – the only possible answer to that question – is a novel.

4

'The transition is now history,' wrote the sociologist Juan J. Linz in 1996. 'It is not today the subject of debate or political struggle.' A decade later Linz could no longer say that: for some time now the transition has not only been subject to debate, but also – sometimes implicitly and sometimes explicitly – the subject of political struggle. It occurs to me that this change is the consequence of at least two factors: the first is a generation of leftists coming to political, economic and intellectual power, my generation, who took no active part in the change from dictatorship to democracy and who consider this change to have been done badly, or that it could have been done much better than it was; the second is the renewal in the intellectual centres of an old far-left discourse that argues that the transition was the consequence of a fraud negotiated between Francoists wanting to stay in power at any cost, led by Adolfo Suárez, and supine leftists led by Santiago Carrillo, a fraud the result of which was not an authentic rupture with Francoism and which left real power in the same hands that had usurped it during the dictatorship, shaping a dull, insufficient and defective democracy.* In part as a consequence of a conscience as

---

* To those two facts a philosopher could add another, less circumstantial and maybe more profound: human beings' growing capacity for dissatisfaction, a paradoxical result of Western society's growing capacity to satisfy our needs. 'Where cultural progress is genuinely successful and ills are cured, this progress is seldom received with enthusiasm,' writes Odo Marquard. 'Instead, it is taken for granted and attention focuses on those ills that remain. And these remaining ills are subject to the law of increasing annoyance. The more negative elements disappear from reality, the more annoying the remaining negative elements become, precisely because of this decrease.'

clear and rock hard as those of the *golpistas* of 23 February, of an irre-
pressible nostalgia for the clarities of authoritarianism and sometimes a
simple ignorance of recent history, both factors run the risk of deliver-
ing the monopoly of the transition to the right – which has rushed to
accept it, glorifying the time to a ridiculous extent, that is mystifying it
– while the left, caving in to the combined blackmail of narcissistic
youth and an ultramontane left, seems at times ready to wash its hands
of it the way one washes one's hands of an awkward bequest.

I think it's a mistake. Although it didn't have the joy of an instantaneous collapse of a frightful regime, the rupture with Francoism was a
genuine rupture. To achieve it the left made many concessions, but
practising politics involves making concessions, because it involves
giving way on the incidentals in order not to give way on the essentials;
the left gave way on the incidentals, but the Francoists gave way on the
essentials, because Francoism disappeared and they had to renounce
the absolute power they'd held for almost half a century. It's true that
justice was not entirely done, that the Republican legitimacy violated
by Francoism was not restored, those responsible for the dictatorship
did not face trial, its victims were not fully and immediately compensated, but it's also true that in exchange a democracy was constructed
that would have been impossible to construct if the prime objective
hadn't been that of crafting a future but – *Fiat justitia et pereat mundus*
– making amends for the past: on 23 February 1981, when it seemed the
system of liberties was no longer at risk after four years of democratic
government, the Army attempted a coup d'état, which was on the
brink of succeeding, so it's easy to imagine how long democracy would
have lasted if four years earlier, when it had barely got started, a government had decided to bring justice to all, though the world perish. It's
also true that political and economic power did not change hands overnight – which would probably not have happened either if instead of a
negotiated rupture with Francoism there had been a direct rupture –
but it's evident that power soon began to operate under the restrictions
imposed by the new regime, which brought the left to government
after five years and long before began a profound reorganization of
economic power. Furthermore, to state that the political system that
arose out of those years is not a perfect democracy is to state the

obvious: perhaps a perfect dictatorship exists – they all aspire to it, in some way all feel they are – but there's no such thing as a perfect democracy, because what defines a true democracy is its flexible, open, malleable character – that is, permanently improvable – in such a way that the only perfect democracy is one that can be for ever perfected. Spanish democracy is not perfect, but it is real, worse than some and better than many, and anyway, incidentally, more solid and deeper than the fragile democracy General Franco overthrew by force. All this was to a great extent a triumph for anti-Francoism, a triumph for the democratic opposition, a triumph for the left, which obliged the Francoists to understand that Francoism had no future other than its total extinction. Suárez understood that immediately and acted accordingly; all this we owe him; all this and, to a great extent, also the obvious: the longest period of freedom Spain has enjoyed in its entire history. That's what the last thirty years have been. Denying it is to deny reality, the inveterate vice of a certain section of the left that continues to inconvenience democracy and certain intellectuals whose difficulty in emancipating themselves from abstraction and the absolute prevents them from connecting ideas to experience. All in all, Francoism was a bad story, but the end of that story has not been bad. It could have been: the proof is that in the middle of the 1970s the most lucid foreign analysts were predicting a catastrophic exit from the dictatorship; maybe the best proof is what happened on 23 February. It could have been, but it wasn't, and I see no reason why those of us who didn't participate in that story owing to age should not celebrate it; nor do I think that, had we been old enough to participate, we would have committed fewer errors than our parents did.

5

On 17 July 2008, the day before Adolfo Suárez last appeared in the newspapers, photographed in the garden of his house in La Florida in the company of the King – when he'd already seemed to be dead for a long time or everyone had talked about him for a long time as if he were dead – I buried my father. He was seventy-nine, three years older than Suárez, and he'd died the previous day at home, sitting in his favourite armchair, in a gentle, painless way, perhaps without understanding he was dying. Like Suárez, he was an ordinary man: he came from a rich family that had come down in the world settled since time immemorial in a village in Extremadura, he'd studied in Córdoba and in the 1960s had emigrated to Catalonia; he didn't drink, he'd been an obstinate smoker but didn't smoke any more, in his youth he'd belonged to Acción Católica and the Falange; he'd been a handsome young man, kind, conceited, a lady's man and gambler, a good *verbena* dancer, although I'd swear he was never cocky. He was, however, a good veterinary surgeon, and I suppose he could have made money, but he didn't, or no more than necessary to support his family and put three of his five children through university. He had few friends, no hobbies, didn't travel and for his last fifteen years lived on his pension. Like Suárez, he was dark-haired, thin, handsome, frugal and transparent; unlike Suárez, he tried to go unnoticed, and I think he managed it. I won't presume to declare that he was never involved in any crooked deal in those crooked times, but I can say, as far as I know, there was no one who didn't take him for a decent man.

We always got along well, except maybe, inevitably, during my adolescence. I think at that time I was a little embarrassed to be his son,

I think because I thought I was better than him, or that I was going to be. We didn't argue much, but whenever we did argue we argued about politics, which is strange, because my father wasn't terribly interested in politics, and neither was I, from which I deduce that this was our way of communicating at a time when we didn't have much to communicate to each other, or when it wasn't easy to do so. I said at the beginning of this book that my father was a *Suarista* then, as was my mother, and that I looked down on Suárez, one of Franco's collaborators, an ignorant and superficial nonentity who through luck and fiddling had managed to prosper in democracy; it's possible I thought something similar of my father, and that's why I was a little bit embarrassed to be his son. The fact is that more than one argument ended in shouts, if not with a slammed door (my father, for example, was outraged and horrified by ETA's murders; I was not in favour of ETA, at least not much, but I understood that it was all Suárez's fault, that he left ETA no choice but to kill); the fact is also that, once adolescence ended, the arguments ended too. We, however, carried on talking about politics, I suppose because having pretended to be interested we'd ended up actually interested. When Suárez retired, my father continued to be a *Suarista*, he voted for the right and occasionally for the left, and although we didn't stop disagreeing we'd discovered by then that it was better to disagree than to agree, because the conversation lasted longer. In reality, politics ended up being our main, almost our only topic of conversation; I don't remember us talking very often about his work, or my books: my father was not a reader of novels and, despite knowing he read mine and that he was proud that I was a writer and that he clipped out and saved articles about me that appeared in the newspapers, I never heard him express an opinion on any of them. In recent years he gradually lost interest in everything, including politics, but his interest in my books grew, or that was my impression, and when I began to write this one I told him what it was about (I didn't deceive him: I told him it was about Adolfo Suárez's gesture, not the 23 February coup, because from the beginning I wanted to imagine that Adolfo Suárez's gesture contained the events of 23 February as if in code); he looked at me: for a moment I thought he'd make some comment or burst out laughing or into tears, but he just frowned absently, I don't know whether sardonically. Later, in the final months of his illness, when he'd wasted away and could barely move or speak, I went on telling him about this book. I talked to him about the years of the political change, about what happened on 23 February, about events and figures we'd argued over years before till we were fed up; now he listened to me distractedly, if he really was listening, to force his attention, sometimes I asked him questions, which he didn't usually answer. But one evening I asked him why he and my mother had trusted Suárez and he suddenly seemed to wake out of his lethargy, trying in vain to lean back in his armchair he looked at me with wild eyes and moved his skeletal hands nervously, almost furiously, as if that fit of anger was going to put him for a moment back in charge of the family or send me back to adolescence, or as if we'd spent our whole lives embroiled in a meaningless argument and finally the occasion had arrived to settle it. 'Because he was like us,' he said with what little voice he had left. I was about to ask him what he meant by that when he added: 'He was from a small town, he'd been in the Falange, he'd been in Acción Católica, he wasn't going to do anything bad, you understand, don't you?'

I understood. I think this time I understood. And that's why a few months later, when his death and Adolfo Suárez's resurrection in the newspapers formed the final symmetry, the final figure of this story, I couldn't help but wonder if I'd started to write this book not to try to understand Adolfo Suárez or Adolfo Suárez's gesture but to try to understand my father, if I'd kept writing it in order to keep talking to my father, if I'd wanted to finish it so my father could read it and know that I'd finally understood, that I'd understood that I wasn't so right and he wasn't so wrong, that I'm no better than him, and that now I never will be.

Bibliography

A substantial part of the information I've used to write this book comes from interviews I've done over the last three years with witnesses and protagonists of the coup d'état and the political transition. As for written sources, it should be remembered that the Supreme Court does not allow the trial proceedings to be consulted, and will not permit it until twenty-five years have passed since the death of the defendants or fifty since the coup; in spite of this, many jurists who took part in the trial have copies of witness statements and those of the defendants, and important fragments of that document have been published in various books, among them those by Juan Blanco, *23-F. Crónica fiel de un golpe anunciado*, Madrid, Fuerza Nueva, 1995, Julio Merino, *Tejero. 25 años después*, Madrid, Espejo de Tinta, 2006, Juan Alberto Perote, *23-F. Ni Milans ni Tejero. El informe que se ocultó*, Madrid, Foca, 2001, Manuel Rubio, *23-F. El proceso: del sumario a la sentencia*, Barcelona, Libros Ceres, 1982, and Santiago Segura and Julio Merino, *Jaque al Rey*, Barcelona, Planeta, 1983. Furthermore, the court's sentence is reproduced in books such as José Luis Martín Prieto's *Técnica de un golpe de estado*, Barcelona, Planeta, 1982, pp. 335–385, José Oneto's *La verdad sobre el caso Tejero*, Barcelona, Planeta, 1982, pp. 381–406, and Manuel Rubio's *23-F. El proceso*, pp. 631–704.

Below I list the titles of a few of the texts that have been especially useful to the writing of mine, dividing them according to the fundamental themes of the book, and after this minimal bibliography I've added a few notes meant only to specify the sources of quotes and, occasionally, to make some clarification about particularly doubtful or controversial aspects.

GENERAL WORKS

Agüero, Felipe, *Militares, civiles y democracia*, Madrid, Alianza, 1995.

Alonso-Castrillo, Silvia, *La apuesta del centro: historia de la UCD*, Madrid, Alianza, 1996.

Attard, Emilio, *Vida y muerte de UCD*, Barcelona, Planeta, 1983.

Calvo Sotelo, Leopoldo, *Memoria viva de la transición*, Barcelona, Plaza y Janés, 1990.

Colomer, Josep Maria, *La transición a la democracia: el modelo español*, Barcelona, Anagrama, 1998.

Fernández Miranda, Pilar and Alfonso, *Lo que el Rey me ha pedido. Torcuato Fernández Miranda y la reforma política*, Barcelona, Plaza y Janés, 1995.

Fraga, Manuel, *En busca del tiempo servido*, Barcelona, Planeta, 1981.

Herrero y Rodríguez de Miñón, Miguel, *Memorias de estío*, Madrid, Temas de Hoy, 1993.

— , ed., *La transición democrática en España*, Bilbao, Fundación BBVA-Fundaçao Mario Soares, 1999.

Guerra, Alfonso, *Cuando el tiempo nos alcanza. Memorias*, Madrid, Espasa Calpe, 2004.

Santos, Juliá, Pradera, Javier, and Prieto, Joaquín, eds., *Memoria de la transición*, Madrid, Taurus, 1996.

— , *Los socialistas en la política española, 1879–1982*, Madrid, Taurus, 1987.

Linz, Juan J., and Stepan, Alfred, *Problems of Democratic Transition and Consolidation. Southern Europe, South America, and Post-Communist Europe*, Baltimore, Johns Hopkins University Press, 1996.

Osorio, Alfonso, *Trayectoria de un ministro de la Corona*, Barcelona, Planeta, 1980.

Prego, Victoria, *Así se hizo la transición*, Barcelona, Plaza y Janés, 1995.

— , *Diccionario de la transición*, Barcelona, Debolsillo, 2003.

Sánchez Navarro, Ángel J., *La transición española en sus documentos*, Madrid, Centro de Estudios Políticos y Constitucionales, 1988.

Sartorius, Nicolás, and Sabio, Alberto, *El final de la dictadura. La conquista de la democracia en España (noviembre de 1975–junio de 1977)*, Madrid, Temas de Hoy, 2007.

Serra, Narcís, *La transición militar*, Barcelona, Debate, 2008.

Sinova, Justino, ed., *Historia de la transición*, 2 vols., Madrid, Diario 16, 1984.

Tusell, Javier, and Soto, Álvaro, *Historia de la transición, 1975–1986*, Madrid, Alianza, 1996.

— , *La transición a la democracia (España, 1975–1982)*, Madrid, Espasa Calpe, 2007.

VV.AA., *Tiempo de transición*, Madrid, Fundación Pablo Iglesias, 2007.

WORKS ON 23 FEBRUARY

Aguilar, Miguel Ángel, Busquets, Julio, and Puche, Ignacio, *El golpe. Anatomía y claves del asalto al Congreso*, Barcelona, Ariel, 1981.

Armada, Alfonso, *Al servicio de la Corona*, Barcelona, Planeta, 1983.

Blanco, Juan, *23-F. Crónica fiel de un golpe anunciado*, Madrid, Fuerza Nueva, 1995.

Calderón, Javier, and Ruiz Platero, Florentino, *Algo más que el 23-F*, Madrid, La Esfera de los Libros, 2004.

Cernuda, Pilar, Jáuregui, Fernando, and Menéndez, Miguel Ángel, *23-F. La conjura de los necios*, Madrid, Foca, 2001.

Colectivo Democracia, *Los ejércitos más allá del golpe*, Barcelona, Planeta, 1981.

Cuenca Toribio, José Manuel, *Conversaciones con Alfonso Armada*, Madrid, Actas, 2001.

Fernández López, Javier, *El Rey y otros militares. Los militares en el cambio de régimen político en España (1969–1982)*, Madrid, Trotta, 1998.

— , *Diecisiete horas y media. El enigma del 23-F*, Madrid, Taurus, 2000.

Fuentes Gómez de Salazar, Eduardo, *El pacto del capó*, Madrid, Temas de Hoy, 1994.

García Escudero, José María, *Mis siete vidas. De las brigadas anarquistas a juez del 23-F*, Barcelona, Planeta, 2005.

Martín Prieto, José Luis, *Técnica de un golpe de estado*, Barcelona, Planeta, 1982.

Palacios, Jesús, *23-F: El golpe del CESID*, Barcelona, Planeta, 2001.

Pardo Zancada, Ricardo, *23 F. La pieza que falta*, Barcelona, Plaza y Janés, 1998.

Prieto, Joaquín, and Barbería, José Luis, *El enigma del Elefante. La conspiración del 23-F*, Madrid, Aguilar, 1991.

Urbano, Pilar, *Con la venia . . . yo indagué el 23-F*, Madrid, Argos Vergara, 1982.

ON ADOLFO SUÁREZ

Abella, Carlos, *Adolfo Suárez*, Madrid, Espasa Calpe, 1997.

García Abad, José, *Adolfo Suárez. Una tragedia griega*, Madrid, La Esfera de los Libros, 2005.

Herrero, Luis, *Los que le llamábamos Adolfo*, Madrid, La Esfera de los Libros, 2007.

Melià, Josep, *Así cayó Adolfo Suárez*, Barcelona, Planeta, 1981.

— , *La trama de los escribanos del agua*, Barcelona, Planeta, 1983.

Morán, Gregorio, *Adolfo Suárez. Historia de una ambición*, Barcelona, Planeta, 1979.
Powell, Charles, and Bonnin, Pere, *Adolfo Suárez*, Barcelona, Ediciones B, 2004.
Suárez, Adolfo, *Fue posible la concordia*, ed. Abel Hernández, Madrid, Espasa Calpe, 1996.

ON MANUEL GUTIÉRREZ MELLADO

Gutiérrez Mellado, Manuel, *Un soldado de España, conversaciones con Jesús Picatoste*, Barcelona, Argos Vergara, 1983.
Puell de la Villa, Fernando, *Manuel Gutiérrez Mellado. Un militar del siglo XX (1912–1995)*, Madrid, Biblioteca Nueva, 1997.

ON SANTIAGO CARRILLO

Carrillo, Santiago, *El año de la peluca*, Barcelona, Ediciones B, 1987.
— , *Memorias*, Barcelona, Planeta, 1993.
Claudín, Fernando, *Santiago Carrillo. Crónica de un secretario general*, Barcelona, Planeta, 1983.
Morán, Gregorio, *Miseria y grandeza del partido comunista de España. 1939–1985*, Barcelona, Planeta, 1986.

ON THE KING

Powell, Charles T., *El piloto del cambio. El Rey, la monarquía y la transición a la democracia*, Barcelona, Planeta, 1991.
Preston, Paul, *Juan Carlos: A People's King*, London, HarperCollins, 2004.
Vilallonga, José Luis de, *El Rey*, Barcelona, Plaza y Janés, 1993.

ON THE INTELLIGENCE SERVICES

Cernuda, Pilar, Bardavío, Joaquín, and Jáuregui, Fernando, *Servicios secretos*, Barcelona, Plaza y Janés, 2000.
Díaz Fernández, Antonio M., *Los servicios de inteligencia españoles: desde la guerra civil hasta el 11-M. Historia de una transición*, Madrid, Alianza, 2005.
Perote, Juan Alberto, *23-F. Ni Milans ni Tejero. El informe que se ocultó*, Madrid, Foca, 2001.

NOTES

PROLOGUE. EPILOGUE TO A NOVEL

p. 5. The poll is mentioned in Umberto Eco's article, 'Érase una vez Churchill', *El Mundo*, 20.3.2008. See also articles on the same poll in the *Mirror* 04.02.2008 and the *Telegraph* 03.02.2008.

p. 8. The article is called 'La tragedia y el tiempo', *La Repubblica*, 23.2.2006, later published in *La verdad de Agamenón*, Barcelona, Tusquets, 2006, pp. 39–42.

p. 9. The Cortes declaration can be found in Amadeo Martínez Inglés, *Juan Carlos I, el último Borbón*, Barcelona, Styria, 2007, p. 264.

p. 10. Jorge Luis Borges, tr. Norman Thomas di Giovanni, 'The Life of Tadeo Isidoro Cruz', in *The Aleph & Other Stories*, New York, Dutton, 1970.

p. 11. Julián Marías, *Una vida presente*, Madrid, Páginas de Espuma, 2008, p. 740.

[p.13. Translator's note: English is intriguingly short of home-grown words for the act of over-throwing governments and the people who do such things. We generally rely on the French coup d'état and occasionally turn to the Swiss-German putsch, or putschist. Since this particular *golpe de estado* came very close to happening in Spain, I have chosen to stick to the Spanish word *golpista* for the soldiers and politicians discussed in this book.]

PART ONE. THE PLACENTA OF THE COUP

p. 26. Hans Magnus Enzensberger, 'Los héroes de la retirada', *El País*, 25.12.1989. Also published as 'Europe in Ruins', translated by Piers Spence, in *Granta* 33, 1990, pp. 136–142.

p. 27. Leopoldo Calvo Sotelo, *Memoria viva de la transición*, p. 52.

pp. 28–29. ' "The only way they're going to get me out of here is by beating me in an election . . ." ' One of the visitors to Moncloa to whom Suárez made a statement of this sort was Fernando Álvarez de Miranda, *Del 'contubernio' al consenso*, Barcelona, Planeta, 1985, p. 145. Alfonso Guerra's quote comes from *Cuando el tiempo nos alcanza*, p. 297; Hemingway's is from an interview with Dorothy Parker, 'The Artist's Reward', *New Yorker*, 30 November 1929, p. 20; the Camus quote is from *The Rebel*, tr. Anthony Bower, London, Penguin, 2006; Meliá's, from *La trama de los escribanos del agua*, pp. 55–56. Meliá's conjecture – that Suárez's first thought on hearing the Civil Guards' gunshots was the next day's front pages – is endorsed by various statements from Suárez himself: see Luis Herrero, *Los que le* *llamábamos Adolfo*, pp. 224–225, or Jorge Trías Sagnier, 'La cacería de Suárez y el 23 de febrero', *ABC*, 23.2.2009, who quotes an unpublished projected memoir that Suárez drafted and which is in the personal archive of Eduardo Navarro, one of the former Prime Minister's most loyal and closest collaborators.

p. 29. Suárez is quoted in Leopoldo Calvo Sotelo, *Memoria viva de la transición*, p. 26.

p. 30. '"**Because I was still Prime Minister of His Majesty's government . . ."**' See for example the audio-visual report by Victoria Prego ('Asalto a la democracia', in *El camino de la libertad*, Barcelona, Planeta/De Agostini, 2008), where he says: 'I was the Prime Minister of the government and I did not feel like throwing myself to the floor, simply because I am the Prime Minister. And the Prime Minister should not do that. I understand those who did perfectly; probably if I hadn't been Prime Minister I would have done the same. But I'm the Prime Minister of the government.'

p. 32. '**For this reason we don't need to pay too much attention to the politicians . . .**' Pablo Castellano, PSOE deputy, writes for example: 'When Tejero burst into the chamber I had the feeling that very few of us were surprised. Those who, from one party or another, were not in the know'; *Yo sí me acuerdo. Apuntes e historias*, Madrid, Temas de Hoy, 1994, p. 344. Ricardo Paseyro is quoted in Juan Blanco, *23-F. Crónica fiel . . .*, p. 131.

pp. 34–35. See Sol Alameda's interview with Suárez in Santos Juliá et al, eds., *Memoria de la transición*, p. 454. 'Everything is tied up and well tied.' The first Franco quote can be found in *Discursos y mensajes del jefe del estado. 1968–1970*, Madrid, Publicaciones Españolas, 1971, p. 108; the second, in *Discursos y mensajes del jefe del estado, 1960–1963*, Madrid, Publicaciones Españolas, 1964, p. 397. As for Jesús Fueyo's phrase, see *Pueblo*, 24.11.1966, quoted by Juan Pablo Fusi, *España, de la dictadura a la democracia*, Barcelona, Planeta, 1979, p. 236. Franco's will can be read in Stanley G. Payne, *The Franco Regime 1939–1975*, Madison, University of Wisconsin Press, 1987, p. 620.

p. 35. The first time Tarradellas speaks of the necessity for a touch on the rudder is 14 June 1979; see Juan Blanco, *23-F. Crónica fiel . . .*, p. 49; the quote comes from *El Alcázar*, 4.7.1980; but on the first Sunday in May of that year the former Catalan premier had already declared to *El País*: 'If there is not a firm and swift touch on the rudder, a scalpel will have to be used.' Quoted by Santiago Segura and Julio Merino, *Las vísperas del 23-F*, Barcelona, Plaza y Janés, 1984, p. 286. **Footnote.** I took the first two statistics from Mariano Torcal Loriente, 'El origen y la evolución del apoyo a la democracia en España', *Revista española de ciencias políticas*, no. 18, April, 2008, p. 50, and the third from Joaquín Prieto, *El País*, 28.10.2007.

pp. 37–38. Joaquín Aguirre Bellver, 'Al galope', *El Alcázar*, 2.12.1980, reprinted in *El ejército calla*, Madrid, Ediciones Santafé, 1981, pp. 129–130. On the various political operations mentioned, see for example Xavier Domingo, 'Areilza aspira a la Moncloa', *Cambio 16*, no. 456, 31.8.1980, pp. 19–21; Miguel Ángel Aguilar, 'Sectores financieros, militares y eclesiásticos proponen un "Gobierno de gestión" con Osorio', *El País*, 27.11.1980; José Oneto, 'La otra Operación', *Cambio 16*, no. 470, 1.12.1980, p. 21.

p. 38. Pilar Urbano, *ABC*, 3.12.1980.

pp. 40–41. Fernando Latorre, under the pseudonym Merlín, in his usual section 'Las Brujas', *Heraldo Español*, 7.8.1980. Fernando de Santiago, 'Situación límite', *El Alcázar*, 8.2.1981. Antonio Izquierdo, under the pseudonym Telémetro, 'La guerra de las galaxias', *El Alcázar*, 24.1.1981. The three artícles by Almendros, all published in *El Alcázar*, were: 'Análisis político del momento militar', 17.12.1980; 'La hora de las otras instituciones', 22.1.1981; and 'La decisión del mando supremo', 1.2.1981. **Footnote to p. 41.** See Manuel Fraga, *En busca del tiempo servido*, p. 232. Information on the police informant's report can be found in Prieto and Barbería, *El enigma del Elefante*, p. 233. The article from *Spic* is reproduced by Pilar Urbano, in *Con la venia . . .*, p. 363.

p. 43. Emilio Romero, 'Las tertulias de Madrid', *ABC*, 31.1.81.

pp. 43–45. Francisco Medina, *23-F, la verdad*, Barcelona, Plaza y Janés, 2006, pp. 89–117. Armada, *Al servicio de la Corona*, p. 92. The suspicions of connivence between Anson and Armada actually began to circulate immediately after the coup; see José Luis Gutiérrez, 'Armada & Ansón', *Diario 16*, 2.3.1981. As for Armada's government, see **footnote to p. 286**. On the relationship between Suárez and Anson, see Gregorio Morán, *Adolfo Suárez*, pp. 40–42, 189, 297–298 and 305–306, and Luis María Anson, *Don Juan*, Barcelona, Plaza y Janés, 1994, p. 403.

p. 49. '**. . . his diaries of the time abound in notes about dinners . . .**' See Manuel Fraga, *En busca del tiempo servido*, pp. 225–226 (22 November: 'I've received reliable information that General Armada would be prepared to lead a government of national unity') or 231 (3 February: 'Political lunch during which the importance of Armada's promotion [to Deputy Chief of the Army General Staff] was emphasized; several pushing him as "the solution"'). Juan de Arespacochaga, *Carta a unos capitanes*, Madrid, CYAN, 1994, pp. 274–275. Fraga is quoted in Juan Blanco, *23-F. Crónica fiel . . .*, p. 135.

p. 52. '**. . . it's very likely that the nuncio and some bishops were informed . . .**' Juan de Arespacochaga claims that they were in *Carta a unos capitanes*, p. 274. See also, for example, Cernuda, Jáuregui and Menéndez, *23-F. La conjura de los necios*, p. 191; or Palacios, *El golpe del CESID*, p. 385.

pp. 55–57. Armada's version of his interview with Múgica is in *Al servicio de la Corona*, p. 224; Múgica's version is in *El Socialista*, 11–17 March 1981, and in *El País*, 13.3.1981. Armada states that he notified his Captain General, who in turn informed the Zarzuela, and the Palace told Suárez: see Prieto and Barbería, *El enigma del Elefante*, p. 92. Some time later Múgica told Leopoldo Calvo Sotelo that at the meeting in Lérida Armada explained his idea of a government of unity and that, when the general wondered who might lead it, Raventós interrupted: 'Who's going to lead it? You are.' Calvo Sotelo interviewed by Rosa Montero, in Santos Juliá et al, eds., *Memoria de la transición*, p. 522. As for the Socialists' contacts with the leaders of the minority parties – specifically the PNV and Convergència i Unió – see Prieto and Barbería, *El enigma del Elefante*, pp. 93–96, or Antxon Sarasqueta, *De Franco a Felipe*, Barcelona, Plaza y Janés, 1984, p. 137. The interview between Jordi Pujol and a member of PSOE is reported by Andreu Farràs and Pere Cullell in *El 23-F a Catalunya*, Barcelona, Planeta, 1998, pp. 53–54. On the rumours of another no-confidence motion by the PSOE and its plans to enter an interim government, see section 10 of this same chapter and **p. 56.** '**. . . because at that time the leaders of the PSOE often discussed the role the Army . . .**' One example: on 9 January Múgica gave a speech at the Club Siglo XXI in the presence of leading right and centrist politicians involved in different operations against the Prime Minister – Alfonso Osorio and Miguel Herrero de Miñón among others; according to Miguel Ángel Aguilar's write-up for *El País*, the Socialist leader 'described the conditions that would have to exist for legitimately constituted power to find itself obliged to call on its armies to maintain individual rights and the security of the state'; he also 'made a constitutional excursion to article 116, which deals with the proclamation of the state of siege and the guarantees that should apply'.

p. 60. Alfonso Guerra cited in Abella, *Adolfo Suárez*, p. 421.

p. 61. '**. . . it perhaps hastens the departure from the government of Deputy Prime Minister Abril Martorell . . .**' Relations between Suárez and Abril, however, had already deteriorated seriously by that point, and it's likely that Suárez would soon have replaced his Deputy Prime Minister in any case; see Abella, *Adolfo Suárez*, pp. 432–434; Luis Herrero, *Los que le llamábamos Adolfo*, p. 196; and Julia Navarro, *Nosotros, la transición*, Madrid, Temas de Hoy, 1995, p. 17. Miguel Herrero de Miñón's article is called 'Sí, pero . . .', *El País*, 18.9.1980, reprinted in *Memorias de estío*, pp. 211–213.

p. 63. '. . . in the middle of January the rumours that have been circulating with variable intensity since the summer proliferate . . .' See for example articles by Fernando Reinlein and Abel Hernández, in *Diario 16* and *Ya* respectively, published on 24 January. Reinlein writes: 'The far-right offensive against the democratic institutions can back up a soft alternative regression [. . .] A few days ago in political circles *Diario 16* was told that two involutional alternatives were being assessed, one "soft" and the other "hard" [. . .] According to these sources, the second hypothesis being ruled out as not very viable and unnecessary, the first may still be alive in the minds of many.' Hernández is undoubtedly alluding to this latter alternative when he states that, 'according to reliable sources', the hypothesis of a government of national unity or salvation or 'authority' with a soldier in charge is being strongly considered ('and, according to these sources, they have one already prepared'), a government formed basically of centrists and Socialists; according to Hernández, 'it seems beyond doubt that senior military officers have held and are holding conversations with prominent Socialist leaders, as well as those from the centre and other parties' with a view to a manoeuvre that, as the journalist describes it, seems to resemble the soft coup: 'All the sources consulted insist they're not talking about an actual military coup, but a very well-planned attempt to bring order to the situation precisely to avoid a military coup. According to prominent politicians who are involved in the conversations, the "operation" is inevitable and is practically finalized' (Five days after this article Hernández reports again on the pressures to form a government of salvation in 'La tregua', *Ya*, 29.1.1981). That Suárez knew that General Armada was at the forefront of this operation is confirmed by, for example, Fernando Álvarez de Miranda – one of the Christian Democrat leaders in the UCD most critical of the Prime Minister – who held a long conversation with him around that time: 'I told him again, finally, that, in my opinion, the situation was very bad, that the warning lights had been flashing for democracy for a while now and that, not having an absolute majority in Parliament, he should seek a coalition with the opposition party. He looked at me sadly, saying: "Yes, I know full well they all want my head and that's the message even from the Socialists: a coalition government, led by a soldier – General Armada. I won't bow to such pressure even if it means me leaving Moncloa in a coffin" '; *Del 'contubernio' al consenso*, p. 145. (Also in Paul Preston, *Juan Carlos: A People's King*, p. 451.) As for the rumours of a no-confidence vote, years after his resignation Suárez said to Luis Herrero – a personal friend of his and son of his political mentor Fernando Herrero Tejedor – 'I discovered there was a conspiracy at the heart of the parliamentary group to make me lose a no-confidence vote, the second in a few months, which the PSOE was about to table. Several UCD deputies had already stamped their signatures on it and the papers were kept in a safe'; *Los que le llamábamos Adolfo*, p. 213. Furthermore, Miguel Herrero de Miñón admits that they initiated procedures to table the no-confidence motion. See Prieto and Barbería, *El enigma del Elefante*, p. 116.

p. 65–66. In *23-F. La conjura de los necios*, pp. 190–191, Cernuda, Jáuregui and Menéndez give details of the meeting between Armada and Todman, according to them held at an estate belonging to Dr Ramón Castroviejo. There is reliable information about Todman and the American government and his relation to the coup in Calderón and Ruiz Platero, *Algo más que el 23-F*, pp. 203–209.

p. 67. 'Even some Communist leaders [. . .] Even the leaders of the main trade unions . . .' On the first – specifically, on Ramón Tamames – see Santiago Carrillo, *Memorias*, p. 710; on the second – specifically, on Marcelino Camacho and Nicolás Redondo – see Santiago Segura and Julio Merino, *Las vísperas del 23-F*, pp. 266–267.

p. 70. 'Panorama of Operations Under Way' can be found in Prieto and Barbería, *El enigma del Elefante*, pp. 280–293; in Cernuda, Jáuregui and Menéndez, *23-F. La conjura de los necios*, pp. 295–308; or in Pardo Zancada, *23-F. La pieza que falta*, pp. 403–417.

pp. 77–78. 'Many who have investigated 23 February . . .' See for example Fernández López, *Diecisiete horas y media*, pp. 214–218, and Prieto and Barbería, *El enigma del Elefante*, pp. 223–232. **Footnote to p. 78.** See Cernuda, Jáuregui and Menéndez, *23-F. La conjura de los necios*, pp. 116–119.

p. 79. '. . . The two notes from CESID . . .' can be found in Juan Blanco, *23-F. Crónica fiel* . . ., pp. 527 and 529; the edict published by Milans del Bosch in Urbano, *Con la venia . . .*, pp. 360–364, or Pardo Zancada, *23-F. La pieza que falta*, pp. 416–417.

p. 82. General Juste's quote can be found in Pardo Zancada, *23-F. La pieza que falta*, p. 81, whose description of events at the Brunete Armoured Division I essentially follow.

PART TWO. A *GOLPISTA* CONFRONTS THE COUP

pp. 95–96. Gutiérrez Mellado's opinion on Franco's coup d'état can be found in *Al servicio de la Corona. Palabras de un militar*, Madrid, Ibérica Europea de Ediciones, 1981, p. 254.

p. 97. 'A historiographical cliché . . .' On the question of the so-called 'pact of forgetting', exhaustively discussed in recent years, see two indispensable articles by Santos Juliá: 'Echar al olvido. Memoria y amnistía en la transición', *Claves de Razón Práctica*, no. 129, January–February 2003, pp. 14–24; and 'El Francoismo: historia y memoria', *Claves de Razón Práctica*, no. 159, January–February 2005, pp. 4–13. Max Weber, 'Politics as a vocation', *Essays in Sociology*, Ed. H.H. Gerth & C. Wright Mills, Oxford, Routledge, 1991, p. 118.

p. 101. 'One is either in politics and leaves the military . . .' Gutiérrez Mellado expressed the same idea in various ways. See Puell de la Villa, *Manuel Gutiérrez Mellado*, p. 160.

p. 103. Carlos Iniesta Cano, 'Una lección de honradez', *El Alcázar*, 27.9.1976.

p. 105. '. . . as long as it had its current statutes . . .' We don't know what Suárez's exact wording was, but this is, more or less, what he attributed to himself in the interview with Sol Alameda: see Santos Juliá et al, eds., *Memoria de la transición*, p. 452 ('My answer was that with the current statutes of the PCE its legalization was impossible'); or also his statements to Nativel Preciado, quoted by Nicolás Sartorius and Alberto Sabio, *El final de la dictadura*, p. 743. In Alameda's interview Suárez states that he did not speak of legalization of the PCE on his own initiative, as has been claimed on many occasions (see for example what his Deputy Prime Minister of the time, Alfonso Osorio, says in Victoria Prego, *Así se hizo la transición*, pp. 536–537), but rather in reply to the officers' questions. One credible version of what might have happened at that decisive meeting is in Fernández López, *Diecisiete horas y media*, pp. 17–20, which is where General Prada Canillas' quote comes from. The quote from Suárez's speech in the Francoist Cortes is from Prego, *Así se hizo la transición*, p. 477.

p. 106. 'Some military men and democratic politicians have frequently reproached Suárez for this way of proceeding . . .' Among them, for example, Alfonso Osorio (*Trayectoria de un ministro de la Corona*, p. 277), or Sabino Fernández Campo (Javier Fernández López, *Sabino Fernández Campo. Un hombre de estado*, Barcelona, Planeta, 2000, pp. 98–103). As for the time it took Suárez to decide to legalize the Communist Party, in December 1976 the Prime Minister assured Ramon Trias Fargas, a Catalan nationalist, leader of the then still illegal Esquerra Democràtica de Catalunya, that 'he couldn't put the democratization in danger for a detail like negotiating with a Communist' (Jordi Amat, *El laberint de la llibertat Vida de Ramon Trias Fargas*, Barcelona, La Magrana, 2009, p. 317); in January 1977, when a commission of parties of the democratic opposition met with Suárez to tackle the legalization of the political parties, the Prime Minister refused to discuss that of the PCE

(Sartorius and Sabio, *El final de la dictadura*, p. 765); and still in the middle of February, according to Salvador Sánchez-Terán – at that time the civil governor of Barcelona and a few months later adviser to the Prime Minister – 'the unofficial thesis [. . .] was that the legalization of the PCE could not be dealt with by the Suárez government and should be reserved for the first democratic Cortes; which implied that the PCE could not stand as such at the general elections'; see Sánchez-Terán, *Memorias. De Franco a la Generalitat*, Barcelona, Planeta, 1988, p. 248.

pp. 111–112. '**The scene [. . .] could have happened like this . . .**' See for example the account by Pardo Zancada (*23-F. La pieza que falta*, pp. 71–73), who attended General Ortín's funeral.

p. 114. Gutiérrez Mellado is quoted in Puell de la Villa, *Manuel Gutiérrez Mellado*, p. 202; or see the audio-visual report by Victoria Prego, 'Asalto a la democracia', in *El camino de la libertad*, Barcelona, Planeta/De Agostini, 2008.

pp. 117–118. Gutiérrez Mellado's quote is in José Oneto, *Los últimos días de un presidente. De la dimisión al golpe de estado*, Barcelona, Planeta, 1981, p. 152. Josep Melià tells the story in a rather different way in *Así cayó Adolfo Suárez*, p. 111. The anecdote about Suárez and Gutiérrez Mellado was recalled by the former on various radio and television programmes. See the Radio Nacional de España document, *Manuel Gutiérrez Mellado. La cara militar de la Transición*, June 2006, quoted by Manuel de Ramón, *Los generales que salvaron la democracia*, Madrid, Espejo de Tinta, 2007, p. 62.

p. 122. '**His physical health was not bad . . .**' After Suárez's resignation there was much speculation about his health problems, to which some attributed part of the responsibility for it, or at least for his paralysis during the autumn and winter of 1980. The speculation lacked any foundation: Suárez did not have health problems at that time, although he did during the previous autumn, when he suffered excruciating headaches for two months and had to be treated by doctors for several hours a day, until they discovered that he did not have a brain tumour but rather a simple dental problem. Suárez himself tells this in his interview with Sol Alameda; Santos Juliá et al, eds., *Memoria de la transición*, p. 459. See also 'La buena salud del presidente Suárez', in Justino Sinova, ed., *Historia de la transición*, vol. II, pp. 648–649.

p. 125. Josefina Martínez, *ABC*, 27.9.2007.

p. 130. The King is quoted in the extract of *El Príncipe y el Rey*, by José García Abad, published in *El Siglo*, no. 781, 31 March 2008.

p. 131. The text of the King's speech is in Juan Carlos I, *Discursos. 1975–1995*, Madrid, Departamento de Publicaciones del Congreso de los Diputados y el Senado, 1996, pp. 280–281.

p. 132. '**. . . according to some sources . . .**' See Charles Powell, *Juan Carlos, un rey para la democracia*, Barcelona, Ariel/Planeta, Barcelona, 1995, pp. 278–279. A sentence from a UCD leader could endorse this version of what happened between the King and Suárez on 4 January at La Pleta: 'It seems that anyone who could hear heard on Sunday the 25th [of January] a royal commentary: "Arias was a gentleman: when I hinted that his resignation might be needed, he handed it to me"'; Emilio Attard, *Vida y muerte de UCD*, p. 189.

p. 134. The text of Suárez's resignation speech is in Adolfo Suárez, *Fue posible la concordia*, pp. 262–266; on the way it was written, see Josep Melià – who was in charge of preparing the first draft – *Así cayó Adolfo Suárez*, pp. 94–96; and also Fernández López, *Sabino Fernández Campo*, p. 136.

p. 135, footnote. Suárez explains the reasons for his support for González at the PSOE's 28th Party congress in the interview with Sol Alameda; see Santos Juliá et al, eds., *Memoria de la transición*, p. 460. See also, in the same book, the essay by Juliá, *Los socialistas en la política española, 1879–1982*, p. 535.

p. 136. '. . . as he himself had said to a journalist . . .' See Victoria Prego, *Adolfo Suárez. La apuesta del Rey (1976–1981)*, Madrid, Unidad Editorial, 2002, p. 28.

p. 143. '. . . CESID as an agency contributed to the failure of the coup d'état . . .' In reality, the unfounded rumour that Javier Calderón organized the coup as the head of CESID did not start in 1981 but fifteen years later. The story is interesting. In 1996, after more than a decade away from the agency, Calderón returned to CESID as its director general and, as the result of a restructuring he imposed, several dozen people were dismissed. Among them was Diego Camacho López-Escobar. Camacho decided that his expulsion was not due to his professional incompetence, his unstable personality or the shared opinion of the majority of his commanding officers in CESID that he should not continue with the agency, but rather to a punishment by Calderón for his attitude following 23 February, when, as a captain in AOME under the orders of Cortina, he denounced his immediate superior to Calderón for his alleged participation in the coup: expelling him from CESID fifteen years later, Calderón would be getting revenge for the problems that the accusations against his subordinate caused him after the coup, implicating members of the service in it. It is not easy to believe Camacho's version: I've already said that because of the coup Calderón expelled Cortina from CESID – as with all the others suspected of having acted in favour of the rebels – but not Camacho or any of the other agents who informed on the *golpista* actions inside the agency, who carried on working there over the following years (one of them was also dismissed with Camacho in 1996, but at least one other was not); on the other hand, after the coup Camacho and Calderón maintained a strong friendship over the course of fourteen years that had begun before the coup, when Calderón introduced Camacho as an officer to be trusted first into CESID and later AOME; furthermore (or especially), although after the coup Camacho denounced Cortina, not then or any other time over the intervening fourteen years did he denounce Calderón: he never said Calderón had participated in the coup, much less that he'd organized it. Be that as it may, after his dismissal from the intelligence service Camacho was disciplined and arrested for making statements to the press contrary to his oath, and from that moment on his military career was cut short. That was when he began to claim that Calderón and CESID had designed and executed the 23 February coup, an accusation that a little while later inspired the book by Jesús Palacios, *23-F: El golpe del CESID*.

p. 146. '. . . Sabino Fernández Campo, in theory the third authority in the Royal Household . . .' The first authority was General Nicolás Cotoner y Cotoner, Marquis of Mondéjar; the second, commander of the Military Chamber, General Joaquín de Valenzuela. The operation of the Household and the powers of each of the authorities that run it are explained in detail in Javier Cremades, *La casa de S.M. el Rey*, Madrid, Civitas, 1998, pp. 61–105.

p. 148. '. . . Quintana Lacaci is an unwavering Francoist . . .' A few days after the failure of the 23 February coup General Quintana Lacaci told the new Minister of Defence, Alberto Oliart, at the first meeting they held: 'Minister, before I sit down I must tell you that I am a Francoist, that I adore the memory of General Franco. For eight years I served as a colonel in his personal guard. I wear this military medal that I won in Russia. I fought in the Civil War. So you can well imagine my way of thinking. But the Caudillo gave me the order to obey his successor and the King ordered me to stop the coup on 23 February. If he had ordered me to assault the Cortes, I would have done so.' See Paul Preston, *Juan Carlos. A People's King*, p. 485.

PART THREE. A REVOLUTIONARY CONFRONTS THE COUP

p. 164. '. . . he was Secretary General of the Communist Party . . .' See Santiago Carrillo, *Memorias*, p. 712.

p. 165. Max Weber, 'Politics as a vocation', *Essays in Sociology*, p. 160.

pp. 169–170. Fernando Claudín, *Santiago Carrillo*, p. 303.

p. 172. Suárez is quoted in Sánchez Navarro, *La transición española en sus documentos*, p. 288; Carrillo, in 'Tras la inevitable caída . . .', *Mundo Obrero*, 7.7.1976.

p. 177. 'According to his then closest collaborators . . .' See for example Alfonso Osorio, *Trayectoria de un ministro de la Corona*, p. 277, or Rodolfo Martín Villa, *Al servicio del Estado*, Barcelona, Planeta, 1984, p. 62. Perhaps it is Salvador Sánchez-Terán who best sums up the opinion of Suárez's circle on the behaviour of the Communists in reaction to the Atocha murders: 'The PCE won in a few hours – and by the blood of their men – more democratic respectability than in all their demands for restoration of liberties carried out during the entire transition'; *La Transición. Síntesis y claves*, Barcelona, Planeta, 2008, pp. 157–158.

pp. 177–178. The most extensive version I know of the meeting between Suárez and Carrillo – a version the protagonists themselves have approved – is found in Joaquín Bardavío, *Sábado Santo rojo*, Madrid, Ediciones Uve, 1980, pp. 155–171. Carrillo has also described it at length in *Juez y parte. 15 retratos españoles*, Barcelona, Plaza y Janés, 1995, pp. 218–223. Otherwise, shortly after the conversation took place Carrillo told Manuel Azcárate that in the course of it Suárez had told him: 'In this country there are two politicians: you and me'; Manuel Azcárate, *Crisis del eurocomunismo*, Barcelona, Argos-Vergara, 1982, p. 247. As for the change in public opinion in favour of the legalization of the PCE, it was in fact spectacularly fast; see the opinion polls in Tusell, *La transición a la democracia*, p. 116.

p. 179. Carrillo's first quote is in Prego, *Así se hizo la transición*, p. 656; the second, in Morán, *Miseria y grandeza del partido comunista de España. 1939–1985*, p. 542, which is for the most part where I got the description of what happened in the meeting on Calle Capitán Haya: it is Morán himself who claims that the paper read by Carrillo was written by Suárez. But see also Prego, *Así se hizo la transición*, pp. 663–667.

p. 181. *Le Monde*, 22.10.1977. Quoted by Fernando Claudín, *Santiago Carrillo*, p. 279.

p. 182. *Time*, 21.11.1977.

p. 186. Carrillo is quoted in Carlos Abella, *Adolfo Suárez*, p. 455.

p. 187. Carrillo, *Memorias*, p. 712.

p. 187, footnote. It should be said that in his memoirs Guerra regrets having said this – in September 1979, during an extraordinary PSOE conference; see *Cuando el tiempo nos alcanza*, pp. 274–275.

p. 188. Karl Marx, *The Eighteenth Brumaire of Louis Bonaparte*, trans. Daniel De Leon, Chicago, Charles H. Kerr, 1907, p. 5.

p. 189. Nicolás Estévanez, *Fragmentos de mis memorias*, Madrid, Tipográfico de los Hijos de R. Álvarez, 1903, p. 460.

p. 191–192. Santiago Carrillo, *Memorias*, pp. 712–716. What happened in the clock room is also reconstructed by Alfonso Guerra, in *Cuando el tiempo nos alcanza*, pp. 297–301.

p. 194. Santiago Carrillo interviewed by María Antonia Iglesias, *El País semanal*, 9.1.2005. The quote from *El Socialista* is in Fernando Claudín, *Santiago Carrillo*, p. 19.

pp. 195–196. Ian Gibson, *Paracuellos: cómo fue*, Madrid, Temas de Hoy, 1983; Jorge M. Reverte, *La batalla de Madrid*, Barcelona, Crítica, 2004, pp. 673–679, where the minutes of the meeting between the Communists and anarchists, during which the executions of Paracuellos were planned, are reproduced; and Ángel Viñas, *El escudo de la República. El oro* *de España, la apuesta soviética y los hechos de mayo de 1937*, Barcelona, Crítica, 2007, pp. 35–78.

p.196. '. . . the order might have come from Alexander Orlov . . .' Antonio Elorza claims the order did not come from Orlov, and that 'it could only have been issued by the delegate of the Communist International in Spain', Victorio Codovilla; 'Codovilla en Paracuellos', *El País*, 1.11.2008. Carrillo is quoted in Gibson, *Paracuellos*, p. 229.

p. 199. Carrillo is quoted in *Diario 16*, 16.3.1981.

p. 203. Carrillo is quoted in José García Abad, *Adolfo Suárez*, p. 22.

pp. 205–206. M. Vázquez Montalbán, 'José Luis Cortina Prieto. Cocido madrileño nocturno', in *Mis almuerzos con gente inquietante*, Barcelona, Planeta, 1984, p. 91. **'. . . he participated in GODSA . . .'** In fact, GODSA was the culmination of a study group called Team XXI founded by Antonio and José Luis Cortina in the late 1960s and which, in many articles published in magazines at the time, expressed the at once radical and tame Falangism of both brothers. For more on Team XXI, see Jeroen Oskam, *Interferencias entre política y literatura bajo el franquismo*, Amsterdam, Universiteit van Amsterdam, 1992, pp. 215, 226–234, among others; on GODSA, see Cristina Palomares, *Sobrevivir después de Franco*, Madrid, Alianza Editorial, 2006, pp. 198–205.

pp. 215–217. '. . . the most plausible are the following . . .' My account fundamentally follows that of Fernández López, in *Diecisiete horas y media*, pp. 133–134. Tejero's words are quoted by Aramburu in Manuel de Ramón, *Los generales que salvaron la democracia*, p. 99, where one can also read the version offered of the confrontation between Aramburu and Tejero by Aramburu himself and one of Tejero's Civil Guards. **'. . . the Cortes was filled with the rarefied air . . .'** What happened in the Parliament during the evening and night of the 23rd and the morning of the 24th is described in a report commissioned by the President of the Chamber, written by his secretaries – Víctor Carrascal, Leopoldo Torres, Soledad Becerril and José Bono – and sent to the investigating magistrate; it is dated 15 March 1981, consists of thirty-five pages and includes several appendices where the damages caused to the Cortes by the assault are specified right down to the consumption of alcohol – including nineteen bottles of champagne, four of which were Moët Chandon – food and tobacco in the bar. Part of my account comes from this source.

p. 217. '. . . circulating in a fragmentary and confused way as well was the news picked up secretly from a transistor radio by former Deputy Prime Minister Fernando Abril Martorell . . .' According to *El País* (25.2.1981), there was another transistor radio in the Cortes, belonging to the UCD deputy Enrique Sánchez de León; according to José Oneto (*La noche de Tejero*, Barcelona, Planeta, 1981, p. 123), the radio Abril Martorell was listening to belonged to Julen Guimon, also a UCD deputy.

PART FOUR. ALL THE COUPS OF THE COUP

pp. 228–229. Fernández López summarizes some of the hypotheses around the military authority awaited in the Cortes in *Diecisiete horas y media*, pp. 218–223. Suárez's statement was picked up by Agencia EFE on 16 September 1988. See Juan Blanco, *23-F. Crónica fiel . . .*, p. 42.

p. 231–232. The anecdote about General Sanjurjo comes from Pardo Zancada, *23-F. La pieza que falta*, p. 160. Calvo Sotelo is quoted in Victoria Prego, 'Dos barajas para un golpe', *El Mundo*, 4.7.2008. Not long after the coup the journalist Emilio Romero – very close to the *golpistas* – expressed an identical opinion to that which Calvo Sotelo would give years later, in 'De la radio a la prensa', prologue to *La noche de los transistores*, by Rosa Villacastín and

María Beneyto, Madrid, San Martín, 1981, p. 7. On the other hand, the supposed civilian plot was denounced very quickly in *Todos al suelo: la conspiración y el golpe*, Madrid, Punto Crítico, 1981, by Ricardo Cid Cañaveral and other journalists, which led those accused to bring a lawsuit against them; some of those journalists have since retracted their accusations (see Cernuda, Jáuregui and Menéndez, *23-F. La conjura de los necios*, pp. 225–228). If one has a lot of time, see Juan Pla, *La trama civil del golpe*, Barcelona, Planeta, 1982. **Footnote to p. 231.** See Fernández López, *Diecisiete horas y media*, pp. 73–75.

pp. 235–236. Alfonso Armada, *Al servicio de la Corona*, p. 149 and p. 146.

pp. 239–240. Milans del Bosch is quoted in Gabriel Cardona, *Los Milans del Bosch*, Barcelona, Edhasa, 2005, pp. 340–341. Milans' antagonism towards Gutiérrez Mellado was made public after the coup in a letter published by *El Alcázar* (28.8.1981), in which, after claiming that the only adjective that applies to the former Deputy Prime Minister is 'despicable' and before calling him a coward and a traitor, he says among other things: 'No one can receive lessons in military ethics from you, for the simple reason that you do not know them. I'd like to think you are mad, which would justify your very frequent and hysterical reactions . . .'

p. 242. Rafael Sánchez Ferlosio, *God & gun. Apuntes de polemología*, Barcelona, Destino, 2008, p. 273. The anecdote about Tejero and the corpse of the murdered Civil Guard was recounted by José Luis Martín Prieto in one of his articles reporting on the 23 February trial; see *Técnica de un golpe de estado*, p. 269.

p. 243. *El Imparcial*, 31.8.1978.

p. 248. Gutiérrez Mellado, *Un soldado de España*, p. 32.

p. 250. The report sent by Armada to the Zarzuela is usually attributed to a professor of constitutional law; but, according to Fernández López, it was most likely prepared by a professor of administrative law; Fernández López proposes a name: Laureano López Rodó. See *Diecisiete horas y media*, pp. 71–73; and, by the same author, *Sabino Fernández Campo*, pp. 131–132. That the report left the Zarzuela and circulated around the Madrid political village is confirmed by Emilio Romero, in *Tragicomedia de España*, Barcelona, Planeta, 1985, p. 275.

p. 251. Suárez is quoted in, for example, Abella, *Adolfo Suárez*, p. 437.

p. 256. '. . . **and while murmurs circulated in Madrid . . .**' On the rumours that a group of Captains General demanded the King force Suárez to resign, see Pardo Zancada, *23-F. La pieza que falta*, p. 185; on the rumours about the no-confidence motion, see the note to **p. 63.** '. . . **some leaders of political parties were flocking to the Zarzuela . . .**' See Manuel Fraga's lengthy account of his conversation with the King on 24 November, in *En busca del tiempo servido*, beginning on p. 223. Felipe González visits the Zarzuela at the beginning of December; see for example Antonio Navalón and Francisco Guerrero, *Objetivo Adolfo Suárez*, Madrid, Espasa Calpe, 1987, p. 183. As for the King's speech, it is not superfluous to recall that in his memoirs Armada claims that the King showed him a draft of it on 18 December, at the Zarzuela; see *Al servicio de la Corona*, p. 225.

p. 257. '**Although we have only Armada's testimony about what was discussed in those conversations with the King . . .**' See Palacios, *El golpe del CESID*, pp. 282–286, where Armada's recollections are recorded. See also the version offered by Fernández López, *Diecisiete horas y media*, p. 75, and, on Armada's dinner with the monarch mentioned on **pp. 260–261**, see pp. 92–93.

p. 260. '. . . **the newspapers were full of hypotheses of coalition or caretaker or unity governments . . .**' As well as the articles already cited, see for example Josep Tarradellas' statements, published 1 February, picked up by Europe Press and quoted by Palacios, *23-F: El golpe del CESID*, p. 323; or the article by Fernando Reinlein in *Diario 16*, 2.2.1981.

'. . . there's no reason to rule out that he might have had doubts . . .' Manuel Fraga also had the impression at the time that the King was having doubts; on Friday 30 January, the day after Suárez's resignation, he wrote in his diary: 'The King immediately opened constitutional consultations; I had the feeling he was not in a hurry, that he was not taking anything for granted, and that this time the consultations were not a mere formality.' Further on he adds: 'On the 31st the King decided, with good judgement, not to propose a candidate until the UCD crisis was resolved and (without saying so) to allow time for contacts between the political groups'; *En busca del tiempo servido*, pp. 230–231. Fraga also notes that on 1 February the King postponed a planned trip to the United States. As for the possibility of forming governments of various parties as a solution to the political crisis, the parties themselves discussed it publicly and all the newspapers reported it.

p. 262. '. . . according to Armada, he also told him of an imminent military move . . .' See Armada's statements collected by Jesús Palacios, in VV.AA, *El camino de la libertad (1978–2008)*, vol. IV, Madrid, Unidad Editorial, 2008, p. 10, where the former royal secretary also claims to have told Gutiérrez Mellado about a coup; we don't know if, according to Armada, he gave the general the names of the *golpistas*: astonishingly, in 2001 he claimed he did not 'because that seemed to me a lack of loyalty'; see Cuenca Toribio, *23-F. Conversaciones con Alfonso Armada*, p. 99. For his part, Gutiérrez Mellado declared before the examining magistrate concerning his conversation with Armada: 'When I told him my obsession was the permanent union of the Armies, General Armada answered me ironically, as I was later able to realize, that I should rest easy, because the Army was very united'. Quoted by Pilar Urbano, *Con la venia . . .*, p. 37.

p. 265. The journalist who covered the trial – who is quoting an observation of Agatha Christie's – is Pilar Urbano, *Con la venia . . .*, p. 108. The version the trial gave of the preambles to the coup can be read in the sentence of the court martial: see for example Martín Prieto, *Técnica de un golpe de estado*, beginning on p. 335; Tejero's version can be read in his declaration to the prosecutor, published by Merino in *Tejero. 25 años después*, beginning on p. 163.

p. 268. 'There is a theory that has enjoyed a certain renown . . .' It is defended by, for example Pilar Urbano in *Con la venia . . .*, p. 306.

pp. 269–270. Niccolò Machiavelli, *De principatibus*, ed. Giorgio Inglese, Roma, Istituto Storico Italiano per il Medio Evo, 1994, p. 286.

p. 273. 'In spite of the hermetic character of AOME . . .' The declarations before the magistrate by Sergeant Rando Parra and Captain Rubio Luengo – members of Cortina's unit – can be read in Juan Blanco, *23-F. Crónica fiel . . .*, pp. 487–494. Two versions of the so-called Jáudenes Report – containing the declarations about the alleged participation in the coup by various members of AOME – can be found in Cernuda, Jáuregui and Menéndez, *23-F. La conjura de los necios*, pp. 309–327, and in Perote, *23-F: Ni Milans ni Tejero*, pp. 253–270. Javier Calderón and Florentino Ruiz Platero discuss these testimonies in detail in *Algo más que el 23-F*, pp. 165–188.

p. 275, footnote. For information on *Operación Mister* see Prieto and Barbería, *El enigma del Elefante*, pp. 223–232, and Cernuda, Jáuregui and Menéndez, *23-F. La conjura de los necios*, pp. 176–186.

p. 276, footnote. The AOME member is Captain Diego Camacho; Jesús Palacios develops this thesis in *23-F: El coup del CESID*, pp. 230–231.

p. 277. '. . . it's very likely [. . .] that in the days before the coup Cortina turned into a sort of adjutant of Armada's . . .' Some authors maintain that it was Cortina who personally informed the US Ambassador and Papal nuncio of the imminence of the coup; see Cernuda, Jáuregui and Menéndez, *23-F. La conjura de los necios*, pp. 191–198, or Palacios, *23-F: El golpe del CESID*, pp. 344–347.

p. 285. 'As I reconstruct it or imagine it . . .' The version that Tejero gives of the conversation can be read in Merino, *Tejero. 25 años después*, pp. 232–236; that of Armada, in *Al servicio de la Corona*, pp. 242–243, and, in more detail, in Cuenca Toribio, *Conversaciones con Alfonso Armada*, pp. 84–90. There are credible reconstructions of what happened in Fernández López, *Diecisiete horas y media*, pp. 161–165; Prieto and Barbería, *El enigma del Elefante*, pp. 182–187; Pardo Zancada, *23-F. La pieza que falta*, pp. 296–300; Cernuda, Jáuregui and Menéndez, *23-F. La conjura de los necios*, pp. 152–159; or Palacios, *23-F: El golpe del CESID*, pp. 410–415.

p. 286, footnote. Prieto and Barbería, *El enigma del Elefante*, pp. 185–186. Dr Echave's testimony can be seen in the television report *El 23-F desde dentro*, directed by Joan Úbeda, produced in 2001 and given away with the newspaper *Público*, 23 February 2009. Juan de Arespacochaga is one of the people who claim to have had news of Armada's government before the coup; a government in which, as he guessed from the start, 'the person I most respect politically as do millions of Spaniards' (he is undoubtedly referring to Manuel Fraga) would figure and, along with him 'two more members of the commission that wrote the Constitution'; he also claims that a list of the prospective Cabinet was later circulated that included himself and other 'personal exponents of service to Spain above parties and factions'. See *Carta a unos capitanes*, pp. 274–275.

p. 290. Those who advance the theory of a deliberate delay in the broadcast of the royal message – though attributing it to different reasons and drawing different conclusions – go from Pedro de Silva (*Las fuerzas del cambio*, Barcelona, Prensa Ibérica, 1996, p. 204) to Amadeo Martínez Inglés (*23-F. El golpe que nunca existió*, Madrid, Foca, 2001, pp. 145–148), by way of Ricardo de la Cierva (*El 23-F sin máscaras*, Madrid, Fénix, 1999, p. 226).

p. 292. The King's message is in, for example, Fernández López, *Diecisiete horas y media*, p. 166; as well as in Paul Preston, *Juan Carlos: A People's King*, pp. 481–482.

PART FIVE. *VIVA ITALIA!*

p. 303. Adolfo Suárez, 'Yo disiento', *El País*, 4.6.1982.

p. 304. The dialogue between Suárez and General de Santiago is taken from Victoria Prego, *Diccionario de la transición*, p. 557. The incident between Suárez and Tejero is mentioned by, among others, Urbano, *Con la venia . . .*, p. 183, and Charles Powell, *Adolfo Suárez*, p. 180; José Oneto recreates it novelistically in *La noche de Tejero*, p. 195.

pp. 304–305. The anecdote of what happened during the National Defence Council meeting is told in Charles Powell, *Adolfo Suárez*, p. 181.

p. 306. José Ortega y Gasset, *Mirabeau o el político*, in *Obras completas*, vol. IV, Madrid, Taurus, 2005, pp. 195–223.

p. 307. Isaiah Berlin, *The Sense of Reality*, London, Chatto & Windus, 1996, p. 32. *Paris Match*, 28.8.1976, quoted by García Abad, *Adolfo Suárez*, p. 354.

p. 310. 'Some of Suárez's apologists . . .' I'm referring to, for example, Josep Melià, who in *La trama de los escribanos del agua*, pp. 49–56, recounts Suárez's early days in Madrid; in the same book, p. 49, he also tells the anecdote about Suárez with the father of his future wife.

p. 312. See Gregorio Morán, *Adolfo Suárez*, from p. 105.

p. 313. Franco's comment to his personal physician, Vicente Pozuelo, does not come from his own book, *Los 476 días de Franco*, Barcelona, Planeta, 1980, but rather that of Luis Herrero, *El ocaso del régimen*, Madrid, Temas de Hoy, 1995, in whom Pozuelo confided it. Herrero claims Franco's opinion 'was perhaps due to the fact that not long before the intelligence services had delivered to El Pardo a copy of the notes that Suárez – like many other young politicians of the regime – had sent to the Zarzuela summarizing his points of view on the pending political transition'.

p. 315. The King's comment is from July 1972, and the person who heard him say it was his biographer, José Luis Navas; see García Abad, *Adolfo Suárez*, p. 70.

pp. 316. Suárez is quoted in Morán, *Adolfo Suárez*, p. 261. [Puerta de Hierro is one of Madrid's most exclusive neighbourhoods and the Colegio Nuestra Señora del Pilar is one of its best schools, with a long list of prominent alumni.]

pp. 319–321. Suárez's account can be read in Victoria Prego, *Adolfo Suárez*, pp. 26–27; Luis Herrero gives more details about the same episode in *Los que le llamábamos Adolfo*, pp. 135–138.

p. 327. The cartoon by Forges was in *Cambio 16*, 12–18 July 1976, p. 18. The quote from *Le Figaro*, in Sánchez Navarro, *La transición española en sus documentos*, p. 287. The quote from *El País*, from the article 'Nombres para una crisis', 6 July 1976.

p. 328. Machiavelli, *De principatibus*, p. 289. Suárez is quoted in Sánchez Navarro, *La transición española en sus documentos*, p. 288. The second Suárez quote, *Adolfo Suárez, Fue posible la concordia*, p. 26.

[**p. 330.** Guerrilleros de Cristo Rey (literally 'Warriors of Christ the King') was a paramilitary group that operated in the late 1970s.]

p. 331. Miguel Primo de Rivera is quoted in Sánchez Navarro, *La transición española en sus documentos*, p. 355. As well as Primo de Rivera, the Law for Political Reform was defended in the Cortes by Fernando Suárez – who steered the proposal through – Noel Zapico, Belén Landábury and Lorenzo Olarte.

p. 332. *The New York Times* and *Le Monde* headlines from 19 November 1976 are quoted in Abella, *Adolfo Suárez*, p. 149.

p. 338. '. . . he declared himself a Social Democrat to his former Deputy Prime Minister . . .' See Alfonso Osorio, *Trayectoria de un ministro de la Corona*, pp. 327–328. The anecdote about the argument over which part of the chamber the UCD deputies should occupy is recounted in Martín Villa, *Al servicio del Estado*, p. 82, and Herrero de Miñón, *Memorias de estío*, p. 208.

p. 341. The editorial ran under the headline 'Desorden autonómico, desorden partidario', *El País*, 30 December 1980.

p. 344. For Rossellini's opinion of *General Della Rovere*, see Ángel Quintana, *Roberto Rossellini*, Madrid, Cátedra, 1995, p. 187. 'It is reasonable to surmise that any of the young Francoist politicians [. . .] could have done what Suárez did . . .' One of those young politicians, Alfonso Osorio, admitted in 2006: 'In order to carry out the political transition [. . .] someone was needed who had sufficient intelligence, adequate knowledge, capacity for dialogue, infinite patience, exquisite manners and overwhelming sympathy, and none of us politicians in 1976 had all those qualities together [. . .] We had more than enough presumptuousness, arrogance, elitism and prejudices: precisely what Adolfo Suárez didn't have', 'Prologue' to Manuel Ortiz, *Adolfo Suárez y el bienio prodigioso*, Barcelona, Planeta, 2006, p. 20.

p. 347. Michel de Montaigne, 'Of Utility and Honesty', *Essays of Montaigne, vol. 7*, trans. Charles Cotton, revised by William Carew Hazlitt, New York, Edwin C. Hill, 1910, p. 1181. Max Weber, 'Politics as a vocation', *Essays in Sociology*, p. 164.

pp. 348–349. See Adolfo Suárez, *Fue posible la concordia*, p. 331. The anecdote about the safe in Suárez's office comes from Leopoldo Calvo Sotelo, *Memoria viva de la transición*, pp. 187–188.

p. 350. '. . . as he told the journalists . . .' See Adolfo Suárez, *Fue posible la concordia*, p. 359.

p. 351. See Adolfo Suárez, *Fue posible la concordia*, p. 293.

p. 352. Fraga's words were addressed to Ricardo de la Cierva, who reproduces them in *La dere-cha sin remedio*, Barcelona, Plaza y Janés, 1987, p. 391.

p. 354. The anecdote about Suárez and Hernández Mancha is told by, for example, José Díaz Herrera and Isabel Durán, in *Aznar. La vida desconocida de un presidente*, Barcelona, Planeta, 1999, pp. 373–374.

p. 356. Hans Magnus Enzensberger, 'Europe in Ruins', *Granta 33*, p. 138. Adolfo Suárez, 'El amor y la experiencia del dolor', prologue to Mariam Suárez, *Diagnóstico: cáncer*, Barcelona, Debolsillo/Galaxia Gutemberg, 2005, p. 13.

p. 358. There is an account of Suárez's last public appearance in Luis Herrero, *Los que le llamábamos Adolfo*, pp. 297–298.

p. 361. '. . . it was Lieutenant Colonel Tejero's fault that he was prosecuted . . .' Tejero's various declarations before the judge on Cortina's implication are examined by Calderón and Ruiz Platero in *Algo más que el 23-F*, pp. 166–171. For information on the Jáudenes Report, see the note to p. 295. The contradictory versions of Rando Parra and Rubio Luengo, on the one hand, and Cortina, on the other, are also in Palacios, *El coup del CESID*, pp. 31–58, where abundant information on what happened within AOME after the coup can be found.

p. 366. Santa Pau Corzán is quoted in Pardo Zancada, *23-F. La pieza que falta*, p. 324.

p. 370. The text of the conditions of capitulation of those who assaulted the Cortes, the so-called 'Pacto del capó', can be read in the documentary appendix included in the book by Pardo Zancada, *23-F. La pieza que falta*, p. 425. (Pardo Zancada is the one who claims, by the way, that the surrender pact was signed 'on the roof' of one of his vehicles, and not, as Lieutenant Colonel Fuentes tends to say and to repeat – see *El pacto del capó*, p. 135– on the hood.) See also there (beginning on p. 412) the manifesto drawn up by the occupiers of the Cortes and sent to the press, the text of the final telex sent by the Zarzuela to Milans, and Milans' edict annulling the edict that declared the state of emergency in Valencia or the message the Zarzuela sent to Pardo Zancada by way of San Martín to gain his surrender.

EPILOGUE: PROLOGUE TO A NOVEL

p. 380. Martín Prieto, *Técnica de un golpe de estado*, p. 387. The articles collected in Martín Prieto's book form an excellent account of what happened during the trial. See also the previously mentioned book by Milans' defence lawyer, Santiago Segura, written in collaboration with the journalist Julio Merino, *Jaque al Rey*; and those by José Oneto, *La verdad sobre el caso Tejero*, and Manuel Rubio, *23-F. El proceso*, as well as the account by Urbano in *Con la venia . . .*, pp. 311–357. '**Less than a year later the final court . . .**' On the appeals and final sentences of the Supreme Court, see Fernández López, *Diecisiete horas y media*, pp. 195–198.

p. 387. '**The coup d'état reinforced the Crown . . .**' See Santos Juliá, 'El poder del Rey', *El País*, 17.11.2007.

p. 388. '**. . . 23 February brought an end to the war.**' The final date of the transition is a matter of dispute. In general, it tends to be said that democracy was consolidated in October 1982, with the Socialists coming to power, but Linz and Stepan – whose thesis is that a democracy has taken root when it becomes 'the only game in town' – consider that perhaps the key date is 23 February, or more precisely the moment of the imprisonment of General Milans del Bosch and Lieutenant Colonel Tejero when 'there was never a politically significant movement in the military or in civil society to grant them clemency'; *Problems of democratic transition and consolidation*, pp. 108–110.

p. 390. The bullfighter is Rafael de Paula, interviewed by Miguel Mora in *El País*, 31.3.2006; and the poet is José Bergamín, interviewed by Gonzalo Suárez, in *La suela de mis zapatos*, Barcelona, Seix Barral, 2006, p. 207. Alan Pauls, *El factor Borges*, Barcelona, Anagrama, 2004, p. 42.

p. 392. Juan J. Linz, 'La transición española en perspectiva comparada', in J. Tusell and Álvaro Soto, eds., *Historia de la transición*, p. 21. **Footnote.** Odo Marquard, *Filosofía de la compensación: estudios sobre antropología filosófica*, Barcelona, Paidós, 2001, p. 41.

ACKNOWLEDGEMENTS

This book is in debt to many more people than I can mention, but I must thank Miguel Ángel Aguilar, Óscar Alzaga, Luis Alegre, Jordi Amat, Luis María Anson, Jacinto Antón, José Luis Barbería, Josep Anton Bofill, Javier Calderón, Antoni Candela, Jaime Castillo, Diego Camacho, Santiago Carrillo, Jordi Corominas, Carme Chacón, Javier Fernández López, Manuel Fernández-Monzón Altolaguirre, Felipe González, Jordi Gracia, Manuel López, Lídia Martínez (and Gemma Caballer and the rest of the librarians at Pavelló de la República), Carles Monguilod, Joaquim Nadal, Alberto Oliart, Àngel Quintana, Ricardo Pardo Zancada, Javier Pradera, Joaquín Prieto, Francisco Rico, Narcís Serra, Carlos Sobrino, Luis Miguel Sobrino, Mariano Torcal, David Trueba, Miguel Ángel Valladares and Enrique Zapata.

A NOTE ON THE AUTHOR

Javier Cercas was born in 1962. He is a novelist, short-story writer and columnist, whose books include *Soldiers of Salamis* (which sold more than a million copies worldwide, won six literary awards in Spain and was filmed by David Trueba), *The Tenant* and *The Motive*, and *The Speed of Light*. He taught at the University of Illinois in the late 1980s and for many years was a lecturer in Spanish literature at the University of Gerona. His books have been translated into more than twenty languages.

A NOTE ON THE TRANSLATOR

Anne McLean is the translator of works by Julio Cortázar, Héctor Abad, Ignacio Martínez de Pisón and Juan Gabriel Vásquez among others. She has twice won the Independent Foreign Fiction Prize: in 2004 for *Soldiers of Salamis* by Javier Cercas (which also won the Valle Inclán Award) and in 2009 for *The Armies* by Evelio Rosero.

A NOTE ON THE TYPE

The text of this book is set Adobe Garamond. It is one of several versions of Garamond based on the designs of Claude Garamond. It is thought that Garamond based his font on Bembo, cut in 1495 by Francesco Griffo in collaboration with the Italian printer Aldus Manutius. Garamond types were first used in books printed in Paris around 1532. Many of the present-day versions of this type are based on the *Typi Academiae* of Jean Jannon cut in Sedan in 1615.

Claude Garamond was born in Paris in 1480. He learned how to cut type from his father and by the age of fifteen he was able to fashion steel punches the size of a pica with great precision. At the age of sixty he was commissioned by King Francis I to design a Greek alphabet, and for this he was given the honourable title of royal type founder. He died in 1561.